QUEERING SOCIAL WORK EDUCATION

EDITED BY SUSAN HILLOCK
AND NICK J. MULÉ

QUEERING SOCIAL WORK EDUCATION

UBCPress · Vancouver · Toronto

© UBC Press 2016

All rights reserved. No part of this publication may be reproduced, stored in a retrieval system, or transmitted, in any form or by any means, without prior written permission of the publisher, or, in Canada, in the case of photocopying or other reprographic copying, a licence from Access Copyright, www.accesscopyright.ca.

25 24 23 22 21 20 19 18 17 16   5 4 3 2 1

Printed in Canada on FSC-certified ancient-forest-free paper (100% post-consumer recycled) that is processed chlorine- and acid-free.

Library and Archives Canada Cataloguing in Publication

Queering social work education / edited by Susan Hillock and Nick J. Mulé.

Includes bibliographical references and index.
Issued in print and electronic formats.
ISBN 978-0-7748-3270-0 (pbk.). – ISBN 978-0-7748-3271-7 (pdf). –
ISBN 978-0-7748-3272-4 (epub). – ISBN 978-0-7748-3273-1 (mobi)

1. Social work education.   2. Social work with sexual minorities.   I. Hillock, Susan, 1963-, author, editor   II. Mulé, Nick J., 1963-, author, editor

HV11.Q87 2016   361.3071   C2016-904128-X
                                                                        C2016-904129-8

Canada

UBC Press gratefully acknowledges the financial support for our publishing program of the Government of Canada (through the Canada Book Fund), the Canada Council for the Arts, and the British Columbia Arts Council.

This book has been published with the help of a grant from the Canadian Federation for the Humanities and Social Sciences, through the Awards to Scholarly Publications Program, using funds provided by the Social Sciences and Humanities Research Council of Canada.

Printed and bound in Canada by Friesens
Set in Myriad and Minion by Marquis Interscript
Copy editor: Deborah Kerr
Proofreader: Dianne Tiefensee
Indexer: Christine Jacobs
Cover designer: Martyn Schmoll

UBC Press
The University of British Columbia
2029 West Mall
Vancouver, BC V6T 1Z2
www.ubcpress.ca

Contents

Preface / vii
    Susan Hillock and Nick J. Mulé

Introduction / 3
    Susan Hillock

**Part 1: From Absence to Presence –
Queers Positioning Themselves in Social Work**

1   A Queer History / 17
      Susan Hillock

2   Broadening Theoretical Horizons: Liberating Queer in Social Work Academe / 36
      Nick J. Mulé

3   Queer and Trans Collisions in the Classroom: A Call to Throw Open Theoretical Doors in Social Work Education / 54
      Jake Pyne

4   Social Work, the Academy, and Queer Communities: Heteronormativity and Exclusion / 73
      Susan Hillock

Part 2: Coming Out and the Academic Closet – Rainbow Narratives

5   Feminist and Queer Rights: The Lived and Living Experience of Queer Social Work Faculty / 93
    Norma Jean Profitt and Brenda Richard

6   Constructing Alternatives: Reflections on Heterosexism in Social Work Education / 111
    Karolyn Martin and Robyn Lippett

7   Coming Out with God in Social Work? Narrative of a Queer Religious Woman in Academe / 130
    Maryam Khan

8   Challenging Transmisogyny: From the Classroom to Social Work Practice / 148
    Jade Pichette

Part 3: The Queering Project – Gender and Sexual Diversity in Social Work Education

9   Oh Canada: LGBTQ Students and Campus Climates in Canadian Social Work Programs / 163
    Shelley L. Craig, Lauren B. McInroy, and Christopher Doiron

10 Opening Theory: Polyamorous Ethics as a Queering Inquiry in the Social Work Classroom / 185
    Becky Idems

11 Social Work Education: Exploring Pitfalls and Promises in Teaching about Black Queer Older Adults / 205
    Delores V. Mullings

12 Queering Space in Social Work: How Simcoe County Has Moved from Queerful to Queerious / 227
    Jan Yorke, Ligaya Byrch, Marlene Ham, Matthew Craggs, and Tanya Shute

Conclusion / 246
    Nick J. Mulé

List of Contributors / 251

Index / 256

Preface

SUSAN HILLOCK AND NICK J. MULÉ

In Canada, there has been a failure to address queer individuals and communities, queer-based theories, and queer issues in social work education and the social work profession. The co-editors of this volume, Susan Hillock and Nick Mulé (both social work professors who are queer-identified), decided to collaboratively organize the book in the hope that it will be a catalyst to begin the dialogue, scholarship, and research aimed at addressing these gaps in social work education. Where did our collaboration begin? We met in 2012 at the Canadian Association for Social Work Education (CASWE) annual National Conference at the Congress of the Humanities and Social Sciences in Kitchener-Waterloo, Ontario. Nick, a gay white man and chair of the CASWE Queer Caucus, was sitting patiently, waiting for interested social work educators to join him for the caucus meeting. Susan, a bisexual white woman, wandered in, laughed out loud, and expressed her (ironic) surprise that there looked to be only two queer people at the conference. After we waited awhile, another woman entered the room. She quickly clarified that she was straight but wanted to be a queer ally. A gay male social work graduate student eventually joined us. After discussing caucus business, Susan mentioned her frustration and disappointment that at her school of social work, and at the national CASWE conference, queer people and queer issues seemed to be invisible and absent from the discourse. Nick agreed, recounting his yearly efforts to motivate people to become involved in the queer caucus. We then wondered what happens to queer social work students, colleagues, and service users who must cope with this type of silence and vacuum every day. From this recognition

– the lack of presence and visibility of queers in social work – grew the idea for this volume.

When we began to research this topic, we found obvious and disturbing gaps in queer social work knowledge, scholarship, research, and literature. In particular, we noted a lack of current Canadian content and context regarding these issues in the social work discipline and education. To fill these gaps, this volume of original works highlights the queering of social work education and its potential impact on theory, classrooms and curriculum, andragogy and pedagogy, research, and policy. As such, it is the first book in North America to address these issues in social work education. Celebrating the voices, stories, and resistance of queer social work faculty, administrators, colleagues, and students, diverse authors from across Canada present their thinking, stories, and recommendations related to queering social work education. This volume also emphasizes a contemporary, progressive, and innovative approach, utilizes a critical and anti-oppressive social work lens that sheds light on the current realities of social work education and queer communities, and demonstrates how queering social work education contributes to an enlightening of the discipline. Although the ideas, themes, issues, and andragogy discussed here are specifically situated in Canada, we believe they will be of relevance to social work education and other related fields outside our borders.

This book is organized in three thematic parts. Part 1 provides the context for the volume by engaging readers to discover and analyze historical and contemporary background information on all major aspects of queer social work – theories, social activism and movements, histories, communities, resistance, victories, and issues – and how they relate to a queered perspective. Part 2 presents first-person accounts of queer-identified people's experiences in social work education and addresses themes such as coming out, silencing/closeting/passing, safety, identity, expression, sexuality, gender, resistance, and intersectionality (i.e., the intersections of privilege and oppression where people are geographically, institutionally, socially, economically, and culturally situated regarding social work and social work education). Part 3 questions and challenges the current state of Canadian social work education. It presents alternative perspectives and highlights that social work education can be queered without jettisoning the principles and standards of practice of the profession. In this part of the book, we argue for the queering project – the queering of social work education: why queer social work education is important; how it is congruent with the profession's code of ethics, standards of practice, and academic freedom; and how a queer lens and sensibility will contribute positively to social work theory, andragogy/pedagogy, research, policy, and by extension, practice.

We hope that this book will be useful and of interest to those who engage in research and teaching not only in social work, but in sexuality/queer/gender studies, andragogy, anthropology, psychology, sociology, human rights, counselling, mental health, corrections, human services, health care, and/or higher education. Its major contribution to these disciplines of study is the focused look at queer perspectives in the social work profession in the Canadian academic environment, with potential for broader influences, as an untapped contribution to knowledge and research.

We would like to thank the contributors. We have appreciated their hard work and refreshing openness to editorial critique. For more information about the authors, please refer to the Contributors' section on page 251. We would also like to thank Darcy Cullen at UBC Press, who was especially helpful in offering feedback and support through the publishing process. Additionally, we thank UBC Press for its support of this important issue and willingness to publish this unique contribution to the literature. Also, both editors thank each other for the shared passionate concern with illuminating queer issues in social work education and the hard work and dedication required to complete this book. The intent on all our parts – the contributors, Darcy Cullen, UBC Press, and the co-editors – is to both broaden and deepen social work education so that it becomes inclusive of queer issues and better serves queer individuals and communities.

QUEERING SOCIAL WORK EDUCATION

Introduction

SUSAN HILLOCK

A comprehensive review of the literature illustrates a dearth of scholarship and research regarding lesbian, gay, bisexual, trans, queer, intersex, and polysexual (LGBTQIP) people, communities, theories, and related issues. This is true in Canadian academic literature generally and social work practice, research, and education specifically (Bacon, 2006; Bird, 2004; Ford, 2004; Ruffolo, 2006; Walker, 2004). The acronym LGBTQIP captures the great diversity of queer experiences and identities, but this volume will use LGBTQ. Although some literature does discuss queering the broader academy, it does not examine social work (Bacon, 2006; Bird, 2004; Ford, 2004; Ruffolo, 2006; Walker, 2004). And yet, social work is rooted in the work of Jane Addams, who lived and worked alongside same-sex partners, supported female-centred practice, and was key to the creation of progressive social work and the development of community practice.

Furthermore, the queer literature that does exist in Western academia tends to be divided into three main thematic areas. The first summarizes the rise of gay and lesbian liberation movements over time and provides historical reviews of gay and lesbian social and political activism (Adam, 1995; Fish, 2012; Kinsman and Gentile, 2010; Knegt, 2011; McLeod, 1996; Q-team, 2011; Smith, 1999; Warner, 2002). These works are significant as they help us to understand the origins of queer-based oppression and how queer communities organized into powerful resistance movements.

The second type of literature attempts to teach "straight" people and students in mainstream society and social work, mental health, criminal justice, and human services programs how to be sensitive to and work with queer-identified individuals and communities (and other diverse "oppressed" groups). This literature is based on what have been called anti-oppressive practice (AOP), minority sensitivity, and human rights approaches (Logie, Bridge, and Bridge, 2007; Messenger and Morrow, 2006; Moore, Dietz, and Jenkins, 1996; Willis, 2007).

In the third thematic area, queer-based theories question, resist, and challenge hegemonic notions of normalcy, gender, and sexuality, and attempt to deconstruct the artificial binaries of straight and homosexual, normal and abnormal, male and female, and so on. Queer-based theorists and writers critique minority approaches, choosing instead to interrogate the status quo and work toward dismantling homophobia and heterosexist and cisgender privilege. According to MacKinnon (2011), queer theory invites "a questioning of all sexuality and a critical unpacking of how we know what we think we know" (p. 141). This genre of progressive, critical, queer sexuality-based theoretical literature includes works by Angelides (2006), Edwards (1998), Fryer (2012), Hart and Richardson (1981), Jagose (1996), Jones and Ward (2009), Kirsch (2006), Lovaas, Elia, and Yep (2006), and Wishik and Pierce (1995).

Although these works are important, it is clear that we know very little about what individual social work academics, students, and practitioners actually know about queer-based theories, communities, people, and issues, how they learn, articulate, and use knowledge about the LGBTQ community members and their issues, or how they choose to teach and practise in these areas. Overall, LGBTQ issues, discussion, and theorizing are absent from the social work literature (Mallon, 1998; Trotter, 2000, as cited in Willis, 2007; Van Voorhis and Wagner, 2001). Due to these gaps in social work research, education, and practice, social work educators, field instructors, and practitioners have limited knowledge and understanding of queer people, their communities, histories, theories, and issues. Since, for the most part, these understandings often start in the social work classroom and field practicum, we believe that social work educators have a responsibility to assist students to develop their understanding, sensitivity, and analytical, assessment, and practice skills with LGBTQ individuals and communities. This volume has been compiled to assist both educators and students to begin to build and/or further their knowledge, develop skills, and work toward completing these essential tasks.

As the first book of its kind in North America, *Queering Social Work Education* moves readers along a trajectory: Part 1 provides a contextual historical background for LGBTQ history, activism, and theories; Part 2 examines first-person lived experiences of oppression (such as harassment, silencing, and discrimination), resistance, and celebration; and Part 3 reflects on the challenge of mapping social change in social work education to make it more inclusive of queers and their sensibilities. In addition, academics, social work educators, practitioners, field instructors, administrators, and students, as well as criminal justice, psychology, and human services, mental health practitioners, faculty, and students, will gain valuable insight to inform their practical skills and aid their work.

Although we recognize that debates, tensions, and variance regarding language preferences exist across queer individuals, theorists, activists, and communities, we have chosen to use the word "queer" in this volume because it serves as an umbrella term for the range and diversity of our communities and because it most closely fits our theoretical and political understandings of queer communities, theories, and social work. For us, the word meets four important goals: it comes closer than any other term in describing our own sexual orientation and gender expression; in using it, we reclaim it, transitioning it from meaning weird, unusual, and abnormal to celebrating diversity, resistance, and uniqueness; it recognizes queer contributions to Canadian society; and it serves to destabilize and deconstruct the notion of fixed identities such as male/female, homosexual/heterosexual, normal/abnormal, and so on. In addition, as white academics, contributors, editors, and authors, we recognize that our experiences and what we know as a gay man and a bisexual woman are necessarily situated, shaped, and limited by our particular social, economic, race, gender, class, and political locations and identities.

Thus, we endeavoured to include and reflect multiple Canadian perspectives, experiences, and narratives. We sought out diverse and divergent opinions among social work educators, students, administrators, and practitioners about what queering social work might look like. We also wanted to encourage social work education to engage more fully with a wide range of theoretical, personal, and political projects and perspectives that queer activists, theorists, and social workers have developed and are currently developing. Thus, there is deliberate variation across chapters in terms of conceptual and theoretical complexity, with some authors engaging with queer-based theories and others distancing themselves from theory in favour of queer politics and/or personal narratives. The book interweaves thoughtful, engaged, academic reflection in a collective project, sometimes dipping into a politicized and polarizing voice from those who have been silenced and marginalized. Some authors speak to allies who are interested in furthering the project of queering social work. Other authors focus on educating and conscious-raising for people who are new to these issues. Still others launch a strong critique of the establishment and traditional social work education. In addition, this range of content, tone, and analysis means that some chapters grapple with teasing apart complicated theoretical tensions and intensely unpacking the queering project, whereas others offer a more general scan and introduction to the topic and current issues. In many ways, this collection reflects the vastness of the possible positions in the project of queering social work education, and thus, it appeals to readers at all stages in that continuum. These debates, twists and turns, and contradictions are seen as invaluable to help deepen understanding, thinking, and dialogue. Moreover, it is important for social work not to have a singular template or definition of queering the education project, but rather to engage with fluidity.

As social work educators, we recognize that academia often requires in-depth knowledge rather than broad generalist knowledge. Even so, social work educators attempt to address a broad range of issues, and their ability to navigate every area (whether queerness, spirituality, sexuality, race, or income inequality) will always be uneven. In addition, though we tried to recruit and discuss as many aspects of the queer community as possible, we accept that bisexuality has not been covered in great detail. Although we focus on social work education, we believe that some of the thinking, dialogue, analyses, and suggestions provided in the following chapters can be applied to practice situations. We also recognize that our recommendations may not be suitable for every social worker or classroom or student. However, we hope that this book provides new knowledge and perspectives, and that it will be a valuable contribution to social work theory and education, here in Canada and internationally.

This volume is structured to articulate a clear conceptualization and application of queering social work education. Part 1: From Absence to Presence, is the contextual section of the book, and it provides a historical overview of Canadian LGBTQ communities, issues, movements, rights, theories, critiques, and presence/absence in social work education. It also reviews the use of terminology over time. The social work profession's understanding and positions on LGBTQ populations and their implications for theory, andragogy/pedagogy, policy, and practice are also highlighted.

To build on past gains and ensure that queer people are fully present, participating and/or appropriately represented, and actively engaged in critical social work thinking, discussion, teaching, research, services, curriculum, and policy making, we need to review their past efforts and struggles. To accomplish this, we need to understand the history of a once stigmatized and shamed hidden existence and how it transformed through activism and resistance into diverse queer communities and movements. In Chapter 1, Susan Hillock provides an overview of the history of queer absence and presence from the early seventh century BC to current times. She discusses the evolving views of homosexuality (as sin, crime, or sickness) and corresponding patterns of judgment, punishment, and persecution. She also critiques the relative absence of LGBTQ issues and those identified as "other" in mainstream history, literature, and scholarship. This chapter also gives a synopsis of Canadian LGBTQ communities, issues, movements, rights, and evolving absence/presence in society, historical records, activism, and social movements.

In Chapter 2, Nick J. Mulé focuses on broadening the theoretical horizons of social work. For the most part, it has managed to sidestep the debates between past concepts of gay and lesbian studies and queer theory, the latter of which is becoming increasingly dominant in sexuality studies. Yet the implications of such debates are incalculable for social work and all its aspects. Is theory adequately serving practice and vice versa when it comes to gender, sexual diversity, and social work? In addressing this question, Mulé compares current social work theories and concepts with those of sexuality studies debates. In addition, he politicizes the terminology that differentiates LGBTs from queers and that distinguishes their respective social agendas, all toward a critical, progressive understanding of LGBTQ populations and communities and the social work discipline's relationship to them. In seeking to broaden the theoretical horizons that uphold social work's commitment to social justice, Mulé finds queer theory unequal to the task. He highlights its limiting effects and suggests that a return to and resurrection of the principles of gay liberation would better aid the development of a modernized queer liberation theory.

Chapter 3, by Jake Pyne, takes us into the world of the classroom. In social work education, queer and trans subjects are often discussed as inhabiting a shared minority subject position. When trans is selected for specific treatment, it is often to celebrate the transgender figure as a symbol of queer transgression. Yet more than a decade of debate in gender and sexuality studies has raised serious concerns regarding queer theory readings of trans subjectivity. Most prominent is the charge that queer theory has functioned to roll back recognition for (some) trans subjects by casting a sex-change trajectory as the uncritical antithesis of a more politically desirable gender queer performance. Indeed, in the drama of the queer academe, the transsexual has played the unfashionable and antiquated foil to the more enlightened, cosmopolitan queer. Despite important analyses offered up by queer theory, this chapter argues that overreliance on a queer theory framework for gendered difference makes insiders of some trans subjects and outsiders of others. In the project of queering social work, Pyne calls for a pause. If some trans bodies and narratives are not examples of queer transgression, what are they examples of? What does the queer theory movement make possible and impossible for trans subjects? What alternative analyses are available? Recalling the historical context of the queer eye for transgender, this chapter reviews key ontological and epistemological debates over the gendered self, medical meaning, and the authority of the speaking subject. Ultimately, Pyne explores how queer theory and trans subjectivities may collide in the social work classroom, and in response, the theoretical doors we are called upon to open.

In Chapter 4, Susan Hillock examines the introduction and development of LGBTQ studies in North America and discusses issues related to and attempts directed at queering the academy and social work education. Her review of the current literature on queering educational systems reveals an emphasis on school bullying and uncovers specific gaps in professional teacher and social work training, education, and research. This chapter posits that social workers tend to be homophobic and to demonstrate high levels of heterosexism; thus, social work educators need to find ways of assisting students to challenge and transform these traditional beliefs. Finally, the chapter highlights the social work profession's literature, understanding, positions, and tensions related to queering social work practice, social workers, schools of social work, students, and research.

Part 2: Coming Out and the Academic Closet, presents first-person narratives that address queer themes as they impact personal lives, such as coming out, silencing/closeting/passing, identity, sexuality, resistance, and intersectionality. In-depth analyses of topics such as subjectivity are addressed, and stories of being queer in social work education and working with straight and queer students, colleagues, and administrators are shared.

In Chapter 5, Norma Jean Profitt and Brenda Richard discuss their experiences of being queer in social work practice and education. Their analyses interweave personal experience with the history of the feminist and queer rights movements and what they see as social work values and ethics. In presenting their experiences as white queer social workers and faculty, this chapter highlights the pivotal place of political movements in making meaning in their lives. In addition, directions for retheorizing gender, sexuality, and sex in social work are explored. The authors also critique current social work theories, knowledges, and approaches to LGBTQs in social work practice and education, and they recommend strategies to queer social work.

Currently, social work education perpetuates heterosexism. In Chapter 6, queer-identified social work students Karolyn Martin and Robyn Lippett recount their experiences in an Atlantic Canada social work program. In their classrooms and learning community, they encountered tokenization and minoritization (though perhaps not intentional) during discussions of sexualities. They advocate for the adoption of a queer approach to social work education – one rooted in social constructionism and queer theory – that would enable investigation of the privileging of heterosexuality and the dismantling of binary approaches to sexualities. Thus, a queer approach promotes an understanding of sexualities and identities as fluid, diverse, and socially constructed. Martin and Lippett offer two recommendations for implementing a queer approach to social work education: emphasis on self-reflexivity in the social work program and promotion of student opportunities for praxis beyond the classroom.

In Chapter 7, Maryam Khan suggests that exploration of religion and spirituality is warranted in social work courses when such dimensions comprise the social identities of both faculty and student constituencies. She argues that if social work is to be inclusive of queer Muslims and other religious queers, it must examine the nexus of religiosity, spirituality, and sexuality. This chapter debunks conceptions of a secular queer identity and challenges contemporary notions of secular spirituality. The author discusses her experiences, as a student and a part-time post-secondary educator, of incorporating a faith-based spirituality in social work andragogy and practice.

Chapter 8, by Jade Pichette, focuses on transmisogyny – the interaction between transphobia and misogyny that particularly targets trans women. Even in anti-oppressive social work education, this topic is rarely addressed. If trans women are mentioned at all in social work, it is usually by authors who appropriate their lives. Increasingly, there is a need to address gaps in education that render trans women an invisible part of the LGBTQ community. Pichette discusses her own experiences as a trans woman social worker and offers suggestions on addressing transmisogyny in the classroom. Transmisogyny breeds in social work in many forms, such as not mentioning the lives of trans women, listening to cis authors talk about trans women, and expressing micro-aggression or outright bigotry toward trans women. Pichette sheds some light on the exclusion of trans women in social work and provides constructive solutions.

Part 3: The Queering Project, challenges the current state of Canadian social work academe. It focuses on the queering project – providing alternative perspectives and exploring diverse ways in which social work education can be queered while remaining true to the profession's principles and standards of practice. Thus, this project is very much aligned with the values of social work itself: the celebration of diversity; the pursuit of social justice; and engagement with praxis. This part of the book discusses how social work education and the discipline can better assist queer-identified academics and students to be safely out. In terms of community and collective action, it also examines how to connect the queering project and interested stakeholders (i.e., service users, academics and students, field instructors and social workers, administrators, policy makers, researchers, and activists). This is congruent with social work education's commitment to community collaboration in the ongoing development of the profession, one that will be inclusive of queers and their sensibilities.

In Chapter 9, Shelley L. Craig, Lauren B. McInroy, and Christopher Doiron note that negative experiences remain relatively common for LGBTQ students on post-secondary campuses, yet the perceptions of LGBTQ social work students at their institutions and in their programs have received little consideration, particularly in Canada. Assessment of these educational climates is essential to encourage safe and productive classrooms for LGBTQ students and to ensure that their identities are adequately represented in the social work profession. This chapter describes a recent study of the educational climates for LGBTQ students in the bachelor of social work and master of social work programs at English-language Canadian institutions. Participants generally reported that their institutions were at least somewhat accepting of LGBTQ issues, yet a third of them also encountered homophobia in their programs. Many stated that their instructors were poorly informed regarding non-discrimination policies and that LGBTQ issues were underrepresented in curriculum content. Students felt that their classmates and faculty were uncomfortable with their LGBTQ identities and noted that faculty was often unsupportive: 19 percent reported that faculty expressed homophobia, and 22 percent indicated that faculty expressed transphobia. The authors offer systemic recommendations to address these challenges.

Recent societal gains for LGBTQ people have led to an increasing emphasis on aligning anti-homophobia advocacy with social work's core values and embracing cultural competence approaches in curriculum and practice. These approaches encourage practitioners to challenge their own homophobic and heterosexist beliefs and attitudes, and offer them resources to work confidently with LGBTQ service users. In Chapter 10, Becky Idems builds on queer and postmodern scholarship to challenge the normalizing and conservatizing function of shifts toward competency and traces their alignment with the neo-liberal project. Furthermore, Idems argues for a deliberate and politicized queered approach to social work within neo-liberal contexts. Thus, she explores the potential of using queerness as a mode of inquiry, rather than as a practice outcome or a knowable certainty. Outlining the politicized emergence of polyamorous communities, and discussing three principles at the heart of poly ethics, Idems explores polyamory as an "outlaw theory" that has the potential to broaden student notions of inclusion and exclusion while simultaneously challenging and expanding andragogical strategies to help students explore tensions between social control and social justice. In doing so, the chapter traces a path for the adoption of all manner of queering inquiries in classrooms.

In Chapter 11, Delores Mullings focuses on older black LGBTQ adults. Social workers remain largely unaware of the concerns, potential interventions, and practices relating to this population, from both a research and an andragogical perspective. Although ongoing dialogue and research increasingly attempt to engage LGBTQ communities in discussions about aging-related concerns, black queer people have been largely excluded from this discussion in Canada. Nor do they tend to figure in research, which means that they are virtually non-existent in the educational content of social work schools. Mullings adds to the discussion about queer older adults from a black perspective, emphasizing gaps in social work education and offering teaching strategies and recommendations to help prepare students to engage in ethical and socially just field work with this population.

Rural and northern experiences for LGBTQ individuals are frequently isolating and fraught with abuse, sexual prejudice, sexual stigma, and homonegativity, experiences that can be seen as paralleling those of other non-dominant groups. Bringing the concerns and needs of LGBTQ communities to the forefront in rural areas can be challenging and may take efforts on a number of fronts. Queering social work has an important role to play in this regard. With this in mind, Chapter 12, written by Jan Yorke, Ligaya Byrch, Marlene Ham, Matthew Craggs, and Tanya Shute, explores the barriers, opportunities, and contexts that face LGBTQ communities in the rural and northern setting of Simcoe County, Ontario, including a discussion of socio-cultural, political, and ideological factors. The chapter also examines the relationship between rural and northern educational institutions and the queer community, and it uncovers how academia has legitimized queerness in Simcoe County and transformed "queerful" (fearful) to "queerious" (curious). Finally, through the examination of LGBTQ history in Simcoe County and the use of a community engagement model, the authors demonstrate how social work students and academics have used community-level knowledge to work toward local LGBTQ policy development and implementation.

It is the position of this book, and of its contributors, that social work educators have an ethical obligation and responsibility to support students in the following ways: developing awareness of heterosexist cisgendered privilege; strengthening their knowledge and use of analytical, assessment, practice, and research skills with LGBTQ individuals and communities; working toward dismantling heterosexism, homophobia, and cisgenderism; and creating the conditions necessary for social change. Although Canadian LGBTQ communities and individuals have made some gains in terms of public education, legal rights, and Pride organizing, "homophobia and heterosexism remain dominant, both officially – such as in the Canadian education and health systems – and even more unofficially" (Knegt, 2011, p. 128). If we do not act to queer social work and academia, we run the risk of harming queer-identified colleagues, students, service users, and their allies. Supporting this conclusion, Logie, Bridge, and Bridge (2007) emphasize that "it is imperative that social workers address personal biases in order to prevent perpetuating the oppression and further marginalizing the LGBT populations" (p. 201). They also suggest that failure to remedy these gaps in the research, education, literature, and practice can negatively affect care, empathy, and service delivery, and can decrease the quality of education that students receive. The failure to address these issues has also resulted in the relative obscurity of queer-based theories, issues, and people in the Canadian social work profession. This makes inquiring about and queering social work a virtually untapped topic in Canada. Our hope is that this volume will begin the dialogue, scholarship, and research aimed at addressing these gaps in social work education.

References

Adam, B.D. (1995). *The rise of a gay and lesbian movement.* New York: Twayne.
Angelides, S. (2006). "Historicizing (bi) sexuality." *Journal of Homosexuality* 52 (1–2): 125–58. http://dx.doi.org/10.1300/J082v52n01_06.
Bacon, J. (2006). "Teaching queer theory at a normal school." *Journal of Homosexuality* 52 (1–2): 257–83. http://dx.doi.org/10.1300/J082v52n01_11.
Bird, L. (2004). "A queer diversity: Teaching difference as interrupting intersections." *Canadian Online Journal of Queer Studies in Education* 1 (1). http://jqstudies.library.utoronto.ca/index.php/jqstudies/issue/view/233.
Edwards, T. (1998). "Queer fears: Against the cultural turn." *Sexualities* 1 (4): 471–84. http://dx.doi.org/10.1177/136346098001004005.
Fish, J. (2012). *Social work and lesbian, gay, bisexual, and transpeople: Making a difference.* Bristol: Policy Press.
Ford, Tracy. (2004). "Queering education from the ground up: Challenges and opportunities for educators." *Canadian Online Journal of Queer Studies in Education* 1 (1). http://jqstudies.library.utoronto.ca/index.php/jqstudies/issue/view/233.
Fryer, D.R. (2012). *Thinking queerly.* Vancouver: UBC Press.
Hart, J., and D. Richardson. (1981). *The theory and practice of homosexuality.* London: Routledge and Kegan Paul.
Jagose, A. (1996). *Queer theory: An introduction.* New York: New York University Press.

Jones, R.L., and R. Ward. (2009). *LGBT issues: Beyond categories.* Edinburgh: Dunedin.

Kinsman, G., and P. Gentile. (2010). *The Canadian war on queers: National security as sexual regulation.* Vancouver: UBC Press.

Kirsch, M. (2006). "Queer theory, late capitalism, and internalized homophobia." *Journal of Homosexuality* 52 (1–2): 19–45. http://dx.doi.org/10.1300/J082v52n01_02.

Knegt, P. (2011). *About Canada:Queer rights.* Halifax: Fernwood.

Logie, C., T.J. Bridge, and P.D. Bridge. (2007). "Evaluating the phobias, attitudes, and cultural competence of master of social work students toward the LGBT populations." *Journal of Homosexuality* 53 (4): 201–21. http://dx.doi.org/10.1080/00918360802103472.

Lovaas, K.E., J.P. Elia, and G.A. Yep. (2006). "Shifting ground(s): Surveying the contested terrain of LGBT studies and queer theory." *Journal of Homosexuality* 52 (1–2): 1–18. http://dx.doi.org/10.1300/J082v52n01_01.

MacKinnon, R.V. (2011). "Thinking about queer theory in social work education: A pedagogical (in)quiry." *Canadian Social Work Review* 28 (1): 139–44.

Mallon, G.P. (1998). *We don't exactly get the welcome wagon: The experiences of gay and lesbian adolescents in child welfare systems.* New York: Columbia University Press.

McLeod, D.W. (1996). *Lesbian and gay liberation in Canada: A selected annotated chronology, 1964–1975.* Toronto: ECW Press/Homewood Books.

Messenger, L., and D.F. Morrow, eds. (2006). *Case studies on sexual orientation and gender expression in social work practice.* New York: Columbia University Press.

Moore, L., T.J. Dietz, and D.A. Jenkins. (1996). "Beyond the classroom: Taking action against heterosexism." *Journal of Gay and Lesbian Social Services* 5 (4): 87–98. http://dx.doi.org/10.1300/J041v05n04_06.

Q-team. (2011). *Queers made this: A visual archive of queer organizing in Montreal* [Documentary film]. Montreal: Q-team.

Ruffolo, D. (2006). "Reading students as queer: Disrupting (hetero) normativity for an equitable future." *Canadian Online Journal of Queer Studies in Education* 2 (1): http://jqstudies.library.utoronto.ca/index.php/jqstudies/article/view/3289/1417.

Smith, Miriam. (1999). *Lesbian and gay rights in Canada: Social movements and equality-seeking, 1971-1995.* Toronto: University of Toronto Press.

Van Voorhis, R., and M. Wagner. (2001). "Coverage of gay and lesbian subject matter in social work journals." *Journal of Social Work Education* 37: 147–59.

Walker, R. (2004). "'Queer'ing identity/ies: Agency and subversion in Canadian Education." *Canadian Online Journal of Queer Studies in Education* 1 (1). http://jqstudies.library.utoronto.ca/index.php/jqstudies/article/view/3274/1406.

Warner, T. (2002). *Never going back: A history of queer activism in Canada.* Toronto: University of Toronto Press.

Willis, P. (2007). "'Queer eye' for social work: Rethinking pedagogy and practice with same-sex attracted young people." *Australian Social Work* 60 (2): 181–96. http://dx.doi.org/10.1080/03124070701323816.

Wishik, H., and L. Pierce. (1995). *Sexual orientation and identity: Heterosexual, lesbian, gay, and bisexual journeys.* Laconia, NH: New Dynamics.

PART 1

**From Absence to Presence –
Queers Positioning Themselves in Social Work**

1

A Queer History

SUSAN HILLOCK

Social work administrators, educators, and field instructors have a responsibility to assist students to develop awareness of heterosexist cisgendered privilege, strengthen their knowledge and use of analytical, assessment, practice, and research skills with lesbian, gay, bisexual, trans, and queer (LGBTQ) individuals and communities, work toward dismantling heterosexism, homophobia, and cisgenderism, and create social change. To do this, social workers, educators, and students need to understand queer history and past struggles and victories, including the history of queer communities, resistance, activism, and social movements. To this end, I present a brief history of LGBTQs over time; describe evolving views of homosexuality and corresponding patterns of judgment, punishment, and persecution; and analyze the absence of LGBTQ issues and those identified as "other" in mainstream history, literature, scholarship, and research. I also provide an overview of Canadian LGBTQ communities, their issues and movements, sought-after and achieved rights, and their changing absence/presence in society, archived historical records, and activism resulting from their engagement in social movements.

Historical Presence and Absence

As early as the seventh century BC, there is mention of same-sex attraction in the women-to-women love poems of Sappho on the Greek island of Lesbos (Miller, 1995). According to Adam (1995), ancient Greek and Roman literature frequently describes behaviours that are deemed homosexual today. However, most of this literature and history focuses exclusively on male relationships. He argues that, in the classical era, "it was common for many (sometimes all) males to have homosexual relationships, at least for a period of their lives" (p. 1). There is little documentation about same-sex relationships through the Dark Ages and the Christian crusades, but one might assume that they did continue. Monter (1981) claims that "a continuous homosexual subculture has existed since as early as the 12th century" (p. 42). Moreover, Sylvestre (1983) argues that same-sex relationships between males were common, especially in monasteries, armies, and colleges. Thus, a tradition of same-sex relationships survived in gender-segregated monastic life over the twelfth to fifteenth centuries. With an emphasis on punishment for what was seen as immoral, fifteenth-century records report same-sex behaviours in the Venetian mercantile elite, and the sixteenth-century Spanish Inquisition also documented same-sex behaviours (Miller, 1995). Similarly, sodomy trials involving noblemen and their servants were recorded in the seventeenth century (Adam, 1995).

During the eighteenth and nineteenth centuries, the industrial revolution and a massive rural-to-urban migration brought networks of people together who shared common interests and sexual orientations. Interesting questions have been asked regarding how sexual behaviours and identities intersect to transform urban landscapes and vice versa (Houlbrook and Cocks, 2006). This period of the eighteenth and nineteenth centuries in gay history is often called the "Belle Époque" (Miller, 1995, p. 76). Indeed, there are indications that at this time same-sex relationships, at least in the upper classes, seemed almost fashionable in England and France. This is evidenced by the proliferation of Molly houses (same-sex gathering places) and the recorded practices of club members who participated in same-sex relationships and behaviours, androgyny, drag, and cross dressing (Miller, 1995). In fact, in 1791, the penal code of France actually decriminalized homosexuality (Miller, 1995). The Belle Époque also embodies a long history of queer individuals and communities resisting heterosexist societal norms by gathering together in ways that defied cultural, religious, and social mores.

In 1869, Karl Maria Kertbeny was the first to use the word "homosexuality" in print (as cited in Miller, 1995, p. 13). A Hungarian doctor, K.M. Benkart, initially defined homosexuality as a "congenital condition" (Warner, 2002, p. 22). In addition, at this same time in Western Europe, there were signs that a male homosexual underground was being established, which demonstrated the beginnings of a burgeoning gay semi-public presence and resistance to heterosexist dictates and expectations (Adam, 1995; Miller, 1995). By 1891, early inquiry, research, and scholarship related to same-sex relationships and behaviours had also begun. For instance, John Addington Symonds, an English scholar, wrote and printed fifty copies of *A Problem in Modern Ethics*, which offered "a systematic review of the existing scholarly literature on homosexuality" (Adam, 1995, p. 17). The new field of sexology – the study of sexuality and sexual behaviours – also arose during this period (Houlbrook and Cocks, 2006). Furthermore, British sexologist Havelock Ellis famously outed several exceptional men in history, including "Erasmus, Leonardo da Vinci, Michelangelo, ... and Cellini" (Miller, 1995, p. 16). Miller (1995) suggests that homosexuality was fairly common in English prep schools, colleges, and universities. Gay society and culture continued to grow and strengthen through the early to mid-twentieth century. The Institute for Sex Research was founded, films with gay subject material were being made and shown (though censored), gay bars and clubs were flourishing in major urban centres, and the World League for Sexual Reform was created (Adam, 1995; Hirschfeld, 1975a, 1975b). In the United States, these gains culminated in 1924, with the incorporation of the first gay rights group – the Society for Human Rights (Adam, 1995, p. 46). Space does not permit a full discussion of how queer sexuality has been practised and taken up in the broader realm of sexuality across the ages, but it is worth noting that it has always had, and will continue to have, a place in the social, cultural, and historical phenomenon of sexuality (Houlbrook and Cocks, 2006).

Homosexuality as Sin and Crime

Clearly, same-sex relationships, behaviours, activities, communities, activism, and resistance have been present for a long time. They have also been accompanied by long-standing and corresponding patterns of judgment, punishment, and persecution. These patterns evolved in societies, religions, and states that viewed homosexuality "as a sin, as a crime, and more recently, as a sickness" (Vogel and North, 2012, p. 127). For centuries, the churches and states that labelled homosexuality as a sin and/or a crime went to great lengths to repress and punish it (Warner, 2002). As early as 527 A.D., Emperor Justinian "introduced the first civil law against homosexuality," which was based on the Mosaic laws of the ancient Hebrews (p. 17). In Europe, from as early as the twelfth century, individuals who were accused of sodomy were persecuted and put to death (Adam, 1995). Later, during the Inquisition, those accused of or found to participate in same-sex relationships were burned at the stake as witches. In the sixteenth century, Britain formalized a statute prescribing death as the penalty for the "Abominable Act of Buggery" (Warner, 2002, p. 18).

In 1885, England also added laws against oral sex, which was called "indecent behavior" (Miller, 1995, p. 47). In 1895, famous flamboyant playwright and poet Oscar Wilde was charged for indecent behaviour (Miller, 1995). After a trial that resulted in a hung jury and a subsequent retrial, he was convicted and served two years of hard labour in prison. English society was simultaneously shocked and titillated by the uncovering of Wilde's same-sex behaviours. He became the symbol of masculine homosexuality in the Western world, and his trials epitomized negative nineteenth-century social attitudes about homosexuality (Miller, 1995).

In Canada, the first documentation of punitive law regarding homosexuality dates from 1648, when a male in New France, which later became Canada, was convicted for same-sex activity (Kinsman, 1987). In addition, homosexuality, masturbation, prostitution, bawdy houses, and pornography were added to the Canadian Criminal Code during the nineteenth century (Warner, 2002). In 1890, a new offence of gross indecency was enshrined in the Criminal Code to punish male-on-male sex acts. However, in 1892, Canada changed the laws and reclassified buggery as an offence against morality, no longer punished by death (Warner, 2002). Homosexuality remained a crime in Canada until the late 1960s, when many of these unjust laws were finally repealed. In contrast, anti-sodomy laws in the United States were repealed in all states only as late as 2003 (Fields, 2004).

Homosexuality as Sickness

The nineteenth and twentieth centuries saw the rise of psychiatry, Victorian attitudes, the social sciences, the Christian, Social Purity, and public health movements, and McCarthyism (Adam, 1995; Miller, 1995; Warner, 2002). From the long-standing state practice of criminalizing same-sex relationships, it was not a major transition, in more modern times, to move from viewing homosexuality as sin and crime to labelling it as disease and deviance. According to Warner (2002), by medicalizing same-sex behaviours and desires as illness, the developing health professions acted to support church and state battles "to suppress homosexual acts and simultaneously define them in clinical terms" (p. 22). As mentioned previously, K.M. Benkart defined homosexuality as a medical condition. In 1886, Richard von Krafft-Ebing's book *Psychopathia Sexualis* described it as "a physiologically based psychiatric pathology ... a weakness of the nervous system" (as cited in Warner, 2002, p. 22). Pursuant to this, homosexual males were labelled as "Inverts" (men who, for congenital reasons, behaved like women). In a peculiar social twist, this label soon changed in popular culture to "Perverts," and homosexual men were seen as abnormal and unnatural. Warner (2002) states that the writings of Sigmund Freud connected homosexuality with arrested sexual development. According to him, Freud believed that all people were born with innate bisexuality but that they matured into monosexuality as adults. In contrast, Hodges (2011) contends that Freud's explanations of normative sexual desire may not be so straightforward and are more complicated than Warner suggests. Indeed, Hodges hypothesizes that a queer reading of Freud's work can challenge heteronormativity in psychoanalytic theory.

The framing of homosexuality as illness was met with resistance, particularly from gay men who attempted to shift the scientific discourse away from illness and psychiatric disorders. Nonetheless, by the 1950s, the psychiatric profession had chosen to diagnose homosexuality as a "mental disorder caused by environmental and psychological conditions" (Warner, 2002, p. 24). Indeed, psychiatry's first *Diagnostic and Statistical Manual of Mental Disorders* (DSM) classified homosexuality as "sexual deviance" (Warner, 2002, p. 24). This definition soon became prevalent in the social and behavioural sciences, and in medical circles; it was institutionalized in 1968, when homosexuality was listed as a mental disorder in the DSM3 (Ivey, D'Andrea, and Ivey, 2012; Warner, 2002). In the name of medical science, attempts were then made to cure these "mentally ill" people. These misguided (and often heinous) interventions included "psychoanalysis, drugs, aversion therapy, and even lobotomies" (Warner, 2002, p. 24). After much social protest, civil unrest, and direct action by gay and lesbian activists in the early 1970s, homosexuality was finally removed from the DSM in 1973 (Jagose, 1996).

The Absence of Lesbian Women

Other than the poems of Sappho (mentioned above), female same-sex relationships have received scant attention in the literature. Since the study of history usually consists of men writing about other men, documentation has typically overlooked women. Furthermore, in terms of social mores and beliefs, especially related to civil law and property rights, women have usually been deemed as non-persons and therefore non-sexual, so their sexual activities have largely been ignored (Warner, 2002). As well, because no penis is involved, "women's relationships were usually thought not to be sexual by definition" (Adam, 1995, p. 5). Indeed, it is rare to find historical records in which gay and lesbian people speak for themselves, and for centuries women had been forbidden to read or write.

Although for the most part, women-attracted women have been ignored in historical records, there are a few exceptions. Of course, Sappho's poems are one example. There is also some evidence that, during the Belle Époque, female-to-female sexual relationships were common among some upper-class groups. Adam (1995) highlights another rare example of queer women being mentioned in history. He describes the unique situation of Eleanor Butler and Sarah Ponsonby, known as the ladies of Llangollen, Wales. Eighteenth-century correspondence and diaries reveal that wealthy upper-class women were expected to marry, but they chose to live with each other instead. In Britain, there were also documented cases of women living together as "husband and wife" (Jennings, 2007). Since women were seen as non-sexual beings, "there was little reason for such relationships to be called sexual or homosexual and no warrant for women to identify themselves in terms of sexual orientation" (p. 5).

Interestingly, the period of the American Revolution produced some instances of gender bending or women passing as men (Miller, 1995). As well, documented acknowledgment of female same-sex relationships exists for a brief period in early-nineteenth-century America, when bright young privileged women left home to pursue education and chose to participate in same-sex relationships (Miller, 1995, p. 57). These relationships were known as Boston marriages, and their same-sex proclivities were called "smashing." Indeed, they became so prevalent on university and college campuses that the US Association of Collegiate Alumnae appointed a research committee in the 1880s to study the phenomenon (Miller, 1995).

Except for these infrequent examples, lesbian and bisexual women have largely been absent from society's view, historical records, research, and literature. This has made finding evidence of their existence as well as tracing and documenting the many and varied expressions of their sexuality very challenging (Jennings, 2007). Such is the case even in social work, which could be called the queerest of the helping professions as it was founded on Jane Addams's female-centred community development work at Hull House. Although Addams would not have been seen as a lesbian in her day, her long-term living arrangements with same-sex partners, female friendships, intimate relationships, and work with and on behalf of women could be described as the beginning of queer social work. According to Stebner (1997), in a world of nineteenth-century ideals related to femininity and womanhood, Addams (along with six female colleagues) was revolutionary in producing woman-centred spaces and woman-identified practices. Indeed, their contributions and sexualities were not acknowledged for many years, partially because they were female, were unaffiliated with any university, and were conducting their social change work in a male-dominated field (Stebner, 1997). As a result, these roots of queer social work have been ignored and are rarely discussed or taught in social work education.

When female-to-female sexual desire was finally recognized in the mid-twentieth century, the response tended to be punitive. For example, the Canadian Criminal Code was amended in the 1950s to include same-sex acts involving women (Warner, 2002). Incredibly, it was not until 1966 that William Masters and Virginia Johnson (1966) scientifically proved that women had orgasms. Furthermore, the limited information on female same-sex relationships that did exist in the literature and research tended to be medicalized and to attribute female homosexuality to the immature, irresponsible, and abnormal personalities of lesbians. In the psychiatric community, lesbians were seen as "masculine women who had rejected femininity" (Miller, 1995, p. 23). One could argue that this erroneous belief lingers today. Like gay men, lesbians were diagnosed as abnormal and unnatural, and were called "Female Inverts" (Miller, 1995, p. 54). Accordingly, "hysterectomies and estrogen injections were then seen as a curative to these unnatural urges and behaviours" (Warner, 2002, p. 24). Disturbingly, before the 1950s, female genital mutilation was commonly practised as a supposed cure for lesbianism (Koso-Thomas, 1987).

The Absence of Racialized Queers

Historically, this denial of female same-sex relationships also extended to the same-sex activities, relationships, and presence of all queer individuals who were defined as "other" – such as people of colour, elderly people, and those with diversability. For the most part, unless their bodies were exploited as objects for sale by the dominant culture (as in colonization, the sex trade, breeding, and slavery), those who have been identified as other or even as non-human have mostly been viewed as non-sexual (Butler, 1990). Furthermore, the histories, issues, and experiences of racialized queer individuals are very different from those of white queers (Barnard, 1999). They not only had to deal with heterosexism and homophobia in mainstream society and their own racial communities but they also had to navigate racism (and classism, poverty, forced labour, residential schools, and slavery) from the broader society and the mostly white-centric gay and lesbian rights movement.

One exception to the invisibility trend in the literature is the early anthropological (albeit voyeuristic) study of gender-flexible individuals and same-sex behaviours among many Indigenous peoples in "North and South America,

Polynesia, Indonesia, and eastern Siberia" (Adam, 1995, p. 2). According to Wilson (1996), although we should be cautious of records and "histories" that are grounded in androcentric and Eurocentric perspectives, historical records document the observations and reactions of the first European colonizers who chronicled what they saw as individuals expressing same-sex gender roles and sexualities in Indigenous groups. Usually male, they were characterized as effeminate, as performing female gender roles, and as having same-sex relationships. Anthropologists used the word "Berdache," a Persian term for "a young captive or slave," to describe these men (Roscoe, 1998, p. 7). However, Wilson (1996) explains that although Berdaches sometimes did have sexual relationships with other men, their characteristics were often more consistent with gender androgyny than with homosexuality. In some Indigenous communities, they were also revered as spiritual leaders (Alderson, 2013). According to these historical records and interpretations, many Indigenous cultures and communities seemed much more accepting of gender and sexual diversity than was the norm in dominant white cultures. Of course, since there is much diversity within and across Indigenous peoples, not all Indigenous queer individuals were accepted, and many experienced oppression and discrimination in their communities and from elders (Baskin, 2011; Roscoe, 1998; Wilson, 1996). It could be argued that this acceptance has been uneven at best and that, at worst, the treatment of queer individuals has been deeply damaging and oppressive.

Canada's first organized Indigenous queer group, called the Nichiwakan Native Gay and Lesbian Society, was established in Winnipeg in 1986 (Knegt, 2011). Three years later, the Two-Spirited People of the First Nations was formed in Toronto (p. 113). The first pow wow for queer Aboriginal people was held at the 1990 Winnipeg Third Annual Inter-tribal Native American, Gay and Lesbian conference (Knegt, 2011). Many North American Indigenous groups have adapted the tradition of the Berdaches and now refer to a wide range of queer individuals/identities as "two spirit" (Meyer-Cook and Labelle, 2004). Meyer-Cook and Labelle (2004) explain that this term was conceived in Minnesota in 1988 and adopted at the 1990 "Native American/First Nations gay and lesbian conference" in Winnipeg (p. 31). For more information exploring Indigenous history in Canada (particularly contextualized in social work) and the presence, experiences, issues, and social activism of two-spirited people, see Baskin (2011), Meyer-Cook and Labelle (2004), Roscoe (1998), Sinclair, Hart, and Bruyere (2009), Strega and Carrière (2009), and Wilson (1996).

Similarly, bisexual, trans, and intersexed people, as well as queer immigrants, refugees, and migrants, although active and resisting heterosexism for generations, have historically been absent/ignored in the literature. Indeed, it was not until the late 1980s and early 1990s that these diverse groups and their identities, issues, strengths, and needs were more publicly recognized and moved to the forefront of LGBTQ activism, research, education, and scholarship. (For more detailed explorations, see Chapter 3, on trans theories and issues; Chapter 7, on Muslim queers; Chapter 10, on polytheory and ethics; Chapter 8, on trans women; and Chapter 11, on older black queers.) In addition, see Knegt (2011) for a discussion related to queer immigrants, refugees, and migrants.

Resistance and the Rise of Queer Rights and Activism

In England, gay men resisted state repression of and action against their communities as early as the Middle Ages (Cook, Mills, Trumbach, and Cocks, 2007), and lesbians followed suit soon afterward (Jennings, 2007). Both lesbians and gays seemed to increase their presence at the turn of the eighteenth century (Vogel and North, 2012). In 1725, a police raid on a Molly house in Covent Garden was met with "determined and violent resistance" by the household residents (Kinsman, 1987, p. 53). In nineteenth-century Germany, activists in the homosexual community organized the first documented homosexual rights movement (Adam, 1995; Vogel and North, 2012). It was led by the Scientific-Humanitarian Committee, which was founded on May 15, 1897 (Adam, 1995; Miller, 1995). This movement publicly supported the advancement of civil rights and equality for homosexual people.

Also in the nineteenth century, governments began to change their criminal laws and to decrease sanctions related to homosexuality. In Canada, the legal penalties for some homosexual behaviours were no longer prosecuted by 1836, and the penalties were finally abolished by 1861 (Warner, 2002). In addition, as mentioned above, the Criminal Code was amended in 1892 to declare buggery an offence against morality and thus no longer a capital crime.

Unfortunately, by the Second World War, these historical gains had been undone by the rise of fascism, Hitler and the Nazi Party, and Stalinism. Under these regimes, homosexual activism was suppressed, individuals lived in a climate of fear, and many were tortured and murdered (Miller, 1995). After the war, in the late 1940s and early 1950s, communism in Eastern Europe and the Soviet Union continued to suppress homosexual rights. In America, McCarthyism terrorized the homosexual community (Adam, 1995; Miller, 1995).

Furthermore, many years elapsed before Canada removed buggery and sodomy from the Criminal Code, which was amended only in 1969 (Warner,

2002). Also in that year, the Liberal government finally "decriminalized sex between men under certain circumstances" (Vogel and North, 2012, p. 129). Retrospectively, however, these changes can be seen as a partial victory, since the legislation was still fairly restrictive. Although unjust laws were repealed, the new laws were framed in a public/private binary, placing homosexuality in the private realm, restricting its focus to two consenting adults. Such framing did little for the public recognition of same-sex desires and relations or of the variance in sexual behaviours and expression (including having more than one partner) (Kinsman, 1987). Furthermore, although laws may have changed, Canadian attitudes and beliefs did not necessarily shift, as evidenced by continued homophobia and heterosexism. Today, although numerous gains have been made, many religions and states still see homosexuality as sinful and illegal. Globally, LGBTQ individuals are often forced to live under extreme risks of violence, encounter persecution and discrimination, and can be incarcerated, tortured, and even executed (Itaborahy and Zhu, 2013).

Documenting Modern Gay and Lesbian Liberation Movements

Several sources have summarized the rise of Western gay and lesbian liberation movements, including Adam (1995) *The Rise of a Gay and Lesbian Movement;* Canadian Lesbian and Gay Archives (1971–87) *The Body Politic,* a gay rights magazine; Crawford (1984) *Homosexuality in Canada: A Bibliography;* Fish (2012) *Social Work and Lesbian, Gay, Bisexual, and TransPeople: Making a Difference;* Fraser and Miller (1982) *Lesbian and Gay Heritage of Toronto;* Kinsman (1987) *The Regulation of Desire: Sexuality in Canada;* Kinsman and Gentile (2010) *The Canadian War on Queers: National Security as Sexual Regulation;* Knegt (2011) *About Canada: Queer Rights;* McLeod (1996) *Lesbian and Gay Liberation in Canada: A Selected Annotated Chronology, 1964–1975;* Q-team (2011) *Queers Made This: A Visual Archive of Queer Organizing in Montreal,* a documentary film; Smith (1999) *Lesbian and Gay Rights in Canada: Social Movements and Equality-Seeking, 1971–1995;* Vogel and North (2012) "Living Rooms, Bedrooms and the Streets"; and Warner (2002) *Never Going Back: A History of Queer Activism in Canada.*

These sources describe and analyze queer presence, resistance, and activism over time. They also celebrate what the movement has achieved, such as Pride organizing, public education, legal equality rights, the 2005 federal legalization of same-sex marriage, the ratification of same-sex benefits, and bringing the queer community, issues, sexual orientation, and expression out of the closet (Fitzgerald and Rayter, 2012). Although these works are important additions to queer history, presence, and scholarship, some have been criticized for privileging the interests of white, middle-class gays and lesbians, thus failing to consider intersectionality – how racialization, gender, diversability, socio-economic class, and other factors intersect to create differences between LGBTQ individuals and within communities (Cosis Brown and Cocker, 2011; Van Wormer, Wells, and Boes, 2000).

North American Gay and Lesbian Rights Movements

In Western cultures and countries, the postwar era saw the rise of the "Homophile movement," which decriminalized homosexual activity and emphasized equal rights for homosexual people (Vogel and North, 2012, p. 129). As in the Belle Époque, when gay culture flourished in urban settings, major North American cities, such as Chicago, Montreal, New York, San Francisco, Toronto, and Vancouver, quickly became vibrant places for gay men to meet, network, and develop new ways of living (Vogel and North, 2012).

As early as the 1920s, American gays and lesbians began organizing to protest against unfair laws and to work toward equality. As mentioned previously, the first gay rights organization was formed in 1924 (Adam, 1995). Much of this work stalled during the Second World War, but civil liberty efforts were quickly revived when the war ended. In 1948, the Kinsey Report shocked the world by claiming that homosexuality was widespread in America (Adam, 1995). Subsequently, two significant influential queer organizations were constituted. In Los Angeles, the Mattachine Society (whose members challenged homosexual persecution and attacks) was created in 1951, and San Francisco's Daughters of Bilitis – "the first post-war lesbian organization" (Adam, 1995, p. 69) – was established in 1955.

These groups represented the inauguration of queer political organizing that contributed to community development and direct public social activism. This new form of contestation contrasted with that of the individualized or contained institutional queer activism and resistance of the past. Several significant factors influenced the evolution of modern queer activism in North America. These include the women's liberation and anti-war movements, Black Power, and the Stonewall riots, all of which were based on marginalized social locations and counter-cultural reaction to social norms. The social context of the time was one of intense oppression imposed by religious, medical, and legal institutions (including persecution via police repression and the

1968 insertion of homosexuality as a mental disorder in the DSM3, as mentioned above). A confluence of all these awakened sensibilities led to the formation of new gay and lesbian groups.

The women's movement was a key civil rights influence. The late 1950s and the 1960s saw thousands of women organizing to challenge intimate partner violence, the gendered relations of power, the meanings of sexuality, gender, and identity, and the socially constructed divisions between the private and public, and normal and abnormal (Smith, 1999). Unsurprisingly, as Knegt (2011) notes, lesbians were basically excluded from the early gay rights movement, as men controlled its debates, issues, and physical/political spaces. Like the racialized individuals who confronted racism in the gay and lesbian rights movement, lesbians, bisexual women, and trans people soon found that sexism was alive and well in the gay liberation movement. Therefore, lesbian women soon began setting up their own independent organizations. In Canada, a lesbian group calling itself the Cunts announced in 1971 that it was starting an independent support and activism group (Knegt, 2011, p. 110). In 1973, gay women in Montreal published "the first strictly lesbian journal in Canada," titled *Long Time Coming* (Knegt, 2011, p. 110).

Along with the women's movement, the American Indian, Black Power, and anti-war movements also had significant effects on the gay liberation movement. Under the ministry and leadership of Martin Luther King Jr., black people and their allies were mobilizing to make changes in the American South. Simultaneously, American Indigenous groups were organizing to press for land claims and to combat inequality and racism, and students and their allies were protesting the Vietnam War. Modern-day Indigenous gay activism also got its start with the 1975 San Francisco founding of a group called the Gay American Indians (Meyer-Cook and Labelle, 2004, p. 42).

The religious, medical, social, and legal persecution of queer people and communities reached a breaking point in the late 1960s. Warner (2002) suggests that certain social themes worked together to set up the conditions necessary for massive social change, such as the outlaw status of queer people, police harassment, state repression and regulation, the notion that heterosexuality was normal and mandatory, the inclusion of homosexuality as a mental disorder in the DSM3, and the nationwide efforts of queers to force social and legal change. Vogel and North (2012) report that police raids on gay establishments and publications were a common occurrence during the 1960s, with bathhouses being a particularly popular target. On one infamous night, June 27–28, 1969, New York City police "raided a Greenwich Village gay bar called the Stonewall" (Adam, 1995, p. 81). Instead of peacefully co-operating with their arrests, several people, including drag queens, trans individuals, sex trade workers, and gay men, bravely resisted police, "first with jeers and high camp and then with a hail of coins, paving stones, and parking meters" (Adam, 1995, p. 81). Twentieth-century queers had had enough. From these courageous acts of resistance, the gay liberation movement was born. The Mattachine Action Committee called for "organized resistance" (Adam, 1995, p. 81); protests and marches were soon swelling across the nation; gay, lesbian, and allied students organized meeting spaces and protest marches; Carl Wittman's 1970 Gay Manifesto was published; and in 1973, due to the gay liberation movement and its organized protests, homosexuality as a mental disorder was finally removed from the DSM3 (Adam, 1995). Less than three years later, gay and lesbian "liberation movements emerged in every major city and campus in the US, Canada, Australia, and Western Europe" (Adam, 1995, p. 89).

Canada's LGBTQ Rights Movement

1960s Era

Adam (1995), McLeod (1996), and Smith (1999) suggest that, as in the United States, homosexual rights and activist groups have existed in Canada since the early 1960s. Both the Vancouver Association for Social Knowledge (1964) and the Ottawa Council on Religion and the Homosexual (1965) were established to advocate for the rights of Canadian gays and lesbians (Adam, 1995). These early groups focused on educating the public about "homosexuality in order to counter bigotry" (Smith, 1999, p. 28). Emphasis was also placed on queering public spaces and creating gay-friendly and safe bars, clubs, and coffee houses (Goldie, 2001). By 1967, gay and lesbian activists were leading the struggle to decriminalize homosexuality in Canada. This was finally achieved in 1969. Also in that year, gay and lesbian university students formed political action campus groups, starting at the University of Toronto (2001).

1970s Era

By 1972, these student groups had spread across Canada to several cities and universities (Adam, 1995). Some key organizations and events in Canada's gay and lesbian liberation movement include the 1970 establishment of the Gay Liberation Front in Vancouver; the 1972 founding of the Montreal Front de libération homosexuel; the 1971 Gay Action and Community Homophile Association of Toronto; the first gay and lesbian groups' march on Parliament, in

1971; the 1972 plan for a national federal election strategy to advocate equality and the rights of homosexual people; the first gay and lesbian clubs in Saskatoon (1973) and London, Ontario (1975); and the 1975 development of the National Gay Rights Coalition/Coalition nationale pour les droits des homosexuels (Adam, 1995; McLeod, 1996; Warner, 2002). As well, language had changed, and the word "homosexual" was supplanted with the preferred terms "gay" and "lesbian" (Miller, 1995).

The Pride movement, which arose from the original organizing of the early 1970s, used events and parades to enhance public visibility as it promoted its politics and celebrated the strength of its communities in the face of heteronormativity. Changing laws, organizing around common identities, and staging parades were just some aspects of the gay and lesbian liberation movement. An important goal was to change social ideologies and attitudes in popular culture related to homosexuality. Thus, new theoretical concepts and terms were being developed in the research, writing, and scholarship to explain the complexities inherent in trying to transform popular culture. According to Knegt (2011), the term "homophobia" was created to describe and analyze "the cause of oppression and discrimination against homosexuals" (p. 7). In addition, heterosexism was newly defined as a "social system that favours opposite sex relationships including a presumption that everyone is heterosexual – normal and superior" (Knegt, 2011, p. 8). Queer theory, as a body of study and research, also started to make inroads in the academy. Edwards (1998) defines queer theory as "a set of theoretical ideas, informed by post structural theory that primarily aims to deconstruct or disassemble sexual categories, such as straight, gay, and lesbian, and, in particular, trouble the gendered and sexual boundaries between heterosexual and homosexual populations" (p. 483). For more information on queer theory, see Chapter 2 in this volume and Sullivan's (2003) *A Critical Introduction to Queer Theory*.

1980s Era

The 1980s brought the AIDS epidemic to public attention and with it, the abysmal failure of the state to deal with the disease. With numerous social workers on the front lines of this crisis, and the negative impact of the illness on gay men in particular, the wide reach of the virus led to a querying of identity categories that challenged the notion that queer sexualities were uniform and congruent. This reformulation of sexuality as fluid opened the space for multiple ways of being queer and transformed gay and lesbian activism into a large-scale social movement designed to fight HIV infection, promote awareness, and advocate for funding, stepped-up research, support services, and health resources for AIDS survivors and their families. Along with this social and healthcare crisis, social oppression and discrimination, as well as police suppression, continued to be inflicted on gay and lesbian communities. In 1981, an ongoing series of police raids against gay clubs, bars, bathhouses, and other establishments culminated in a violent police intervention in Toronto that led to what were then the "largest mass arrests" in Canadian history (Knegt, 2011, p. 6). According to Knegt (2011), the raid resulted in massive public protests and demonstrations for lesbian and gay equality, human rights, and freedom of sexual expression, as had been the case after the police raid on the Stonewall gay bar in Greenwich Village. This newly acquired public presence culminated in campaigns to enshrine queer equality and rights in the Canadian Charter of Rights and Freedoms (Department of Canadian Heritage, 2014). Section 15 of the Charter, protecting the rights, freedoms, and equality of individuals from discrimination, came into effect in 1985, but sexual orientation was not read into the Charter by the Supreme Court of Canada until 1995 (Knegt, 2011; Smith, 1999). During the 1980s, sexual orientation was increasingly included in provincial and territorial human rights codes across the country (Knegt, 2011).

Along with Pride events, public protests, and Charter challenges, the 1980s gay and lesbian movements also emphasized the evolution of, and theorizing related to, identity politics. Smith (1999) and Warner (2002) explain that identity politics strive to decentre notions of stable identity, subjectivity, queer difference, gender, and marginality. The 1980s witnessed the emergence of bisexual presence and identities in gay and lesbian circles. Also, a wide variety of diverse racial and ethnic queer groups began to organize early in the decade. Both the first black queer group and the Gay Asians of Toronto were formed in Toronto in 1984 and 1980 (respectively) (Knegt, 2011). By the late 1980s and early 1990s, several racialized queer groups had established themselves and spread throughout Canada. Organizing groups interested in acknowledging and reflecting national diversity and intersecting oppressions coalesced into the 1990 formation of Queer Nation, an inclusive "high energy activist movement" (p. 118). A natural outcome of this evolution was the identification and recognition of differences within and across racialized groups and communities (Barnard, 1999).

1990s Era

The 1990s saw a shift in activist language from liberation to human rights and from LGBT to LGBTQ (sometimes LGBTQI) to "queer." Although "queer" was an offensive term that referred to deviance and abnormality, Jagose (1996) explains that queer communities reclaimed the word as an "umbrella term for a coalition of culturally marginal sexual self-identifications ... and to describe a nascent theoretical model" (p. 1). Since the 1990s, the word has often been applied to "all non-heterosexual people" (Knegt, 2011, p. 7). The 1990s also saw an acknowledgment of the presence, experiences, identities, and issues related to transgendered and intersexed individuals, a continued emphasis on creating gay-friendly spaces, and a major political thrust to secure benefits, spousal rights, and marriage for same-sex couples (Smith, 1999; Warner, 2002). The decade also saw a more sophisticated postmodern analysis of intersecting identities and issues, including a consideration of diversity, such as transgender, two-spirit, and intersex people and discourses, and a discussion of a variety of intersecting sources, from sexism to global/transnational issues and policies.

2000s Era

Some commentators have lauded Canada's July 2005 legalization of same-sex marriage as the outstanding accomplishment of the 2000s era (Fitzgerald and Rayter, 2012, p. xvi). This progressive law has been held up as an example of respect, inclusion, and equality for the rest of the world to emulate. However, LGBTQ communities, queer activists, and theorists were divided about both the campaign that pushed for the legislation and its subsequent "victory." Many critiqued the law as regressive and saw the notion/ideal of family, couples, reproduction, and monogamy (married parents with children), which was originally constructed and contextualized within patriarchy and capitalism, as being a restrictive heterosexist norm (Wiegman, 1997) and as catering to heteronormative concepts of class, privilege, and respectability (Mulé, 2010; Polikoff, 2008; see also Chapters 2 and 10 in this volume). The most current literature, debate, and scholarship continue to expand post-structural analyses and the deconstruction of identity(ies), and to criticize the corporatization of queers as objects, commodities, and consumers (Warner, 2002).

As AIDS shifted in North America from a terminal illness to a manageable chronic condition, the broader health and well-being of LGBTQs came into increased focus (Mulé et al., 2009). Related to this is the unprecedented rise of trans communities and their demands regarding identity issues, appropriate and sensitive health interventions, and human rights protections in general (Irving and Raj, 2014). Moves to queer the academy, orchestrate gay-straight alliances, decrease queer youth suicide, stop bullying and queer baiting in schools, and promote "It Gets Better" campaigns have also been highlighted. In addition, rural, urban, and international migration, experiences, and differences; refugees and immigrants; disability issues; racism and cultural minorities; two-spirited people; and queering the arts remain topical subjects (Fitzgerald and Rayter, 2012; Knegt, 2011).

Conclusion

History is important. As the Spanish philosopher George Santayana (1905) stated, "those who can not remember the past are condemned to repeat it" (p. 284). To ensure that queer people are actively engaged in critical social work debates, teaching, research, services, curriculum, and policy making, we need to understand the LGBTQ struggles of the past. Moreover, we need to acknowledge and celebrate the history of diverse queer communities, issues, resistances, activism, and movements. Thus, this chapter has provided an overview of the history of queer absence and presence from the early seventh century BC, has discussed evolving views of homosexuality, and has critiqued the absence of many LGBTQ people in history, literature, scholarship, and research.

In queering social work education, understanding the progress as well as the defeats of LGBTQs is crucial, particularly given the discipline's involvement with queer communities. Ensuring a queer presence in social work curriculum and andragogy, recognition and inclusion in social work policy, and representation among social work faculty and staff will not only educate current and future social work students but will also help to queer social work education and the discipline itself.

References

Adam, B.D. (1995). *The rise of a gay and lesbian movement*. New York: Twayne.
Alderson, K.G. (2013). *Counseling LGBTI clients*. Thousand Oaks, CA: Sage.
Barnard, I. (1999). "Queer race." *Social Semiotics* 9 (2): 199–212. http://dx.doi.org/10.1080/10350339909360432.
Baskin, C. (2011). *Strong helpers' teachings: The value of Indigenous knowledges in the helping professions*. Toronto: Canadian Scholars' Press.
Butler, J. (1990). *Gender trouble: Feminism and the subversion of identity*. New York: Routledge.
Canadian Lesbian and Gay Archives. (1971–87). *The body politic*. Retrieved from http://www.clga.ca.
Cook, M., R. Mills, R. Trumbach, and H.G. Cocks. (2007). *A gay history of Britain: Love and sex between men since the Middle Ages*. Oxford: Greenwood World.
Cosis Brown, H., and C. Cocker. (2011). *Social work with lesbians and gay men*. Los Angeles: Sage.
Crawford, W. (1984). *Homosexuality in Canada: A bibliography*. 2nd ed. Toronto: Gay Archives.

Department of Canadian Heritage. (2014). *Your guide to the Canadian Charter of Rights and Freedoms*. Retrieved from http://www.pch.gc.ca/eng/1356631760121/1356631904950.

Edwards, T. (1998). "Queer fears: Against the cultural turn." *Sexualities* 1 (4): 471–84. http://dx.doi.org/10.1177/136346098001004005.

Fields, J. (2004). "Same-sex marriage, sodomy laws, and the sexual lives of young people." *Sexuality Research and Social Policy: A Journal of the NSRC* 1 (3): 11–23. http://dx.doi.org/10.1525/srsp.2004.1.3.11.

Fish, J. (2012). *Social work and lesbian, gay, bisexual, and trans people: Making a difference*. Bristol: Policy Press.

Fitzgerald, M., and S. Rayter, eds. (2012). *Queerly Canadian: An introductory reader in sexuality studies*. Toronto: Canadian Scholars' Press.

Fraser, J., and A.V. Miller. (1982). *Lesbian and gay heritage of Toronto*. Toronto: Gay Archives.

Goldie, T., ed. (2001). *In a queer country: Gay and lesbian studies in the Canadian context*. Toronto: Arsenal Pulp Press.

Hirschfeld, M. (1975a). "Berlins drittes Geschlecht 1905." In *Documents of the Homosexual Rights Movement in Germany, 1836–1927*, ed. Jonathan Katz, 1–77. New York: Arno.

–. (1975b). "M. Sappho und Sokrates 1902." In *Documents of the Homosexual Rights Movement in Germany, 1836–1927*, ed. Jonathan Katz, 1–36. New York: Arno.

Hodges, I. (2011). "Queering psychoanalysis: Power, self and identity in psychoanalysis therapy with sexual minority clients." *Psychology and Sexuality* 2 (1): 29–44. http://dx.doi.org/10.1080/19419899.2011.536313.

Houlbrook, M., and H. Cocks, eds. (2006). *The modern history of sexuality*. Basingstoke, UK: Palgrave Macmillan.

Irving, D., and R. Raj, eds. (2014). *Trans activism in Canada: A reader*. Toronto: Canadian Scholarly Press.

Itaborahy, L.P., and J. Zhu. (2013). State-sponsored homophobia: A world survey of laws – Criminalisation, protection and recognition of same-sex love. International Gay and Lesbian Association (ILGA). Retrieved from http://old.ilga.org/Statehomophobia/ILGA_State_Sponsored_Homophobia_2013.pdf.

Ivey, A.E., M. D'Andrea, and M. Ivey. (2012). *Theories of counselling and psychotherapy: A multicultural perspective*. Los Angeles: Sage.

Jagose, A. (1996). *Queer theory: An introduction*. New York: New York University Press.

Jennings, R. (2007). *A lesbian history of Britain: Love and sex between women since 1500*. Oxford: Greenwood World.

Kinsman, G. (1987). *The regulation of desire: Sexuality in Canada*. 2nd ed. Montreal: Black Rose Books.

Kinsman, G., and P. Gentile. (2010). *The Canadian war on queers: National security as sexual regulation*. Vancouver: UBC Press.

Knegt, P. (2011). *About Canada: Queer rights*. Halifax: Fernwood.

Koso-Thomas, O. (1987). *The circumcision of women: A strategy for eradication*. London: Zed.

Masters, W., and V. Johnson. (1966). *Human sexual response*. St. Louis: Reproductive Biology Research Foundation.

McLeod, D.W. (1996). *Lesbian and gay liberation in Canada: A selected annotated chronology, 1964–1975*. Toronto: ECW Press/Homewood Books.

Meyer-Cook, F., and D. Labelle. (2004). "Namaji: Two-spirited organizing in Montreal, Canada." *Journal of Gay and Lesbian Social Services* 16 (10): 29–51.

Miller, N. (1995). *Out of the past: Gay and lesbian history from 1869 to the present*. New York: Random House.

Monter, E.W. (1981). "Sodomy and heresy in early modern Switzerland." *Journal of Homosexuality* 6 (1–2): 41–55. http://dx.doi.org/10.1300/J082v06n01_05.

Mulé, N.J. (2010). "Same-sex marriage and Canadian relationship recognition: One step forward, two steps back – A critical liberationist perspective." Special issue of *Journal of Gay and Lesbian Social Services* 22 (1–2): 74–90. http://dx.doi.org/10.1080/10538720903332354.

Mulé, N.J., L.E. Ross, B. Deeprose, B.E. Jackson, A. Daley, A. Travers, and D. Moore. (2009). "Promoting LGBT health and wellbeing through inclusive policy development." *International Journal for Equity in Health* 8 (18). Retrieved from http://equityhealthj.biomedcentral.com/articles/10.1186/1475-9276-8-18.

Polikoff, N. (2008). *Beyond (straight and gay) marriage: Valuing all families under the law.* Boston: Beacon Press.

Q-team. (2011). *Queers made this: A visual archive of queer organizing in Montreal* [Documentary film]. Montreal: Q-team.

Roscoe, W. (1998). *Changing ones: Third and fourth genders in Native North America.* New York: St. Martin's Press.

Santayana, G. (1905). *The life of reason.* Vol. 1, *Reason in common sense.* Amherst: Prometheus Books.

Sinclair, R. (Otiskewapiwskew), M.A. Hart (Kaskitemahikan), and G. Bruyere (Amawaajibitang), eds. (2009). *Wicihitowin: Aboriginal social work in Canada.* Winnipeg: Fernwood.

Smith, Miriam. (1999). *Lesbian and gay rights in Canada: Social movements and equality-seeking, 1971-1995.* Toronto: University of Toronto Press.

Stebner, E.J. (1997). *The women of Hull House: A study in spirituality, vocation and friendship.* Albany: State University of New York Press.

Strega, S., and J. Carrière, eds. (2009). *Walking this path together: Anti-racist and anti-oppressive child welfare practice.* Winnipeg: Fernwood.

Sullivan, N. (2003). *A critical introduction to queer theory.* New York: New York University Press.

Sylvestre, P.F. (1983). *Bougrerie en Nouvelle-France.* Hull: Editions Homoreux.

Van Wormer, K.S., J. Wells, and M. Boes. (2000). *Social work with lesbians, gays, and bisexuals: A strengths perspective.* Boston: Allyn and Bacon.

Vogel, C., and R. North. (2012). "Living rooms, bedrooms and the streets." In *Talking Radical Gender and Sexuality: Canadian History through the Stories of Activists,* ed. S. Neigh, 123–45. Halifax: Fernwood.

Warner, T. (2002). *Never going back: A history of queer activism in Canada.* Toronto: University of Toronto Press.

Wiegman, R. (1997). "Queering the academy." In *The Gay '90s: Disciplinary and Interdisciplinary Formations in Queer Studies,* ed. Thomas Foster, Carol Siegel, and Ellen E. Berry, 3–22. New York: New York University Press.

Wilson, A. (1996). "How we find ourselves: Identity development and two-spirited people." *Harvard Educational Review* 66 (2): 303–18 http://dx.doi.org/10.17763/haer.66.2.n551658577h927h4.

2

Broadening Theoretical Horizons: Liberating Queer in Social Work Academe

NICK J. MULÉ

Taking up issues of gender and sexual diversity in social work education has entailed unravelling society's traditional and hegemonic notions regarding gender identity and expression, sexual desires and sexuality, types of relationships, and the ways in which families and communities are constituted. By "gender and sexual diversity," I mean communities of lesbians, gays, bisexuals, transsexuals, transgender, two-spirit, intersex, queer, and questioning people, referred to herein as LGBT or LGBTQ. From past complicity with society's cisgendered and heterosexist norms, to the emergence of gender and sexually diverse voices in society and academia – and the fight for legitimacy in both – to the teachings of feminist/gender/lesbian and gay/sexuality studies and queer theory in particular, social work is implicated by the very obligations of the profession to take up such issues both theoretically and for practical purposes. "Cisgendered" refers to those whose biologically assigned sex at birth aligns with normative perceptions of gender. For example, a cisgendered woman is deemed female at birth and grows up to identify with the female gender. "Heterosexism" refers to the notion that heterosexuality is normative and superior to all other sexualities. As much as social work posits the dialectical relationship between theory and practice (Payne, 2014), it is important for us to question whether theory is adequately serving practice and vice versa when it comes to gender and sexual diversity. This chapter seeks to address this, not merely as an academic question, but as one with material implications for social work as a discipline, for LGBT communities and the queer movement, for social work faculty who teach in this area, and for aspiring social work students who will be serving in the field. Social work theories that absent gender and sexuality are in essence limiting, with detrimental implications for practice; thus, focusing on these characteristics will help address this gap. More specifically, I will examine and critique the roles of queer theory and its prominence in sexuality studies from approximately 1990 to the present. In what follows, I employ a queer liberationist perspective that is grounded in my experience as a queer activist.

Before the modern LGBT movement emerged in North America during the late 1960s and the 1970s, social work as a discipline mirrored society's moralizing, pathologizing, and criminalizing of our communities via medical/ psychiatric, legal, and religious institutions. Rigid gender binary expectations, lack of recognition of same-sex attractions, desires, and relationships (Peterson, 2013), and repression of two-spirit (Meyer-Cook, 2008; Owa-Li, 2010), intersex (Kalev, 2012), queer, and questioning people have been and continue to be played out in cisgendered and heterosexist policies, programs, and services that have marginalized our communities (Mulé, 2008). In the past, these included lack of same-sex relationship recognition in benefits or marriage, adoption restrictions (Mulé, 2010; Young and Boyd, 2006), and various versions of the *Diagnostic and Statistical Manual of Mental Disorders* (DSM). The DSM has had detrimental effects on LGBs, a harm that persists today with trans populations (Daley and Mulé, 2014; Westbrook and Schilt, 2014). Currently, we see a lack of adequate funding for populations that do not have an HIV/AIDS focus (Mulé et al., 2009); limited access to hormones and sex-reassignment surgery (Butler, 2001; Lev, 2004; Lombardi, 2009); exclusionary access requirements for trans people in shelter systems (Project 10, 2013); forced decision making regarding the gender of intersex infants and children (Dreger, 2002, n.d.; Hidalgo et al., 2013); and faith-based publicly funded high schools that will not permit the establishment of gay-straight alliances (GSAs) (Callaghan, 2012).

In keeping with temporal changes in social-political contexts, teachings in social work from the 1990s onward have increasingly been sensitized to issues of diversity through many models inclusive of anti-oppressive practice (Baines, 2011), personal empowerment through strengths-based approaches (Saleebey, 2009), and critical social work (Fook, 2012). Anti-oppressive practice addresses a multitude of subjective social locations, such as race, ethnicity, age, disability, gender, gender identity and expression, sexual orientation, and socio-economic status, and how our very locations in a power-imbalanced society can leave us vulnerable to oppression (Dominelli, 2002; Thompson, 2012). Strengths-based approaches provide a practical means of empowerment, urging individuals to tap into their personal, family, community, and cultural strengths as a means not only to resolve their issues but to increase personal growth as well (Parton and O'Byrne, 2000). Critical social work, based on critical theory, points to systemic forms of oppression and discrimination, noting that numerous social problems are socially constructed, with detrimental effects on minorities and the disenfranchised (Allan, Briskman, and Pease, 2009; Fook, 2012; Mullaly, 2007). Although these perspectives and approaches opened up spaces for the issues of gender- and sexually diverse communities to be taken up, nuanced specificities such as addressing the diverse experiences of LGBTQs are lacking (Mulé, 2006), risking an andragogy that merely skims the surface.

More specific to the issues of the gender- and sexually diverse are teachings in sexuality studies and queer theory. During the 1970s and even more so in the 1980s, a significantly pronounced component of sexuality studies was that of modernist (i.e., an understanding of structures and systems and their power dynamics) gay and lesbian studies that engaged with identity politics as a means to challenge the predominantly heterosexist and homophobic views of the time. Identity politics for LGBTs incorporated the powerful and unique act of coming out, publicly self-identifying as non-heterosexual and asserting this minoritized sexuality as a counter-cultural identity that contests heteronormativity (Lovaas, Elia, and Yep, 2006; Quart, 2013; Slagle, 2006). Such studies (and by extension teachings) were designed to rupture heteronormative, hegemonic societal discourses into triggering a more diversified perspective and understanding of sexuality (Lovaas et al., 2006). In the early 1990s, queer theory took up a prominent space in postmodernist thought (i.e., a questioning of metanarratives and powerful and hegemonic discourses), challenging identity-based, fixed, essentialist notions of gender and sexuality (Butler, 1990, 1993; Foucault, 1990). It troubled and deconstructed normative and restrictive understandings of gender (feminine, masculine), sex (female, male), and sexuality (heterosexual, homosexual, bisexual), espousing instead, fluidity and variance in all three and questioning binary concepts within each (Jagose, 1996; Sullivan, 2003; Turner, 2000).

However, tensions still exist between postmodernist queer theory, based and developed in academia, and the modernist perspectives of the queer movement, based and developed in the community, due to the former's lack of practical applications and the latter's activist-rooted drive for material social change (Crosby et al., 2012; Mulé, 2015). Although positive developments have occurred, including the sharing of ideas between modernism and postmodernism, this chapter focuses on the differences between the two schools of thought. Hence, modernist gay and lesbian studies, with their defined identities, sought to effect material changes within systems and structures by disrupting hegemonic heteronormative policies, laws, funding, programs, and services. Material changes included a structural/systemic recognition of the specific and unique needs of queer people so that they could live their lives as they chose. This could come in the form of housing, employment, health care, and social services. This contrasts directly with a humanities-based queer theory and its emphasis on the micro. This focus on fluidity, non-essentialism, and the eschewing of identities leaves the theory without a material applicable strategy. Policies, programs, and services that are designed to address social problems often do so from a population-based approach such as those specifically focused on the needs of LGBTQ youth or seniors – a material application for which queer liberation advocates but queer theory is unable to employ. Social work, with its emphasis on social justice, needs to consider how these diverse, and sometimes diametrically opposed, approaches can be taken up in the discipline.

Proponents of queer theory have advocated for its applicability in social work practice as an alternative to past social work framing of LGBTQ populations, but their argument is based on the inaccurate premise that gay and lesbian liberation is conceptualized in binary notions (Coates and Sullivan, 2005). Another approach is to perpetuate some form of identity or seek its expansion (Burdge, 2007). A major theme here is the creation of new, alternative spaces that accept how LGBTQs define themselves (McPhail, 2004), whether it be in narrative therapy (Willis, 2007) or broader counselling and therapeutic modalities (Hodges, 2008). In particular, Hodges (2008) highlights dilemmas in using queer theory in therapeutic settings, then resorts to liberatory space-making strategies (which may include identities) as a queer theory strategy. Even when queer theory is used as a form of divestment from identity categories, it falls short of examining the power of identities within society and cites queer activism and collectivism as a means of effecting change, particularly in addressing structural inequalities beyond psychic structures (Hodges, 2008). In essence, what is argued as a means of applying queer theory is at worst a co-optation of the liberationist principles that preceded it or at best the overlapping of the two, though crediting only the former (Hicks, 2000, 2005, 2008).

Taking into consideration current social work theoretical and practice-based approaches and tensions between sexuality studies and queer theory, I will begin by contextualizing politicized terminology and its relationship to dominant social agendas. I then critique the effects of queer theory's dominance in academic teachings, highlighting the importance of respecting subjectivities, self-determination, and social justice – three principles in the social work discipline that are pertinent to this issue. I argue for a return to the original tenets and principles of gay liberation and suggest ways in which they can be developed into a current-day critical queer liberation perspective and theory. Determining whether theory and practice are adequately serving each other with regard to gender and sexual diversity lends itself to queering social work academe.

Politicized Terminology and the Social Agenda

One way to contextualize the complexities and specificities in gender- and sexually diverse social movements is to define terminology and identify long-lasting and current political tensions in these movements and their implications for broader social agendas (i.e., maintaining and sustaining heteronormative and gender binary world views). LGBTQ populations are no different from other minoritized and/or marginalized groups, in that their political perspectives are non-monolithic. I define "queer" as having non-normative sexual orientations, gender identities, and expressions. In addition, "gender queer" is sometimes used to signify a departure from restrictive bio-medical definitions of sex and binary notions of gender (Queer Ontario, 2013). In this chapter, "queer" is also defined politically as those of us who have deliberately reclaimed a once pejorative label, believe in a queer culture that is distinct, are disinterested in being part of the mainstream, are proud of and celebrate our differences, possess politicized views, and resist assimilation (Brown, 2007).

What I have experienced in political action/activist movement work is that politically, "LGBTs" tend to seek equality within the acceptable confines of cis-gendered, heterosexual standards, whereas "queers" generally seek to define their lives as they choose. What follows are divergent political motivations – assimilation for LGBTs and societal transformation for queers. Queer liberationists believe that by adhering to traditional gender binary and heteronormative constructs, LGBTs ascribe to such socially controlling forces by shaping their lives and social relations to reflect those of cisgendered heterosexuals in order to be palatable and thus respected and accepted in mainstream society. However, by rejecting such forces and offering alternatives (i.e., creating gender identities and forming social relations outside rigid gender roles and couplist constructs), not only for themselves but for society in general, queer liberationists contribute to social change (see Chapter 10 in this volume). In activist circles, this results in two very different end goals: for LGBTs, the goal is about acceptance and respect within cisgendered and heteronormative constructs, whereas for queers, it is about freedom and emancipation from these very constructs.

Typically, what emerges from these multiplicities is a heightened profile for LGBTs, who are seen as tending toward acceptance and respectability; homonormative standards (Duggan 2003) help them to fit in, with the result that they are effectively mainstreamed (Rimmerman, 2008). One example is following the heteronormative order and family structure of same-sex marriage, followed by having or adopting children. Another is transitioning one's gender to the opposite gender within the confines of a traditional binary based on social expectation (i.e., traditional constructs of masculinity or femininity). Hence, mainstreamed popularized notions of LGBTs have the effect of pushing radical queers to the margins. This has direct implications for the social agendas of both groups (i.e., for LGBTs, the fight is for equality with heterosexuals, whereas for queers, the struggle is to broadly transform society). A deeper, and somewhat uncomfortable, conversation needs to occur in which we explore our various desires, determine why some of them are more socially sanctioned than others and thus more privileged, and decide how to address this issue.

Worth noting at this point is the fluidity and variance of language itself, as the meaning of terminology such as "LGBT" and "queer" is not fully agreed upon in LGBTQ communities. In this chapter, I employ terms and definitions drawn from my experiences as a queer activist in the queer liberation movement in Toronto and across Ontario, but they are also commonly used in national and international social movements and discourse. Also, it is important to note that such concepts as "LGBTs" and "queers" are not necessarily diametrically opposed, lest such terminology be viewed as binary in and of itself. In reality, there is not always a fine line between the two. Depending on the experiences, values, and views of individuals, their political positions can vary on the issues at hand (Edelman, 1998). For example, some LGBTs may see the same-sex marriage victory as a radical improvement in the institution of marriage, whereas queers tend to see it as assimilationist. On the other hand, some queers who oppose same-sex marriage would not want to limit same-sex couples from having that choice. Like all political movements, the LGTBQ movement consists of a spectrum of political positions. In this section, I have highlighted two that are not necessarily or explicitly distinct.

Dominance of Queer Theory and Its Limiting Effects

As the broad LGBTQ movement diverged, queer theory rose to prominence in academia. In sexuality studies, "queer" swiftly became synonymous with queer theory, especially in the humanities (its birthplace) and the social sciences (Crosby et al., 2012; Slagle, 2006). This synonymy not only represses the history of the term, but seriously restricts its multiple current meanings, simultaneously silencing opposing political stances in its usage. Queer theory neither coined nor has a monopoly on the word "queer," which originated in the sixteenth century and referred to oddness and eccentricity. Later, it was associated with people who were in financial difficulties. By the late nineteenth century, it had begun to denote sexual deviance and was increasingly applied to homosexuality and/or effeminate males (Weeks, 2011). The word experienced a highly politicized resurgence during the early 1990s as the once pejorative term was reclaimed to disarm heterosexist and homophobic bigots, while also contesting heteronormative and cisgendered hegemonic world views. Far from the ivory towers of academia, this was (and continues to be) played out in the streets via community activist groups. For examples, see ACT UP (http://www.actupny.org/), AIDS Action Now! (http://www.aidsactionnow.org/), Audre Lorde Project (http://alp.org/), Lesbian Avengers (http://www.lesbianavengers.com/), OutRage! (http://outrage.org.uk/), Queer Nation (http://queernationny.org/), Queer Ontario (http://queerontario.org/), and Transexual Menace (http://www.transexualmenace.org/). In the larger LGBT movement, the counter-cultural, critical queer movement defines itself as an anti-normative, anti-assimilationist queer site that celebrates difference. These grassroots initiatives are an important part of the queer movement's history, and they continue to contribute greatly to our understanding of a queer sensibility. To limit our knowledge of "queer" within the confines of queer theory is to deny an important history and to ignore sites of queer that the theory fails to take up. This is not necessarily to blame queer theorists for the dominance of queer theory, but rather to remind academics and educators of the importance of teaching comprehensively, whether one aligns with queer theory or not. For example, an academic/educator who teaches from a queer theory perspective could embark on a collective project by including the additional histories and aspects mentioned above.

Interestingly, with their self-defined and deliberately pronounced presence on the ground, queers began to contest the social agenda just as queer theory was developing in academia. Yet, their respective discourses could not have been more different. The queer activist/community groups used their identities politically to rupture society's binaristic and hegemonic perspectives (Brown, 2007). Queer theory ruptured the same target by eschewing identities, challenging fixed notions of gender and sexuality, and promoting the concept of fluidity across the gender and sexual spectrum (Jagose, 1996). The contributions of both to social agendas are not to be underestimated. In asserting its defined difference, the former concretized the diversity of gender and sexuality in society, whereas the latter forced society to rethink its binary notions and why it assigns such rigid boundaries to gender and sexuality. Nonetheless, unresolved divides do persist, premised on a proud positioning of diversity and the need for associated material social changes for queer activists and a vision in which traditional gender and sexual delineations dissipate for queer theorists. These differences are not necessarily theoretically or philosophically based, as overlap can occur within such discourses. Rather, they rest on how to apply either of the progressive perspectives to create the conditions necessary for social change.

Progressive, critical, queer activists draw from the traditions of the gay liberation movement that involve the politicized act of coming out, the proud staking of one's stance on the terrain of diversity, and the demand not only for equality via legal rights, but for equity via social rights on the path toward social justice (Adam, 1987; Altman, 1971; Smith, 1999; Warner, 2002). In other words, given the persistence of discrimination based on sexual orientation and gender identity/expression, winning human rights legislation does not necessarily translate into social rights on the ground. Examples include not being publicly ridiculed, humiliated, scorned, or attacked because of one's sexual orientation or gender identity/expression. What underscores such activism is a political identity that troubles cisgendered and heteronormative social structures, offering alternatives that liberate our genders and sexualities (Brown, 2007; Mulé, 2015), such as broadening rigid categories on intake forms and training service providers in the use of inclusive language and sensitive and equitable interventions. Because aligning with identities is its antithesis, queer theory has rendered itself incapacitated when having to deal with practical applications. This leaves it vulnerable to inadvertently contributing to neo-liberalism, for it risks disappearing the individual (anti-identitarianism) (Crosby et al., 2012), who is often required to contest systemic oppressions. It is difficult to challenge social structures and systems, whether individually or collectively, in the absence of an identity from which one can base assertions or social actions. Without shared interests, which often translate into a collective identity, even if for strategic essentialist reasons (Spivak, 2006), individuals are left to fend for themselves in trying to survive in neo-liberal market forces.

The study of social work involves both the understanding of theories and the practical means of applying them. Social work studies also take up the dialectical relationship between theory and practice (Payne, 2014), which returns us to my question: Do theory and practice adequately serve each other? In the next section, I deconstruct this question in the context of critical social work education that upholds social justice as its goal. I examine queer theory and a queer liberation perspective, both in terms of their respective discourses and how they contribute to effecting social change. Their implications for social work are extensive if social work is to seriously take up LGBTQs and a commitment to queering academe. To begin, social work needs to enter into, and process through, these debates rather than sidestepping them.

Subjectivities, Self-Determination, and the Politicization of Essentialism and Fluidity

Self-determination and social justice are two core principles in the social work discipline (CASWE, 2005a, 2005b). The former speaks to the subjective power of individuals at a micro level to make decisions that they believe are right and meaningful for themselves, provided that the decisions harm neither themselves nor others (CASW, 2005). Social workers who respect this principle will not engage in power-over dynamics with their service recipients (Sakamoto and Pitner, 2005). Recognition of subjectivities in those we serve requires us to keep an open mind, as their experiences and values may be quite foreign to our own. A heterosexual-identified social worker working with a service recipient who identifies as LGBTQ is an example of a situation in which both individuals are quite differently situated. Reciprocal learning about our own and our service recipients' subjectivity (i.e., identities and social locations) engenders a respectful working relationship, which is very much a part of what we do when we engage people with integrity.

A second core principle is social justice, which can be applied at micro, mezzo, or macro levels (CASWE, 2005a, 2005b). To engage in social justice work is to try to effect change in society that will better the lives of the marginalized, disenfranchised, and oppressed (Mullaly, 2007). It is a commitment to equality, to ensure equal treatment and opportunities for all. More importantly, on the point of equity, it recognizes that some people are far more disadvantaged than others – systematically, systemically, and for the benefit of privileged groups – and hence, they require material responses that address their specific needs. The needs of a closeted queer-identified youth who attends high school will be very different from those of a straight-identified youth at the same school. Social justice work, regardless of the level at which it is practised, usually involves advocacy that raises consciousness regarding an issue and its history, public education (that may or may not entail research for evidentiary material), a clear naming and articulation of the issues, a critical analysis, and a proposed solution for social change toward emancipation of the targeted population or communities (Hoefer, 2012).

In addition to these principles, a social work ethos calls for respect of subjectivities, not only to keep value judgments in check but to challenge us to be truly open to the variance of each and every individual with whom we work (Fook, 2012). It is on the point of variance, which makes up the subjectivities of each individual, that queer theory provides a relevant contribution. From its postmodern perspective, it strongly emphasizes fluidity, particularly in the areas of gender and sexuality, as based on personal feelings and experiences. Like all theories, it functions on a spectrum in which its challenge to identities as transparent, congruent, stable, and contained calls for a careful and sensitive approach to social work intervention, respecting that people are often in excess of their identities. What becomes problematic is the extreme end of the queer theory spectrum, from which non-essentialism asserts fluidity to the point of defying identity. On one hand, queer theory supports an open-minded approach regarding variance in subjectivities in social work practice, but it can fall short on recognizing that essentialism is the true subjectivity for some (see Chapter 3 in this volume, regarding trans individuals). As mentioned, queer theory lacks practical application. Particularly in social work, how does one apply queer theory without identities (think policy, funding, programming, and services to specified populations) or advocacy work such as collectivization, mobilization, and social action?

Interestingly, the queer liberation perspective does not concern itself with the essentialism versus fluidity argument. The very essence of people having the freedom to conduct their lives as they choose (Altman, 1971; Warner, 2002) does not leave room for judgment on whether their subjectivities are aligned with essentialism or fluidity, but rather with the freedom to simply and honestly be who they are with integrity. This is clearly an open-minded approach that directly aligns with the social work principles of self-determination and social justice. In addition, queer liberation provides material applicability, based on its history of activism and its influences from the black civil rights and feminist movements (see Chapter 1 in this volume; Warner, 2002). One example, among many instances of social work services that increasingly recognize LGBTQs in either specialized or mainstream services, is the ongoing process of getting gender-based shelters to recognize trans people (Project 10, 2013).

So, do theory and practice serve each other well with regard to queer theory and the queer liberation perspective in the social work context? Both queer theory and the queer liberation perspective provide interesting world views that at once overlap and are contrasting but can assist in the training of social workers who serve LGBTQ communities. Nevertheless, with regard to practice, queer theory has far less to offer due to its anti-identitarian stance (Crosby et al., 2012). Queer liberation has over forty years of activism and social change experience that include dealing with the serious health crisis of AIDS (Gould, 2009) and advocating for inclusive health care and social services for LGBTQs (Mulé et al., 2009). Given this, the dialectical relationship between theory and practice in informing social work may be better served by the queer liberation perspective, though queer theory should not be entirely discarded.

Queer Liberation: Critical Perspective, Burgeoning Theory

A disadvantage of the queer liberation perspective in academic settings, whether it be in gender and sexuality studies or in social work, is that it is not a formal theory and is rarely taken up, other than studying it as it existed during its heyday, when it arose as the gay liberation movement. I think it is a mistake to reduce teachings in this area to a mere historical rendering. Many tenets of the original gay liberationist thinkers remain relevant today, as I have previously argued. Although the word "liberation" fell out of favour for a time, and the mainstream LGBT movement has captured the attention and support of heterosexual society by mimicking its norms and standards, queer liberation as a concept and perspective is experiencing a resurgence of late (Queer Ontario, 2010b). It offers an alternative perspective that strikes a critical note, questions the status quo, and creatively conjures up new existences and ways of living that break with social norms. Importantly, such a perspective can benefit all of society, not just queers.

This is not to say that queer liberation does not have its issues or detractors. Its very founding and early development were led by gay white men who did not necessarily embrace intersectional issues (i.e., women's and race issues) as sensitively as they could have, which eventually resulted in an internal split and the formation of autonomous lesbian, race, and ethnicity-based organizing (Warner, 2002). Queer theorists often criticize gay liberation for its strategic approach of engaging in rights claims via identity politics (MacKinnon, 2011), but in doing so they miss the point. In reality, gay liberationists pursued human rights as a means to an end, not as an end in itself. It was always clear that seeking legal justice on specific issues was a way of attracting people to the movement, but that the social justice work would be ongoing (Warner, 2002). This is also precisely where mainstream LGBTs and queer liberationists part company: the former are content with legal justice, believing they have achieved equality (see Berger, Searles, and Neuman, 1988, for a feminist perspective on this), whereas the latter do not rest at legal justice, believing that the real work will involve a fight for social justice. This vision of social justice involves making changes on the ground level to ensure that both attitudes and behaviours toward queers change for the better, beyond what is iterated in human rights legislation. In other words, although legal justice and social justice can have a dialectical relationship, they are not necessarily one and the same, particularly in connection with outcomes. Legal justice often operates within conservative, equality-based constraints, whereas the vastness of social justice operates in an equity-based, liberationist, emancipatory mode that simultaneously exposes the inaccessibility of legal justice for the socially marginalized or disenfranchised.

Queer-identified liberationists today subscribe to a highly politicized meaning of the word "queer," which serves as a pronounced identity and distinguishes them from mainstream LGBTs (Brown, 2007; Queer Ontario, 2010a). The very embracing of such an identity (despite its huge variance across non-normative gender identities/expressions and sexual orientations) smacks of essentialism to some queer theorists, but it holds meaning for liberationists in effecting material change. This can be quite pronounced in comparison to some in the mainstream LGBT movement, who think they have reached an end-point victory when they achieve a rights claim that is equal to or mimics heteronormative models (such as same-sex marriage). Herein, how one frames progress becomes complicated, because even those LGBTs who strive to fit into a mainstream heteronormative model can claim progress by their very presence, which in and of itself is a disruption. Progression is taken to another level by queer liberationists, who challenge heterosexual models and strive to create alternative models in which they can live a more liberatory existence. The problem with the former is that it ascribes privileges by nature of being part of the mainstream, which in turn, further marginalizes the latter.

By focusing this chapter on linking the tenets of the queer liberation perspective to two social work principles, I have illustrated that there is potential for a burgeoning queer liberation theory, as there are numerous other linkages that can be made within social work and other disciplines. The very early principles of gay liberation and their development into today's queer liberation as a means of counteracting neo-liberalism and homonormativity also lend queer liberation to a potential theoretical conceptualization. Even though queer liberation is not a formal theory, it certainly offers an alternative counter-cultural perspective that dovetails well with social work principles. As such, it is worth consideration in connection with teaching and the project of queering social work education.

Queering Social Work Academe

Social work has lagged behind in entering the discussion regarding gender and sexuality studies (there is an absence of social-work-based literature in the debates; see also Chapter 4 in this volume). Thus, it risks not being current on the latest discourses, theories, and perspectives. Also, given the potential implications for practice, I argue that social work academe has a responsibility to take up both the studies and the issues to provide social work students with a nuanced understanding of LGBTQ communities and how to work with them. Doing so will inevitably require addressing theoretical conundrums and practical challenges, given the complexity of the debates and the dialectical theory-practice relationship. Nevertheless, none of this is new, as theories and perspectives vary and challenge each other, not to mention their malleability when practice is factored in. The infusion of these LGBTQ perspectives in social work academe involves interdisciplinary andragogy. By incorporating the discourses offered by queer theory and the queer liberation perspective, among others in social work teachings, we will provide our students with a more comprehensive array of theoretical knowledge and practice considerations that have very real implications for LGBTQ communities.

Ways and means of queering social work academe include beginning with a more open and more broad palette by which we consider what knowledges we want to impart that engage a mutual dialogical andragogical process that encourages queer-focused dialogue between students and faculty. In essence, we need a process in which teaching and learning are transferable in class discussions between faculty and students. Hence, providing theoretical and perspective-based knowledge that is inclusive of queer theory, the queer liberation perspective, and the debates therein will contribute to a more comprehensive understanding of the issues. Course readings and text(s) need to encompass this broader scope. Case studies and community development work need to consider the varying approaches. Films, documentaries, and guest speakers whose perspectives differ from those of the mainstreamed LGBT movement, which is committed to assimilationism, are sure to provoke discussion and challenge both heteronormative and homonormative thinking. In addition, varied field placements that expose students to LGBTQ populations, whether in mainstream or specialized services, would provide hands-on experience in which students can play out the theory-practice dialectic and recognize the differences, complexity, and subtleties across and within LGBTQ groups and theorists. Ultimately, it is very important that this approach to queering social work academe not be relegated to specialized courses that deal solely with LGBTQs, for, as electives, they may not necessarily be offered on a consistent basis. Although having such courses is perfectly acceptable, I suggest that this varied and comprehensive knowledge needs to be integrated across the social work curriculum so that LGBTQs are not othered as a pathologized and oppressed population in need of social work assistance.

I also argue that what underscores the project of queering social work academe is the need to get political, in terms of grappling with both theoretical discourses and practical applications. Tensions exist between theories and practice, and although it is important to consider where they overlap and complement each other, it is also essential that the social work discipline not lose sight of fundamental differences that can serve to marginalize or enrich. It is not in our best interests to shy away from the complexities and their potential implications; rather, we need to untangle, examine, and critique them – that is, to engage in the very politics of progressive social work. Anything less would be a failure to meet our responsibilities to those whom we serve.

Conclusion

This chapter has outlined the trajectories of the broad LGBTQ movement and the divergences found therein, particularly between LGBT assimilationists and queer liberationists, and has discussed sexuality studies in general and the dominance of queer theory. The very politic of the LGBTQ movement was contextualized by defining terminology, particularly the word "queer" at both the community level and in queer theory. The chapter also highlighted the importance of recognizing these differences due to their potential implications for social agendas. Although both queer theory and the queer liberation perspective contribute to the social work tenets of recognizing subjectivities, respecting self-determination, and advocating for social justice, I argued for a return to and development of the principles of the early gay liberation movement in composing a modern-day queer liberation perspective that counteracts neo-liberalism and homonormativity. In this, I began to address the question as to whether theory and practice are adequately serving each other in social work education. Recognizing that there is no clear answer, I suggest that if social work academe is to be queered, such questions must be attempted if we are to do justice to the integrity of our andragogy, to our students, to the LGBTQ communities, and to the service recipients therein.

References

Adam, B.D. (1987). *The rise of a gay and lesbian movement*. Boston: Twayne.
Allan, J., L. Briskman, and B. Pease. (2009). *Critical social work: Theories and practice for a socially just world*. 2nd ed. Crow's Nest, Australia: Allen and Unwin.
Altman, D. (1971). *Homosexual oppression and liberation*. New York: Outerbridge and Deinstfrey.
Baines, D., ed. (2011). *Doing anti-oppressive practice: Social justice social work*. 2nd ed. Black Point, NS: Fernwood.
Berger, R.J., P. Searles, and L. Neuman. (1988). "The dimension of rape reform legislation." *Law and Society Review* 22 (2): 329–58. http://dx.doi.org/10.2307/3053439.
Brown, G. (2007). "Mutinous eruptions: Autonomous spaces of radical queer activism." *Environment and Planning* 39 (11): 2685–98. http://dx.doi.org/10.1068/a38385.
Burdge, B.J. (2007). "Bending gender, ending gender: Theoretical foundations for social work practice with the transgender community." *Social Work* 52 (3): 243–50. http://dx.doi.org/10.1093/sw/52.3.243.
Butler, J. (1990). *Gender trouble: Feminism and the subversion of identity*. New York: Routledge.
–. (1993). *Bodies that matter: On the discursive limits of sex*. New York: Routledge.
–. (2001). "Doing justice to someone: Sex reassignment and allegories of transsexuality." *GLQ: A Journal of Lesbian and Gay Studies* 7 (4): 621–36. http://dx.doi.org/10.1215/10642684-7-4-621.
Callaghan, T. (2012). Holy homophobia: Doctrinal disciplining of non-heterosexuals in Canadian Catholic schools. Unpublished thesis, University of Toronto.
CASW (Canadian Association of Social Workers). (2005). "Code of ethics." Retrieved from http://www.casw-acts.ca/sites/default/files/attachements/CASW_Code%20of%20Ethics.pdf.
CASWE (Canadian Association for Social Work Education). (2005a). *Canadian Association of Social Workers (CASWE) code of ethics*. Ottawa: CASWE-ACFTS.
–. (2005b). *Canadian Association of Social Workers (CASWE) guidelines for ethical practice*. Ottawa: CASWE-ACFTS.
Coates, J., and R. Sullivan. (2005). "Achieving competent family practice with same-sex parents: Some promising directions." *Journal of GLBT Family Studies* 1 (2): 89–113. http://dx.doi.org/10.1300/J461v01n02_06.
Crosby, C., L. Duggan, R. Ferguson, K. Floyd, M. Joseph, H. Love, R. McRuer, F. Moten, T. Nyong'o, L. Rofel, et al. (2012). "Queer studies, materialism and crisis: A roundtable discussion." *GLQ: A Journal of Lesbian and Gay Studies* 18 (1): 127–47. http://dx.doi.org/10.1215/10642684-1422170.
Daley, A., and N.J. Mulé. (2014). "LGBTQs and the DSM-5: A critical queer response." *Journal of Homosexuality* 61 (9): 1288–312. http://dx.doi.org/10.1080/00918369.2014.926766.
Dominelli, L. (2002). *Anti-oppressive social work theory and practice*. Basingstoke, UK: Palgrave Macmillan.
Dreger, A. (2002). *Intersex*. Retrieved from http://www.Fathermag.com/206/intersex/.
–. (n.d.). *Shifting the paradigm of intersex treatment*. Retrieved from http://www.intersexinitiative.org/pdf/dreger-compare.pdf.

Duggan, L. (2003). *The twilight of equality? Neoliberalism, cultural politics, and the attack on democracy*. Boston: Beacon Press.

Edelman, L. (1998). "The future is kid stuff: Queer theory, disidentification, and the death drive." *Narrative* 6: 18–30.

Fook, J. (2012). *Social work: A critical approach to practice*. 2nd ed. Los Angeles: Sage.

Foucault, M. (1990). *The history of sexuality*. Vol. 1, *An introduction*. New York: Pantheon. (Original work published 1976.)

Gould, Deborah B. (2009). *Moving politics: Emotion and ACT UP's fight against AIDS*. Chicago: University of Chicago Press. http://dx.doi.org/10.7208/chicago/9780226305318.001.0001.

Hicks, S. (2000). "'Good lesbian, bad lesbian …': Regulating heterosexuality in fostering and adoption assessments." *Child and Family Social Work* 5 (2): 157–68. http://dx.doi.org/10.1046/j.1365-2206.2000.00153.x.

–. (2005). "Queer genealogies: Tales of conformity and rebellion among lesbian and gay foster carers and adopters." *Qualitative Social Work: Research and Practice* 4 (3): 293–308. http://dx.doi.org/10.1177/1473325005055597.

–. (2008). "Thinking through sexuality." *Journal of Social Work* 8 (1): 65–82. http://dx.doi.org/10.1177/1468017307084740.

Hidalgo, M.A., D. Ehrensaft, A.C. Tishelman, L.F. Clark, R. Garofalo, S.M. Rosenthal, N.P. Spack, and J. Olson. (2013). "The gender affirmative model: What we know and what we aim to learn." *Human Development* 56 (5): 285–90. http://dx.doi.org/10.1159/000355235.

Hodges, I. (2008). "Queer dilemmas: The problem of power in psychotherapeutic and counseling practice." In *Feeling Queer or Queer Feelings*, ed. L. Moon, 7–21. New York: Routledge.

Hoefer, R., ed. (2012). *Advocacy practice for social justice*. 2nd ed. Chicago: Lyceum Books.

Jagose, A. (1996). *Queer theory: An introduction*. New York: New York University Press.

Kalev, H.D. (2012). "Sarah was a butch: Sexual identity, gender practices, and Sarah's Place as mother in the Jewish national pantheon." *Journal of Lesbian Studies* 16 (2): 220–237.

Lev, A.I. (2004). "Deconstructing sex and gender: Thinking outside the box." In *Transgender Emergence: Therapeutic Guidelines for Working with Gender-Variant People and Their Families*, ed. Thomas Laqueur, Virginia Goldner, and Judith Butler, 79–109. Binghampton, NY: Haworth Press.

Lombardi, E. (2009). "Varieties of transgender/transsexual lives and their relationship with transphobia." *Journal of Homosexuality* 56 (8): 977–92. http://dx.doi.org/10.1080/00918360903275393.

Lovaas, K.E., J.P. Elia, and G.A. Yep. (2006). "Shifting ground(s): Surveying the contested terrain of LGBT studies and queer theory." *Journal of Homosexuality* 52 (1–2): 1–18. http://dx.doi.org/10.1300/J082v52n01_01.

MacKinnon, K.V.R. (2011). "Thinking about queer theory in social work education: A pedagogical (in)query." *Canadian Social Work Review* 28 (1): 139–44.

McPhail, B.A. (2004). "Questioning gender and sexuality binaries: What queer theorists, transgendered individuals, and sex researchers can teach social work." *Journal of Gay and Lesbian Social Services* 17 (1): 3–21. http://dx.doi.org/10.1300/J041v17n01_02.

Meyer-Cook, F. (2008). "Two-spirit people: Traditional pluralism and human rights." In *Intersections: Cultures, Sexualités et Genres*, ed. S. Brotman and J.J. Lévy, 245–279. Boisbriand, QC: Presses de l'Université du Quebéc.

Mulé, N.J. (2006). "Equity vs. invisibility: Sexual orientation issues in social work ethics and curricula standards." *Social Work Education* 25 (6): 608–22.

–. (2008). "Demarcating gender and sexual diversity on the structural landscape of social work." *Critical Social Work* 9 (1). Retrieved from http://www.criticalsocialwork.com/units/socialwork/critical.nsf/982f0e5f06b5c9a285256d6e006cff78/ebb5ace61ebf5d368525744c00802bdf?OpenDocument.

–. (2010). "Same-sex marriage and Canadian relationship recognition: One step forward, two steps back – A critical liberationist perspective." Special issue of *Journal of Gay and Lesbian Social Services* 22 (1–2): 74–90. http://dx.doi.org/10.1080/10538720903332354.

–. (2015). "The politicized queer, the informed social worker: Dis/re-ordering the social order." In *LGBTQ People and Social Work: Intersectional Perspectives,* ed. B.J. O'Neill, T.A. Swan, and N.J. Mulé, 17–36. Toronto: Canadian Scholars' Press.

Mulé, N.J., L.E. Ross, B. Deeprose, B.E. Jackson, A. Daley, A. Travers, and D. Moore. (2009). "Promoting LGBT health and wellbeing through inclusive policy development." *International Journal for Equity in Health* 8 (18). Retrieved from http://equityhealthj.biomedcentral.com/articles/10.1186/1475-9276-8-18.

Mullaly, B. (2007). *The new structural social work.* 4th ed. Don Mills, ON: Oxford University Press.

Owa-Li, D. (2010). "Doubleweaving two-spirit critiques building alliances between Native and queer studies." *GLQ: A Journal of Lesbian and Gay Studies* 16 (1–2): 69–92.

Parton, N., and P. O'Byrne. (2000). *Constructive social work: Towards a new practice.* Basingstoke, UK: Palgrave Macmillan.

Payne, M. (2014). *Modern social work theory.* 4th ed. Chicago: Lyceum Books.

Peterson, C. (2013). "The lies that bind: Heteronormative constructions of 'family' in social work discourse." *Journal of Gay and Lesbian Social Services* 25 (4): 486–508. http://dx.doi.org/10.1080/10538720.2013.829394.

Project 10. (2013, January 25). "Transsexual and transgender women denied access to shelters as temperatures drop in Montréal." Retrieved from http://p10.qc.ca/uncategorized/transsexual-and-transgender-women-denied-access-to-shelters-as-temperatures-drop-in-montreal.

Quart, A. (2013). "Beyond feminism." In A. Quart, *Republic of Outsiders: The Power of Amateurs, Dreamers, and Rebels,* 31–52. New York: New Press.

Queer Ontario. (2010a). "'Queer' in name." Retrieved from http://queerontario.org/about-us/foundational-ideas/queer-in-name/.

–. (2010b). "Queer liberation." Retrieved from http://queerontario.org/about-us/foundational-ideas/queer-liberation/.

–. (2013). "About us." Retrieved from http://queerontario.org/about-us/.

Rimmerman, C.A. (2008). "The assimilationist and liberationist strategies in historical context." In C.A. Rimmerman, *Lesbian and Gay Movements: Assimilation or Liberation?* 11–29. New York: Basic Books.

Sakamoto, I., and R.O. Pitner. (2005). "Use of critical consciousness in anti-oppressive social work practice: Disentangling power dynamics at personal and structural levels." *British Journal of Social Work* 35 (4): 435–52. http://dx.doi.org/10.1093/bjsw/bch190.

Saleebey, D., ed. (2009). *The strengths perspective in social work practice.* 5th ed. Boston: Pearson.

Slagle, R.A. (2006). "Ferment in LGBT studies and queer theory: Personal ruminations on contested terrain." *Journal of Homosexuality* 52 (1–2): 309–28. http://dx.doi.org/10.1300/J082v52n01_13.

Smith, M. (1999). *Lesbian and gay rights in Canada: Social movements and equality-seeking, 1971–1995.* Toronto: University of Toronto Press.

Spivak, G.C. (2006). *Other worlds: Essays in cultural politics.* Abingdon, UK: Routledge.

Sullivan, N. (2003). *A critical introduction to queer theory.* New York: New York University Press.

Thompson, N. (2012). *Anti-discriminatory practice: Equality, diversity and social justice.* 5th ed. Basingstoke, UK: Palgrave Macmillan.

Turner, W. (2000). *A genealogy of queer theory.* Philadelphia: Temple University Press.

Warner, T. (2002). *Never going back: A history of queer activism in Canada.* Toronto: University of Toronto Press.

Weeks, J. (2011). *The languages of sexuality.* New York: Routledge.

Westbrook, L., and U.K. Schilt. (2014). "Doing gender, determining gender: Transgender people, gender panics, and the maintenance of the sex/gender/sexuality system." *Gender and Society* 28 (1): 32–57. http://dx.doi.org/10.1177/0891243213503203.

Willis, P. (2007). "'Queer eye' for social work: Rethinking pedagogy and practice with same-sex attracted young people." *Australian Social Work* 60 (2): 181–96. http://dx.doi.org/10.1080/03124070701323816.

Young, C., and S. Boyd. (2006). "Losing the feminist voice? Debates on the legal recognition of same-sex partnerships in Canada." *Feminist Legal Studies* 14 (2): 213–40. http://dx.doi.org/10.1007/s10691-006-9028-8.

3

Queer and Trans Collisions in the Classroom: A Call to Throw Open Theoretical Doors in Social Work Education

JAKE PYNE

> I made one of my participants cry. Jessie, a self-identified male-to-female transsexual, was dismayed after reading a completed study in which I examined the narrative construction of her gender. Wiping tears from her eyes, she said, "You have taken away the identity I have worked all my life to build"... I was pained, for my desire was to deconstruct gender, not erase her identity ... How did I make such a mess?
>
> – J. Kaufmann, "Trans Representation"

In these opening lines from an article about trans representation, Kaufmann (2010) describes the "mess" that can result when the post-structural (and often queer) method of deconstruction is brought to bear on transsexual embodiment. Though the prospect of a distraught research participant is indeed cause for alarm, I believe this is the tip of the iceberg with respect to what is at stake in the theories we use to read, think, and speak of trans experience. Further, I believe a similar mess can occur in the queered social work classroom.

In social work education, trans and queer subjects are often discussed as inhabitants of a shared identity category – the ill-fitting "sexual minority" (see Phillips, McMillen, Sparks, and Ueberle, 1997). When trans is selected out, it is often to celebrate the transgender figure as a symbol of queer transgression (see Burdge, 2007; Markman, 2011; McPhail, 2004). Yet over a decade of debate in gender and sexuality studies has raised serious concerns with queer readings of trans subjectivity (Elliot, 2010; Namaste, 2000; Prosser, 1998; Rubin,

1998; Stryker, 2004). Most prominent is the charge that queer theory of the 1990s functioned to roll back recognition for (some) trans subjects by casting a sex-change trajectory as the uncritical antithesis of a more politically desirable gender queer performance (Prosser, 1998). Indeed, in the drama of the queer academe, the transsexual has, at times, played the unfashionable and antiquated foil to the more enlightened, cosmopolitan queer. Despite vital analyses offered up by queer theory, this chapter suggests that an overreliance on a queer framework for gendered difference makes insiders of some trans subjects and outsiders of others. In the project of queering social work, I argue for a pause. If some trans bodies and narratives are not examples of queer transgression, what are they examples of? What does the queer moment make possible and impossible for trans subjects? What alternative analyses are available? Recalling the historical context of queer and trans subject positions, this chapter reviews key ontological and epistemological battles over the gendered self, medical meaning, and the authority of the speaking subject. Ultimately, I explore how queer and trans may collide in the social work classroom, and in response, the theoretical doors we are called upon to open.

Language and Terminology

As Bettcher (2009) notes, it is impossible to draw hard lines between "queer," "transgender," and "transsexual." Many subsume transgender and transsexual people under the queer umbrella. Many do not. Many transgender and transsexual people subsume themselves under that umbrella. Again, many do not. One individual might identify as all three, as I in fact do. Yet the imprecise distinction between these terms is precisely what is called into play in andragogical settings in which the gendered self is up for discussion. In this chapter, I use "queer" to refer to a politicized identity and a movement demarcating itself from heteronormativity. Queer theory developed out of queer studies and poststructural feminism to critique the assimilation that had come to be associated with gay and lesbian equality projects. Though the term "transgender" is often mobilized to refer to a broad range of identities that challenge gender norms, I distinguish between transgender as a relatively recent queer-aligned politicized identity and movement, versus "transsexuals," as those who seek to medically alter the sexed body. In my use of "transsexual," I allow that some transsexuals do identify with radical transgender politics, whereas others do not, viewing themselves instead as ordinary men and women. I use the shorthand "trans" to denote everyone on the gender non-conforming spectrum, including transgender, transsexual, transitioned, gender queer, non-binary, and some two-spirit people. As trans people have multiple intersecting identities (such as race, class, ability, and so on), these terms are far from adequate or exhaustive, but they do serve temporarily for discussion. It should be noted that queer theory would probably be critical of the move to define identities in this way.

The Trans Subject in Social Work

The social work figure of a transgender person has shifted substantially over time. Though the troubling psychopathological disease model went unquestioned during the 1970s and 1980s (see Levine, 1978), new calls for advocacy emerged in social work literature during the 1990s, repositioning trans people as an oppressed minority (see Mallon, 1999). In the context of the postmodern turn in theory, and in the wake of 1990s queer and transgender theorizing, social work literature in the 2000s began to celebrate transgender people as symbols of the dissolution of modern categories (Burdge, 2007; McPhail, 2004). Transgender came to stand as the cutting edge of gender, with the empowering social work task defined as disrupting the gender binary (Markman, 2011; Nagoshi and Brzuzy, 2010) or ending gender altogether (Burdge, 2007). Despite the transsexual objections I will outline, social work educators have been urged in some texts to teach queer theory as the framework for practice with trans communities (Burdge, 2007; McPhail, 2004, 2008).

To be clear, social work scholars who address trans issues, whether in text or in the classroom, overwhelmingly do so in support of trans communities. My hope is that they continue to do so. The analysis offered up by queer theory has been vital for creating political possibilities and livable lives for a multitude of genders. Yet assertions such as those made above (trans as destabilization and trans as outside and beyond gender) require our attention in that they cohere for some trans subjects but run absolutely counter to the lived experience of others (Kirby, 2008). Though ostensibly positive, these celebrations mire us in a decade of debate over queer readings of trans lives (Butler, 2004; Elliot, 2010; Halberstam, 1998; Kaufmann, 2010; Namaste, 2000; Prosser, 1998; Rubin, 1998). In the project of queering social work, we run the risk of unwittingly lending support for a moral contest over gender legitimacy – a contest I am not the first to suggest we must disengage from (Elliot, 2010).

The Birth of Queer

It would be an understatement to say that the queer movement of the 1990s, and the tandem academic field of queer theory, reconfigured the political landscape of sexuality and gender. Emerging from the union of feminism and sexuality studies, queer theory gained ground at a time when the salience of identity solidarity was starkly in question. Foucault and the post-structuralists were advancing discourse analysis and deconstruction in the academy, calling attention to the ways in which language constitutes rather than simply describes reality (Jagose, 1996). Multiple marginalized communities (lacking any unified identity) were devastated by the AIDS crisis, including a substantial number of men who engaged in sex with other men yet did not identify as "gay" (Beasley, 2005; Stryker, 2006a). Further, the gay and lesbian movement had achieved some success in consolidating a public gay identity, prompting those whose sexual identifications and practices did not fit this image to increasingly voice their dissent (Jagose, 1996). In this context, the political efficacy of identity categorization (homosexual and heterosexual, man and woman) was hotly debated. As Jagose (1996) remarks, the emergence of "queer" was inevitable.

Whereas a segment of the gay and lesbian movement increasingly sought state legitimacy for a stable "born that way" identity, queer theory argued against this grain, eschewing the reliance on a known or essential self. Building on the work of Foucault, queer theorists rejected the notion of fixed identity, charging instead that the fictional act of labelling identities reifies the differences that these labels purport to describe, obscuring the instability of all identity (Butler, 1990). Calling for the destabilizing of sexuality, queer theory troubled the line between homo and hetero, and promised to turn sexual categories on their heads (Halperin, 1995). It did not disappoint. Rejecting gender categorization as a normalizing project, queer theory promised liberation from prescription through anti-essentialist gender trouble. Unfortunately, in this respect, some trans scholars and activists would come to say that it did disappoint. Though transgender phenomena were commonly offered as examples of desirable queer performance, queer theorists came under fire from trans scholars who argued that queer theory had failed to do justice to transsexual experience (see Namaste, 1996; Prosser, 1998; Rubin, 1998). Yet if trans subjects were ostensibly framed positively by queer theory, how can we explain this critique? To answer requires a review of transgender and transsexual positions, and the uses to which queer theory has been put.

Queer and Trans Collisions

Though the term "transgender" is now commonly used in English-speaking Europe and North America (and to some extent elsewhere), this has been the case only since the 1990s (Stryker, 2006a). Prior to this, "transsexual" was the primary English-language word to describe a person with cross-gender identification. Coined during the development of sex-change technologies (from the 1940s to the 1960s), it came to be used as both a psychiatric diagnosis and a term of self-representation (Meyerowitz, 2002). In the context of an almost total information vacuum about the concept of sex-change, the word was adopted by would-be transsexuals who searched, often alone, for a solution to their unnamed bodily dilemma. Meyerowitz (2002) notes that the concept of a gender identity conflict and the development of clinical pathways and technologies to redress it were the products of ongoing negotiation between transsexuals and the medical community. Yet clinicians maintained an astonishing level of discursive and material control over their new "patients." In addition to defining "true" and "false" transsexuals and the (often unattainable) criteria for sex-change eligibility, clinicians defined a successful transition: passing unnoticed in the "normal" heterosexual cisgender world (Stone, 1991). Indeed, eligibility was often contingent on the foreseeable capacity to "pass" and on the candidates' match with the expected transsexual narrative (see Green and Money, 1969). Though passing was – and is – indeed a goal of many transsexuals, no alternative had yet been publicly articulated.

During the latter half of the twentieth century, transsexual autobiographies began to pepper the public sphere (Stone, 1991). These narratives kept closely to the clinical texts in their descriptions of coherent identities that rarely deviated from the expectations of the target gender role. Primarily penned by transsexual women, they attracted the scorn of 1970s and 1980s radical feminists, who launched public attacks on transsexual women, whom they regarded as inauthentic parodies of femininity and a danger to "real" women (see Daly, 1978; Raymond, 1979). Although the modernist radical feminist critique of transsexualism is at odds with the later postmodern queer critique of transsexualism, a family resemblance is noticeable in the distrust of transsexual self-narratives and the disapproval of medical transition procedures. At the time, transsexuals were not in speaking positions to reply. However, a self-published pamphlet by trans woman Caroll Riddell articulated an early public response to Raymond's (1979) *Transsexual Empire,* a book-length attack on trans women. Riddell (1996) bluntly stated, "My living space is threatened by this book" (p. 189).

In 1991, trans scholar Sandy Stone launched the first academic response to Raymond – an essay titled "The Empire Strikes Back" – considered by many to be the generative text of the field of transgender studies (Stryker and Whittle, 2006). Naming her intervention "A Posttranssexual Manifesto," Stone used a post-structural analysis to respond to both mainstream medical discourses and radical feminist discourses that had both worked to nullify transsexuals' perspectives on their own lives. Revisiting early autobiographical texts, Stone deconstructed the conditions under which they were produced, including the requirements of the clinicians who authorized sex-change procedures. Stone called for transsexuals to refuse to disappear into their new lives and to speak instead from their specific subject positions to disrupt "conventional gender discourse" (p. 296). When she called for a "post-transsexual" politic of visibility, Stone did not yet have the term "transgender"; it was proposed by those who answered her (see Bornstein, 1994; Feinberg, 1996; Stryker, 2006b; Wilchins, 1997). As Stryker (2006a) remarks, "transgender" moved trans subjects "from the clinics to the streets" (p. 2).

"Transgender" emerged in the context of the new queer interest in gender subversion, instability, and transgression. In *Gender Trouble,* an inaugural work of queer theory, Butler (1990) argued that marginalized identities are complicit in their marginalization through the reification of their own identity boundaries. An essential identity of "woman," Butler suggested, contributes to women's abjection. Further, the harmful heterosexualization of desire is made possible by the construct of two stable biological sexes, extended to two social gender roles, inevitably attracted to one another (Butler, 1990). Claiming instead that all gender is imitative, Butler (1990) proposed that repetitive gendered acts give rise to the categories we think of as biological sex, rather than the other way around. Redeeming drag and butch-femme expression from accusations of heteronormativity, Butler (1990) contended that queer gender practices use mimicry to subvert rather than reify norms; thus, drag makes visible the mimicry in all gender expression. In this vein, queer theory advanced a politic built on trouble and subversion, with transgender phenomena often serving as example (Prosser, 1998).

The impact of early queer theory on feminism, gay and lesbian studies, and the social sciences and humanities more broadly was atomic. Stryker (2004) is not alone in her admission that the 1990s radical vision of queer took her breath away (p. 213). Yet as queer theory increasingly articulated itself, it did so against that which was unqueer. And transsexuals, with their "true selves" and their "wrong body" metaphors, appeared to be *very* unqueer. Contributing to a corpus of anti-transsexual moral critique from radical feminists (Raymond, 1979), social scientists (Billings and Urban, 1982), psychoanalytic scholars (Millot, 1990), and feminist post-structuralists (Hausman, 1995), queer theory added a novel twist to the familiar refrain that transsexuals do gender wrong. Unlike the mainstream, which chided transsexuals for their transgressions, queer theory rebuked them for their failure to more fully transgress – for buying into conservative gender norms and as Davy (2011) notes, for basically having "bad politics" (p. 169). Butler's (1993) controversial discussion of the transsexual subjects who appeared in Jennie Livingston's (1990) documentary *Paris Is Burning* became a flashpoint for this debate.

Paris Is Burning depicted the cultural moment of the 1980s New York City gay "ball" scene, which was led by black and other racialized queer communities. Although Livingston primarily followed subjects who would not have been described as transsexual, the film did feature Venus Xtravaganza, a transsexual Latina sex worker living and working as a woman. In one particular scene, Xtravaganza and another transsexual woman recount their desires for the camera, perhaps at the prompting of Livingston. In a series of rapidly cut segments, the women list what they long for. As a (potentially heterosexual) transsexual woman living in urban poverty, Xtravaganza mentioned the sex-change operation that she could not afford, a home in the suburbs, and a husband. Not long after this scene, the viewer learns that Xtravaganza has been murdered, presumably by a client, possibly by a client who discovered her status as a transsexual. Her friend states matter of factly, "That's just part of being a transsexual in New York City." To the dismay of trans scholars and activists, Butler (1993) used the events of Xtravaganza's (actual) death as a backdrop against which to stage an argument about the merits of subversion, taking the opportunity to comment on the heteronormativity of Xtravaganza's desires and the symbolic meaning of a death that came while pursuing those desires. Butler further remarked that Xtravaganza's death "testifies" to her "tragic misreading of the social map of power," and drew links between transsexualism and what Butler called the "uncritical miming of the hegemonic"(p. 131). Appearing alongside uplifting depictions of drag, this belittling of transsexual desire, and transsexual death, inspired outrage.

The critiques came quickly and covered much ground. Namaste (2000) charged that queer theory in general, and Butler in this instance, showed a lack of regard for the lives of its celebrated gender transgressors – a disregard made possible by what she described as the methodological weakness of a field that evolved from literary, cultural, and film studies. Queer theory, argued Namaste (2000), had abandoned Foucault's detailed examination of social and institutional power in favour of representational analysis. For example, the lack of state funding for transsexual health care, the disposability of racialized transsexual lives, and the social and legal vulnerability of sex workers were pushed aside to comment on the symbolism of Xtravaganza's death. In his lengthy critique of Butler, Prosser (1998) pointed out that Xtravaganza's disparaged desires (for surgery, for a home, and for a husband) are desires that, had they been fulfilled, might have saved her life. Prosser (1998) charged that Butler's critique "perversely" invested subversive value "in that which makes the subject's real life most unsafe" (p. 49). Rubin (1998) remarked that the gap between queer theory and the communities it spoke to had grown into an "abyss" (p. 279).

The Opening of Theoretical Doors

Though Namaste (2000) called for the rejection of queer theory on "theoretical and political grounds" (p. 9), I would argue that the critiques offered by queer theory (and its post-structural forebears) are indispensable. Historical studies of sexual and gender categories (Chauncey, 1994; Foucault, 1990; Valentine, 2007) have shown us that our taken-for-granted identities are often historically specific and delivered to us through networks of power, with effects that fall short of liberation. Such is the case for transsexual and transgender identities as well. Yet the undoing of identity can reduce and endanger the space available for those identities that are on the margins, and so there is a need to find a way forward. A number of feminist theorists have attempted to account for the value of both queer and trans (transgender and transsexual) positions (Elliot, 2010; Heyes, 2003; MacDonald, 1998), and this chapter builds on their important work. I propose that our ability to craft what Riddell (1996) and Prosser (1998) called for, our ability to craft theory with more "living space," is contingent upon our willingness to open new doors – doors to meaning with respect to the ontology of gender, the medical body, and the self-knowledge of speaking subjects.

The Ontology of Gender: Contesting the Gendered Self

At the beginning of the debate between queer-theory-aligned transgender versus transsexual positions is a question of ontology – a question of what gender *is*. The all-too-familiar status quo is that biology is the bedrock of gender. The relationship between sex and gender is mechanical; gender is the social mirror of biological sex, and thus males are inevitably masculine and females inevitably feminine; biology is destiny, as they say (Stryker, 2006a). In an early sociological theorization, Garfinkel (1957) referred to this as the "natural attitude" toward gender. This problematic attitude is now most commonly termed "gender essentialism": the belief that men are naturally a certain way and that women are naturally another way, by nature of their essences (Bialystock, 2013). As Butler (1990) and other feminists effectively pointed out, this has long been used to naturalize woman's subordinate position. Yet Butler (1990) cast the anti-essentialist net wider with the post-structural proposal that investing in the identity of "woman" (as most feminist projects do) is detrimental to women. Queer theory concurred that investing in a gay identity is subject to the same fatal limitations (Halperin, 1995). Anti-essentialism thus came to be a crucial marker of queer theory, along with the celebration of fluidity and the rejection of identity.

For queer-theory-based and some queer-aligned transgender people, a refusal of gendered "realness" is vital. Rejecting the terms of medicalized transsexuality (the *insistence* on an unambiguous crossing as remedy for misalignment) lifts categorical constraints and opens up new possibilities for "outlaw" bodies and genders to flourish. Indeed, transgender advocates have made anti-essentialist claims central to their political strategy, refusing to pass as, or circulate the discourse of, "real" men and women (Bornstein, 1994; Nobel, 2006; Wilchins, 1997). Bornstein (1994) summarizes her position: "the idea of gender itself ... needs to be done away with" (p. 114). To be clear, I understand these claims to be nothing short of life sustaining for *some*. Yet the liberatory potential of this begins to fracture when applied to some transsexuals. For example, a common feature of transsexual narratives is a claim to *constancy* – to have always been one's felt gender; thus, transition makes it possible to become the person who one always knew one was (Bialystock, 2013; Elliot, 2010; Rubin, 1998). The concept of fluidity in fact may not be relevant to some transsexuals, if they experience their gender identity as having preceded and survived the forces of socialization, including their own attempts at self-suppression (Bialystock, 2013). In the end, for some transsexuals, it is sex (the body) not gender (the identity) that proves fluid and changeable, albeit within limitations.

This sense of fixedness can of course be viewed as a claim to essence and thus subject to substantial critique. Indeed, transsexuals have been read through a post-structural or queer lens to be terminally attached to the "fiction" of gender. Hausman (1995) believes that transsexuals tame the radical potential of non-conformity, asserting that "transsexuals are the dupes of gender" (p. 140). Even queer/transgender texts that are more sympathetic to trans subjects suggest that transsexuals erroneously imagine the significance of sex and gender. Halberstam (1994) writes, "it is perhaps preferable therefore to acknowledge that gender is defined by its transitivity, that sexuality manifests as multiple sexualities, and that therefore we are all transsexuals. There are no transsexuals" (p. 226). It probably does not need saying that most if not all transsexuals would disagree with both the assertion that everyone is a transsexual and the idea that no one is. Rubin (1998) argues that the denial of gender identity's significance "invalidates the categories by which the subject makes sense of its own experience" (p. 265).

Distilled down, this debate turns on the presumed error of the essential self. Fuss (1989) remarks of essentialism, "few other words in the vocabulary of contemporary critical theory are so persistently maligned, so little interrogated, and so predictably summoned as a term of infallible critique" (p. xi). Prosser (1998) points out that anti-essentialism has become a "routine" of theory, supporting Sedgwick and Frank's (1995) proposal that at times we must "take the risk of essentialism" (Prosser, 1998, p. 17). Speaking specifically to transsexual narratives, Bialystock (2013) proposes that we must learn to distinguish between *essentialisms* – between archaic notions about the nature of *all* men and women, versus the very intimate, very urgent question of "who am I?" (p. 129). Although Foucault (1990) and the queer theorists who followed certainly gave us a sense of history regarding how subjects are incited to answer the question "who am I?," this alone does not make the answers that are proffered unquestionably false. Critics who remain skeptical point to the "danger" of such admissions to prop up gender hierarchies, in particular male domination (Halberstam, 1998; Heyes, 2003). This projected end point is by no means certain, but if we grant that an essential understanding of the gendered self can be viewed as dangerous, so too can the denial of another's foundational claim to that self. Danger is a matter of perspective.

Stone's (1991) post-structural analysis of what she deemed the rigidity of the transsexual script pointed out that a word was missing from these totalizing narratives: the word "some." Yet queer scripts have often reproduced a problematic reversal, with (paradoxically) universalist anti-claims to a total fluidity. I propose a loosening of the essentialist/anti-essentialist chokehold to allow the full range of gender narratives to breathe. If, for some trans people, the claim to gender fluidity is vital and necessary, yet for others, it is an imposition that denies their specificity, then Stone's missing word "some" may indeed be our needed tonic. For *some*, gender may be fluid and untethered, and for *some*, it may be fixed and unambiguous, thus compelling, for *some*, the medical interventions explored below.

Medical Meaning

A common post-structural analysis of transsexualism is that transsexual bodily modifications (i.e., sex-change) are conservative and assimilationist, and capitulate to, rather than challenge, gender norms. This is not a compliment.

Advancing a queer feminist position, Hausman (1995) argues that transsexual surgery props up gender norms and should therefore be discontinued. Others share variations of her criticism. Garber (1992) remarks that transsexuals "essentialize their genitalia" (p. 98). Reich (1992) states that transsexuality "works to stabilize the old sex/gender system by insisting on the dominant correspondence between gender desire and biological sex" (p. 121). Davy (2011) notes that this evaluative approach to bodies results in a moral dichotomy, pitting the subversive (good) against the docile (bad).

Among those who are opposed to transsexual body modification, a common view is that transsexuals are the passive products of technology and are thus docile, not subversive. Feminist theorists such as Jeffreys (1997) cast transsexuals as the victims of their own gender transitions. Further, poststructural scholars, drawing on a Foucauldian analysis, have tended to regard medicine as always and only a normalizing force (Davy, 2011). Yet what this perspective does not consider is transsexual agency. Meyerowitz (2002) chronicles the complex negotiations that took place between transsexuals and medical professionals during the 1960s development of sex-change technologies. Indeed, early clinicians described the desire of the transsexuals whom they encountered as "a fierce and demanding drive" and complained about the lengths they would go to in pursuit of their goals (Meyerowitz, 2002, p. 130). Devor and Matte (2006) recount that one wealthy transsexual (Reed Erickson) personally funded early surgical development. Thus, these individuals can hardly be described as the passive victims of science. In the rush to depict transsexuals as constructed, Prosser (1998) points out that such theorists have failed to recognize transsexuals as "constructing subjects" and furthermore, failed to detect anything positive about construction (p. 8).

What queer-theory-based critics of transsexual practices miss is the body underneath the discourse about the body – the material flesh in question as the "contingent ground of all our knowledge" (Stryker, 2006a, p. 12). As Rubin (1998) states, "Bodies are the ultimate point of view" (p. 268). With an analysis that rarely dipped below the surface of discourse, early queer theory missed this crucial sign, a space that has since been filled by a proliferation of theorizing about trans embodiment (Davy, 2011; Elliot and Roen, 1998; Prosser, 1998; Rubin, 1998), including proposals for alternative methodologies (such as phenomenology) that might better grasp the somatic experience, which discourse analysis overlooks (Davy, 2011; Rubin, 1998). Although the queer-theory-based transgender position proposes gender incoherence as a form of subversion (Halberstam, 1998; Nobel, 2006), Prosser (1998) reminds us that for many, incoherence is a "barely livable zone," gesturing to the profound exclusion and abhorrent violence that can await those who occupy the space between genders (p. 12). Instead, Prosser (1998) theorizes the transsexual move toward coherence as a journey on the path to integration and wholeness (p. 80). For some trans subjects, the body need not be altered, or it may deliberately be partially altered for a visibly queer or trans "aesthetic" (Davy, 2011). For others, a disjoint must be healed for a livable life, and for these latter subjects, our theoretical doors must open onto new questions about the meaning of shaping "flesh to self" (Prosser, 1998, p. 59) and the methods by which we ascertain such meanings.

Self-Knowledge and the Speaking Subject

> The sounds that come out of my mouth
> can be summarily dismissed.
>
> – S. Stryker, "My Words to Victor Frankenstein"

In early medical gender clinics, the clinicians who presided over access to sex-change technologies were invested with a staggering level of institutional power. For transsexuals who found their original role unlivable, the stakes were high. Successfully "mapping the relations of power" in the clinic (Stryker and Whittle, 2006) depended on producing the correct autobiographical narrative, featuring, among other things, an unequivocal lifetime identification with the new role, an asexual past and heterosexual future, and sexist ideologies too numerous to list (Stone, 1991). It is generally acknowledged by both sides of the adversarial clinician-patient dyad that transsexuals took it upon themselves to study the available texts about transsexuality and to counsel one another in preparation for their assessments (Stone, 1991). Clinicians, for their part, coached each other on how to distinguish authentic accounts from stories that they saw as duplicitous and as frustrating their task of discerning "true" from "false" transsexuals (see Lothstein, 1983).

Post-structural trans scholar Sandy Stone (1991) was the first to publicly blast the imposition of these requisite narratives, referring to the virtual library of identical autobiographical stories as "suspicious" (p. 289). Stone (1991) called for transsexuals to deploy the complexity of their subjectivity as a means to wrest themselves out from under clinical control, as well as to respond to the ire of radical feminists who had seized on the sexist elements in transsexual autobiographies. The transgender movement answered Stone's call and continues, with great pleasure, to queerly disrupt the accepted trans narrative

(Bornstein, 1994; Spade, 2006; Wilchins, 1997). Though the official story of transsexuality still structures the clinic encounter in many jurisdictions (Namaste, 2000), the proliferation of multiple narratives has loosened its hold considerably. No tears will be shed about that. Yet Stone's inclusion of the word "suspicious" suggests that post-structural and queer theories may have left the trope of the duplicitous transsexual intact, establishing new hierarchies of gender legitimacy and ultimately failing to achieve justice for the diversity of trans subjects.

The sticking point in queer theory interpretations of trans narratives is the authority that is given (or not) to the speaker. Faithful to the methods of discourse analysis and deconstruction, queer theory scours texts to undercut implicit essentialist statements that limit radical potential. In the transsexual narrative, the enthusiastic theorist need not look far; many transsexuals convey the sense that they have "always" been their felt gender, that they are "trapped in the wrong body," and that they are compelled to express their "true" self. These binaries of wrong body/right body and true self/false self are absolute anathema to queer theory, and some queer (including transgender) authors have stated as much. Halberstam (1998) asks rhetorically, "Who might we ask, can afford to dream of a right body? Who believes such a body exists?" (p. 172). Yet if we are to take transsexuals seriously, which I argue that we must do, the self-evident answer to Halberstam's question is that many transsexuals believe in a right body, or at least in a body that is "righter." Attempting to undermine the official clinical gender story, Bornstein (1994) comments that the "wrong body" metaphor merely reflects cultural norms and is not an "honest reflection of our transgender feelings" (p. 66). By this, she may simply have meant her own "transgender feelings," yet by universalizing her claim, she ascribes to more traditional transsexuals a false consciousness that has become almost classic.

Rubin (1998) points out that theory's denial of transsexual self-description plays into "patterns of domination" (p. 264). At the heart of modernist transphobia is the rejection of the transsexual claim to self. The suspicion in the gender clinic, the refusal of chosen names and pronouns, the denial of access to gender-specific spaces and services, and all manner of symbolic and literal violences enacted on trans bodies are seen as acceptable responses to people who "lie" about who they are (Bettcher, 2007). What begs our attention is the concern that a skeptical postmodern theory may recycle this offence, refusing the transsexual self-account not because it is inauthentic or unreal, but because it appeals to the concepts of authenticity and realness, resolutely discarded by some theorists. Lacanian Catherine Millot (1990) states, "In their requirement of truth ... transsexuals are the victims of error" (p. 143).

To be sure, the "wrong body" metaphor remains contested for many reasons, not the least of which is that it requires us to concede that something is wrong with trans bodies (Bettcher, 2014). Yet to evade Kaufmann's (2010) "analytic erasure," we must explore, as Bettcher (2014) does, how such narratives might be resistant, while, admittedly, also being insufficient. For example, Rubin (2003) took note of the ahistorical and essentialized narratives of the transsexual men in his study – who often reported that they had *always* been men – yet Rubin suggests that we ask "what matters to people, not what is the matter with them" (p. 10). Scholars have brought attention back to the function of the transsexual narrative – the need to render somatic sensation as story, sensation that may not lend itself well to story at all. Elliot and Roen (1998) note that the transsexuals interviewed in their study often had difficulty articulating their experience: "It's very hard to put into words" (p. 256). In Meadow's (2011) study with parents of gender-variant children, one mother recalled that her transgender daughter (once her son) described her sense of being a girl as coming from "deep down where the music plays" (p. 740). Meadow (2011) concludes that the discourses often used to account for gender difference (biology, psychology, and secular spirituality) can be regulatory but can also serve as ready tools for the subject to speak its account. Such accounts, Salah (2007) writes, "straddle and confound the social, biological and symbolic registers" (p. 152).

In his analysis of transsexual autobiography, Prosser (1998) suggests that the construction of narrative can function to heal the painful split that many transsexuals describe. Like surgery itself, the metaphorical story, the story of continuity, sews the seams of the past and the future, and narrates the journey "home" (Prosser, 1998). Scholars of trans narratives have since offered strong critiques of this theory that takes body narratives as a priori truths. For example, Bhanji (2013) considers "migration" metaphors in trans narratives, suggesting that the concept of "home" may be available to some trans subjects and not others, on the basis of race and national belonging. Salamon (2010) argues that the material body is not as available to our consciousness as Prosser would like to suggest. In addition, Kapusta (2013) and Crawford (2013) point out that our identities and our bodily sensations are never solely our own interior phenomena but are always delivered to us via the social and are thus subject to discursive influence. Yet whether or not we take essentialized transsexual narratives as presumptively true, it behooves us to open theoretical doors to their meaning. If we are to maintain a suspicion of essentialized narratives, let us also develop a suspicion of theory that claims false consciousness for the subjects about which it opines. This new suspicion may in fact serve as what Prosser (1998) calls our "crucial braking mechanism" in our rush to deconstruct (p. 17). What a human being can know of the somatic self and what a human being can articulate of that self are questions that must remain open.

Implications for Social Work Education

Some major theorists, perhaps as a result of these debates, did eventually shift or clarify their positions. In her later work, Butler (2004) acknowledged, "The transsexual desire to become a man or a woman is not to be dismissed as a simple desire to conform to established identity categories" (p. 8). Similarly, Halberstam (2005) recognized that "transsexual is not simply the conservative medical term to transgender's transgressive vernacular" (p. 54). Yet the debates discussed in this chapter were widely circulated and arguably remain in play in contemporary queer politics. To address what is at stake, I want to return to Rubin's (2003) suggestion that we ask "what matters to people, not what is the matter with them" (p. 10). What I have proposed is that what matters to different trans subjects is, well, different. For some, who may identify with the radical visibility and fluidity of queer and transgender movements, what matters is the removal of identity's constraints – the possibility of motion – the opening of gendered *space*. Halberstam (1994), for example, champions gender's "transitivity" (p. 226). For those transsexuals who seek to quietly make their crossing or who feel they have always been their felt selves, what matters is stability and continuity – a sense of gendered *place*. Prosser (1998) reminds us, "there's no place like home" (p. 171). This is not an exhaustive account of what matters to trans subjects – indeed, multiple intersecting identities would make such a list impossibly problematic – but the space/place distinction remains useful for securing contradictory gender trajectories as legitimate.

For social work educators, what might this mean in the classroom? To begin, those who seek to include trans-themed texts in course syllabi, which I sincerely hope that they do, can be thoughtful about their selections. Does a particular text position trans people (however positively) as outside and beyond gender, as gender's outer *space*? If so, this text can be paired with a reading that speaks to transsexual concerns of authenticity, embodiment, stability, and place, as a way of exploring the diversity of claims emanating from marginalized groups. Educators who engage trans guest speakers or trans students in the classroom about their personal experience can be mindful of an individual's alignment within the space/place identity framework and supplement the discussion with alternative perspectives. In lectures about post-structural concepts of the self, the contested nature of those concepts can be explored by presenting transsexual objections to the proposed fiction and fluidity of identity. When teaching queer theory, educators can avoid the assumption that queer is a synonym for trans (though it might be for some), or that queer theory is the most appropriate framework with which to explore trans lives (though again, it might be for some). Lastly, these debates can serve as an entry point for inquiring about the implications of our theories and the (in)ability of those theories to help us understand, in Rubin's (2003) words, "what matters to people" (p. 10).

Beyond these concerns over classroom content, I would also suggest that we direct Rubin's question to ourselves as well – that we ask ourselves what matters to *us*. As scholars, educators, activists, theorists, and students, what is it that matters? bell hooks (1994) famously said, "I came to theory because I was hurting." "I saw in theory," she went on to say, "a location for healing" (p. 59). Yet as we look back on the theoretical contests over trans legitimacy, it is clear that theory's potential for healing is matched by its potential for injury. Consider the opening moment of this chapter – Kaufmann's (2010) admission that she made one of her research participants cry (p. 104). For the participant, a transsexual woman, the post-structural queer dissection of her identity brought her to tears: death by deconstruction.

Although, of course, there exists the possibility of ill intent in scholarly debate, in many instances the elisions recalled in this chapter seem to be rooted more in a belief in the soundness of one's own analysis and the error of another's. For social work educators, these debates provide a forum for thinking through how binaristic social justice analyses (progressive versus regressive, subversive versus docile, good versus bad) may themselves contribute to injustice. As we look for and find these binaries threaded through a post-structural tradition that is so opposed to binaries, what does this tell us about what matters to us? What can we learn about our attachment to our progressive identities, our willingness to claim a higher truth, and our tendency to value theoretical consistency over genuine curiosity? As social work interest grows in queer theory, in post-structural concepts of self, and in the desire to represent trans lives in the classroom, we have a responsibility to do justice to trans experience by opening theoretical doors that have been prematurely shut – doors to the meaning of the gendered self, the medical body, and the authority of the speaking subject. Ultimately, what matters is that we use theory as a tool to grow, rather than shrink, our "living space" (Riddell, 1996).

References

Beasley, C. (2005). *Gender and sexuality: Critical theories, critical thinkers*. London: Sage.
Bettcher, T.M. (2007). "Evil deceivers and make-believers: On transphobic violence and the politics of illusion." *Hypatia* 22 (3): 43–65. http://dx.doi.org/10.1111/j.1527-2001.2007.tb01090.x.
–. (2009). "Feminist perspectives on trans issues." In *The Stanford Encyclopedia of Philosophy*. Retrieved from https://leibniz.stanford.edu/friends/preview/feminism-trans/.
–. (2014). "Trapped in the wrong theory: Rethinking trans oppression and resistance." *Signs* (Chicago) 39 (2): 383–406. http://dx.doi.org/10.1086/673088.
Bhanji, N. (2013). "Trans/scriptions: Homing desires, trans(sexual) citizenship and the racialized bodies." In *Transgender Studies Reader 2*, ed. S. Stryker and A. Aizura, 512–27. New York: Routledge.
Bialystock, L. (2013). "Authenticity and trans identity." In *Talk about Sex: A Multidisciplinary Discussion*, ed. R. Stewart, 122–245. Sydney: Cape Breton University Press.
Billings, D., and T. Urban. (1982). "The socio-medical construction of transsexualism: An interpretation and critique." *Social Problems* 29 (3): 266–82. http://dx.doi.org/10.2307/800159.
Bornstein, Kate. (1994). *Gender outlaws: Men, women and the rest of us*. New York: Routledge.
Burdge, B. (2007). "Bending gender, ending gender: Theoretical foundations for social work practice with the transgender community." *Social Work* 52 (3): 243–50. http://dx.doi.org/10.1093/sw/52.3.243.
Butler, J. (1990). *Gender trouble*. New York: Routledge.
–. (1993). *Bodies that matter: On the discursive limits of sex*. New York: Routledge.
–. (2004). *Undoing gender*. New York: Routledge.
Chauncey, G. (1994). *Gay New York: Gender, urban culture and the making of the gay male world*. New York: Basic Books.
Crawford, L.C. (2013). "Transgender without organs? Mobilizing a geo-affective theory of gender modification." In *Transgender Studies Reader 2*, ed. S. Stryker and A. Aizura, 473–82. New York: Routledge.
Daly, M. (1978). *Gyn/ecology: The metaethics of radical feminism*. Boston: Beacon Press.
Davy, Z. (2011). *Recognizing transsexuals: Personal, political and medicolegal embodiment*. Aldershot, UK: Ashgate.
Devor, A., and N. Matte. (2006). "ONE Inc. and Reed Erickson: The uneasy collaboration of gay and trans activism, 1964–2003." In *The Transgender Studies Reader*, ed. S. Stryker and S. Whittle, 387–406. New York: Routledge.
Elliot, P. (2010). *Debates in transgender, queer and feminist theory: Contested sites*. Farnham, UK: Ashgate.
Elliot, P., and K. Roen. (1998). "Transgenderism and the question of embodiment: Promising queer politics?" *GLQ: A Journal of Lesbian and Gay Studies* 4 (2): 231–61.
Feinberg, L. (1996). *Transgender warriors: Making history from Joan of Arc to RuPaul*. Boston: Beacon Press.
Foucault, M. (1990). *The history of sexuality*. Vol. 1, *An introduction*. New York: Random House. (Original work published 1978.)
Fuss, D. (1989). *Essentially speaking: Feminism, nature and difference*. New York: Routledge.
Garber, M. (1992). *Vested interests: Cross dressing and cultural anxiety*. New York: Routledge.
Garfinkel, H. (1957). *Studies in ethnomethodology*. Oxford: Polity Press.
Green, R., and J. Money. (1969). *Transsexualism and sex reassignment*. Baltimore: Johns Hopkins University Press.
Halberstam, J. (1994). "F2M: The making of female masculinity." In *The Lesbian Postmodern*, ed. L. Doan, 210–28. New York: Columbia University Press.
–. (1998). *Female masculinity*. Durham, NC: Duke University Press.

—. (2005). *In a queer time and place: Transgender bodies, subcultural lives*. New York: New York University Press.
Halperin, D. (1995). *Saint Foucault: Towards a gay hagiography*. New York: Oxford University Press.
Hausman, B. (1995). *Changing sex: Transsexualism, technology and the idea of gender*. Durham, NC: Duke University Press.
Heyes, C. (2003). "Feminist solidarity after queer theory: The case of transgender." *Signs* (Chicago) 28 (4): 1093–120. http://dx.doi.org/10.1086/343132.
hooks, b. (1994). *Teaching to transgress: Education as the practice of freedom*. New York: Routledge.
Jagose, A. (1996). *Queer theory: An introduction*. New York: New York University Press.
Jeffreys, S. (1997). "Transgender activism: A lesbian feminist perspective." *Journal of Lesbian Studies* 1 (3–4): 55–74. http://dx.doi.org/10.1300/J155v01n03_03.
Kapusta, S. (2013). "Trans authenticity and the feminist legacy of relationality." In *Talk about Sex: A Multidisciplinary Discussion*, ed. R. Stewart, 144–53. Sydney: Cape Breton University Press.
Kaufmann, J. (2010). "Trans representation." *Qualitative Inquiry* 16 (2): 104–15. http://dx.doi.org/10.1177/1077800409350699.
Kirby, A. (2008). "What is trans? Tools for an open dialogue." *Women's Studies Quarterly* 36 (3–4): 292–93. http://dx.doi.org/10.1353/wsq.0.0133.
Levine, C.O. (1978). "Social work with transsexuals." *Social Casework* 59 (3): 167–74.
Livingston, J. (1990). *Paris is burning* [Documentary film]. United States: Academy Entertainment Off White Productions.
Lothstein, L. (1983). *Female to male transsexualism: Historical, clinical and theoretical issues*. New York: Routledge.
MacDonald, E. (1998). "Critical identities: Rethinking feminism through transgender politics." *Atlantis* 23 (1): 3–12.
Mallon, G.P. (1999). "A call for organizational trans-formation." *Journal of Gay and Lesbian Social Services* 10 (3–4): 131–42.
Markman, E. (2011). "Gender identity disorder, the gender binary, and transgender oppression: Implications for ethical social work." *Smith College Studies in Social Work* 81 (4): 314–27. http://dx.doi.org/10.1080/00377317.2011.616839.
McPhail, B. (2004). "Questioning gender and sexuality binaries: What queer theorists, transgendered individuals, and sex researchers can teach social work." *GLQ: A Journal of Lesbian and Gay Studies* 11 (2): 3–21.
—. (2008). "Re-gendering the social work curriculum: New realities and complexities." *Journal of Social Work Education* 44 (2): 33–52. http://dx.doi.org/10.5175/JSWE.2008.200600148.
Meadow, T. (2011). "Deep down where the music plays: How parents account for childhood gender variance." *Sexualities* 14 (6): 725–47. http://dx.doi.org/10.1177/1363460711420463.
Meyerowitz, J. (2002). *How sex changed: A history of transsexuality in the United States*. Cambridge, MA: Harvard University Press.
Millot, C. (1990). *Horsexe: An essay on transsexuality*. Trans. K. Hylton. New York: Autonomedia.
Nagoshi, J.L., and S. Brzuzy. (2010). "Transgender theory: Embodying research and practice." *Affilia* 25 (4): 431–43. http://dx.doi.org/10.1177/0886109910384068.
Namaste, V. (1996). "Tragic misreadings: Queer theory's erasure of transgender subjectivity." In *Queer Studies: A Lesbian, Gay, Bisexual and Transgender Anthology*, ed. B. Beemyn and M. Eliason, 183–203. New York: New York University Press.
—. (2000). *Invisible lives: The erasure of transsexual and transgendered people*. Chicago: University of Chicago Press.
Nobel, J. (2006). *Sons of the movement: FtMs risking incoherence on a post-queer cultural landscape*. Toronto: Women's Press.

Phillips, S., C. McMillen, J. Sparks, and M. Ueberle. (1997). "Concrete strategies for sensitizing youth-serving agencies to the needs of gay, lesbian, and other sexual minority youth." *Child Welfare* 76 (3): 393–409.

Prosser, J. (1998). *Second skins: The body narratives of transsexuality.* New York: Columbia University Press.

Raymond, J. (1979). *The transsexual empire: The making of the she-male.* Boston: Beacon.

Reich, J. (1992). "Genderfuck: The law of the dildo." *Discourse* 15 (1): 112–127.

Riddell, C. (1996). "Divided sisterhood: A critical review of Janice Raymond's transsexual empire." In *Blending Genders: Social Aspects of Cross-Dressing and Sex-Changing,* ed. R. Ekins and D. King, 171-89. London: Routledge.

Rubin, H. (1998). "Phenomenology as method in trans studies." *GLQ: A Journal of Lesbian and Gay Studies* 4 (2): 263–81.

–. (2003). *Self-made men: Identity and embodiment among transsexual men.* Nashville: Vanderbilt University Press.

Salah, T. (2007). "Undoing trans studies." *Topia: Canadian Journal of Cultural Studies* 17: 150–55.

Salamon, G. (2010). *Assuming a body: Transgender and rhetorics of materiality.* New York: Columbia University Press.

Sedgwick, E.K., and A. Frank. (1995). "Shame in the cybernetic fold: Reading Silvan Tomkins." In *Shame and its sisters: A Silvan Tomkins reader,* ed. E.K. Sedgwick and A. Frank, 1-28. Durham and London: Duke University Press.

Spade, D. (2006). "Mutilating gender." In *The Transgender Studies Reader,* ed. S. Stryker and S. Whittle, 315–32. New York: Routledge.

Stone, S. (1991). "The empire strikes back: A posttranssexual manifesto." In *Body Guards: The Cultural Politics of Sexual Ambiguity,* ed. K. Straub and J. Epstein, 280–304. New York: Routledge.

Stryker, S. (2004). "Transgender studies: Queer theory's evil twin." *GLQ: A Journal of Lesbian and Gay Studies* 10 (2): 212–15. http://dx.doi.org/10.1215/10642684-10-2-212.

–. (2006a). "(De)subjugated knowledges: An introduction to transgender studies." In *The Transgender Studies Reader,* ed. S. Stryker and S. Whittle, 1–17. New York: Routledge.

–. (2006b). "My words to Victor Frankenstein above the village of Chamounix: Performing transgender rage." In *The Transgender Studies Reader,* ed. S. Stryker and S. Whittle, 244–56. New York: Routledge.

Stryker, S., and S. Whittle, eds. (2006). *The transgender studies reader.* New York: Routledge.

Valentine, D. (2007). *Imagining transgender: An ethnography of a category.* Durham, NC: Duke University Press. http://dx.doi.org/10.1215/9780822390213.

Wilchins, R.A. (1997). *Read my lips: Sexual subversion and the end of gender.* Ithaca: Firebrand.

4

Social Work, the Academy, and Queer Communities: Heteronormativity and Exclusion

SUSAN HILLOCK

Social work research and literature have covered many diverse topics related to queer people and their communities. However, the literature has not explored what individual social work academics, students, and practitioners know about queer-based theories, people, and issues, and how they teach and practise in these areas. Many commentators have mentioned this absence (Mallon, 1998a, 1998b; Trotter, 2000; Van Voorhis and Wagner, 2001; Willis, 2007). In addition, gender identity and expression, trans content and transphobia, and cisgenderism have historically been ignored. Generally speaking, although queer faculty and students have contributed to raising awareness and making change, minimal attention has been paid to how social workers learn, articulate, and use knowledge about LGBTQ community members and issues. Unfortunately, other literature regarding queering the broader academy, which could potentially have been helpful, does not discuss social work (Bacon, 2006; Bird, 2004; Ford, 2004; Ruffolo, 2006; Walker, 2004).

Although it seems clear that social work educators and field instructors have a responsibility to assist students to develop their understanding, sensitivity, and analytical, assessment, and practice skills with LGBTQ communities – and for most social workers, this process starts in the social work classroom and field practicum – there is limited information about how social work schools and educators achieve these ends. To fill this gap, this chapter describes the introduction and evolution of gay and lesbian studies. It also reviews attempts to queer the academy and highlights the social work profession's literature, understanding, and positions related to queering social work practice, social workers, social work schools, students, and research.

History of Gay and Lesbian Studies

Gay and lesbian studies (GLS) – the study of and research into issues related to sexual orientation and gender identity – began in the United States during the early 1970s. As part of a wider gay and lesbian liberation movement, queer students and faculty acted as instigators, raising awareness and demanding inclusivity and equality, and became the catalysts for the development of GLS programs. The University of California-Berkeley pioneered GLS undergraduate courses in the spring of 1970 (McNaron, 1997). The City College of San Francisco lays claim to developing one of the first American gay literature studies course, in 1972. In 1989, it formed the first American gay and lesbian studies department (City College of San Francisco, n.d.). In 1973, Lambda Legal was founded to provide legal aid, advice, education, and support to gays and lesbians (Lambda Legal, n.d.). In 1986, the City University of New York began the first comprehensive university student centre and gay and lesbian studies program (Center for LGBTQ Studies, n.d.).

Canadian LGBTQ Studies

In 1985, Concordia University introduced the first undergraduate course in lesbian studies curriculum at the Simone de Beauvoir Institute, Concordia's centre for women's studies (Simone de Beauvoir Institute, n.d.). In 1989, Concordia also developed the first gay studies' literature and film course. In 1992, it hosted the first worldwide research conference on gay and lesbian studies. Fifteen hundred researchers and scholars attended this conference, called La Ville en Rose (Simone de Beauvoir Institute, n.d.). Gradually, more courses and programs related to queer studies and gay, lesbian, bisexual, trans, and intersex issues, sexualities, gender, and sexual orientation were developed across Canada, particularly in urban areas.

In fact, most large Canadian universities now feature "sexuality studies (including LGBT/queer studies) programs and courses" (Fitzgerald and Rayter, 2012, p. xvii). Currently, ten Canadian universities have undergraduate and/or graduate programs and courses specializing in topics emphasizing gender, sexuality, sexual orientation/expression, heterosexism and cisgenderism, and trans, intersex, and queer theory/studies. As well, in 1998, the Mark S. Bonham Centre for Sexual Diversity Studies (http://www.uc.utoronto.ca/sexualdiversity) was founded at the University of Toronto. The largest and best-resourced LGBTQ program in the country, it offers undergraduate and graduate programming.

Community-based researchers, students, and scholars can also refer to archival holdings if they wish to study LGBTQ topics. The second-largest LGBTQ archives in the world, the Canadian Lesbian and Gay Archives, a huge repository that was established in 1973, is located in Toronto (http://www.clga.ca/). The University of Saskatchewan is known for developing extensive LGBTQ resources and services, including libraries and a rich archive (http://library.usask.ca/archives/collections/sexualdiversity.php). Also, the Pride library at Western University (http://www.uwo.ca/pridelib/) features the Hudler Archives (named after long-time queer activist and retired social worker Richard Hudler), with a number of LGBTQ holdings.

Queers, the Educational System, and Discrimination

The North American, British, and Australian literature regarding queering educational systems is somewhat limited. Most of the relevant books and articles are produced by gay/lesbian studies and gender and women's studies, are often outdated, and are heavily contextualized within the experience of and deal largely with American universities, faculty, and students (Bacon, 2006; Bird, 2004; Ford, 2004; Ruffolo, 2006; Walker, 2004). A comprehensive review and analysis of current Canadian literature found that little is known about Canadian queer history (Fitzgerald and Rayter, 2012) and that "most edited collections on sexuality for use in the classroom have little Canadian content" (p. xvii). For the most part, this literature does not mention social work.

Much of the work on queer issues and education has focused on the experiences of queer youth and the problem of bullying in schools. This makes sense, as "suicide is still the leading cause of death among queer youth" (Knegt, 2011, p. 73). Much media and international attention has concentrated on youth suicide and bullying, particularly in kindergarten to grade 12 (K-12) school systems, related to issues of sexuality, gender, and sexual orientation. In a national survey titled *Every Class in Every School,* Taylor et al. (2011) conclude that many students who identify as gay, lesbian, bisexual, or transgendered (or are perceived to be) experience verbal and physical harassment and/or are assaulted on a daily or weekly basis. Furthermore, two-thirds of these students reported feeling unsafe in schools, citing bathrooms and change rooms as the most dangerous places (Taylor et al., 2011).

Due to homophobia, heterosexism, oppression, and discrimination, queer youth and adults experience higher rates of mental illness, depression, anxiety, paranoia, and loneliness than the straight population (Canadian Mental Health Association Ontario, n.d.). Queer people also face discrimination in education, health care, housing, policing, social services, and employment. In 1996, a research study from Gay and Lesbian Health Services in Saskatoon demonstrated that queer Canadians experience a range of physical and mental health and social problems, including increased unemployment and lower life expectancy rates that are significantly out of proportion with the rest of society. Although this study found that homophobia, cisgenderism, and heterosexism are linked with major health and social issues for queers, few national, provincial, and municipal programs have been developed to intervene in these areas, and healthcare, mental health systems, and social services fail to adequately respond to homophobia and its impact on the well-being of queer individuals (Banks, 2003, pp. 8-15).

In addition, according to Knegt (2011), homophobic hate crimes are on the rise, and "nearly 75% go unreported" (p. 90). Furthermore, an American study found that gays and lesbians were the "most frequent victims of hate crimes" and that "school is the primary setting for this type of violence" (Herek, 1989, as quoted in Schneider, 1997, p. 294).

One might assume that "it gets better" for young people as they enter postsecondary and graduate education and/or the workforce. However, in Rankin's (2005) university study, most faculty, students, administrators, and staff felt that campus climates were homophobic toward LGBTQs. T. Warner (2002) underlines the importance of developing strategies and campaigns to dismantle heterosexism and eradicate homophobia in education because "schools, universities, and colleges of this country [Canada] are often hostile and unsafe places for lesbians, gays, bisexuals, and transgendered people" (p. 336). Furthermore, in a 2002 Quebec study, the majority of teachers surveyed acknowledged that they were aware of school-based homophobia, but three-quarters of them also admitted that they knew very little about homosexuality and needed more information (Fitzgerald and Rayter, 2012, p. 303). T. Warner (2002) argues that part of the problem is that information and resources on sexual orientation and homophobia are generally not available and that "teachers and counsellors seldom receive training on how to deal with students or with the harassment they receive" (p. 336). In addition, other studies have demonstrated that few queer teachers have come out, especially in the K-12 school systems, and that "education faculties at universities are paying limited attention to sexual diversity, heterosexism, and homophobia in professional teacher training" (Fitzgerald and Rayter, 2012, p. 303). There are significant gaps in education in this area. However, we also know that not everyone wishes to learn about heterosexism or is willing to change their homophobic beliefs and attitudes. Unfortunately, there are still many professionals who lack awareness and remain uneducated about queer people and their issues (T. Warner, 2002).

Queer students are not alone in facing harassment and discrimination: queer teachers and staff are also forced to deal with institutionalized homophobia (Knegt, 2011). Some classic examples include the 1976 case of Doug Wilson, a graduate student who was not allowed to supervise other students after he tried to organize an association for gay students at the University of Saskatchewan; the 2000 case of a grade 4 teacher who was reprimanded by an Ontario school board for bringing her same-sex partner to a social event and admitting to students that they were indeed lesbians; and the April 2010 case of a teacher, Lisa Reimer, who was fired by her Vancouver Catholic school board, allegedly because she and her same-sex partner had a child (Knegt, 2011). Thus, the risks and consequences for coming out on the job in education, as in other sectors, are very high. Fears of being fired, harmed, undermined, ostracized, not supported, and accused of child molestation are all valid reasons to keep queer teachers in the closet (Khayatt, 1992). Therefore, it is not surprising that many queer educators (and students) choose not to come out.

Queer Changes in Schools, Colleges, and Universities

Queer activism, successful Charter of Human Rights and Freedoms challenges and human rights complaints, the high rates of bullying, school shootings (mostly in the United States), and suicide among queer youth have forced schools, colleges, and universities to acknowledge problems and initiate changes. In the late 1990s, the education faculties of the University of Saskatchewan and the University of Alberta initiated teaching and research programs related to sexuality (Fitzgerald and Rayter, 2012, p. 299). Knegt (2011) notes that Toronto's York University hosted a Queer Nation conference in March 1996, featuring research presentations and discussion papers on lesbian and gay perspectives and approaches related to the field of Canadian studies. In addition, in the early 2000s, the University of Toronto and its Ontario Institute for Studies in Education created an in-service course on homophobia for teachers (Fitzgerald and Rayter, 2012, p. 299).

At the forefront of social changes, young students in the United States led the creation and development of a school-based gay-straight alliance (GSA) movement. In 1996, the US Gay Lesbian Straight education network initiated a nationwide "day of silence" to dramatize the silencing of sexual minorities in schools (p. 300). A Canadian version of this resistance movement is the Day of Pink, established by Jeremy Dias of the Canadian Centre for Gender and Sexual Diversity (formerly Jer's Vision) and based on a Nova Scotia teen's experience of being bullied with homophobic slurs because he wore a pink shirt to school (International Day of Pink, n.d.). In 2000, the BC Teachers' Federation, a long-time supporter of LGBTQ equality and rights, strongly endorsed the formation of GSAs and developed guidelines and bursaries in support (Clarke, 2000). By late 2004, half of Vancouver's high schools had GSAs, which soon spread across Canada. In 2006, the Canadian Teachers' Federation created and distributed a handbook on how to develop GSAs (Canadian Teachers' Federation, 2006). In 2002, after years of schools banning queer-positive books, the Supreme Court of Canada finally ruled these acts as unconstitutional and approved three specific children's books (*Chamerlain v. Surrey School District No. 36*, 2002). On a positive note and as an optimistic sign of change, Knegt (2011) points out that "in 2007, Canada's Human Rights Commission Report called for all schools – including religious ones – to engage in campaigns to combat homophobia, training for all school personnel on issues related to sexual diversity, and more inclusive curricula in faculties of education" (p. 89). Unfortunately, there has been strong resistance to these human rights advancements. A case in point is Bill 44, passed in 2009 by the Alberta government to allow parents to withdraw their children from classes if religion, sex, or sexual orientation lessons or content were being taught (Knegt, 2011; Bill 44, Human Rights, Citizenship and Multiculturalism Amendment Act, 2009). Also, in 2012, Ontario passed Bill 13, Accepting Schools Act, which supports the formation of GSAs in all publicly funded schools (including Catholic schools) (Bill 13, Accepting Schools Act, 2012), yet it has not been fully implemented, particularly in Catholic school settings (Moore, 2014).

Queer Presence and Absence in Social Work

A comprehensive review reveals minimal literature about LGBTQ theories, queer-identified people, and LGBTQ-related issues in Canadian academic literature generally and more particularly in social work practice and education. On the whole, as previously mentioned, how social workers learn, articulate, and use knowledge about LGBTQs or how they understand the related issues are infrequently taken up in the literature. Mallon (1998a, 1998b), Van Voorhis and Wagner (2002), and Willis (2007) note the glaring absence of LGBTQ content in the social work literature.

Most of the sparse professional social work research and scholarship that does focus on queer subject matter tends to consist of articles about the HIV/AIDS crisis (Van Voorhis and Wagner, 2001). To some degree, the social services literature has also featured LGBTQ youth work, particularly in foster care, public schools, and child welfare systems (Dame, 2004; Mallon, 1998b; Staller and Kirk, 1997; Wilber, Ryan, and Marksamer, 2006). Berger (1977, 1983, 1990, 1996) has written extensively about gay and lesbian social work practice in the United States. Other American scholarship in the area of practice includes Alderson (2013), Cosis Brown and Cocker (2011), Hidalgo, Peterson, and Woodman (1985), and Van Wormer, Wells, and Boes (2000). Important works related to social work with LGBTQ populations in Britain include Brown (1998) and Martin and Hunter (2001). In Canada, works contributing in this area include Brotman and Ou Jin Lee (2011), Dame (2004), Filax (2007), Gibson (2010), and Kwong-Lai Poon (2011). Overall, the discipline and its researchers, scholars, and publications have been slow in "recognizing the legitimacy of homosexuality in the professional literature" (Mallon, 1998a, p. 7). Consequently, Cosis Brown and Cocker (2011) maintain that, compared to other subjects and fields of study, "social work with lesbians and gay men attracts little academic and practice debate" and thus "remains a marginalised area of practice, research, and teaching" (p. 2).

Social Workers

According to Mackelprang, Ray, and Hernandez-Peck (1996), "because virtually every practitioner will work with gay, lesbian and bisexual clients, it is important that all practitioners develop ... competence in this area" (p. 29). Obviously, to be effective, social workers should be knowledgeable about service users' socio-cultural experiences in order to apply appropriate interventions (Vasquez and Eldridge, 1994). Homophobia, transphobia, cisgenderism, heterosexism, and discrimination (related to queer people) proliferate as long as social work and healthcare professions fail to educate and engage their workers in these subject areas (Gates, 2006). T. Warner (2002) makes the case that this bigotry persists due to a lack of knowledge, self-awareness, training, and information among practitioners but also because dominant medical models still see homosexuality as "deviant, abnormal, or dysfunctional" (p. 343). As he explains, these antiquated views cause harm to service users, who often experience a "refusal to recognize same-sex relationships, denial or inappropriate services, judgemental, hostile, patronizing, and moralizing responses" (p. 345) because of them.

Like teachers, social workers receive minimal training, information, and resources about LGBTQ populations and related issues (Gates, 2006). Trotter, Brogatzki, Duggan, Foster, and Levie (2006) also found that they were not very "informed about work with gay people or with broader issues of sexuality" (p. 369). From their own personal and professional experiences, Trotter et al. also noted that most social workers whom they knew "regarded sexuality as a minor issue that they need not address in any routine way" (p. 384). One might argue that sexuality in general and sexual orientation in particular are treated as taboo subjects in social work, perhaps reflecting a lack of awareness and discomfort about our own (and others') sexuality and identity.

Schools of Social Work

Given the values and beliefs of social work (CASW, 2005a, 2005b; CASWE, 2012), one might assume that homophobia, biphobia, transphobia, heterosexism, and cisgenderism would not be prevalent in its schools and faculties. Indeed, the Canadian Association of Social Workers' "Code of Ethics" (CASW, 2005a) clearly states that social workers must "recognize and respect the diversity of Canadian society" (p. 4). It also emphasizes that they must "not tolerate discrimination based on ... sexual orientation" (p. 3). In dealing with heterosexism, the "Guidelines for Ethical Practice" (CASW, 2005b) adds that social workers must also "acknowledge and respect the impact that their own heritage, values, beliefs, and preferences can have on their practice and on clients whose background and values may be different than their own" (p. 4). Significantly for education, these guidelines state that social workers must "endeavor to provide instruction based on the most current information and knowledge available in the profession" (p. 15). As well, the Canadian Association for Social Work Education's "Standards for Accreditation" (CASWE, 2012) highlights several principles that guide accreditation. These include a respect for human diversity and the requirement to promote social and economic justice, address structural sources of inequities, eliminate conditions that infringe human and civil rights, and encourage and support diversity and social justice related to gender and sexual identities (pp. 3–4). In addition, the jointly developed codes of ethics of the International Federation of Social Workers and the International Association of Schools of Social Workers state that there is an "international requirement to promote social justice for lesbian, gay, and bisexual people" (Fish, 2012, p. 15).

Given these ethical standards and responsibilities, one would think that social work schools would garner high marks for recognizing heterosexism, decreasing homophobia, sharing appropriate LGBTQ knowledge, and working collectively with LGBTQ communities to ensure human dignity, respect, equality, and safety for all individuals and to create the conditions necessary for social change. In fact, the limited scholarship that does exist shows that such is not the case. Indeed, one could argue that social work's performance in these areas is dismal.

Significantly, Mulé (2006) found that ethics codes and curricula standards were inconsistent in their inclusion of sexual orientation and that they did not address issues of gender identity and gender expression. Moreover, the social work profession can be viewed as "having a troubled relationship" with queer communities and even as being "historically engaged in their oppression" (Cosis Brown and Cocker, 2011, p. 2). According to Moore, Dietz, and Jenkins (1996), "even within the social work profession and schools of social work, there is much evidence that homophobia and heterosexism still dominate" (p. 88). Indeed, a 1987 study by Wisniewski and Toomey found "one third of social workers to be homophobic" (as quoted in Logie, Bridge, and Bridge, 2007, p. 201). According to Logie et al. (2007), this means that social workers are "more homophobic than psychologists and other mental health professionals" (p. 205). Social workers have also demonstrated high levels of heterosexist bias (Logie et al., 2007; Trotter et al., 2006). Unfortunately, attempts to decrease the homophobic and heterosexist prejudices of social work students have proven unsuccessful (Berkman and Zinberg, 1997; Cramer, 1997). In addition, Mackelprang et al. (1996) suggest that "providing content on gay and lesbian issues has been a relatively low priority in social work education" (p. 28). In an ad hoc survey of twenty-seven social work textbooks, Morrow (1996) found that "social work programs perpetuate bias and discrimination" and that "44 percent of all textbooks had low or no gay and lesbian content" (p. 1). More recent works, including Bacon (2006), Bird (2004), Chinell (2011), Fish (2012), and Foreman and Quinlan (2008), indicate that little has improved on this front. Altogether, these are powerful indicators that significant gaps in social work LGBTQ education, research, theorizing, analysis, debate, and coverage have continued over time.

Social Work Role Models

A clear example of queer absence in social work is the lack of positive role models in the literature, profession, and education, as is the case in Canadian society generally. Research shows that, although they may not identify as homosexual, 1.0 to 1.5 percent of the population in Western cultures have had homosexual contact, and as many as 10.0 percent of the population may be considered homosexual (Ernulf, Innala, and Whitam, 1989). Thus, one might assume that there are significant numbers of LGBTQ students, faculty, practitioners, and service users who are not visible in the research and literature. In fact, most social workers are probably unable to name a famous queer Canadian other than k.d. lang (singer), Libby Davies (NDP MP), Kathleen Wynne (Ontario premier), or Rick Mercer (comic), let alone a well-known queer social worker. This is predictable, as we have no way of knowing how many queer-identified social workers, social work academics, policy makers, field instructors, researchers, students, and administrators exist in Canada.

Indeed, there are no Canadian surveys or statistics regarding this subject. None of the provincial and territorial social work organizations, whether regulatory or association, has any statistics, documents, or research on queer academe, social work educators, social workers, social work students, or service users. These include the Canadian Association for Social Work Education (CASWE, http://caswe-acfts.ca/), Canadian Association of Social Workers (CASW, http://www.casw-acts.ca/), and Canadian Association of University Teachers (CAUT, https://www.caut.ca/) (personal communications, April-July 2013). A representative from CASWE did suggest that the accreditation self-study reports for individual schools of social work may contain some information about LGBTQ faculty, students, curricula, policies, and issues, but these are not on public record and are thus inaccessible (personal communication, April 2013).

To be sure, social work students, faculty, and administrators may also be very reluctant to identify as queer and be out at their work sites. Not surprisingly, queer social workers are "fearful of disclosing because of the detrimental effect on careers" (Trotter et al., 2006, p. 384). Indeed, Van Soest (1996) suggests that "gay and lesbian faculty may experience considerable personal and social stress if found out" (p. 61). According to Van Soest (1996), even when schools, colleges, and universities develop and implement anti-discriminatory policies, they are "often ignored by those controlling jobs, tenure, and promotion" (p. 56). This may also explain why scholars and authors rarely identify themselves as lesbian, gay, bisexual, transgendered, intersex, or queer in scholarly publications. Indeed, only a few articles are written by queer-identified or allied social work academics, who discuss their experiences in teaching students about LGBTQ theory, content, and related issues from a queer-identified perspective (Brownlee et al., 2005; Chinell, 2011; Erich, Bouttè-Queen, Donnelly, and Tittsworth, 2007; Foreman and Quinlan, 2008; Gerdes and Norman, 2008; McPhail, 2004; Todd and Coholic, 2007; Willis, 2007). Perhaps the fear of being outed, the devaluing of research on queer people and issues, and the potential of academic and personal backlash, discrimination, and harassment keep these authors from queer identifying (Van Voorhis and Wagner, 2002).

Another example of this queer invisibility/silencing in social work is the story of Mary Richmond and Jane Addams (Hamington, 2010). Richmond (1917) wrote *The Social Diagnosis,* and Addams established the Settlement House movement (Hamington, 2010). These women and their conflicting perspectives on the root causes and "treatments" of personal and social problems had major influences on the evolution of the social work profession and created what is now seen as a binary tension between micro and macro social work practice and theory. Many introductory social work classes discuss these founding foremothers, but what is often unmentioned, and therefore invisible and uncelebrated, is the fact that Jane Addams had female companions throughout her life. In 1889, she and Ellen Gates Starr co-founded the first settlement house in America (Hull House, Chicago), and it is likely that they were intimate partners (Tierney, 1997). Addams was also said to have had a same-sex relationship with Mary Rozet Smith that lasted for years (Hamington, 2010). Ironically, the social work ideals and ethics that we value today and associate with community development and anti-oppressive practice (AOP) – social justice, collectivity, respect, shared leadership, grassroots organizing, advocacy, empowerment, and democracy – and the evolution of social work practice itself, may be due more to Addams's neophyte version of queer social work theory and practice than we ever knew. Indeed, progressive social work has therefore always been queer, and failing to teach it as such not only distorts the values and beliefs that we hold dear but also ignores a social work grounded in the realities of women understanding and helping other women.

Social Work Students

In broader academic education and the social work education literature, attempts have been made to study and present teaching models aimed at assisting students to recognize heterosexism and decrease homophobia (Bacon, 2006;

Bird, 2004; Black, Oles, Cramer, and Bennett, 1999; Brotman and Ou Jin Lee, 2011; Ford, 2004; Oles, Black, and Cramer, 1999; Telesco, 2009; Walker, 2004). Most of these emphasize cultural competency models and frameworks for teaching "straight" people and students in mainstream society and social work, mental health, criminal justice, and human services programs how to be sensitive to and work with queer-identified individuals and communities (and other diverse "oppressed" groups). This type of literature is based on what have been called AOP, minority sensitivity, and human rights approaches (Logie et al., 2007; Messenger and Morrow, 2006; Moore, Dietz, and Jenkins, 1996; Willis, 2007).

However, these models have been critiqued for essentializing homosexuality, privileging masculinity and whiteness, reinforcing differences in identity as always fixed and knowable, and not taking into account nuances of human sexuality and gender expression (MacKinnon, 2011, pp. 139–40; Razack, 1999). As well, many of these models implicitly countenance the heterosexist notion of teaching the "normal" about the "abnormal" and straight social workers about rescuing and/or liberating "oppressed" LGBTQ individuals, which "underscores heterosexuality as dominant and normative and LGBT as marginalized and oppressed" (MacKinnon, 2011, p. 140). Ironically, these models also presume that straight students (often the intended audience) are comfortable, knowledgeable, aware, and open about their own sexualities, identities, and orientations, which may not necessarily be the case.

In addition, the effectiveness of these approaches has been challenged, as social work educators and practitioners may not have the knowledge and competence to teach/practice in these areas or may not be comfortable discussing their own (and others') sexualities. For their part, students may not receive current and accurate information, and may not be receptive to deconstructing their heterosexism, cisgenderism, and homophobia. There is little evidence to suggest that such models work to decrease homophobic bias (Berkman and Zinberg, 1997; Cramer, 1997; MacKinnon, 2011; Telesco, 2009). Consequently, one may conclude that social work faculty are "not current or sufficiently informed" to teach in this area (Vasquez and Eldridge, 1994, p. 5). Furthermore, there is little evidence that the situation in social work education has improved since the 1980s and 1990s (Chinell, 2011; Fish, 2012; Foreman and Quinlan, 2008). Indeed, Craig, McInroy, and Doiron's latest research (Chapter 9 in this volume) underscores continuing heterosexist and homophobic attitudes in schools of social work and social work students. These findings highlight the need for further LGBTQ research and study in these areas.

Social Work Research

There is also minimal research about or involving LGBTQ communities and issues. Indeed, Herek, Kimmel, Amaro, and Melton (1991) argue that "most scientific research in the social and behavioural sciences has ignored sexual orientation and behaviours or uncritically adopted societal prejudices against gay and lesbian populations" (p. 957). Wheeler (2003) also notes that most research that "has focused on gay men has been slim in comparison with other groups" and that the "research that has specifically focused on lesbians is even more sparse" (p. 66). In terms of social work education, Logie et al. (2007) claim that though some research has examined social workers' attitudes about working with LGBQT service users, "little research has been conducted to examine Master of Social Work (MSW) students" (p. 205). The same could be said about bachelor of social work students. On a positive note, some new developments have occurred in LGBTQ research since the early 1980s. Efforts have been made to develop queer-friendly, queer-specific, and queer-appropriate research methods (Levy and Johnson, 2012; Meezan and Martin, 2003). The late 1990s and early 2000s also saw a burgeoning of new research, led by queer educators, researchers, and students, with and about lesbian, gay, bisexual, transgendered, intersexed, and racialized individuals, communities, and related issues (Meezan and Martin, 2003; Tully, 1996; D.N. Warner, 2004).

Conclusion

This chapter examined the introduction and evolution of LGBTQ studies in North America. It revealed that the literature on queering educational systems focuses on school bullying, and showed that gaps exist in professional teacher and social work training, education, and research. Sadly, it also determined that many social workers are homophobic and that they demonstrate high levels of heterosexism. For the most part, social work education has failed to embrace trans issues and concerns, and attempts to decrease the biases of social work students have been unsuccessful. Clearly, there is a need for new and updated andragogical theories, methods, research, and strategies related to LGBTQ topics.

References

Alderson, K.G. (2013). *Counseling LGBTI clients*. Thousand Oaks, CA: Sage.
Bacon, J. (2006). "Teaching queer theory at a normal school." *Journal of Homosexuality* 52 (1–2): 257–83. http://dx.doi.org/10.1300/J082v52n01_11.

Banks, C. (2003). *The cost of homophobia: Literature review on the human impact of homophobia in Canada*. Saskatoon: Community–University Institute of Social Research. Retrieved from http://www.usask.ca/cuisr/sites/default/files/BanksHumanCostFINAL.pdf.

Berger, R.M. (1977). "An advocate model for intervention with homosexuals." *Social Work* 22 (4): 280–83.

–. (1983). "What is a homosexual? A definitional model." *Social Work* 28 (2): 132–35.

–. (1990). "Passing: Impact on the quality of same-sex couple relationships." *Social Work* 35: 328–32.

–. (1996). *Gay and gray*. 2nd ed. Boston: Alyson.

Berkman, C.S., and G. Zinberg. (1997). "Homophobia and heterosexism in social workers." *Social Work* 42 (4): 319–32. http://dx.doi.org/10.1093/sw/42.4.319.

Bill 13, Accepting Schools Act. (2012). S.O. 2012, c. 5. Retrieved from http://ontla.on.ca/web/bills/bills_detail.do?locale=en&BillID=2549.

Bill 44, Human Rights, Citizenship and Multiculturalism Amendment Act. (2009). RSA 2000, cH-14. Retrieved from http://www.assembly.ab.ca/ISYS/LADDAR_files/docs/bills/bill/legislature_27/session_2/20090210_bill-044.pdf.

Bird, L. (2004). "A queer diversity: Teaching difference as interrupting intersections." *Canadian Online Journal of Queer Studies in Education* 1 (1). http://jqstudies.library.utoronto.ca/index.php/jqstudies/issue/view/233.

Black, B., T.P. Oles, E. Cramer, and C.K. Bennett. (1999). "Attitudes and behaviours of social work students toward lesbian and gay male clients." *Journal of Gay and Lesbian Social Services* 9 (4): 47–68. http://dx.doi.org/10.1300/J041v09n04_03.

Brotman, S., and E. Ou Jin Lee. (2011). "Exploring gender and sexuality through the lens of intersectionality: Sexual minority refugees in Canada." *Canadian Social Work Review* 28 (1): 151–56.

Brown, H.C. (1998). *Social work and sexuality: Working with lesbians and gay men*. Basingstoke, UK: Macmillan. http://dx.doi.org/10.1007/978-1-349-13415-1.

Brownlee, K., A. Sprakes, M. Saini, R. O'Hare, K. Kortes-Miller, and J. Graham. (2005). "Heterosexism among social work students." *Social Work Education* 24 (5): 485–94. http://dx.doi.org/10.1080/02615470500132756.

Canadian Mental Health Association Ontario. (n.d.). "Lesbian, gay, bisexual, trans & queer identified people and mental health." Retrieved from http://ontario.cmha.ca/mental-health/lesbian-gay-bisexual-trans-people-and-mental-health/.

Canadian Teachers' Federation. (2006). *Gay-Straight Student Alliance Handbook*. Ottawa: Canadian Teachers' Federation.

CASW (Canadian Association of Social Workers). (2005a). "Code of ethics." Retrieved from http://casw-acts.ca/sites/default/files/attachements/CASW_Code%20of%20Ethics.pdf.

–. (2005b). "Guidelines for ethical practice." Retrieved from http://casw-acts.ca/sites/default/files/attachements/CASW_Guidelines%20for%20Ethical%20Practice.pdf.

CASWE (Canadian Association for Social Work Education). (2012). "Standards for accreditation." Ottawa, CASWE-ACFTS. Retrieved from http://caswe-acfts.ca/wp-content/uploads/2013/03/CASWE-ACFTS-Standards-11-2014.pdf.

Center for LGBTQ Studies. (n.d.). "About CLAGS." Retrieved from http://www.clags.org/about-clags/.

Chinell, J. (2011). "Three voices: Reflections on homophobia and heterosexism in social work education." *Social Work Education* 30 (7): 759–73. http://dx.doi.org/10.1080/02615479.2010.508088.

City College of San Francisco. (n.d.). "LGBTQQI* Studies: History." Retrieved from http://www.ccsf.edu/en/educational-programs/school-and-departments/school-of-behavioral-and-social-sciences/LGBT.html.

Clarke, P. (2000). "Gay/Straight Alliances." *Teacher: Magazine of the BC Teachers' Federation.* 12(6). Retrieved from https://bctf.ca/publications/NewsmagArticle.aspx?id=12854.

Cosis Brown, H., and C. Cocker. (2011). *Social work with lesbians and gay men.* Los Angeles: Sage.

Cramer, E.P. (1997). "Effects of an educational unit about lesbian identity development and disclosure in a social work methods course." *Journal of Social Work Education* 33: 461–72.

Dame, L. (2004). "Queer youth care in Manitoba: An examination of their experiences through their voices." *Canadian Online Journal of Queer Studies in Education* 1 (1). Retrieved from http://jqstudies.library.utoronto.ca/index.php/jqstudies/article/view/3270/1397.

Erich, S., N. Bouttè-Queen, S. Donnelly, and J. Tittsworth. (2007). "Social work education: Implications for working with the transgender community." *Journal of Baccalaureate Social Work* 12 (2): 42–52.

Ernulf, K.E., S.M. Innala, and F.L. Whitam. (1989). "Biological explanation, psychological explanation, and tolerance of homosexuals: A cross-national analysis of beliefs and attitudes." *Psychological Reports* 65 (3): 1003–10. http://dx.doi.org/10.2466/pr0.1989.65.3.1003.

Filax, G. (2007). *Queer youth in the province of the severely normal.* Vancouver: UBC Press.

Fish, J. (2012). *Social work and lesbian, gay, bisexual, and transpeople: Making a difference.* Bristol: Policy Press.

Fitzgerald, M., and S. Rayter, eds. (2012). *Queerly Canadian: An introductory reader in sexuality studies.* Toronto: Canadian Scholars' Press.

Ford, Tracy. (2004). "Queering education from the ground up: Challenges and opportunities for educators." *Canadian Online Journal of Queer Studies in Education* 1 (1). http://jqstudies.library.utoronto.ca/index.php/jqstudies/issue/view/233.

Foreman, M., and M. Quinlan. (2008). "Increasing social work students' awareness of heterosexism and homophobia: A partnership between a community gay health project and a school of social work." *Social Work Education* 27 (2): 152–58. http://dx.doi.org/10.1080/02615470701709485.

Gates, T. (2006). "Challenging heterosexism: Six suggestions for social work practice." *The New Social Worker.* Retrieved from http://www.socialworker.com/feature-articles/ethics-articles/Challenging_Heterosexism%3A_Six_Suggestions_for_Social_Work_Practice/.

Gerdes, K.E., and J. Norman. (2008). "Teaching social work students the breadth of gay and lesbian identity development." *Journal of Teaching in Social Work* 17 (1–2): 137–54.

Gibson, Margaret E. (2010). "Building research, building justice: Epistemology, social work, and lesbian parents." *Canadian Social Work Review* 27 (2): 239–58.

Hamington, M., ed. (2010). *Feminist interpretations of Jane Addams.* University Park: Pennsylvania State University Press.

Herek, G.M., D.C. Kimmel, H. Amaro, and G.B. Melton. (1991). "Avoiding heterosexual bias in psychological research." *American Psychologist* 46 (9): 957–93. http://dx.doi.org/10.1037/0003-066X.46.9.957.

Hidalgo, H., T.L. Peterson, and N.J. Woodman, eds. (1985). *Lesbian and gay issues: A resource manual for social workers.* Washington, DC: National Association of Social Workers.

International Day of Pink. (n.d.). "About." Retrieved June 22, 2016, from http://dayofpink.org/about/.

Khayatt, D. (1992). *Lesbian teachers: An invisible presence.* Albany: State University of New York Press.

Knegt, P. (2011). *About Canada: Queer rights.* Halifax: Fernwood.

Kwong-Lai Poon, M. (2012). "Writing the racialized queer bodies: Race and sexuality in social work." *Canadian Social Work Review* 28 (1): 145–50.

Lambda Legal. (n.d.). "History." Retrieved from http://www.lambdalegal.org/about-us/history.

Levy, D.L., and C.W. Johnson. (2012). "What does the Q mean? Including queer voices in qualitative research." *Qualitative Social Work: Research and Practice* 11 (2): 130–40. http://qsw.sagepub.com/content/11/2/130.

Logie, C., T.J. Bridge, and P.D. Bridge. (2007). "Evaluating the phobias, attitudes, and cultural competence of master of social work students toward the LGBT populations." *Journal of Homosexuality* 53 (4): 201–21. http://dx.doi.org/10.1080/00918360802103472.

Mackelprang, R.W., J. Ray, and M. Hernandez-Peck. (1996). "Social work education and sexual orientation: Faculty, student, and curriculum issues." *Journal of Gay and Lesbian Social Services* 5 (4): 17–32. http://dx.doi.org/10.1300/J041v05n04_02.

MacKinnon, R.V. (2011). "Thinking about queer theory in social work education: A pedagogical (in)quiry." *Canadian Social Work Review* 28 (1): 139–44.

Mallon, G.P., ed. (1998a). *Social work practice with lesbian, gay, bisexual, and transgender people.* 2nd ed. New York: Routledge.

–. (1998b). *We don't exactly get the welcome wagon: The experiences of gay and lesbian adolescents in child welfare systems.* New York: Columbia University Press.

Martin, J.I., and S. Hunter. (2001). *Lesbian, gay, bisexual, and transgender issues in social work: A comprehensive bibliography with annotations.* Alexandria, VA: Council on Social Work Education.

McNaron, T. (1997). *Poisoned ivy: Lesbian and gay academics confronting homophobia.* Philadelphia: Temple University Press.

McPhail, B.A. (2004). "Questioning gender and sexuality binaries: What queer theorists, transgendered individuals, and sex researchers can teach social work." *Journal of Gay and Lesbian Social Services* 17 (1): 3–21. http://dx.doi.org/10.1300/J041v17n01_02.

Meezan, W., and J. Martin, eds. (2003). *Research methods with gay, lesbian, bisexual, and transgender populations.* Binghamton, NY: Haworth Press.

Messenger, L., and D.F. Morrow, eds. (2006). *Case studies on sexual orientation and gender expression in social work practice.* New York: Columbia University Press.

Moore, L., T.J. Dietz, and D.A. Jenkins. (1996). "Beyond the classroom: Taking action against heterosexism." *Journal of Gay and Lesbian Social Services* 5 (4): 87–98. http://dx.doi.org/10.1300/J041v05n04_06.

Moore, O. (2014). "Human-rights tribunal probing student's complaints of homophobic discrimination." *Globe and Mail* (Toronto). Retrieved from http://www.theglobeandmail.com/news/toronto/tribunal-to-hear-gay-discrimination-case-following-complaints-by-student/article18073812/.

Morrow, D.F. (1996). "Heterosexualism: Hidden discrimination in social work education." *Journal of Gay and Lesbian Social Services* 5 (4): 1–16. http://dx.doi.org/10.1300/J041v05n04_01.

Mulé, N.J. (2006). "Equity vs. invisibility: Sexual orientation issues in social work ethics and curricula standards." *Social Work Education* 25 (6): 608–22. http://dx.doi.org/10.1080/02615470600833527.

Oles, T.P., B. Black, and E. Cramer. (1999). "From attitude change to effective practice: Explaining the relationship." *Journal of Social Work Education* 35 (1): 87–100.

Rankin, S.R. (2005). "Campus climates for sexual minorities." *New Directions for Student Services* 111: 17–23. http://dx.doi.org/10.1002/ss.170.

Razack, N. (1999). "Anti-discriminatory practice: Pedagogical struggles and challenges." *British Journal of Social Work* 29 (2): 231–50. http://dx.doi.org/10.1093/oxfordjournals.bjsw.a011444.

Richmond, M.E. (1917). *The social diagnosis.* New York: Russell Sage.

Ruffolo, D. (2006). "Reading students as queer: Disrupting (hetero)normativity for an equitable future." *Canadian Online Journal of Queer Studies in Education* 2 (1). http://jqstudies.library.utoronto.ca/index.php/jqstudies/article/viewFile/3289/1418.

Schneider, M.S., ed. (1997). *Pride and prejudice: Working with lesbian, gay, and bisexual youth.* Toronto: Central Toronto Youth Services.

Simone de Beauvoir Institute. (n.d.). "About the program." Retrieved from https://www.concordia.ca/finearts/cinema/programs/undergraduate/sexuality-minor/about-sexuality-minor.html.

Staller, K.M., and S.A. Kirk. (1997). "Unjust freedom: The ethics of client self-determination in runaway youth shelters." *Child and Adolescent Social Work Journal* 14 (3): 223–42. http://dx.doi.org/10.1023/A:1024521720170.

Taylor, C., and T. Peter, with T.L. McMinn, T. Elliott, S. Beldom, A. Ferry, Z. Gross, S. Paquin, and K. Schachter. (2011). *Every class in every school: Final report on the first national climate survey on homophobia, biphobia, and transphobia in Canadian schools.* Toronto: Egale Canada Human Rights Trust.

Telesco, G.A. (2009). "Case studies on sexual orientation and gender expression in social work practice." *Journal of Teaching in Social Work* 29 (3): 363–67. http://dx.doi.org/10.1080/08841230802325281.

Tierney, W.G. (1997). *Academic outlaws: Queer theory and cultural studies in the academy.* London: Sage. http://dx.doi.org/10.4135/9781483327877.

Todd, S., and D. Coholic. (2007). "Christian fundamentalism and anti-oppressive social work pedagogy." *Journal of Teaching in Social Work* 27 (3–4): 5–25. http://dx.doi.org/10.1300/J067v27n03_02.

Trotter, J. (2000). "Lesbian and gay issues in social work with young people: Resilience and success through confronting, conforming, and escaping." *British Journal of Social Work* 30 (1): 115–23. http://dx.doi.org/10.1093/bjsw/30.1.115.

Trotter, J., L. Brogatzki, L. Duggan, E. Foster, and J. Levie. (2006). "Revealing disagreement and discomfort through auto-ethnography and personal narrative: Sexuality in social work education and practice." *Qualitative Social Work: Research and Practice* 5 (3): 369–88. http://dx.doi.org/10.1177/1473325006067366.

Tully, C., ed. (1996). *Lesbian social services: Research issues.* Binghamton, NY: Haworth Press.

Van Soest, D. (1996). "The influence of competing ideologies about homosexuality on non-discrimination policy: Implications for social work education." *Journal of Social Work Education* 32: 53–64.

Van Voorhis, R., and M. Wagner. (2001). "Coverage of gay and lesbian subject matter in social work journals." *Journal of Social Work Education* 37: 147–59.

–. (2002). "Among the missing: Content on lesbian and gay people in social work journals." *Social Work* 47 (4): 345–54. http://dx.doi.org/10.1093/sw/47.4.345.

Van Wormer, K.S., J. Wells, and M. Boes. (2000). *Social work with lesbians, gays, and bisexuals: A strengths perspective.* Boston: Allyn and Bacon.

Vasquez, M.J.T., and N.S. Eldridge. (1994). "Bringing ethics alive: Training practitioners about gender, ethnicity, and sexual orientation issues." *Women and Therapy* 15 (1): 1–16. http://dx.doi.org/10.1300/J015v15n01_02.

Walker, R. (2004). "'Queer'ing identity/ies: Agency and subversion in Canadian Education." *Canadian Online Journal of Queer Studies in Education* 1 (1). http://jqstudies.library.utoronto.ca/index.php/jqstudies/article/view/3274/1406.

Warner, D.N. (2004). "Towards a queer research methodology." *Qualitative Research in Psychology* 1 (4): 321–37. http://dx.doi.org/10.1191/1478088704qp021oa.

Warner, T. (2002). *Never going back: A history of queer activism in Canada.* Toronto: University of Toronto Press.

Wheeler, D. (2003). "Methodological issues in conducting community based health and social services research among black and African American LGBT populations." *Journal of Gay and Lesbian Social Services* 15 (1–2): 65–78. http://dx.doi.org/10.1300/J041v15n01_05.

Wilber, S., C. Ryan, and J. Marksamer. (2006). *Serving LGBT youth in out-of-home care: CWLA best practice guidelines*. Washington, DC: Child Welfare League of America.

Willis, P. (2007). "'Queer eye' for social work: Rethinking pedagogy and practice with same-sex attracted young people." *Australian Social Work* 60 (2): 181–96. http://dx.doi.org/10.1080/03124070701323816.

PART 2

Coming Out and the Academic Closet – Rainbow Narratives

5

Feminist and Queer Rights: The Lived and Living Experience of Queer Social Work Faculty

NORMA JEAN PROFITT AND BRENDA RICHARD

In this chapter, we offer a reflection of our lived, and living, experience of being queer in social work education and practice. As long-time feminists, we intend to show how feminism as a political movement has illuminated, and intersected with, our understanding of queer rights and theorizing, and how, in turn, both feminist and queer struggles have unquestionably shaped our social work values and ethics. In presenting our experience as white queer social workers and faculty, we highlight the pivotal place of political movements in making meaning about our lives. We then briefly offer directions for retheorizing gender, sexuality, and sex in social work. Finally, to concretize our vision of social justice and ethics, we suggest strategies to queer social work.

As we wrote this piece, the process of revisiting the past and contemplating the present was much more than an intellectual exercise detached from the personal and political. For us, it was an emotionally laden and often painful recounting of events, comments, omissions, and silences that have shaped, and continue to shape, our daily lives as queers. Although growing social work attention to queer issues is undoubtedly encouraging (Martinez, Barsky, and Singleton, 2011; Moffatt and Todd, 2011; O'Neill, Swan, and Mulé, 2015), our experience, spanning the 1980s to the 2010s, has shown that there has been little real recognition of either the social, cultural, and political contexts of heteronormativity that envelop us in social work or of the costs of survival in such milieus. We hope that offering up our narratives in the service of social justice will contribute to recognizing heteronormative conditions in all schools of social work and universities, and will encourage the much needed queering of social work.

First, we want to explain our use of terms. "Queer" encompasses gender, sexual, and sex diversity, and non-hetero/gender/sexual/sex normative identities, including non-identifications. An expression of pride, it challenges traditional heterosexual ideas of gendered sexuality. We also use "gay and lesbian" because this terminology, dominant in the early part of the gay and lesbian movements, continues to the present day. Our understanding of heteronormativity is best captured by Berlant and Warner (1998): "A whole field of social relations becomes intelligible as heterosexuality, and this privatized sexual culture bestows on its sexual practices a tacit sense of rightness and normalcy. This sense of rightness – embedded in things and not just in sex – is what we call heteronormativity" (p. 551). This concept calls attention to how social institutions and policies reinforce the belief that there are male and female human beings who are gendered and complementary, and that each gender has certain "natural" roles in life. Our communities are thus organized around "heteronormative family and kinship structures that connote our most meaningful interactions and lived experiences through reproduction and generational succession" (Fox, 2007, p. 504). Despite the general perception that the public sphere is asexual, heterosexuality is inscribed within it as the dominant ideology (Richardson and May, 1999).

Second, before recounting our experience, we want to briefly comment on the notion of "experience." As academics, we are cognizant of the socially contested nature of experience as well as of critiques of the concept; see, for example, Scott's (1992) incisive essay on "experience" and Mohanty's (1992) call to attend to the historically and culturally specific contexts of "experience." As Bannerji (1995) asserts, critical reflection of experience is a process of meaning making about the relation between the personal and the social that validates the ways in which we experience and define ourselves and thus exercise our agency: "Experience, therefore, is that crucible in which the self and the world enter into a creative union called 'social subjectivity' ... Since political agency, experience and knowledge are transformatively connected, where but in ourselves and lives can we begin our explanatory and analytical activities?" (pp. 86–88). Therefore, our accounts of our experience reflect our meaning making about the world. Since the meaning of experience is a site of political struggle, we do make claims in this discussion about the oppression of queers and what is needed to queer social work. We argue that although social work education and practice have increasingly acknowledged gender and sexual diversity, there is still much work to do in creating non-heteronormative and non-sexist environments for all.

Brenda Richard's Narrative

I have taught in an eastern Canadian school of social work for thirty years. I am the only "out" tenured faculty member in the history of the school, which was founded in 1941. Though this reflects a stark political reality, the personal experience sheltered in this statistic is also profound. For queer academics, the university, with its promise of academic freedom, presented itself as a unique refuge, protection in a world that criminalized and pathologized people and ideas (Young, 2003). Here, one hoped to contribute to fundamental change in the education of social workers and thus to the practice of social work, which itself deified the heteronormative nuclear family concept and reified "homosexuality" as criminal and as illness (Bergler, 1962; Ruttenbeck, 1973). A central contradiction anchored this idyll, however, since most academic discourse in classrooms and coffee rooms excluded that of queer thought. One felt free to discuss anything except the central unifying component of one's life and work.

In the early seventies, feminist thought and activism provided a conceptual framework for the articulation of women's disconnection from sources of power in society (Friedan, 1963; Greer, 1970; Millett, 1970). Feminist theories were the first to encapsulate the social, economic, and political position of women and to name the consequences of lived realities – rape and physical violence, sexual abuse of children, economic deprivation, and marginalization in all governing social and political bodies. Although the Canadian second-wave feminist movement did not speak to the struggles of lesbians, women with (dis)abilities, or African Canadian and Aboriginal women, it did provide the first energized understanding of a binary society of male and female that was designed to produce order for the privileged and disorder in the lives of those without social sanction (Cohen, 1993; Pierson, 1993). For many academics, it was life-saving, intellectually and spiritually, as the connections forged with other activists began to have tangible results in the creation of transition houses, women's centres, greater equity in educational and employment opportunities, and language that disrupted the comfort and complacency of the status quo (Pierson and Cohen, 1993; Pierson, Cohen, Bourne, and Masters, 1993; Spender, 1980). I entered the social work profession as a feminist, and I entered the academy bolstered by a feminist vision, determined to add my effort to the collective dismantling of privilege entrenched in the premises of traditional social work.

The school at which I work is a progressive one. Over the years, it has revisioned its theories as radical, structural feminist, anti-oppressive, postmodernist, and critical (Mullaly, 2009; Payne, 2005). Queer theory is now included in its undergraduate and graduate courses. Over the course of these developments, a primary point of tension remained within parts of the practice community in the false dichotomy of "theory" and "practice," as if one could practise responsibly without both. Social work education struggled to ensure that such bifurcation was not embodied in curricula, for knowledge of one without the other is of little use. Yet, in the university, heteronormativity as a hegemonic device for ordering social relations required the bifurcation of one's self if one identified as queer. There was an unstated expectation to collude silently in one's own oppression, remaining invisible as queer while teaching structural feminist and anti-oppressive theory and practice. This expectation was also manifested in the dearth of reading, discussion, and conversation about queer issues in general as well as the lack of interest in, and funding for, queer research initiatives. The inattention to queer people in the university and in social work practice was so profound that it parched the environment. Such absence reinforced one's lack of safety, and the hush when overt homophobia was displayed but not addressed in conferences, classrooms, washrooms, lounges, and hallways triumphed with its resounding silence.

A culture of coerced invisibility prevailed wherein survival required adherence to, or at least co-operation with, a code of silence. The environment felt unsafe, and one occupied that unnamed space in which all real danger awaits and from which survival strategies derive unknowingly, even, and especially to, the survivor. One did not talk about one's private life; one did not request to be heard; one did not anticipate particularized proactive support from administration. One even grew used to one's place in the "isms" – queers were so often appended in phrases such as "racism, sexism, disableism, ageism, etc." that they could have formed a singing group called the Et Ceteras. Therein, as queers, we resided in obscurity. If a topic related to sexual orientation emerged in research, writing, or the media, it was not presented as a development of interest but was prefaced universally with the word "controversial" to warn that a sinister element lurked within. This alert served to skew its reception and sabotage discussion. No one commented on the narrow focus of research on queer issues, such as the seemingly exhaustive pathologizing preoccupation with alcoholism and enmeshment in the lives of lesbian women and the "promiscuity" of gay men (Hunter and Nickerson, 2003; Mallon, 1998). The identification of mental illness or anti-social behaviour in gays and lesbians boosted the identifiers' profiles as experts with empirical, clinical evidence of pathology while it diminished the possibilities for true understanding of gay women and men, who were already forced to live careful lives on the periphery of society (Fisher, 2004; Hunter and Nickerson, 2003).

As late as the early 1980s and into the 1990s, standard social work texts were either silent or devoid of substance on gay and lesbian issues (Hepworth and Larsen, 1986; Mullaly, 1993; Sheafor, Horejsi, and Horejsi, 1997). If the issues were touched upon, the texts simply advised social workers to "refer" them to a specialized practitioner (Hepworth and Larsen, 1986). How these practitioners were expected to emerge was unclear, given the taint of the issues themselves and the fact that most gay and lesbian social workers remained unidentified for fear of losing their jobs. Their invaluable experience for serving "clients" was subverted. Issues related to gays and lesbians (transgender was not yet a concept in social work) were designated as "other," creating a new professional category for the "we" and "they" binary, with the practitioner as healthy heterosexual and the gay person as "other" (O'Brien, 1999). The knowledge of the social worker could thus be further compartmentalized to suit a social arrangement and traditional model of expert and dependant.

Such practices solidified the marginalization of queer people as service users. Non-disclosure was the only protection available to maintain personal and professional safety. Until the Nova Scotia Human Rights Act was amended in 1991, after a sustained lobby by Lesbian Gay Rights Nova Scotia (Fisher, 2004), discrimination was legal in matters of employment and housing. In a meeting I attended during the 1980s, the minister of social services, whose department was the largest employer of social workers in the province, boasted with a smile, "I discriminate on a daily basis against homosexuals" to prevent them from being hired to work with children. In the silence that followed his pronouncement, and in a room full of social workers whose discomfort or shock rendered them unwilling or unable to speak, his remark flashed with power. My voice strangled by disbelief, and desperate for ethical action on my part and redress on his, I managed to say that his approach belied the statistical data on sexual offences against children. No other voices emerged and the discussion moved on. Afterward I confided my distress to a social worker, who agreed to request a meeting with the minister. The deputy minister was sent to our meeting instead. Perhaps thinking to assuage us as presumed straight women, he laughingly said that he had told the minister not to say such things in public. Then, I suppose because he also presumed that we would understand, he added, as if it were amusing, that a close member of his family simply "did not like black people"; similarly, he indicated that the minister simply had an antipathy to gay people. To say that there was "some" racism and "some" homophobia in Nova Scotia at the time is to seriously understate the reality of life in the Maritimes.

Understandably, almost all gay and lesbian social workers were closeted then – the only viable option, it seemed, for inclusion in the profession. An exception was the late Ken Belanger, who forged new ground as a gay social worker (Nova Scotia Association of Social Workers, n.d.). The "closet" as a social construct was intended to enforce social control. As singular spaces, closets also reduced the threat of collective discovery that heteronormativity is harmful to *all* people. If the rights to security, personal safety, and political inclusion were accorded to all, who would choose to live in a closet? Queer social workers were made to feel as if they somehow skirted the edges of respectability; this was validated by the judgments of those privileged by heterosexist entitlement in a world that condemned queers. Those judgments, rendered in the form of whispers and innuendo, contained an awareness of the power to derail careers and to dismantle professional reputations. Queer social workers were forced to compartmentalize their professional and private lives in pursuit of a personal commitment to social work practice and education.

This history of social work's subjugation of queers carries critical implications for social work education and practice today. Much of the content of "direct practice" still involves traditional family issues situated within a heteronormative framework. In its preoccupation with fixing "marital" discord, family dysfunction, and divorce – no stone, except one, too heavy to overturn – the social work profession adhered to the presumptions of heteronormativity and failed to understand the complexities of queer people's lives. Such adherence to heteronormative world views, approaches, and practices is detrimental to the well-being of those who entrust us with their lives, either as students or service users. A deliberate invocation of the righteousness of privilege, this posture has long been shown to be an ill-fit for queers (Hunter and Nickerson, 2003).

Today, we understand more about the context of adolescent suicide and its causes and prevalence among queer youth (Taylor, 2008). We recognize that partner relationships may, in fact, be same-sex. We know that chosen family members can supersede biological ones and that identity is not limited to that prescribed by tradition. We can still unknowingly overlook the impact that the history of subjugation has on the lives of queers today, especially older citizens. We can still miss the outrage of queer professionals when they are subjected to limiting assumptions about queers. When conventional training in assessments and treatment modalities fails to consider the realities of queer lives, social work practice is incompetent practice.

In social work with lesbian, gay, bisexual, two-spirit, transgender, transsexual, queer, questioning, and intersex issues, the past continues to define and shape our understanding of the present. Survival strategies are still required in schools of social work and universities, albeit modified in accordance with changing times. In my case, the support of feminist colleagues was pivotal to my survival. In our progressive social justice initiatives, mutual learning bolstered our resistances. During the last decade, so much has changed in the university, in social work education, in the profession of social work, and in society, and yet so much heteronormativity remains.

Norma Jean Profitt's Narrative

Feminist – until all women are free! Although this rallying cry might seem an anachronism in today's social, political, and economic climate, it still moves me to act for equity, fairness, and freedom. I became a feminist in the early 1980s, after I graduated from Wilfrid Laurier University with a master of social work degree. Sadly, I was not exposed to feminist theories at the university but luckily was introduced to them by a feminist classmate. That exposure, my practicum at Anselma House (a refuge for abused women in Kitchener-Waterloo, Ontario), and my exploration of early Canadian maternal feminist and pro-choice (abortion) movements in an undergraduate religion course coalesced with personal experience of women's oppression into a desire to volunteer at the women's centre in Halifax, Nova Scotia.

To use a fundamental concept of the feminist movement, I had my "consciousness raised" at the women's centre (Rebick, 2005). We devoured radical and socialist feminist theories of women's paid and unpaid labour, occupational segregation, caregiving, gendered poverty, rape, sexual harassment, woman abuse, and pornography, and we talked fervently of philosophy and the kinds of change that the feminist movement sought (Jaggar, 1988). I had finally found a language that spoke to me. The feminism that I forged with others at the centre was about theories, strategies, and political movements, a personal and political practice enacted in individual and collective struggle (Jaggar, 1988). This vision of feminism guided my work as director of Bryony House, a Halifax shelter for abused women, itself born of the feminist movement.

Central to feminism were critical analyses of the organization of patriarchal power, including the vital role of violence against women in enforcing women's subordination in the familial and public spheres (Jaggar, 1988). Feminism thus demanded fundamental change in social structures, ways of thinking, and everyday practices (Pierson and Cohen, 1993). Although I still labour to grasp its full import, one of the essays most influential on my thinking was "The Combahee River Collective Statement," written by the Combahee River Collective (1983). This collective, composed of black feminists such as Barbara Smith, named the simultaneity of oppressions and linked capitalism, sexism, racism, and heterosexism.

Another incisive moment occurred when a friend explained that her lesbianism was a political statement. Her claim prompted me to think about why my colleagues at the women's centre felt threatened by lesbian critiques of feminist theory and practice (Pierson, 1993; Rebick, 2005). Adrienne Rich's (1980) "Compulsory Heterosexuality and Lesbian Existence" brought everything together; it exposed and connected patriarchal control over women's sexuality with the privileging of heterosexuality. Feminism had challenged the ideology of the family, questioning its patriarchal structure and insularity, and now it opened up a new notion of "relationships" and "family." Rich affirmed that until lesbians were free, heterosexual women would not be free.

Intuitively, I knew then that gay and lesbian people challenged not only the dominant sexuality of (hetero)sexuality but the fundamental premise of heteronormativity: that female and male human beings are gendered and complementary. In contemporary Western society, femininity and masculinity are located as fixed internal essences within female and male bodies. Desire is assumed to flow from sex/gender, with gender reflecting or expressing desire (Butler, 1999). I had a personal stake in contesting these notions of femininity and masculinity. Even though I felt pressured in my youth to conform to cultural scripts of being a girl, such as hiding my intelligence so that a male classmate could come first in class, I have never been able to relate to "femininity." Questioning the assumed links between the sex categories of "male" or "female," gender, and sexuality made sense to me, and so the concept of queerness has always signified liberation from prescribed (hetero)sexual and gender norms and the hope that social struggle would bring gender and sexual freedom and expression.

In 1987, under the auspices of CUSO, I worked with two women's organizations in Costa Rica, a rural grassroots effort (Women United in Health and Development) and a feminist collective (Women's Collective Pancha Carrasco) that was dedicated to organizing with poor women. In the latter, we painstakingly examined how heterosexism manifested in ourselves, our philosophy, and our practice, and accordingly, we incorporated our analysis of heterosexism into the Marxist feminism of the collective (Chinchilla, 1991). Although I had understood that power and politics were central to feminism, my experience with the Women's Collective moved me from a liberal ideology to structural analyses of class, gender, heterosexism, imperialism, colonialism, and so forth (Farmer, 1996).

Rather than springing fully formed from my being, like Athena from the forehead of Zeus, my current thinking about gender and sexuality has evolved over thirty years of personal experience and collective struggle. My theorizing has been influenced by structural social work (Mullaly, 1993), queer theory (McPhail, 2004), "Third World" feminisms (Mohanty, Russo, and Torres, 1991), cultural studies (Hall, 1991), postmodernism, and post-structuralism (Nicholson, 1990; Weedon, 1987). Nevertheless, from the outset of my social work practice, I carried with me knowledge and insights from my activism and the feminist and gay and lesbian liberation movements. Feminism schooled me to see the broader landscape, and in this, Marilyn Frye's (1983) image of a birdcage is apt. Feminism allows me to discern, not just one wire of the cage, but its multiple wires of constraints – the "network of systematically related barriers" that comprise oppression (p. 5). I consider this to be one of feminism's greatest gifts.

Shortly after I began teaching in a Maritime school of social work in 1999, I designed and taught, on four occasions, a bachelor of social work elective called "Social Work and Lesbian, Gay, Bisexual and Two-Spirit Peoples" (LGBT-S course). One of my political objectives for students who took the course was to examine the ways in which heteronormativity and heterosexism construct heterosexuality "as the 'natural' and 'normal' sexuality, by which all 'Other' sexualities are measured and subordinated" (Ferfolja, 2007, p. 148). My experience as faculty in the social work school, however, was one of being caught within the dominant liberal humanist framework of the university institution, where "systemic heterosexism and heteronormativity" (Kopelson, 2002, p. 20) are integral to the fabric of everyday life.

In teaching the LGBT-S course, I grasped more deeply the pervasiveness of heteronormativity as well as the experience of marginalization of some queer students whom I supported during their social work studies. After leaving academia in 2011, I realized that the offering of the LGBT-S elective stood in for a more thorough and much deeper examination and dismantling of heteronormativity and heterosexism in the curriculum and environment of the school. Simply "including queers and queer relationships within a heteronormative frame of reference" (Fox, 2007, p. 505) is not enough. In my experience, oppression is about more than the absence of overt or hostile discourse and actions; it is also about silence, omission, and assumption (Ferfolja, 2007). A professed "acceptance" of queers assumes that the necessary deep transformative work has already been done.

Although acceptance of gender and sexual diversity may be a desired end point for some, I see it as a station along the way. "Acceptance" does not entail critical analyses of heteronormativity or an abiding engagement in challenging and changing existing conditions. It suggests that there is something to accept (Riddle, 1996). It also suggests that positive attitudes toward queers somehow eradicate the very real trappings of heteronormativity. In my view, acceptance has often meant that though people profess to hold positive attitudes, they take for granted the privilege associated with heterosexual status or feel uncomfortable with queer displays of affection. They may view all sexual orientations as the same because they perceive no meaningful differences in life experiences, thus invisibilizing queer people's realities and failing to acknowledge the actualities of heterosexism for those who do not fit heterosexual gender, sexual, and sex moulds. Furthermore, they may overfocus on the sexuality of queers and encourage disclosure without appreciating the potentially harmful consequences (Hunter and Nickerson, 2003).

Institutions, too, can profess acceptance and assert that queer students can explore any of their issues in family and other courses, although the reality is that the curriculum is heteronormative and geared toward heterosexuals (Hunter and Nickerson, 2003). At its most profound level, heteronormativity is a "form of violence deeply embedded in our individual and group psyches, social relations, identities, social institutions, and cultural landscape" (Yep, 2002, p. 168). At the school where I taught, heteronormativity and heterosexism were also reflected in institutional policies, such as those relating to sexual harassment and affirmative action, that did not recognize sexual and gender diversity and expression.

In this liberal humanist stance of acceptance, silence, omission, and assumption operate to perpetuate a heteronormative and heterosexist climate. For example, faculty and students often assume they are open-minded, non-heterosexist, and already enlightened and knowledgeable. They claim to know what it is like to be non-hetero/gender/sex normative and feel entitled to comment on others' presumed sexuality or gender. Assumptions are in play when queers are defined by their sexuality but heterosexual persons are not, thus ignoring other aspects of subjectivity (Ferfolja, 2007), or are spoken about as if they were a separate species, when heterosexuals are not perceived as such (Willis, 2007). The gender and sexual status quo is also maintained through silence – about everyday lives, relationships, difference, and the meaning of "family"; about feelings of grief that would be remarked upon if they were experienced by a heterosexual partner; and about student comments that queers should not be allowed to adopt children. The absence of discourse about sexual and gender diversity – in everyday talk, in discussions of curriculum, in appraisals of how students are doing – signals to faculty and students alike both non-existence and erasure.

The political position of acceptance also veils omission and active ignorance – of how a particular theory attends to gender and sexual diversity; of the tension among human rights, religious beliefs, and social work ethics; of the suffering of queer students who are subjected to psychic violence; of the vigilance required to always be at the ready to respond; and of the inordinate amount of energy needed to get through class material that does not speak to queer lives. At the same time that sexuality stands in for the whole identity of queers, there is a curious silence about actual lived experience and a minimization of "how often and casually vehemence is unleashed by the ignorant" (personal communication with former BSW student, April 13, 2012).

Queer survival in a liberal humanist system of social work knowledge that privileges "*ways of not knowing*" (Jeyasingham, 2008, p. 141, emphasis in original) has its costs. For me, one of them was the growing disjuncture between my commitment to social work as an ethical-political project and my lived experience of social work. My formation in the feminist movement prepared me for resistance and activism over the long term, yet I did not see social work education and practice as a vanguard on the queer or feminist front. Dismissals of transgender demands for gender-neutral washrooms, and of feminism as too narrow because it does not include men, press home the labour that social work education still needs to do to constitute "safer" non-heteronormative environments for queer faculty and students alike.

Despite the climate of heteronormativity in the university institution, I did have the privilege of witnessing, in the LGBT-S course, the diversity and complexity of student experience of genders and sexualities that were otherwise obscured by heteronormative discourse and practice. As I have noted elsewhere, imparting the LGBT-S course was the richest experience of my teaching career (Profitt, 2015). Not only did I perceive then the urgent and vital need to queer social work, as advanced by the editors and authors of this book, but also came up against the limits of my own knowledge and understanding of trans- and intersexuality.

An imagined other world, born of my teaching and learning with students, exposed how claims of acceptance position people as innocent bystanders to oppressive power systems rather than as actors implicated in gender and sexual dominance (Ford, 2004). This position is dangerous to those of us who live outside of dominant heterosexual, gender, and sex scripts. My hope is still that a belief in social justice and ethics along with a reconceptualization of gender, sexuality, and sex in social work can move us toward an ethical-political commitment to change, building a freer non-heteronormative and non-sexist social work education and profession. Imagine!

Retheorizing Gender, Sexuality, and Sex in Social Work

Consequently, both of us have thought carefully about what might be required to theorize and comprehend sexual and gender diversity inclusively in order to queer social work. Given that attitudes of sexism and heterosexism are closely interrelated with negativity expressed toward individuals who are perceived as transgressing sex and gender norms (Black, Oles, and Moore, 1996; Martinez et al., 2011), it is imperative to push the boundaries of our thinking to conceptualize gender, sexuality, and sex in ways that break open the categories, operating systems, and processes of heteronormativity and heterosexism. We can then explore how gender, sexuality, and sex inform each other and how they inform, and are informed by, other axes of inequity and oppression.

As queer theorists and feminists have advocated, to achieve a deeper understanding of gender, sexual, and sex diversity in social work, we need to unhook the binaries of sex (male and female), sexuality (homosexuals and heterosexuals), and gender (women and men) from each other (Lorber, 1996; McPhail, 2004). According to Johnson and Repta (2012), letting go of stagnant notions of gender and sex involves two elements: "reconsidering how we have conceptualized distinctions between the masculine/feminine and male/female" (p. 17) and shaking up the notion that gender is strictly social and that sex is strictly biological since "physiological sex affects social gender and vice versa" (p. 25). McPhail (2004) further affirms that "by not challenging the gender binary, masculinity and femininity are reified and heterosexuality is institutionalized," thus maintaining the social order and hierarchies of gender and sexuality (p. 7). At the very least, it is essential to "disturb the assumption that heterosexuality and the sex/gender dichotomy are natural states of being" (Willis, 2007, p. 185). In this regard, Butler's (1999) work is edifying because it shows how "gender" and "sex" are socially and culturally constructed, posits non-essentialist conceptions of gender, and theorizes gender as performative rather than a stable identity or essence.

If social work were to vigorously push its theorizing of gender, sexual, and sex diversity, it has the potential to deeply unsettle hegemonic masculinity and femininity. Gender diversity disrupts our understandings of male/female and gay/straight as well as our notion of men and women as separate and different. This can be more challenging than the "acceptance" of non-heterosexual identities such as gay or lesbian or simplistic discourses of biological determinism ("gays and lesbians are born that way") that do not interrogate the sex/gender system that reifies sex "as a biological base from which the social world of gender is built" (Drabinski, 2011, p. 13). In the face of "the pervasive conflation of sex, gender, and sexuality in broader society" (Bailey, 2011, p. 371), theorizing about gender, sexual, and sex diversity must be supple enough to theorize fixed and stable identities, fluidities and continuities, and the absence of determinative self-identifications.

In reimagining the relationship between gender and sexuality, Richardson (2007) suggests that we consider

> how gender's link to sexuality is not determinate or unidirectional, but complex, dynamic, contingent, fluid and unstable ... To do this we require theoretical frameworks that allow more complex analyses of the dynamic, historically and socially specific relationship between sexuality and gender, as well as the gendered and sexualized specificity of their interconnections. That will enable understanding of gender and sexual diversity and, related to this, avoid the past tendency to presume western frameworks, acknowledging non-western localized understandings of gender's relationship to sexuality that demonstrate the complexities and variability involved. (pp. 464–65)

Such an approach would permit consideration of gender and sexuality as both distinct and conjoint, and would bring cultural and material analyses together (Richardson, 2007).

The project of reconceptualizing gender, sexuality, and sex as integral to social work is potentially revolutionary. As West and Zimmerman (1987) point out, these elements are not simply the essential properties or characteristics of individuals but are biological, social, and cultural processes that constitute the integral dynamics of our hegemonic social order. Gender structure is deeply embedded in the institutional and cultural levels of our society and in all social relationships (Richardson, 2007; West and Zimmerman, 1987). Theorizing in ways that disrupt what are normatively thought of as gender, sexuality, and sex does therefore require that we think about a myriad of often taken-for-granted aspects of our lives; examples include the politics of sexual choice and reproduction, and the sexual division of labour in which women's work is seen as part of what they are, not what they do (Nestle, Howell, and Wilchins, 2002; Richardson, 2007; West and Zimmerman, 1987).

In this reconceptualization project, structural social work can contribute significantly to theorizing diversity through its focus on the structural and material aspects of oppressive power systems and structures, lived experience, and collective activism (Mullaly, 2007). Structural social work theory, including feminist theory, has been critiqued for its additive approach and conceptions of simplified and fixed social identities of those who belong to "oppressed social groups" (Payne, 2005). This need not be the case. As well as the constitution of individual subjectivities, any framework that we develop to theorize and understand gender, sexual, and sex diversity in social work must necessarily encompass analyses of how domination and oppression operate on the cultural, symbolic, structural, and interpersonal levels, thus including language and meaning, social structures and institutions, and everyday interactions and practices (Grosz, 1990).

Structural social work can offer important critical analyses of how normative understandings and practices of gender, sexuality, and sex are reproduced through social structures and institutions so that we do not lose sight of structural roots and material conditions of domination and oppression. For example, as noted above, gender as a social structure is still very relevant and salient in our social world in specific concrete and material ways notwithstanding the insights of queer theory and the cultural turn that posits gender and sexuality as fluid, plural, and situated. Despite the ongoing tension between queer theory and queer struggles for liberation, our hope is that social work can simultaneously theorize the existence of oppressive systems of power, the constitution of multiple non-prescriptive intersectional identifications and non-identifications, and the need for structural, cultural, discursive, and material change to be sought through individual and collective action.

Queering Social Work Education

Given that all students have the right to an inclusive education, they must be encouraged throughout the curriculum to examine the operation of heteronormativity in their own and others' lives. All social work courses should be reviewed for content on queer issues, paying attention to where such examination occurs and where content in each complements and reinforces content in another. Furthermore, presentation and discussion of all critical issues in social work should encompass queer perspectives and experiences, and be appropriately grounded in such.

One of the challenges in social work education is to address the concrete inequities in the lives of those who are marginalized by a rigid social structure without reinforcing its attendant binaries and hierarchies of power. For example, queers are still persecuted in many societies around the world

(Human Rights Watch, 2009); how do we present these realities while recognizing the heterogeneity of experience and breaking down "us and them" categories? "Diversity" initiatives must carefully elucidate both the individuality and intersectionality of queer lives rather than glossing over differences. Despite advances brought about by the queer movement, queer persons are still affected on a daily basis by heteronormativity in a myriad of ways. In this regard, the deliberate lack of exposure in social work curricula to the realities of queer lives remains an obstacle to student learning.

Affirmative action for queer students, faculty, and staff must recognize both historical and present-day oppression. Historically, for queer people, the fundamentals of life have been at stake. So creative is hegemonic oppression and marginalization that distinct forms of them are designed for particular groups. For example, queer people have been brutalized and ridiculed, have feared expulsion from their families, experienced the loss of financial stability by dropping out of unsafe schools, and absorbed denouncements of themselves in texts, popular culture, and political, medical, religious, and educational institutions. We know that recognition of the barriers to equitable education that queer students face does not threaten or diminish opportunities for other marginalized applicants.

Education about heteronormativity and gender, sexual, and sex diversity should examine relations, processes, practices, and behaviours that implicate all of us in gender, sexual, and sex dominance and the production of difference rather than focusing only on queers. Ownership of one's own place in power systems would help shift the dynamics of binary thinking and provide greater safety for queer students, who cannot be the sole representatives of diversity. Students can thrive in the classroom and field placement when they are free from heterosexism and able to be who they are.

All faculty must be engaged in a process of teaching and learning about heteronormativity and gender, sexuality, and sex diversity, and must collectively commit to it as a social justice issue. This requires more than a general awareness of social issues. Faculty uncertainty about how to manage this complex terrain can impede comprehensive dialogue with students and faculty alike. To address this, schools can provide opportunities for instructors to become educated on queer issues so that their level of comfort is enhanced. As well, queer faculty should not be constricted by the fear of having tenure and promotion denied.

Such comprehensive measures necessarily require leadership and support from all levels of administration, from presidents to directors. Directors must be explicit about their support of school policies and practices that facilitate inclusion and strongly endorse faculty members' work. As a result of the marginalization of their lives and work, including activism and survival, queer academics have rarely received recognition for either.

In conclusion, as queer social workers and academics, we were often left to fend for ourselves in social work education and practice, the profession, and the university. Students, our most important constituents, hold the promise of change in their approaches to social work. Hopefully, our contribution can fortify that promise.

References

Bailey, M.M. (2011). "Gender/racial realness: Theorizing the gender system in ballroom culture." *Feminist Studies* 37 (2): 365–86.

Bannerji, H. (1995). *Thinking through: Essays on feminism, Marxism, and anti-racism.* Toronto: Women's Press.

Bergler, E. (1962). *Homosexuality.* New York: Collier Books.

Berlant, L., and M. Warner. (1998). "Sex in public." *Critical Inquiry* 24 (2): 547–66. http://dx.doi.org/10.1086/448884.

Black, B., T.P. Oles, and L. Moore. (1996). "The relationship between attitudes: Homophobia among students in social work programs." *Journal of Baccalaureate Social Work* 2 (1): 23–41.

Butler, J. (1999). *Gender trouble: Feminism and the subversion of identity.* 2nd ed. New York: Routledge.

Chinchilla, N.S. (1991). "Marxism, feminism, and the struggle for democracy in Latin America." *Gender and Society* 5 (3): 291–310. http://dx.doi.org/10.1177/089124391005003003.

Cohen, M.G. (1993). "The Canadian women's movement." In *Canadian Women's Issues: Strong Voices*, ed. R.R. Pierson, M.G. Cohen, P. Bourne, and P. Masters, 1–31. Toronto: James Lorimer.

Combahee River Collective. (1983). "The Combahee River Collective Statement." In *Home Girls: A Black Feminist Anthology*, ed. B. Smith, 272–82. New York: Kitchen Table: Women of Color Press.

Drabinski, K. (2011). "Identity matters: Teaching transgender in the women's studies classroom." *Radical Teacher* 92: 10–20.

Farmer, P. (1996). "On suffering and structural violence: A view from below." *Daedalus* 125 (1): 261–83.

Ferfolja, T. (2007). "Schooling cultures: Institutionalizing heteronormativity and heterosexism." *International Journal of Inclusive Education* 11 (2): 147–62. http://dx.doi.org/10.1080/13603110500296596.

Fisher, J. (2004). *Outlaws and inlaws: Your guide to LGBT rights, same-sex relationships and Canadian law.* Toronto: Egale Canada Human Rights Trust.

Ford, T. (2004). "Queering education from the ground up: Challenges and opportunities for educators." *Canadian Online Journal of Queer Studies in Education* 1 (1). Retrieved from http://jqstudies.library.utoronto.ca/index.php/jqstudies/article/view/3273/1403.

Fox, C. (2007). "From transaction to transformation: (En)countering white heteronormativity in 'safe spaces.'" *College English* 69 (5): 496–511.

Friedan, B. (1963). *The feminine mystique.* New York: W.W. Norton.

Frye, M. (1983). *The politics of reality: Essays in feminist theory.* Trumansburg, NY: Crossing Press.

Greer, G. (1970). *The female eunuch*. London: MacGibbon and Kee.
Grosz, E. (1990). "Philosophy." In *Feminist Knowledge: Critique and Construct*, ed. S. Gunew, 147–74. London: Routledge.
Hall, S. (1991). "Ethnicity, identity and difference." *Radical America* 3: 9–22.
Hepworth, D.H., and J. Larsen. (1986). *Direct social work practice: Theory and skills*. 2nd ed. Chicago: Dorsey Press.
Human Rights Watch. (2009). *Together, apart: Organizing around sexual orientation and gender identity worldwide*. New York: Human Rights Watch.
Hunter, S., and J.C. Nickerson. (2003). *Affirmative practice: Understanding and working with lesbian, gay, bisexual, and transgender persons*. Washington, DC: NASW Press.
Jaggar, A.M. (1988). *Feminist politics and human nature*. Totowa, NJ: Rowman and Littlefield.
Jeyasingham, D. (2008). "Knowledge/ignorance and the construction of sexuality in social work education." *Social Work Education* 27 (2): 138–51. http://dx.doi.org/10.1080/02615470701709469.
Johnson, J.L., and R. Repta. (2012). "Sex and gender: Beyond the binaries." In *Designing and Conducting Gender, Sex and Health Research*, ed. J. Oliffe and L. Greaves, 17–37. Thousand Oaks, CA: Sage. http://dx.doi.org/10.4135/9781452230610.n2.
Nova Scotia Association of Social Workers. (n.d.). "Ken Belanger Memorial Award." Retrieved from http://www.nsasw.org/site/recipients2.
Kopelson, K. (2002). "Dis/integrating the gay/queer binary: 'Reconstructed identity politics' for a performative pedagogy." *College English* 65 (1): 17–35. http://dx.doi.org/10.2307/3250728.
Lorber, J. (1996). "Beyond the binaries: Depolarizing the categories of sex, sexuality, and gender." *Sociological Inquiry* 66 (2): 143–60. http://dx.doi.org/10.1111/j.1475-682X.1996.tb00214.x.
Mallon, G.P. (1998). *Foundations of social work practice with lesbian and gay persons*. New York: Routledge.
Martinez, P., A. Barsky, and S. Singleton. (2011). "Exploring queer consciousness among social workers." *Journal of Gay and Lesbian Social Services* 23 (2): 296–315. http://dx.doi.org/10.1080/10538720.2010.541026.
McPhail, B.A. (2004). "Questioning gender and sexuality binaries: What queer theorists, transgendered individuals, and sex researchers can teach social work." *Journal of Gay and Lesbian Social Services* 17 (1): 3–21. http://dx.doi.org/10.1300/J041v17n01_02.
Millett, K. (1970). *Sexual politics*. New York: Doubleday.
Moffatt, K., and S. Todd. (2011). "Gender and sexuality: Introduction." *Canadian Social Work Review* 28 (1): 127–28.
Mohanty, C. (1992). "Feminist encounters: Locating the politics of experience." In *Destabilizing Theory: Contemporary Feminist Debates*, ed. M. Barrett and A. Phillips, 74–92. Stanford, CA: Stanford University Press.
Mohanty, C.T., A. Russo, and L. Torres, eds. (1991). *Third World women and the politics of feminism*. Bloomington: Indiana University Press.
Mullaly, B. (1993). *Structural social work: Ideology, theory, and practice*. 1st ed. Toronto: McClelland and Stewart.
–. (2007). *The new structural social work: Ideology, theory, practice*. 3rd ed. Don Mills, ON: Oxford University Press.
–. (2009). *Challenging oppression and confronting privilege*. 2nd ed. Don Mills, ON: Oxford University Press.
Nestle, J., C. Howell, and R. Wilchins. (2002). *Genderqueer: Voices from beyond the sexual binary*. Los Angeles: Alyson Books.
Nicholson, L., ed. (1990). *Feminism/postmodernism*. New York: Routledge, Chapman and Hall.

O'Brien, C. (1999). "Contested territory: Sexualities and social work." In *Reading Foucault for Social Work*, ed. A.S. Chambon, A. Irving, and L. Epstein, 131–55. New York: Columbia University Press.

O'Neill, B.J., T.A. Swan, and N.J. Mulé, eds. (2015). *LGBTQ people and social work: Intersectional perspectives*. Toronto: Canadian Scholars' Press.

Payne, M. (2005). *Modern social work theory*. 3rd ed. Chicago: Lyceum Books.

Pierson, R.R. (1993). "The mainstream women's movement and the politics of difference." In *Canadian Women's Issues: Strong Voices*, ed. R.R. Pierson, M.G. Cohen, P. Bourne, and P. Masters, 186–214. Toronto: James Lorimer.

Pierson, R.R., and M.G. Cohen. (1993). *Canadian women's issues: Bold visions*. Toronto: James Lorimer.

Pierson, R.R., M.G. Cohen, P. Bourne, and P. Masters, eds. (1993). *Canadian women's issues: Strong voices*. Toronto: James Lorimer.

Profitt, N.J. (2015). "Somewhere over the rainbow: Reflections on teaching a LGBT-S bachelor of social work course." In *LGBTQ people and social work: Intersectional perspectives*, ed. B.J. O'Neill, T.A. Swan, and N.J. Mulé, 297-316. Toronto: Canadian Scholars' Press.

Rebick, J. (2005). *Ten thousand roses: The making of a feminist revolution*. Toronto: Penguin Canada.

Rich, A. (1980). "Compulsory heterosexuality and lesbian existence." *Signs* (Chicago) 5 (4): 631–60. http://dx.doi.org/10.1086/493756.

Richardson, D. (2007). "Patterned fluidities: (Re)imagining the relationship between gender and sexuality." *Sociology* 41 (3): 457–74. http://dx.doi.org/10.1177/0038038507076617.

Richardson, D., and H. May. (1999). "Deserving victims? Sexual status and the social construction of violence." *Sociological Review* 47 (2): 308–31. http://dx.doi.org/10.1111/1467-954X.00174.

Riddle, D. (1996). "Riddle homophobia scale." In *Social Diversity and Social Justice: Gay, Lesbian, and Bisexual Oppression*, ed. M. Adams, P. Brigham, P. Dalpes, and L. Marchesani, 31. Dubuque, IA: Kendall/Hunt.

Ruttenbeck, H.M. (1973). *Homosexuality*. London: Souvenir Press.

Scott, J. (1992). "Experience." In *Feminists Theorize the Political*, ed. J. Butler and J. Scott, 22–40. New York: Routledge.

Sheafor, B.W., C.R. Horejsi, and G.A. Horejsi. (1997). *Techniques and guidelines for social work practice*. 4th ed. Boston: Allyn and Bacon.

Spender, D. (1980). *Man made language*. Boston: Routledge and Kegan Paul.

Taylor, C. (2008). "A human rights approach to stopping homophobic bullying in schools." *Journal of Gay and Lesbian Social Services* 19 (3–4): 157–72. http://dx.doi.org/10.1080/10538720802161672.

Weedon, C. (1987). *Feminist practice and poststructuralist theory*. Oxford: Basil Blackwell.

West, C., and D.H. Zimmerman. (1987). "Doing gender." *Gender and Society* 1 (2): 125–51. http://dx.doi.org/10.1177/0891243287001002002.

Willis, P. (2007). "'Queer eye' for social work: Rethinking pedagogy and practice with same-sex attracted young people." *Australian Social Work* 60 (2): 181–96. http://dx.doi.org/10.1080/03124070701323816.

Yep, G.A. (2002). "From homophobia and heterosexism to heteronormativity: Toward the development of a model of queer interventions in the university classroom." In *Addressing Homophobia and Heterosexism on College Campuses*, ed. E. Cramer, 163–76. New York: Harrington Park Press. http://dx.doi.org/10.1300/J155v06n03_14.

Young, I.M. (2003). "Five faces of oppression." In *Oppression, Privilege and Resistance*, ed. L. Heldke and P. O'Connor, 37–63. Boston: McGraw-Hill.

6

Constructing Alternatives: Reflections on Heterosexism in Social Work Education

KAROLYN MARTIN AND ROBYN LIPPETT

In recent years, Canadian educators have been urged by non-governmental organizations, such as Egale Canada, to address homophobia and transphobia in educational settings (Taylor et al., 2011). Despite these efforts, universities and colleges often remain challenging and unsafe for queer-identified people (Beemyn and Rankin, 2011; Yost and Gilmore, 2011). Although social work in Canada is guided by ethics of social justice (CASW, 2005), social work programs continue to be troubling for queer-identified people (Brownlee et al., 2005; Hafford-Letchfield, 2010). Indeed, though experiences of queer-identified social work students vary, research suggests that many have encountered homophobia, transphobia, and heterosexism at school (Brownlee et al., 2005; Chinell, 2011; Hylton, 2005, 2006). Social work education is embedded within the wider homophobic and transphobic socio-political contexts that Canadian educators are being called upon to address (Brown and Kershaw, 2008; Crisp, 2007; Hylton, 2006). Rooted in these contexts, social workers and students often possess assumptions and attitudes about queer-identified people that perpetuate oppression (Berkman and Zinberg, 1997; Chinell, 2011; O'Brien, 1999). In light of this, social work educators are seeking to develop new andragogies of sexualities that will ameliorate the experiences of queer-identified social work students and transform the discourse of sexualities in the wider profession (Hafford-Letchfield, 2010).

In this chapter, we reflect on our own experiences as queer-identified students in a bachelor of social work (BSW) program at an Atlantic Canadian university. Discussions of sexualities in our classroom were often related to the harmful impacts of homophobia and hatred on the lives of LGBTQ individuals. Rarely, however, did we critically explore the idea that sexuality and sexual identity are social constructions. Because we live in a heterosexist sociopolitical world, this lack of critical discussion led to the privileging of heterosexuality as normative, a priori, and "natural." In these discussions, we often felt minoritized into a homogeneous group of "others" and tokenized as "experts" of a static queer culture. Our experiences have been that social work education does not sufficiently challenge heterosexism, and we argue throughout this chapter that our experiences are not unique, as is confirmed in the current literature. We believe that a gap exists across several local contexts in how sexualities are explored in social work education.

To improve upon social work education's treatment of sexualities, we advocate the adoption of a *queer approach*. Drawing upon social constructionism and queer theory, we envision this approach as promoting an understanding of sexualities, gender, and identities as fluid and contextual (Burdge, 2007; McPhail, 2004; Willis, 2007). It would trouble existing sexual and gender categories (Willis, 2007). It would also allow social work learning communities to explore the social construction of all sexualities, the relations of power that privilege heterosexuality, and the way in which this privilege mediates all experiences. This would better position social work education to challenge heterosexism, homophobia, transphobia, and homonormativity in the educational context and in social work more generally (Brownlee et al., 2005; Camilleri and Ryan, 2006; Chinell, 2011; Crisp, 2007; Fish, 2008).

Our motivation for promoting this approach is rooted in our experiences of negotiating our queer sexualities in the social work classroom. We acknowledge that our sexualities intersect with other aspects of our identities, such as our genders and ethnicities, and that we are granted several unearned privileges because of them. For instance, we both identify as cisgender, meaning that our self-perceptions of our gender identities are congruent with the genders we were assigned at birth (Schilt and Westbrook, 2009). Karolyn Martin grew up in the Maritimes and identifies as a white woman who is queer/lesbian. Robyn Lippett grew up in Toronto and identifies as a white woman who is queer. In addition to our cisgender and white privileges, we both have considerable privilege in terms of our ability, social class, citizenship, and educational backgrounds. Our experiences, then, do not represent those of all queer-identified people who are in our program and/or studying social work. Although it is currently beyond the scope of this chapter, we continually explore how these intersecting identities have mediated our experiences in the classroom.

In this chapter, we explore the theoretical and discursive framings that inform a queer approach to social work education; discuss our own experiences as queer-identified social work students, highlighting how heterosexism has affected us through minoritization and tokenization; and conclude by offering two recommendations for adopting a queer approach to social work education. These recommendations are central to the development of queer andragogies that seek to meaningfully integrate analyses of heterosexism into all aspects of social work education.

Theoretical and Discursive Framings of a Queer Approach

According to Dr. Charlie Glickman (2012), to "queer" something is to critically examine its foundations and our assumptions about it. Because social work is "based on the concepts and assumptions of heterosexuality" (Fish, 2012, p. 7), heterosexuality often goes unquestioned and unexamined in social work education. Indeed, the literature suggests that sexualities in general are under-theorized in its discourses and andragogies (Camilleri and Ryan, 2006; Chinell, 2011; Fish, 2008; Hicks, 2008b). When sexualities are studied in social work education, it is most often "other" sexualities that are discussed (Hicks, 2008a, 2008b). Social work education focuses primarily on the problems associated with identifying as non-heterosexual – such as stigma, legal rights, and inequalities in areas such as adoption – rather than concentrating on the social and material relations that cause these problems (Hicks, 2008b). In these discussions, heterosexuality often remains unquestioned, thus perpetuating heterosexism (Berkman and Zinberg, 1997). Heterosexism, or the assumption that heterosexuality is the superior and natural sexuality, has shaped our own social work educational experiences. Indeed, it has disturbing implications for how social work students of all sexualities envision themselves in the classroom. We suggest a queer approach to social work education because of its potential for troubling these foundations and opening up new possibilities (Glickman, 2012).

As mentioned above, we see a queer approach as being rooted in theories of social constructionism and queer theory. Social constructionism emphasizes that knowledge is mediated by particular experiences, social and material relations, and discourses (Gergen, 2009; Parker and Burman, 1993). Discourses are the "historically, socially, and institutionally specific structure[s] of statements, terms, categories, and beliefs" that shape our social worlds and material relations (Scott, 1988, p. 35). Some discourses are afforded "master status" in our society, and as such, "seem to be reflections of the world as it 'actually' is" rather than particular versions of "reality" and "truth" (Talbot, Bibace, Bokhour, and Bamberg, 1996, p. 225). Social constructionism questions how, and at whose expense, this master status is afforded and maintained.

Heterosexuality is one discourse that has achieved master status (Adams, 1997). Since the Victorian era, Western heterosexuality (marriage between one cisgendered man and one cisgendered woman) has been privileged above all other sexualities, relationships, and desires by powerful institutions such as religion(s), government(s), and capitalism (Adams, 1997; Barker, 2013). Because of its privileged master status, the discourse of heterosexuality structures virtually all aspects of life in Western cultures, including the family and the economy (Adams, 1997; Butler, 1998, 1999; Foucault, 1978). Indeed, it is instrumental in the social construction of a binary system of gender (i.e., men and women) (Butler, 1999; Foucault, 1978). Each gender has a socially constructed role in society and in the labour force: men are normalized as breadwinners who participate in the paid labour force, and women are normalized as caregivers (Adams, 1997). The gendered division of labour is dependent upon the discourse of heterosexuality that naturalizes heterosexual kinship (Butler, 1999). It is also one of the foundations of the capitalist economic system that developed out of the industrial revolution (Adams, 1997; Butler, 1998). For instance, for men to participate in factory work, women needed to provide the "free" caregiving labour to support the current workforce and raise the next (Butler, 1998). Although gender roles have shifted somewhat in the capitalist economy, women and men are still largely expected to perform in their traditional roles (Brodie, 1998).

The discourse of heterosexuality gains its master status by othering, or excluding, all sexualities that fall outside of its narrow definition (Dominelli, 2002, p. 18). The process of othering occurs through the creation of binary oppositions between hetero and other sexualities that are then grouped together as a homogeneous and identifiable category (Butler, 1999). Heterosexuality is encoded in our culture as a priori, natural, and the sexual identity of the majority, whereas the other sexualities are encoded as abject and unnatural (Butler, 1999; Foucault, 1978). Although we are not looking to critique heterosexuality as a sexual identity, we are interested in dismantling the heterosexist structures that afford it these privileges.

In addition to social constructionism, we use queer theory to inform our critique of the heterosexism currently perpetuated by social work education. We understand queer theory to be a post-structural theory that troubles the stability and "naturalness" of sexual and gender categories (Edwards, 1998; Willis, 2007). Queer theory has also prompted critical consideration of the language and identities associated with non-heterosexuality (Wilchins, 2004). In the context of queer theory, sexualities are argued to be "discursively constructed" in particular socio-historical contexts (Sullivan, 2003, p. 1). In other words, our definitions of, and identification with, sexualities are constrained by existing definitions and identities in our particular social, geographical, and historical locations. For instance, as Foucault (1978) argues, only since the seventeenth century has sexuality been seen as a distinct aspect of human experience, a conceptualization that is unique to Western culture.

From this perspective, many have argued that sexualities, sexual identities, and desires change across lifetimes, situations, and contexts, and that identifying sexualities in terms of binary opposites does not represent the fluidity of human sexualities (Barker, 2013; Burdge, 2007; Butler, 1999; Diamond, 2008; Kimmel and Plante, 2004; Messner, 2008; Seidman, 2006; Sullivan, 2003). Because it destabilizes the "naturalness" and superiority of heterosexuality and stresses the constructedness of all sexualities, we use "queer" to inform our approach to social work education. The word "queer" has been reclaimed by scholars and activists seeking to challenge categories that suggest that sexualities "are stable, fixed and stand in direct relationship to a set of Eurocentric, hierarchically organized binary categories that organize human subjectivity (homosexual/heterosexual; female/male)" (Crath, 2010, p. 124). Despite its historical purpose of shaming and threatening, "queer" has become both an active and an empowering political subjectivity (Butler, 1993; Clare, 1999; Crath, 2010; Wilchins, 2004).

However, using "queer" is not without its challenges. Labelling any identity, culture, or experience runs the risk of essentializing it by suggesting that a common understanding is achievable (Bersani, 1995). Further, "queer" activism has often marginalized and/or silenced people who identify as trans, and "queer" has been used in ways that do not recognize the experiences of many (non-white) racialized individuals, economically disenfranchised individuals, and individuals who still see it as pejorative (Anzaldúa, 2009; Butler, 1993; Crath, 2010; Wilchins, 2004; Willis, 2007). Although the term can essentialize and exclude, it is often used in contexts that resist essentialist understandings of sexualities (Crath, 2010; Willis, 2007). Indeed, it can act as a "standpoint for tearing apart dominant ways of knowing about sex, gender, and sexualities" (Willis, 2007, p. 183). We use "queer" because of the possibilities it offers for "social workers to expand and strengthen [their] practice" (Willis, 2007, p. 187). The word "queer" offers similar possibilities for expanding social work andragogies, as such efforts are often "absent from most ordinary, everyday social work" (Hicks, 2008b, p. 133). In the next section, we examine how heterosexism has shaped our experiences in order to highlight the necessity of a queer approach to social work education. However, we use the term "queer" mindfully and with recognition of its limitations.

Our Experiences in Social Work Education

The Canadian Association for Social Work Education's "Standards for Accreditation" (CASWE, 2012) stipulates that social work educational programs must "encourage and support diversity and social justice in all aspects/domains" (p. 4). Multiple studies, however, have confirmed that social work education (in Canada and elsewhere) has not sufficiently encouraged and supported sexual diversity and social justice for people who are LGBTQ- or queer-identified (Berkman and Zinberg, 1997; Hylton, 2005, 2006; Van Soest, 1996). Further, the voices and experiences of queer-identified social work students are rarely included in conversations about the andragogies used in social work education (Chinell, 2011). We believe that such experiences must be added in more meaningful ways to these conversations. Heterosexism continues to impede social justice for queer-identified people in social work programs and in our society, as we have seen in our own classrooms. Our experiences provide further evidence for the necessity of adopting a queer approach to social work education.

Experiences of Minoritization

Our intention in sharing our experiences is to engage in conversation on how to improve discussions of sexualities in social work programs. In our case, our learning community has expressed commitment in working with us to develop a queer approach to social work education. Our BSW program does include course content related to LGBTQ-identified people, and our learning community is inclusive, respectful, and open to exploring new ideas and topics. Nevertheless, we have encountered heterosexism in our classroom. In this section, we discuss our experiences of being minoritized as queer-identified people in our learning community and tokenized as "experts" of "queer culture."

Traditional andragogies of sexualities in the social work classroom have positioned queer-identified social work students as members of a minority group (Hafford-Letchfield, 2010; McPhail, 2004). Indeed, as Rich (1996) argues, heterosexuality is assumed to be the compulsory sexual identity, until stated otherwise. Despite the fluidity of sexualities across lifetimes and contexts, queer sexualities are seen as the static experiences of a few people. Thus, issues affecting them are positioned as pertaining to "a small, relatively fixed homosexual minority" (McPhail, 2004, p. 8). This adoption of what Sedgwick (1990) refers to as the minoritizing view sends the message that discussions of queerness pertain only to those service users, social workers, and students who are queer-identified – or to any heterosexual-identified people who work with queer-identified service users. Minoritizing is deeply disconcerting, not only for queer-identified people, but arguably for everyone; it positions heterosexuality as normal and represents queerness as potentially insignificant for those who do not currently identify as queer, or who do not expressly intend to work with queer-identified service users. This lack of knowledge and/or ignorance contributes to the continued subjugation of queer knowledges, identities, and experiences (Butler, 1993; Jeyasingham, 2008; McPhail, 2004).

We were minoritized in our classroom on some occasions, not because of overt heterosexism (we recall only one incident of this, which we describe below), but rather, because of the infrequent opportunities for critical reflection upon sexualities. In class, case studies and guest speakers offered rich material for learning and discussion. These andragogical strategies were used in every course, yet sexualities were rarely their focus. The limited course content on sexualities made us feel that the topic was not relevant to the majority of our class and our community of practice. Thus, we felt minoritized by the dearth of critical discussion of, and reflection on, sexualities. We believe it is crucial to recall that all social workers and service users have diverse sexualities, not just those who identify as LGBTQ or queer, and that our sexualities are part of what shapes our experiences of the world around us. On occasion, such discussions were presented as optional, not as core content for social work education.

In addition, we often found ourselves initiating and leading these class discussions of sexualities. In them, we often shared our experiences as queer-identified women and raised the topic of sexualities as they relate to social work. We found that these discussions tended to be brief compared with those on other topics. DePalma and Atkinson (2006) write that heterosexual-identified students often cite political correctness as a barrier for engaging in discussions of queer sexualities. For instance, as mentioned in our discussion of the term "queer," the language that diverse queer-identified people apply to themselves often retains pejorative connotations in society. Because queer sexualities have been minoritized in our classroom, the terminology with which to discuss them was rarely a focus of our conversations.

We felt we were constantly "waving the rainbow flag" by introducing and leading discussion on sexualities. As we describe in more detail below, we sometimes hesitated to start these discussions for fear of positioning ourselves as experts in queer culture and queer experience. We worried that our learning community would see us as having authoritative knowledge of sexualities solely because we are queer-identified. We believe that having more formalized and critical discussions of sexualities in our classroom would have provided more opportunities to discuss the multiple and intersecting oppressions faced by queer-identified people. These discussions would clarify how such oppressions are directly related to heterosexism and the privileging of heterosexuality in our society. Further, they would enable our learning community to discuss the language of queer identities and sexualities, increase its competencies and abilities to ally with queer- and LGBTQ-identified people in the field, and challenge any notion that presumes to dictate what is normal about anyone's sexuality.

To illustrate how our learning community could have benefitted from more opportunities to discuss sexualities in class, we reflect on an instance in which a guest speaker was overtly heterosexist. While giving a presentation on provincial social policy, the speaker made remarks that some of us (including other queer- and LGBTQ-identified people) interpreted as outright disapproval of LGBTQ adoption and same-sex families. The speaker explained that the province's policy on adoption had been amended in recent years to allow (in theory) for same-sex couples to adopt children. At several points, the speaker shared their religious beliefs and said that they were opposed to same-sex families. With their implication that only heterosexual families can properly care for children, these comments were overtly heterosexist. We were shocked to find that many attendees did not immediately perceive this and that they were surprised by our reaction to the presentation. Rather than seeing this incident as an isolated event that was relevant solely to us (the "sexual minorities"), we suggest that it could have been transformed into a critical class discussion (Garcia and Van Soest, 1999), not only of the heterosexism that characterizes social work education, but of society in general. That many people did not perceive the speaker's comments to be problematic speaks to the insidious nature of heterosexism. If our class had engaged in more formalized discussions of heterosexism, perhaps more people would have recognized the comments as offensive and complicit in perpetuating social injustices.

Experiences of Tokenization

Heterosexism in the social work classroom can also result in queer-identified students being tokenized as experts in an essentialized queer culture and queer experience (O'Brien, 1999; Swank and Raiz, 2008). As mentioned above, because of the master status of heterosexuality, the only intelligible way of talking about sexualities within this discourse is to frame them in binary terms: as heterosexual versus other (Butler, 1999; Willis, 2007). The acronym LGBTQ illustrates this well by homogenizing a diverse range of experiences and identities into a unified category, whereas in reality perhaps the only unifying feature of this "group" is that its members are not included in the heterosexual category. A queer approach argues that there is no quintessential queer experience; rather, it suggests that experiences of queerness are diverse and resistant to static descriptions and understandings (Dominelli, 2002; Warner, 2003). In spite of this, queer-identified social work students continue to be cast in the role of expert in the classroom (Chinell, 2011), speaking to and about "queer culture," identities, and experiences.

An overt form of tokenizing occurs when these students are asked to speak on behalf of a universalized queer culture and queer experience solely because they themselves are queer-identified. They are assumed to be both in possession of such knowledge and willing to share it. Although this form of tokenizing rarely arose in our classroom, more subtle forms can occur. In instances when we felt tokenized, our learning community probably solicited our input to avoid speaking on our behalf. Nevertheless, we often felt tokenized, as representatives of a queer culture who could speak objectively about an essentialized queer experience. From our perspective, uneasiness and tokenizing did not seem to occur beyond discussions of sexualities (or race). We feel this reflects our learning community's knowledge of the damage that can occur when people speak from a standpoint that they themselves do not occupy (Harding, 1993). We believe that our learning community wished to avoid this. Greater opportunity for critical reflection on sexualities would have encouraged community members to examine their own sexualities (and other aspects of their identities) as being standpoints from which to speak and learn.

Although we both spoke frequently to our own experiences as queer-identified individuals in the classroom, we still felt conflicted about the implications of our sharing. On some occasions, we appreciated having the opportunity to voice our opinions on subjects pertaining to queerness and sexualities. At other times, we felt that we were cast in the role of authorities who could speak on behalf of queer culture. These instances made us uncomfortable and aware that we were complicit in promoting the idea that categories such as gay, lesbian, bisexual, and queer culture are, as Narayan (1997) explains, "pristine and unchanging" (p. 23). We believe that attempts to speak on behalf of all queer-identified people lead to complicity in essentializing and silencing queer sexualities, identities, and experiences, and that such essentialism perpetuates heterosexism (O'Brien, 1999). Although we recognize that these moments represented important chances for us to address heterosexism, many factors influenced our responses. In certain contexts, we welcomed the opportunity to problematize our framing as experts; in others, we thought that it was strategic for us to refrain from addressing heterosexism.

Recommendations for a Queer Approach to Social Work Education

Because we believe that our experiences of minoritization and tokenization resulted from heterosexism, we advocate for a queer approach to social work education. Indeed, the moments when we felt safest and most valued in our social work classroom occurred when human sexualities were celebrated as diverse and were viewed as fluid social constructs. For example, when the concept of heteronormativity was raised during a class seminar, the ensuing rich discussion encouraged all students to think critically about their own sexualities. This reinforced and for some, introduced, the idea that there are no normal sexualities, but rather, that sexualities are diverse and fluid throughout an individual's lifetime. Through a queer approach to social work education, queerness and "other" sexualities would be interpreted and discussed in ways that recognize that they are "of continuing, determinative importance in the lives of people across the spectrum of sexualities" (Sedgwick, 1990, p. 1).

We offer recommendations for adopting a queer approach, based on our experiences as queer-identified social work students. We believe that curricula and practices in social work education should be amended to expose and dismantle heterosexism. In turn, this would help social work learning communities to avoid minoritizing and tokenizing queer-identified people. We recommend that this be done by emphasizing self-reflexivity in the social work program and by promoting student opportunities for praxis in the area of sexualities beyond the classroom. In the next two sections, we present some key considerations for social work educators in designing curricula and methodology from a queer approach.

Recommendation 1: Self-Reflexivity as a Tool for Unlearning Heterosexism

Because social work education often fails to engage in "pro-active questioning of heterosexist frameworks that inform ... social work" as a profession (Hafford-Letchfield, 2010, p. 245), a queer approach could deepen reflection on the assumptions these frameworks propagate (Fish, 2012). Indeed, social work students should be "challenged to ... engage in an unlearning process" (Ballan, 2008, p. 197). Self-reflexivity could assist students and practitioners to become more aware of how their own conceptualizations of sexualities will affect their practice. We recommend that more opportunities for self-reflexivity be incorporated into discussions of sexualities in social work education. To achieve this, students could examine their own views, assumptions, and stereotypes regarding sexualities, discuss the societal barriers that constrain sexualities, and conceive ways to dismantle them (Ballan, 2008; Jeyasingham, 2008).

We experienced the benefits of "unlearning" through self-reflexivity during a seminar titled "Heteronormativity," which we led with two other students in the fall of 2012 on the relevance of heteronormativity to the social work profession. Adapting the heterosexual questionnaire in Rochlin (1995), we opened with a role-play in which two queer-identified parents listened in shock as their daughter came out as heterosexual. The parents then questioned her about when, where, why, and how she had "discovered" she was heterosexual. Some classmates shared that our presentation encouraged them to consider how their heterosexualities granted them the privilege of never having to come out. We also benefitted from reflection upon those circumstances in which we do not come out for fear of negative repercussions and how we use heterosexual privilege to remain "safe" in these instances. Role-play, then, was an effective strategy in our experience and could be of potential value for other students and educators. Research confirms that role-play "can facilitate deeper individual involvement with, and interest in, the scenario [enacted] by exposing students to previous unconscious attitudes or viewpoints" that can lead to "attitude change, combating ignorance, prejudice and discrimination" (Hafford-Letchfield, 2010, p. 249). However, our experiences in educational contexts outside of social work have taught us that role-play must be done with respectful recognition of the myriad challenges of representing a standpoint that the actors may not occupy.

Another andragogical strategy for unlearning through self-reflexivity is through critical reflection assignments, and/or group discussions, that encourage examination of students' own sexualities and their beliefs, values, and assumptions about sexualities in general. We believe that some critical scholarship on sexualities and queerness (such as Epstein, 2009; Foucault, 1978; Hicks, 2008a, 2008b; Plummer, 1995; Spade, 2011) could provide professors and students alike with an opportunity to explore sexualities in new ways. Students could be asked to reflect upon the following questions in an assignment and/or class discussion: What is sexuality? How is it constructed in Western society? Does it vary over time? (adapted from Barker, 2013). These questions allow students to critically consider the numerous ways that all sexualities are discursively constructed.

Creating a safe space that is amenable to the critical discussion of identities and sexualities is essential for promoting learning and engagement in the classroom (Barrett, 2010). However, literature from the field of education questions the possibility of establishing a space that is truly safe for everyone (Leonardo and Porter, 2010). Safety must be understood as a nuanced and fluid concept that is "not static, but a constant movement between safe and unsafe, individual and collective, agreement and disagreement" (Roestone Collective, 2014, p. 1355). It can never be fully guaranteed; rather, it is constantly negotiated (Barrett, 2010; Leonardo and Porter, 2010). Given the realities of oppression and power imbalances among students (and between students and faculty), these negotiations are of the utmost importance (Barrett, 2010; Weber-Cannon, 1990).

The realities of oppression and privilege must always be acknowledged in classroom discussions. Social work students have intersectional identities, often belonging simultaneously to both "privileged groups (for example, male, white, heterosexual, middle or upper class) and oppressed groups (female, person of color, gay, poor or working class)" (Goodman, 2010, p. 10). As such, they have often had challenging personal experiences of oppression that may affect their ability to discuss sexualities (e.g., sexual violence, childhood abuse). Because of this, requirements for classroom safety will differ, and potentially conflict, from student to student. The question at hand, then, can easily become, "safety for whom?" (Leonardo and Porter, 2010, p. 139). Feelings of "denial and resistance, shame, guilt, anger, and anxiety" can and do come to the forefront during such classroom discussions (Garcia and Van Soest, 1999, p. 150). It is the responsibility of instructors to acknowledge the realities of multiple and conflicting oppressions and to engage students in the ongoing negotiation of classroom safety (Garcia and Van Soest, 1999).

Such negotiation presents many challenges, but it is crucial and necessary for supporting student learning and growth (Goodman, 2010). To work toward classroom safety, Barrett (2010) suggests the integration of safety with civility, which focuses on observable and enforceable behaviours. By promoting civility in class, instructors take steps to ensure that students "will not be subjected to certain behaviours on the part of their peers that threaten the social and physical integrity of the learning environment" (Barrett, 2010, p. 10). Instructors should initiate discussions of behaviours that are acceptable and unacceptable, and should model these behaviours in their interactions with students (Barrett, 2010; Weber-Cannon, 1990). We believe that

Weber-Cannon's (1990) "ground rules" for classroom discussion offer excellent advice on creating guidelines for civility. In addition, having a code of civil conduct may clearly elucidate acceptable behaviours and languages for class discussions (Barrett, 2010). In our experience, students' accountability to such a code can be amplified when, acting on a suggestion from the teacher, they themselves collectively formulate it. Instructors should periodically remind students about the ground rules, and students should monitor their own behaviour in accordance with them. The rules should be revisited and/or amended throughout the semester.

Instructors can also initiate discussions on safety, in which it is viewed as a political and contested concept, and they should ensure that all students have a basic understanding of social inequalities and oppressions before entering into discussions of this nature. During the collective development of classroom guidelines, the instructor could ask the class to critically reflect upon this action and bring awareness to who might become silenced in a call for "civility," given the realities of oppression and privilege, both inside and outside the classroom (Leonardo and Porter, 2010). The class could then discuss ways to ensure that all students are able to express themselves safely and effectively (see Petrie and Naugler, 2001, for a detailed list of activities). Further, when developing written assignments on the topic of sexualities, instructors should provide multiple assignment options that approach the topic from many angles (such as self-reflection on one's own sexuality or on social construction in the media) so that students can determine how they feel most comfortable engaging with the subject matter.

Recommendation 2: Opportunities for Praxis

We believe that self-reflexivity is vital in problematizing assumptions of normalcy and naturalness, with regard to sexualities, but this alone will not dismantle the binaries between "gay and straight as distinct kinds of persons" (Sedgwick, 1990, p. 83). Thus, it will not dismantle heterosexism. We also need to engage in praxis, which is both "reflection and action upon the world in order to transform it" (Freire, 2007, p. 51). Good intentions, then, are not sufficient for complete transformation of current conditions; we also need to take action (hooks, 1994). A queer approach requires that social work education provide ample opportunities for social action to disassemble heterosexism and heteronormativity in social work practice.

One such opportunity for developing meaningful praxis is through field placements (Fish, 2012). Hylton (2005) argues that "the dearth of agencies providing services to the lesbian and gay community precluded many [students] from realizing their goal of working with lesbian-, gay- or bisexually identified people" (p. 74). Although the city in which our school is located has virtually no agencies dedicated primarily to serving queer and LGBTQ communities, our university was able to find a placement where Robyn had the opportunity to work with queer and LGBTQ-identified youth. Other students could be encouraged to pursue similar placement opportunities in the future. In addition, social work schools in cities where services for queer and LGBTQ communities are lacking could take a more active role in advocating for the creation of such resources, such as asset mapping and the establishment of faculty and student working groups on such issues as bullying and harassment. As they prepare for their field placements, all social work students should be taught to employ respectful language when interacting with service users (such as honouring their preferred gender pronouns and not making assumptions regarding the gender and sexuality of their partners). Our school already promotes the use of inclusive and respectful language, but this could be integrated into the evaluation process. In addition, students preparing for field placements should reflect on how their own identities, including their sexualities, might influence their perceptions and interactions with agencies and service users. Another opportunity for praxis is to invite guest speakers who integrate theories regarding the constructedness of sexualities into their social work practice. Earlier, we mentioned that our program did not invite speakers on sexualities into the classroom. However, speakers must be invited with the understanding that being queer-identified does not offer them the authority to speak on behalf of all queer-identified people (Johnston, 2009).

Conclusion

The Canadian Association of Social Workers "Code of Ethics" (CASW, 2005) states that respect for the diversity of Canadian society is essential to social work practice and that social workers are obligated to work toward creating a just society. We believe that a queer approach to social work education would prepare future social workers to practise in more socially just ways by equipping them with tools for respectful practice. Through a queer approach, greater care will be taken when discussing sexualities in the classroom to avoid tokenizing and minoritizing queer- and LGBTQ-identified people. This approach would challenge students to think critically about sexualities. In addition, it would encourage them to think about queer- and LGBTQ-identified people and sexualities outside of those topics with which they are commonly associated, such as coming out, queer families and adoption, same-sex marriage, oppression, and homophobia. Adichie (2009) warns about the danger of telling a "single story" about a diverse group of people; having only one story limits the actions and potentials for people belonging to a group. Indeed, as discussed earlier, social work education most often focuses on the problems that are associated with being queer-identified (Hicks, 2008b). Discussions and lectures, then, should diversify queerness by cultivating the strength, power, and positivity of queer identities, experiences, and expressions of sexualities. For us, identifying as queer has presented a number of positive opportunities, connections, and possibilities that are too often neglected in wider discussions.

In this chapter, we have argued for a queer approach to social work education. We identified that heterosexism has shaped our experiences by making us feel minoritized and tokenized in what have otherwise been respectful conversations. Rather than seeing this as the "fault" of our learning community, we believe that social work educational discourse does not adequately problematize the master status of heterosexuality and the binary framing of sexualities, and thus does not sufficiently challenge heterosexism. This has troubling implications for the experiences of queer-identified social work students, as well as for social work practice in general. We recommend that a queer approach to social work education be implemented through greater self-reflexivity related to sexualities in course content and greater opportunities for praxis through field placements and guest speakers. By providing more opportunities for such discussions, stories like ours will help to diversify the single story that is perpetuating heterosexism in social work education. We are hopeful that these discussions will lead to the implementation of a queer approach in our learning community.

References

Adams, M.L. (1997). *The trouble with normal: Postwar youth and the making of heterosexuality.* Toronto: University of Toronto Press.

Adichie, C. (2009, October). "Chimamanda Adichie: The danger of a single story" [Video file]. Retrieved from http://www.ted.com/talks/chimamanda_adichie_the_danger_of_a_single_story.

Anzaldúa, G. (2009). "To(o) queer the writer – Loca, escritora y chicana." In *The Gloria Anzaldúa Reader*, ed. A. Keating, 163–75. Durham, NC: Duke University Press. http://dx.doi.org/10.1215/9780822391272-024.

Ballan, M.S. (2008). "Disability and sexuality within social work education in the USA and Canada: The social model of disability as a lens for practice." *Social Work Education* 27 (2): 194–202. http://dx.doi.org/10.1080/02615470701709675.

Barker, M. (2013). *Rewriting the rules: An integrative guide to love, sex and relationships.* New York: Routledge.

Barrett, B.J. (2010). "Is 'safety' dangerous? A critical examination of the classroom as safe space." *Canadian Journal for the Scholarship of Teaching and Learning* 1 (1): 1–12. http://dx.doi.org/10.5206/cjsotl-rcacea.2010.1.9.

Beemyn, G., and S. Rankin. (2011). "Introduction to the special issue on LGBTQ campus experiences." *Journal of Homosexuality* 58 (9): 1159–64. http://dx.doi.org/10.1080/00918369.2011.605728.

Berkman, C.S., and G. Zinberg. (1997). "Homophobia and heterosexism in social workers." *Social Work* 42 (4): 319–32. http://dx.doi.org/10.1093/sw/42.4.319.

Bersani, L. (1995). *Homos*. Cambridge, MA: Harvard University Press.

Brodie, J. (1998). "Restructuring and the politics of marginalization." In *Women and Political Representation in Canada*, ed. M. Tremblay and C. Andrew, 19–37. Ottawa: University of Ottawa Press.

Brown, H.C., and S. Kershaw. (2008). "The legal context for social work with lesbians and gay men in the UK: Updating the educational context." *Social Work Education* 27 (2): 122–30. http://dx.doi.org/10.1080/02615470701709444.

Brownlee, K., A. Sprakes, M. Saini, R. O'Hare, K. Kortes-Miller, and J. Graham. (2005). "Heterosexism among social work students." *Social Work Education* 24 (5): 485–94. http://dx.doi.org/10.1080/02615470500132756.

Burdge, B.J. (2007). "Bending gender, ending gender: Theoretical foundations for social work practice with the transgender community." *Social Work* 52 (3): 243–50. http://dx.doi.org/10.1093/sw/52.3.243.

Butler, J. (1993). "Critically queer." *GLQ: A Journal of Lesbian and Gay Studies* 1 (1): 17–32. http://dx.doi.org/10.1215/10642684-1-1-17.

–. (1998). "Merely cultural." *New Left Review* 1 (227) (January-February): 33–44.

–. (1999). *Gender trouble: Feminism and subversion of identity*. New York: Routledge.

Camilleri, P., and M. Ryan. (2006). "Social work students' attitudes toward homosexuality and their knowledge and attitudes toward homosexual parenting as an alternative family unit: An Australian study." *Social Work Education* 25 (3): 288–304. http://dx.doi.org/10.1080/02615470600565244.

CASW (Canadian Association of Social Workers). (2005). "Code of ethics." Retrieved from http://casw-acts.ca/sites/default/files/attachements/CASW_Code%20of%20Ethics.pdf.

CASWE (Canadian Association for Social Work Education). (2012). "Standards for accreditation." Retrieved from http://caswe-acfts.ca/wp-content/uploads/2013/03/CASWE-ACFTS-Standards-11-2014.pdf.

Chinell, J. (2011). "Three voices: Reflections on homophobia and heterosexism in social work education." *Social Work Education* 30 (7): 759–73. http://dx.doi.org/10.1080/02615479.2010.508088.

Clare, E. (1999). *Exile and pride: Disability, queerness and liberation*. Brooklyn: South End Press.

Crath, R. (2010). "Reading Fanon in homosexual territory: Towards the queering of a queer pedagogy." In *Fanon and Education: Thinking through Pedagogical Possibilities*, ed. G.J.S. Dei and M. Simmons, 123–46. New York: Peter Lang.

Crisp, C. (2007). "Correlates of homophobia and use of gay affirmative practice among social workers." *Journal of Human Behavior in the Social Environment* 14 (4): 119–43. http://dx.doi.org/10.1300/J137v14n04_06.

DePalma, R., and E. Atkinson. (2006). "The sound of silence: Talking about sexual orientation and schooling." *Sex Education* 6 (4): 333–49. http://dx.doi.org/10.1080/14681810600981848.

Diamond, L.M. (2008). *Sexual fluidity: Understanding women's love and desire*. Cambridge, MA: Harvard University Press.

Dominelli, L. (2002). *Anti oppressive social work theory and practice*. Basingstoke, UK: Palgrave Macmillan.

Edwards, T. (1998). "Queer fears: Against the cultural turn." *Sexualities* 1 (4): 471–84. http://dx.doi.org/10.1177/136346098001004005.

Epstein, R., ed. (2009). *Who's your daddy? And other writings on queer parenting*. Toronto: Sumach Press.

Fish, J. (2008). "Far from mundane: Theorising heterosexism for social work education." *Social Work Education: The International Journal* 27 (2): 182–93. http://dx.doi.org/10.1080/02615470701709667.

—. (2012). *Social work with lesbian, gay, bisexual and trans people: Making a difference*. Chicago: Policy Press.

Foucault, M. (1978). *The history of sexuality*. Vol. 1, *An introduction*. New York: Vintage Books.

Freire, P. (2007). *Pedagogy of the oppressed*. New York: Continuum International.

Garcia, B., and D. Van Soest. (1999). "Teaching about diversity and oppression: Learning from the analysis of critical classroom events." *Journal of Teaching in Social Work* 18 (1–2): 149–67. http://dx.doi.org/10.1300/J067v18n01_12.

Gergen, K. (2009). *An invitation to social construction*. 2nd ed. Thousand Oaks, CA: Sage.

Glickman, C. (2012, April 6). "Queer is a verb" [Web log]. Retrieved from http://charlieglickman.com/2012/04/06/queer-is-a-verb/.

Goodman, D. (2010). "Helping students explore their privileged identities." *Diversity and Democracy* 13 (2): 10–12.

Hafford-Letchfield, T. (2010). "A glimpse of the truth: Evaluating 'debate' and 'role play' as pedagogical tools for learning about sexuality issues on a law and ethics module." *Social Work Education* 29 (3): 244–58. http://dx.doi.org/10.1080/02615470902984655.

Harding, S. (1993). "Rethinking standpoint epistemology: What is 'strong objectivity'?" In *Feminist Epistemologies*, ed. L. Alcoff and E. Potter, 49–82. London: Routledge.

Hicks, S. (2008a). "Thinking through sexuality." *Journal of Social Work* 8 (1): 65–82. http://dx.doi.org/10.1177/1468017307084740.

—. (2008b). "What does social work desire?" *Social Work Education* 27 (2): 131–37. http://dx.doi.org/10.1080/02615470701709451.

hooks, b. (1994). *Teaching to transgress: Education as the practice of freedom*. New York: Routledge.

Hylton, M.E. (2005). "Heteronormativity and the experience of lesbian and bisexual women as social work students." *Journal of Social Work Education* 41 (1): 67–82.

—. (2006). "Queer in southern MSW programs: Lesbian and bisexual women discuss stigma management." *Journal of Social Psychology* 146 (5): 611–28. http://dx.doi.org/10.3200/SOCP.146.5.611-628.

Jeyasingham, D. (2008). "Knowledge/ignorance and the construction of sexuality in social work education." *Social Work Education* 27 (2): 138–51. http://dx.doi.org/10.1080/02615470701709469.

Johnston, S. (2009). "Not for queers only: Pedagogy and postmodernism." In *Feminist Pedagogy: Look Back to Move Forward*, ed. R.D. Crabtree, D.A. Sapp, and A.C. Licona, 80–93. Baltimore: Johns Hopkins University Press.

Kimmel, M.S., and R.F. Plante. (2004). "Introduction to sexuality." In *Sexualities: Identities, Behaviors, and Society*, ed. M.S. Kimmel and R.F. Plante, 1–3. New York: Oxford University Press.

Leonardo, Z., and R.K. Porter. (2010). "Pedagogy of fear: Toward a Fanonian theory of 'safety' in race dialogue." *Race, Ethnicity and Education* 13 (2): 139–57. http://dx.doi.org/10.1080/13613324.2010.482898.

McPhail, B.A. (2004). "Questioning gender and sexuality binaries: What queer theorists, transgendered individuals, and sex researchers can teach social work." *Journal of Gay and Lesbian Social Services* 17 (1): 3–21. http://dx.doi.org/10.1300/J041v17n01_02.

Messner, M. (2008). "Becoming 100% straight." In *Feminist Frontiers*, ed. V. Taylor, L. Rupp, and N. Whittier, 400–4. Toronto: McGraw-Hill.

Narayan, U. (1997). *Dislocating cultures: Identities, traditions, and Third World feminism*. New York: Routledge.

O'Brien, C.A. (1999). "Contested territory: Sexualities and social work." In *Reading Foucault for Social Work*, ed. A.S Chambon, A. Irving, and L. Epstein, 131–55. New York: Columbia University Press.

Parker, I., and E. Burman. (1993). "Introduction: Discourse analysis – The turn to the text." In *Discourse Analytic Research: Repertoires and Readings of Texts in Action*, ed. I. Parker and E. Burman, 1–16. London: Routledge.

Petrie, O., and D. Naugler. (2001). "Anti-racist teaching: In the context of the events of September 11th." *Core: York's Newsletter on University Teaching* 11 (1): 1–2.

Plummer, K. (1995). *Telling sexual stories: Power, change and social worlds*. London: Routledge. http://dx.doi.org/10.4324/9780203425268.

Rich, A. (1996). "Compulsory heterosexuality and lesbian existence." In *Feminism and Sexuality: A Reader*, ed. S. Jackson and S. Scott, 130–41. New York: Columbia University Press.

Rochlin, M. (1995). "The language of sex: The heterosexual questionnaire." In *Gender in the 1990s: Images, Realities and Issues*, ed. E.D. Nelson and B.W. Robinson, 38–39. Toronto: Nelson, Canada.

Roestone Collective. (2014). "Safe space: Towards a reconceptualization." *Antipode* 46 (5): 1346–65. http://dx.doi.org/10.1111/anti.12089.

Schilt, K., and L. Westbrook. (2009). "Doing gender, doing heteronormativity: 'Gender normals,' transgender people, and the social maintenance of heterosexuality." *Gender and Society* 23 (4): 440–64. http://dx.doi.org/10.1177/0891243209340034.

Scott, J.W. (1988). "Deconstructing equality-versus-difference: Or, the uses of poststructuralist theory for feminism." *Feminist Studies* 14 (1): 32–50. http://dx.doi.org/10.2307/3177997.

Sedgwick, E.K. (1990). *Epistemology of the closet*. Berkeley: University of California Press.

Seidman, S. (2006). "Theoretical perspectives." In *Introducing the New Sexuality Studies: Original Essays and Interviews*, ed. S. Seidman, N. Fischer, and C. Meeks, 3–13. London: Routledge.

Spade, D. (2011). *Normal life: Administrative violence, critical trans politics and the limits of law*. New York: South End Press.

Sullivan, N. (2003). *A critical introduction to queer theory*. New York: New York University Press.

Swank, E., and L. Raiz. (2008). "Attitudes toward lesbians of practicing social workers and social work students." *Journal of Baccalaureate Social Work* 13 (2): 55–67.

Talbot, J., R. Bibace, B. Bokhour, and M. Bamberg. (1996). "Affirmation and resistance of dominant discourses: The rhetorical construction of pregnancy." *Journal of Narrative and Life History* 6 (3): 225–51. http://dx.doi.org/10.1075/jnlh.6.3.02aff.

Taylor, C., and T. Peter, with T.L. McMinn, T. Elliott, S. Beldom, A. Ferry, Z. Gross, S. Paquin, and K. Schachter. (2011). *Every class in every school: Final report on the first national climate survey on homophobia, biphobia, and transphobia in Canadian Schools*. Toronto: Egale Canada Human Rights Trust. Retrieved from http://egale.ca/wp-content/uploads/2011/05/EgaleFinalReport-web.pdf.

Van Soest, D. (1996). "The influence of competing ideologies about homosexuality on non-discrimination policy: Implications for social work education." *Journal of Social Work Education* 32: 53–63.

Warner, M. (2003). "Introduction." In *Fear of a Queer Planet: Queer Politics and Social Theory*, ed. M. Warner, vii–xxxi. Minneapolis: University of Minnesota Press.

Weber-Cannon, L. (1990). "Fostering positive race, class, and gender dynamics in the classroom." *Women's Studies Quarterly* 18 (1–2): 126–34.

Wilchins, R., ed. (2004). *Queer theory, gender theory: An instant primer.* New York: Alyson Books.

Willis, P. (2007). "'Queer eye' for social work: Rethinking pedagogy and practice with same-sex attracted young people." *Australian Social Work* 60 (2): 181–96. http://dx.doi.org/10.1080/03124070701323816.

Yost, M.R., and S. Gilmore. (2011). "Assessing LGBTQ campus climate and creating change." *Journal of Homosexuality* 58 (9): 1330–54. http://dx.doi.org/10.1080/00918369.2011.605744.

7

Coming Out with God in Social Work? Narrative of a Queer Religious Woman in Academe

MARYAM KHAN

In the name of God, the most Beneficent and the most Merciful.

As a racialized queer Muslim woman, I have a unique perspective on occupying the intersections of social worker, social work student, and post-secondary educator in social work. This is a reflection piece that discusses my perspective on coming out, alongside the constant negotiation of these positionalities.

I want to make clear that I am *not* arguing for the integration of religion or religious doctrine in social work education and practice. There is expansive literature on how religion has served as a tool for colonialism and imperialism in the case of Indigenous, First Nations, Inuit, and Metis persons and communities (Baskin, 2009; Chapman, 2014). Religion and its authority figures have oppressed – and continue to oppress – many groups in society, including sexually and gender-diverse persons of various origins (Fetner, 2008). My intent behind sharing this narrative is to challenge binary tropes that stipulate *religion equals homophobia and transphobia* and that *queer identities and lives are mainly secular*.

How does one come out as a queer Muslim in predominantly Muslim circles in social work? How does one come out as religious in queer circles? How does one come out as a queer Muslim in the classroom, both as a sessional faculty member and as a student? I have found that coming out as a religious queer in social work is an ongoing battle against identity essentialization and ideologies that posit that a queer and a religious identity are antipodal (Al-Sayyad, 2010; Siraj, 2006, 2011); against exoticization of a queer Muslim identity (Yip, 2005a); and against injustices (past and current) inflicted on queer-identified folks in the name of God.

In this chapter, I detail my experience, as a student and a part-time postsecondary educator, of being silenced in the classroom by peers and faculty members who seemed uncomfortable discussing the nexus of spirituality, religiosity, and sexuality's incorporation in social work philosophy and practice. In failing to address queer religious identities through course work and discussions, social work contributes to the silencing of bodies that occupy such spaces and does not honour the myriad lived experiences and knowledges that students and faculty bring to the classroom. To prevent peripheral identities from being further marginalized, it is imperative to destabilize or critique the identities that fall under "falsely unifying rubrics like ... 'Islam' [that] invent collective identities for large numbers of individuals who are actually quite diverse" (Said, 1978, p. xxviii).

Marginalization and othering also transpire when faculty and students assert that a queer identity is antithetical to a religious one (Al-Sayyad, 2010; Henrickson, 2007). This notion is as common in contemporary society as it is in social work (Heyman, Buchanan, Marlowe, and Sealey, 2006). In fact, a growing body of literature posits that queers can be, and are, religious and do not abandon their faith traditions (Hendricks, 2010; Kugle, 2010, 2014).

When I refer to my "Muslim identity," I mean a combination of my spiritual and religious dimensions, in which the teachings of Islam are at the core (spirituality and religiosity will be explored below). My spirituality cannot easily be separated from Islam and my subject position. The epistemological and ontological orientations that inform my Muslim identity are grounded in Islam and the values of peace it fosters, my commitment to social justice, my status as a racialized woman, and my queerness, to name only a few influencing factors (Shahjahan, 2010).

The narrative below is my experience. It should not be taken as the ultimate truth and representation of *all* racialized queer Muslim women; nor should it be considered independent of its cultural, socio-political, and herstorical contexts. My intention here is not to vilify Islam or to demonstrate that all Muslims are rigid and homophobic. It is to critique institutionalized and monolithic understandings of Islam and Muslims. The problem with employing socially constructed identity categories is that they add to discourses on difference and othering (Connolly, 2002; Said, 1978). My use of "queer" signifies politics that challenge traditional ways of knowing and being, and is not intended to essentialize queer identities (Ahmed, 2006). Since the word rejects an actual definition, its vagueness offers "political advantages" (Kaplan, 1997, p. 6) and signifies a certain attitude of resistance (Halperin, 1995). It also subverts notions of normative sexuality and gender categories, allows for multiplicity, and acknowledges diversity in discussions of socially constructed identity categories (Edwards and Brooks, 1999).

Understanding Religiosity and Spirituality

The literature displays a limited consensus regarding either the definition of spirituality and religiosity or the relationship between the two (Carrette and King, 2005). However, there is consensus that spirituality plays an integral role in the development of some individuals' selfhood and a sense of self (Tisdell, 2003). The term "spiritual dimension" is hard to define, since there is little agreement regarding its meaning (Best, 2008). Spirituality can be defined as originating in one's religious practices (Johns and Hanna, 2011; Tan, 2005); however, other conceptions of spirituality posit that it is a secular entity and therefore separate from religion (Helminiak, 1998; Love, Bock, Jannarone, and Richardson, 2005). Queer communities tend to favour the observance of a secular spirituality (Halkitis et al., 2009), since most mainstream religious institutions discriminate against same-sex attractions and relationships (Henrickson, 2007). Tan (2005) argues that organized religion and its institutions are homophobic, which explains why the gay and lesbian participants in his study looked elsewhere to meet their spiritual needs. In fact, there is a growing body of literature on the positive aspects of a faith-based spirituality in the lives of queer individuals, with respect to queer identity development (Lease, Horne, and Noffsinger-Frazier, 2005; Tisdell, 2003; Yip and Khalid, 2010).

Herstorically, social work education has sometimes vilified religion and celebrated and endorsed spirituality (Wong and Vinsky, 2009). Value judgments regarding religiosity and spirituality are well illustrated by Roof and Gesch (1995):

> To be religious conveys an institutional connotation, prescribed rituals, and established ways of believing; to be spiritual is more personal and experiential, and has to do with the deepest motivations of life for meaning and wholeness. The first is "official" religion, standardized and handed down by religious authorities; the second is "unofficial," highly individualistic, religion "à la carte." (p. 72)

Upon reading this passage, one could infer that religiosity is anachronistic, whereas spirituality is fulfilling and wholesome. I suggest that religious individuals are branded as dogmatic and traditional, and as blindly following doctrine, which in turn removes personal agency from faith. On the other hand, practitioners of spirituality are situated as modern individuals who are more in touch with their being, do not require dogma, and are considered whole. In this manner, binaries are constructed in which religious individuals are traditional and their spiritual counterparts are modern and enlightened (Pargament, 1999). This proves problematic for people who operate from a faith-based spirituality and situates them as inferior. Pargament (1999) argues that such polarized constructions of religiosity and spirituality obstruct investigation into the interaction and relationship between the two concepts. Furthermore, this ignores that both religion and spirituality are social constructs and that construction is contingent on socio-political contexts (Carrette and King, 2005). To track the construction of spirituality and religiosity over time and the shift in their meanings, see Carrette and King (2005); Cascio (1998); Fuller (2001); Praglin (2004); and Rindfleish (2005).

Contemporary expressions of spirituality originated in religious traditions and have been hijacked by the neo-liberal state, which is predicated on consumerism of spirituality as a secular entity (Rindfleish, 2005). A consumer-driven spirituality market exists in contemporary society, wherein individuals can pick and choose from a plethora of spiritual practices, mixing and matching components to fulfill their needs (Rindfleish, 2005). For instance, popular secular forms such as First Nations, Inuit, Metis, and Indigenous healing circles, yoga, chanting, and meditation are actually appropriated from religious practices (Wong and Vinsky, 2009). Although some disagree (Helminiak, 1998), it can be argued that spirituality and religion are intertwined and are not "mutually exclusive" (Cashwell and Young, 2005, p. 13). I believe this intertwinement is important to consider since spirituality in contemporary society is often presented as completely independent of any influence of religious traditions (Shahjahan, 2010).

To honour a holistic approach that integrates religiosity and spirituality, I have adopted Shahjahan's (2010) conception of spirituality, which places emphasis on social justice. I selected this definition because it is grounded in Shahjahan's (2010) subject position and because it originated in his Muslim faith. As he explains,

> I use "spirituality" to refer to a way of being in the world characterized by connections to one's cultural knowledge and/or other beings (e.g. one's community,

transcendental beings, and other parts of creation), allowing a movement from inward to outward action in the social world. I also conceptualize spirituality as one knowledge system contextualized among multiple ways of knowing such as revealed knowledge, intuition, and cultural knowledge; it cannot be captured by the empirical and rational perspective that informs people's actions within the social world (p. 478).

Given that there are multiple ways of knowing, social work education can at times downplay emphasis on this premise. Indeed, masculine Eurocentric and Euro-American conceptions of knowledge and ways of being are often privileged and taken as the norm in Canadian universities (Shahjahan, 2010). This is problematic for women, faculty, and racialized students, and for herstorically othered groups who may identify with epistemological and ontological orientations that are not part of popular Eurocentric and Euro-American conceptions (Bernal, 2002). Willinsky (1998) points out that racist and sexist ideas used in colonial expansion and the imperial project have affected local and global knowledge production as well as learning (informal and formal) in the social and natural sciences, biology, linguistics, geography, and arts. Various examples in herstory speak to prejudiced claims made regarding certain races, genders, and sexual identities to oppress and suppress them, as in the case of the Indigenous, First Nations, Inuit, Metis, and racialized people (Said, 1978; Smith, 2012). In short, inclusion of alternative and marginalized knowledges can disrupt the monopoly that dominant imperial powers hold over knowledge production (Shahjahan, 2005).

Social Work Education and Othering

Teaching is not an objective enterprise (Palmer, 2000). Instructors bring their beliefs, research knowledge, expertise and passion for a given topic, value systems, and lived experiences into the equation of what Baurain (2012) refers to as "teacher knowledge" (p. 312). Therefore, an instructor's ontological and epistemological beliefs and values will influence what topics are selected for the course content and the direction of class discussions (Lindholm and Astin, 2008). Where do our beliefs and values originate? Our upbringing, experiences, positionality, sexual identity, socialization, religion, spirituality, and a host of other factors influence our ways of knowing and being. Discussions of religious and spiritual beliefs are often neglected in academic conversations (Northcut, 2004). Baurain (2012) argues that such conversations are essential to understanding how teachers translate their knowledge into the practice of teaching.

In one of my undergraduate social work courses, the instructor stated that she would not be discussing religion, sexual orientation, and identity in class as she was "uncomfortable" and did not feel "equipped to do this topic justice." She politely encouraged me to take elective courses on gender and sexual diversity that were offered elsewhere in other departments. I suggest that what she left unsaid was that such topics were controversial and that she did not want to engage in them (Ai, 2002). Conversations related to religion and spirituality need to occur in classrooms, since these topics are evident in practice, and they play out in the lives of service users and practitioners (Sheridan, 2004). In addition, some literature stipulates that social work students are *not* receiving instruction on how to address spiritual and religious matters (Canda and Furman, 1999; Derezotes, 1995; Sheridan, 2004). Notably, research reveals that students who desire to explore spiritual and religious subjects in social work must seek additional education and training on such topics (Murdock, 2005).

In my experience, most instructors are *not* transparent about their spiritual and religious beliefs. In addition, their course content selection and discussions indiscriminately reflect their politics. Some examples of this are failing to discuss whiteness in an anti-oppressive course; not identifying their social location or theoretical and political lens; or omitting sexuality and gender in a health course. Why the secrecy? Perhaps some instructors see teaching as an objective enterprise and fear that if they were frank about their politics, they could become vulnerable in front of students and somehow lose their authority. This illusion of objectivity needs to be turned on its head by adopting a critical reflexive stance in practice (Rouse, 1996).

It is not uncommon for students to experience discomfort when discussing the nexus of religion, spirituality, and sexuality in class (Ai, 2002). Indeed, it is virtually inevitable that certain students will make hateful comments about sexually and gender-diverse persons, and will assert that their religious beliefs prevent them from accepting and working with such persons (LePeau, 2007; Levy, 2011). Research indicates that religious individuals can tend to be homophobic and transphobic (Morrow, 2000; O'Brien, 2004), and religious social work students are no exception in this regard. Nonetheless, such research creates binaries of *religious as homophobic* and *queer as secular,* and it ignores the existence of religious individuals who are not homophobic and transphobic (Brice, 2014), and of religious queers (Wilcox, 2006). By "queer as secular," I refer to the assumption that queer individuals are not religious and/or not connected to a faith community (Shannahan, 2010). As Rahman (2010) contends, the identities of gay Muslims are intersectional because "cultures and identities are plural and overlap rather than being monolithic and mutually exclusive" (p. 948). This intersection will be explored in more detail below.

I cannot count the number of times that hate-filled Islamophobic, racist, homophobic, and transphobic comments were made in my classes under the guises of ignorance or the innocent wish to learn about the "other." The students who utter these remarks seem unaware of power dynamics in the classroom and do not recognize their own privileged subject positions. As Applebaum (2008) argues, straight people "do not have to take notice of their sexuality because laws, customs, habits assume heterosexual lives as the norm; and, in so doing, oppression and systemic injustice are normalized and not understood as something in need of critical questioning" (pp. 410–11).

Regardless of whether hateful comments are intentionally malicious or innocent queries, disrespect transpires and parties are still offended (Honneth, 2001). For instance, referring to queer attractions and relationships as a "lifestyle" may simply reflect ignorance, but it could offend individuals who have fought against the rhetoric of choice that dominates contemporary society's beliefs about same-sex relationships and attractions.

Can student discomfort and potential class conflict be justified as the impetus for not addressing such topics in social work courses? Should controversial subjects not be mentioned? For example, when topics of religion and spirituality emerge in class, conversations become uncomfortable, and the subject is usually squelched (Ai, 2002; Praglin, 2004). For racialized individuals, discussing race and racism can be emotionally draining, yet controversial racist comments are made in classrooms in the name of *learning* and *reflecting* to become critical social workers. Why should anyone be subject to such taxing processes? It could be argued that discussions of this nature need to transpire so that everyone can engage in critiques of dominant societal structures in order to mobilize deconstruction and system transformation (Heron, 2005). Discussions of issues related to power and the oppression of marginalized individuals, and the manner in which colonialism permeates daily life, need to be front and centre (Heron, 2005). This, among other reasons, is why race and institutionalized racism matter and require critical examination. In a similar vein, sexuality, religion, and spirituality matter and require attention so that essentialized identities can be deconstructed and heteronormativity challenged. Why is it that certain dimensions of my identity (race) are open for discussion, whereas others (religion and spirituality) are to be kept secret? Are certain elements of my identity more worthy of discussion than others? I think not. When I am with heterosexual Muslims, I feel cautious about my queerness. As well, I tread with caution around queers and refrain from discussing my spiritual and religious beliefs. As I write this, I am thinking of Sedgwick's (1990) work on the epistemology of the closet, which explains that queer individuals go in and out of the closet and that they exercise caution when they disclose their queerness for fear of how such information will be read by others. For instance, because of certain language or symbols that I use, people may speculate about my sexual identity. Hence, I am always aware that they might hijack such knowledge to create their interpretative reading of who I am. In addition, because my classroom discussions deal with issues related to Islam and my faith in God, students may assume that I am homophobic. With that hijacked knowledge, they may read me as a homophobic person since I do not embody queerness in a stereotypical sense. In this way, such open secrets create knowledge and a *reading* about queer individuals and their politics – an unknown typecasting that lies beyond their control and that results in knowledge production through speculation regarding their sexual and gender identities (Sedgwick, 1990).

Othered by Queers

In queer theory, religion is branded as a "stultifying, oppressive institution of a heteronormative, sexist social order" (Wilcox, 2006, p. 74). It is no secret that sexually and gender-diverse persons have been oppressed and persecuted in the name of God and religion throughout history, and that many forms of persecution still exist all over the world. I have heard statements such as, "Why do you want to follow a religion that marginalizes women and on top of that queer women?" "You don't live in a South Asian country, so why are you still following rules from 'back home'?" or, my favourite, "I thought you were born and raised here." The othering I have experienced mixes Islamophobia with various "isms" (racism, ageism, sexism), primarily racism. Other queer-identified peers, mostly white, do not seem to grasp that a queer person could subscribe to faith-based spirituality and believe in God. I have been made to feel archaic, as if I have not reached the level of enlightenment that a queer who subscribes to secular forms of spirituality has achieved. I have been made to feel that I am *backward* and unable to let go of cultural chains from *back home*. On the flip side, I have been exoticized for my courage to come out as a queer Muslim. Whenever I came out as a queer Muslim, I had to reassure my white peers that I did *not* face honour-killing or threats of physical violence and that I did not need to be rescued from my *oppressive* and *violent* family. Addressing the popular culture demonization of Islam and of Muslims as savages (Razack, 2010) is an ongoing aspect of coming out as a religious queer Muslim in LGBTQ circles.

Religious queers have demystified antithetical notions of maintaining both a religious identity and an LGBTQ identity (Rahman, 2010; Shannahan, 2010). LGBTQ theologians and writers have already debunked allegedly homophobic passages in the Bible, Torah, and Quran and have exposed the homophobic, heterosexist, transphobic sentiments in popular interpretations of the holy verses (Comstock and Henking, 1997; Kugle, 2010; Whitaker, 2006a). In fact, religious queers are growing in number (Wilcox, 2006) and are challenging heteronormative, sexist, transphobic, and homophobic interpretations of the holy books in their respective religious and spiritual traditions (Cabezón, 1992; Kugle, 2003; Pattanaik, 2002; Perry, 1972).

For the most part, I have difficulty socializing and fitting into the mainstream queer culture, as it tends to be racist, Islamophobic (Yip, 2008), not religious, and not God friendly (Shannahan, 2010). On various occasions, I have been shut down and marginalized in queer circles due to my intersectional identities. That is why it was important for me to locate like-minded queers at various religious LGBTQ groups that share similar values and beliefs, such as the El-Tawhid Juma Circle Mosque in Toronto and the Metropolitan Community Church of Toronto. Being queer has brought me closer to God because, in the face of adversities, I have discovered respite in God's love; thus, my spirituality has been a protective factor in my life.

Othered by Muslims

Coming out as queer in social work courses where the students are predominantly Muslim has been a bitter-sweet victory. It is victorious because it challenges the tendency of Muslims to deny the existence of queer Muslims (Manji, 1999); in my particular social work group, I have received limited positive reactions for coming out (except from other queer Muslims). In coming out as a queer Muslim, I have encountered the following reactions: "You are not Muslim!" "You're going to hell," "You know that's not allowed in Islam," or, my favourite, "Do your parents know?" Yes, I am a Muslim and a proud one. No, I am not going to hell. Yes, it is allowed in Islam. And yes, my parents do know! Islam's compatibility with queerness is beyond the scope of this discussion, but it must be noted that many Muslims fail to see the Quran as a herstorical document embedded in certain socio-political contexts (Kugle, 2010). As Whitaker (2006a) postulates, "Historically, though, Muslim societies have been relatively tolerant of sexual diversity – perhaps more so than others. Evidence of this can be found in classical Arabic literature, in the accounts of early travellers, and in the examples of Europeans who settled in Arab countries to escape sexual persecution at home" (para. 10).

Indeed, the Quran makes no mention of same-sex attractions and relationships between women (Habib, 2007, 2009), and it does not assign a penalty for same-sex acts (Whitaker, 2006b, para. 12). I consider the Quran, Bible, and Torah as representing the words of God, more meaningful than the claims of religious authorities to offer a *true* interpretation of the divine. For a comprehensive review of sexual and gender diversity in Islam and Muslim societies, see Habib (2010), Kugle (2003, 2010, 2014), and Whitaker (2006b).

When my *open secret* of being queer is affirmed, heterosexual Muslim faculty and students tend to see me as an inauthentic Muslim. This discrediting takes the form of ignoring my knowledge of Islam, belittling my faith, and negating my Muslim status. Thus, I wait until mid- to late semester before coming out. Another reason for waiting is to manage student and faculty resistance against my intersectional identity, as, for example, in disparaging or ignoring my ideas and being disrespectful. For similar reasons, I do not come out as Muslim to queer faculty and students. It seems almost that I must establish my credibility as a secular individual, and even then, I have experienced othering. However, lately, I come out when *I* deem necessary and make no attempt to win anyone over. I recognize that some LGBTQ and religious faculty and students may never accept religious queers in theory or practice. My faith-based spirituality supports me in dealing with adversity from both faculty and students who hate and are uncomfortable with who I am. Yet, I have never abandoned my Muslim identity in favour of my sexual identity and vice versa.

Teaching with a Spiritual Praxis

Many scholars and educators in North America have reconnoitered the role of spirituality in building and fostering positive self-image, healthy relationships, and better learning outcomes in educational systems (Miller, 2000; Palmer, 1993, 1998, 2000). The inclusion of spirituality in social work education allows for the recognition of strengths, resilience, the wisdom of oppressed and marginalized groups, and an acknowledgment of Indigenous knowledges among other non-Western social work practices (Al-Krenawi and Graham, 1999; Barise, 2005; Shahjahan, 2009; Yip, 2005b). Much has been written on the topic of incorporating spirituality in social work education and practice (Cascio, 1998; Dalton, Eberhardt, Bracken, and Echols, 2006; Gilbert, 2000; Heyman et al., 2006).

I employ a spiritual praxis in my teaching and research for the following reasons. First, I view my inclusion of a herstorically marginalized sexual identity with a Muslim identity (perceived as antithetical to each other) as a form of resistance to dominant notions of a secular queer identity. This in fact honours the notion that there are multiple ways of being and knowing in the world. A queer Muslim identity invalidates the binaristic thinking of being either Muslim *or* queer. Second, I reject the Cartesian notion of the separateness of mind, body, and spirit, and view this idea as inherently problematic, since it creates false dichotomies and does not honour the wholeness of a person. My epistemology of faith-based spirituality considers the interconnectedness of all living and non-living things. This recognition demands mutual respect for every individual's uniqueness and equal status, which emphasizes "desirable or enforceable attributes of relationships existing between subjects" (Honneth, 2001, p. 45). Incorporating a spiritual dimension in teaching is a direct challenge to the institution of education's status quo (Dillard, Abdur-Rashid, and Tyson, 2000) and to camps that purport that objectivity can be achieved in research and teaching.

Creating a spirituality friendly climate is imperative when introducing spirituality in social work (Heyman et al., 2006). To this end, a place to start is by offering orientations to the administration on various spiritualties and their relevance to social work (Dalton et al., 2006). Further, Dalton et al. (2006) contend that offering electives on spirituality and social work practice can also be a viable strategy. Another strategy is to develop faculty-student and faculty-faculty mentorship programs and/or committees wherein individuals can explore what spirituality looks like in their lives, classrooms, practice, and curriculum (Dalton et al., 2006).

I am not suggesting that social work engage in religious studies and teach religion in its courses. What I am asking for is openness from faculty and students to entertain intersectional identities in their course work and that they not shy away from such discussions in the classroom. There are a number of ways in which faculty can include a spiritual dimension in their teaching. For instance, I have commenced classes with student- and faculty-led grounding exercises, and have paid close attention to not appropriating others' community and/or religious traditions and spiritual practices for my benefit. I have been careful not to present such practices as ahistorical, meaning that I have given credit to their origins (people, faith, community, and so on) and have not tweaked them to fit my needs (Smith, 2012). Below are some other strategies I have employed at the undergraduate level:

- Include readings and reflexive assignments promoting critical reflections on students' spiritual and religious beliefs and the impact on their practice (LePeau, 2007).
- Include literature on the historical construction of spirituality and religiosity (Shahjahan, 2010).
- Include queer-friendly readings on religion and sexuality (LePeau, 2007).
- Invite guest speakers from various faith traditions who can positively demonstrate a religious queer identity (LePeau, 2007).
- Show films and documentaries on spirituality and guided meditation practices (Dalton et al., 2006).
- Create a listserv for faculty and students to circulate pertinent spirituality-related information and events in the community.

Teaching from a spiritual praxis can be a complex process since it is hard to ascertain student response. Starting out as a junior scholar with fewer than six years of teaching at a post-secondary level has made for interesting experiences in integrating a faith-based spiritual praxis. As their undergraduate course evaluations indicate, some students think that in-class discussions of spirituality and religiosity in social work practice are tricky due to their fear of proselytization or attempts to convert. Most students report that issues of spirituality and religiosity need to be discussed in class so that a holistic perspective of service users can be entertained in treatment plans and case management. Regrettably, as sessional faculty, I do not have full support from my colleagues to deal with the complexities of adding a spiritual dimension to my teaching (Shahjahan, 2010). Colleagues may refuse to assist in managing difficult classroom dynamics since they did not agree with the inclusion of a spiritual praxis; there may be no forum to discuss class dynamics; mentorship and support from the department may be inadequate; and gendered and racialized politics of the department may apply to certain teachers. This last point refers to the fact that, during the early stages of their academic careers, racialized teachers "have to invest much energy in establishing themselves as bona fide teachers both in the eyes of their students and in the eyes of their colleagues" (Hoodfar, 1992, p. 310).

It is imperative to note that classrooms are also directed and maintained by the students themselves. As Briskin and Coulter (1992) state, "power dynamics among students manage, constrain, and interrupt learning. Put another way, students are always gendered, raced, and classed subjects, and thus bring differential power and privilege to the classroom" (p. 258). Although instructors possess formal power (granted by the institution), race, age, (dis)ability, class, gender, sexuality, and other social markers are always imbricated in all classrooms. All of these markers influence and produce power dynamics that need to be factored into the equation of class atmosphere and direction. For example, in some of my classes the mix of students has not been diverse, which has implications for how they perceive me, the nature of the discussions, and the classroom atmosphere. In one undergraduate social work course that I taught, I was the only racialized person in the room. As a result, discussing the complexities of oppression, race, and intersectional identities, to name only a few factors, was a tenuous exercise. Adopting a critical perspective in that class, and urging students to do the same, was challenging, since they seemed unable to hear me and were closed to what I was saying. In other words, they had already made up their minds regarding *what I was about* based on my gender and social presentation. In their evaluations of the course, a few students wrote that they assumed I was automatically homophobic due to being religious. Two admitted that they harboured negative ideas about Islam and Muslims prior to the course and were challenged on such beliefs. Only when I decided to come out to them as a queer Muslim and discussed the nexus of spirituality and religion did the ice melt somewhat. At that moment tensions shifted a bit, and students opened up about their understandings of spirituality, Islam, and sexuality.

As I reflected upon their comments, I had disturbing and unsettling thoughts. Did they see me as less of a threat, a *safer* Muslim, because of my sexuality and gender? What had they thought about me before I came out? I suggest that my queerness made the difference in diminishing the classroom tension, since it made me less of an "other" in some ways. Perhaps my visible otherness as a racialized Muslim woman seemed far more threatening than my queerness. The queerness made me accessible to these students, as it is often associated with the West, which is seen as open-minded and civilized (Puar, 2007), unlike Islam, with its *savage* intolerance of diversity (Said, 1978). For me, becoming and being racialized is accompanied by the constant fear that my every action or utterance will somehow be taken as representative of all South Asian queer Muslims (see Fanon, 1952, on the process of bodies made black through the white gaze).

Conclusion

In this chapter, I have argued that the absence of acknowledging intersectional identities has caused the marginalization of certain subject positions. If social work is to be inclusive of identities (such as queer Muslims and other religious queers), it must examine the nexus of religiosity, spirituality, and sexuality. To aid this process, I have suggested the incorporation of strategies to include a spiritual praxis in social work andragogy.

References

Ahmed, S. (2006). *Queer phenomenology: Orientations, objects, others.* London: Duke University Press. http://dx.doi.org/10.1215/9780822388074.

Ai, A.L. (2002). "Integrating spirituality into professional education." *Journal of Teaching in Social Work* 22 (1–2): 103–30. http://dx.doi.org/10.1300/J067v22n01_08.

Al-Krenawi, A., and J.R. Graham. (1999). "Social work and Koranic mental health healers." *International Social Work* 42 (1): 53–65. http://dx.doi.org/10.1177/002087289904200106.

Al-Sayyad, A.A. (2010). "'You're what?' Engaging narratives from diasporic Muslim women on identity and gay liberation." In *Islam and Homosexuality*, Vol. 2, ed. S. Habib, 373–94. Santa Barbara: Greenwood.

Applebaum, B. (2008). "'Doesn't my experience count?' White students, the authority of experience and social justice pedagogy." *Race, Ethnicity and Education* 11 (4): 405–14. http://dx.doi.org/10.1080/13613320802478945.

Barise, A. (2005). Social work with Muslims: Insights from the teachings of Islam. *Critical Social Work* 6 (2). Retrieved from www.criticalsocialwork.com.

Baskin, C. (2009). "Evolution and revolution: Healing approaches with Aboriginal adults." In *Wichitowin: Aboriginal social work in Canada*, ed. R. Sinclair, M. Hart, and G. Bruyere, 132–52. Halifax and Winnipeg: Fernwood.

Brice, T.S. (2014). "Is homophobia a conservative Christian value?" In *Conservative Christian beliefs and sexual orientation in social work: Privilege, oppression, and the pursuit of human rights*, ed. A.B. Dessel and M.R. Bolen, 257-71. Virginia: Council on Social Work Education.

Baurain, B. (2012). "Beliefs into practice: A religious inquiry into teacher knowledge." *Journal of Language, Identity, and Education* 11 (5): 312–32. http://dx.doi.org/10.1080/15348458.2012.723576.

Bernal, D. D. (2002). "Critical race theory, Latino critical theory, and critical raced-gendered epistemologies: Recognizing students of color as holders and creators of knowledge." *Qualitative Inquiry* 8 (1): 105-26. http://dx.doi.org/10.1177/107780040200800107.

Best, R. (2008). "In defence of the concept of 'spiritual education': A reply to Roger Marples." *International Journal of Children's Spirituality* 13 (4): 321–29. http://dx.doi.org/10.1080/13644360802439466.

Briskin, L., and R.B. Coulter. (1992). "Feminist pedagogy: Challenging the normative." *Canadian Journal of Education* 17 (3): 247–63. http://dx.doi.org/10.2307/1495295.

Cabezón, J.I., ed. (1992). *Buddhism, sexuality, and gender.* Albany: SUNY Press.

Canda, E.R., and L.D. Furman. (1999). *Spiritual diversity in social work practice: The heart of helping.* New York: Free Press.

Carrette, J., and R. King. (2005). *Selling spirituality: The silent takeover of religion.* London: Routledge.

Cascio, T. (1998). "Incorporating spirituality into social work practice: A review of what to do." *Families in Society* 79 (5): 523–31. http://dx.doi.org/10.1606/1044-3894.719.

Cashwell, C.S., and J.S. Young. (2005). "Integrating spirituality and religion into counseling: An introduction." In *Integrating Spirituality and Religion into Counseling: A Guide to Competent Practice*, ed. C.S. Cashwell and J.S. Young, 1–29. Alexandria, VA: American Counseling Association.

Chapman, C. (2014). "Five centuries' material reforms and ethical reformulations." In *Disability incarcerated, imprisonment and disability in the United States and Canada*, ed. L. Ben-Moshe, C. Chapman, and A. Carey, 25-44. New York: Palgrave Macmillan.

Comstock, G.D., and S.E. Henking, eds. (1997). *Que(e)rying religion: A critical anthology*. New York: Continuum.

Connolly, W.E. (2002). *Identity/difference: Democratic negotiations of political paradox*. Expanded ed. Minneapolis: University of Minnesota Press.

Dalton, J.C., D. Eberhardt, J. Bracken, and K. Echols. (2006). "Inward journeys: Forms and patterns of college student spirituality." *Journal of College and Character* 7 (8): 1–22.

Derezotes, D.S. (1995). "Spirituality and religiosity: Neglected factors in social work practice." *Arete* 20 (1): 1–15.

Dillard, C.B., D. Abdur-Rashid, and C.A. Tyson. (2000). "My soul is a witness: Affirming pedagogies of the spirit." *International Journal of Qualitative Studies in Education: QSE* 13 (5): 447–62. http://dx.doi.org/10.1080/09518390050156404.

Edwards, K., and A.K. Brooks. (1999). "The development of sexual identity." *New Directions for Adult and Continuing Education* 1999 (84): 49–57. http://dx.doi.org/10.1002/ace.8406.

Fanon, F. (1952). *Black skin, white masks*. Trans. R. Philcox. New York: Grove Press.

Fetner, T. (2008). *How the religious right shaped lesbian and gay activism*. Minneapolis: University of Minnesota Press.

Fuller, R. (2001). *Spiritual, but not religious: Understanding unchurched America*. New York: Oxford University Press. http://dx.doi.org/10.1093/0195146808.001.0001.

Gilbert, M. (2000). "Spirituality in social work groups: Practitioners speak out." *Social Work with Groups* 22 (4): 67–84. http://dx.doi.org/10.1300/J009v22n04_06.

Habib, S. (2007). *Female homosexuality in the Middle East: Histories and representations*. New York, NY: Routledge.

–. (2009). *Arabo-Islamic texts on female homosexuality, 850-1780 A.D.* New York: Teneo Press.

Habib, S., ed. (2010). *Islam and homosexuality*. Vols. 1–2. Santa Barbara: Greenwood.

Halkitis, P.N., J.S. Mattis, J.K. Sahadath, D. Massie, L. Ladyzhenskaya, K. Pitrelli, M. Bonacci, and S.E. Cowie. (2009). "The meanings and manifestations of religion and spirituality among lesbian, gay, bisexual and transgender adults." *Journal of Adult Development* 16 (4): 250–62. http://dx.doi.org/10.1007/s10804-009-9071-1.

Halperin, D. (1995). *Saint Foucault: Towards a gay hagiography*. Oxford: Oxford University Press.

Helminiak, D.A. (1998). "Sexuality and spirituality: A humanist account." *Pastoral Psychology* 47 (2): 119–26. http://dx.doi.org/10.1023/A:1022909628981.

Hendricks, M. (2010). "Islamic texts: A source for acceptance of queer individuals into mainstream Muslim society." *Equal Rights Review* 5: 31-51. http://www.equalrightstrust.org/ertdocumentbank/muhsin.pdf.

Henrickson, M. (2007). "Lavender faith: Religion, spirituality and identity in lesbian, gay and bisexual New Zealanders." *Journal of Religion and Spirituality in Social Work* 26 (3): 63–80.

Heron, B. (2005). "Self-reflection in critical social work practice: Subjectivity and possibilities of resistance." *Journal of Reflective Practice* 6 (3): 341–51. http://dx.doi.org/10.1080/14623940500220095.

Heyman, J.C., R. Buchanan, D. Marlowe, and Y. Sealey. (2006). "Social workers' attitudes toward the role of religion and spirituality in social work practice." *Journal of Pastoral Counselling* 41: 3–19.

Honneth, A. (2001). "Recognition or redistribution? Changing perspectives on the moral order of society." *Theory, Culture and Society* 18 (2–3): 43–55. http://dx.doi.org/10.1177/02632760122051779.

Hoodfar, H. (1992). "Feminist anthropology and critical pedagogy: The anthropology of classrooms' excluded voices." *Canadian Journal of Education* 17 (3): 303–21. http://dx.doi.org/10.2307/1495298.

Johns, R.D., and F.J. Hanna. (2011). "Peculiar and queer: Spiritual and emotional salvation for the LGBTQ Mormon." *Journal of LGBTQ Issues in Counseling* 5 (3–4): 197–219. http://dx.doi.org/10.1080/15538605.2011.633157.

Kaplan, M.B. (1997). *Sexual justice: Democratic citizenship and the politics of desire.* New York: Routledge.

Kugle, S.S. (2003). "Sexuality, diversity and ethics in the agenda of progressive Muslims." In *Progressive Muslims: On Justice, Gender, and Pluralism,* ed. O. Safi, 190–234. Oxford: Oneworld.

–. (2010). *Homosexuality in Islam.* Oxford: Oneworld.

–. (2014). *Living out Islam: Voices of gay, lesbian, and transgender Muslims.* New York: New York University Press.

Lease, S.H., S.G. Horne, and N. Noffsinger-Frazier. (2005). "Affirming faith experiences and psychological health for Caucasian lesbian, gay and bisexual individuals." *Journal of Counseling Psychology* 52 (3): 378–88. http://dx.doi.org/10.1037/0022-0167.52.3.378.

LePeau, L.A. (2007). "Queerying religion and spirituality: Reflections from difficult dialogues exploring religion, spirituality, and homosexuality." *College Student Affairs Journal* 26 (2): 186-92.

Levy, D. (2011). "Journeys of faith: Christian social workers serving gay and lesbian clients." *Social Work and Christianity* 38 (2): 218–27.

Lindholm, J.A., and H.S. Astin. (2008). "Spirituality and pedagogy: Faculty's spirituality and use of student-centered approaches to undergraduate teaching." *Review of Higher Education* 31 (2): 185–207. http://dx.doi.org/10.1353/rhe.2007.0077.

Love, P.G., M. Bock, A. Jannarone, and P. Richardson. (2005). "Identity interaction: Exploring the spiritual experiences of lesbian and gay college students." *Journal of College Student Development* 46 (2): 193–209. http://dx.doi.org/10.1353/csd.2005.0019.

Manji, I. (1999). "Confessions of a Muslim lesbian." In *ReCreations: Religion and Spirituality in the Lives of Queer People,* ed. C. Lake, 22–23. Toronto: Queer Press.

Miller, J. (2000). *Education and soul.* Albany: State University of New York Press.

Morrow, S.L. (2000). "First do no harm: Therapist issues in psychotherapy with lesbian, gay and bisexual clients." In *Handbook of Counseling and Psychotherapy with Lesbian, Gay, and Bisexual Clients,* ed. R.M. Perez, K.A. DeBord, and K.J. Bieschke, 137–56. Washington, DC: American Psychological Association. http://dx.doi.org/10.1037/10339-006.

Murdock, V. (2005). "Guided by ethics: Religion and spirituality in gerontological social work practice." *Journal of Gerontological Social Work* 45 (1–2): 131–54. http://dx.doi.org/10.1300/J083v45n01_08.

Northcut, T.B. (2004). "Pedagogy in diversity: Teaching religion and spirituality in the clinical social work classroom." *Smith College Studies in Social Work* 74 (2): 349–58. http://dx.doi.org/10.1080/00377310409517720.

O'Brien, J. (2004). "Wrestling the angel of contradiction: Queer Christian identities." *Culture and Religion* 5 (2): 179–202. http://dx.doi.org/10.1080/1438300420000225420.

Palmer, P.J. (1993). *To know as we are known: Education as a spiritual journey.* New York: HarperSanFrancisco.

–. (1998). *The courage to teach: Exploring the inner landscape of a teacher's life.* San Francisco: Jossey-Bass.

–. (2000). "A vision of education as transformation." In *Education as Transformation: Religious Pluralism, Spirituality, and a New Vision for Higher Education in America,* ed. V.H. Kazanjian and P.L. Laurence, 17–22. New York: Peter Lang.

Pargament, K.I. (1999). "The psychology of religion and spirituality? Yes and no." *International Journal for the Psychology of Religion* 9 (1): 3-16. http://dx.doi.org/10.1207/s15327582ijpr0901_2.

Pattanaik, D. (2002). *The man who was a woman and other queer tales from Hindu lore*. New York: Harrington Park Press.

Perry, T. (1972). *The Lord is my shepherd and he knows I'm gay*. Los Angeles: Nash.

Praglin, L. (2004). "Spirituality, religion, and social work: An effort towards interdisciplinary conversation." *Journal of Religion and Spirituality in Social Work* 23 (4): 67-84. http://dx.doi.org/10.1300/J377v23n04_05.

Puar, J. (2007). *Terrorist assemblages: Homonationalism in queer times*. Durham, NC: Duke University Press.

Rahman, M. (2010). "Queer as intersectionality: Theorizing gay Muslim identities." *Sociology* 44 (5): 944-61. http://dx.doi.org/10.1177/0038038510375733.

Razack, S. (2010). "Abandonment and the dance of race and bureaucracy in spaces of exception." In *States of Race: Critical Race Feminism for the 21st Century*, ed. S. Razack, M.S. Smith, and S. Thobani, 87-107. Toronto: Between the Lines.

Rindfleish, J. (2005). "Consuming the self: New Age spirituality as 'social product' in consumer society." *Consumption Markets and Culture* 8 (4): 343-60. http://dx.doi.org/10.1080/10253860500241930.

Roof, W.C., and L. Gesch. (1995). "Boomers and the culture of choice: Changing patterns of work, family, and religion." In *Work, Family, and Religion in Contemporary Society: Remaking Our Lives*, ed. N. Ammerman and W.C. Roof, 61-79. New York: Routledge.

Rouse, J. (1996). "Feminism and the social construction of scientific knowledge." In *Feminism, Science and the Philosophy of Science*, ed. L.H. Nelson and J. Nelson, 195-215. Dordrecht, Netherlands: Kluwer. http://dx.doi.org/10.1007/978-94-009-1742-2_10.

Said, E.W. (1978). *Orientalism*. New York: Vintage Books.

Sedgwick, E.K. (1990). *Epistemology of the closet*. Berkeley: University of California Press.

Shahjahan, R.A. (2005). "Mapping the field of anti-colonial discourse to understand issues of Indigenous knowledges: Decolonizing praxis." *McGill Journal of Education* 40 (2): 213-40.

–. (2009). "The role of spirituality in the anti-oppressive higher education classroom." *Teaching in Higher Education* 14 (2): 121-31. http://dx.doi.org/10.1080/13562510902757138.

–. (2010). "Toward a spiritual praxis: The role of spirituality among faculty of colour teaching for social justice." *Review of Higher Education* 33 (4): 473-512. http://dx.doi.org/10.1353/rhe.0.0166.

Shannahan, D.S. (2010). "Some queer questions from a Muslim faith perspective." *Sexualities* 13 (6): 671-84. http://dx.doi.org/10.1177/1363460710384556.

Sheridan, M.J. (2004). "Predicting the use of spiritually-derived interventions in social work practice: A survey of practitioners." *Journal of Religion and Spirituality in Social Work* 23 (4): 5-25. http://dx.doi.org/10.1300/J377v23n04_02.

Siraj, A. (2006). "On being homosexual and Muslim: Conflicts and challenges." In *Islamic Masculinities*, ed. L. Ouzgane, 202-16. London: Zed Books.

–. (2011). "Isolated, invisible, and in the closet: The life story of a Scottish Muslim lesbian." *Journal of Lesbian Studies* 15 (1): 99-121. http://dx.doi.org/10.1080/10894160.2010.490503.

Smith, L.T. (2012). *Decolonizing methodologies: Research and Indigenous peoples*. 2nd ed. London: Zed Books.

Tan, P.P. (2005). "The importance of spirituality among gay and lesbian individuals." *Journal of Homosexuality* 49 (2): 135-44. http://dx.doi.org/10.1300/J082v49n02_08.

Tisdell, E.J. (2003). *Exploring spirituality and culture in adult and higher education*. San Francisco: Jossey-Bass.

Whitaker, B. (2006a, May 5). "What's wrong with being gay and Muslim?" *Guardian*, UK edition. Retrieved from http://www.theguardian.com/commentisfree/2006/may/05/whatswrong withbeinggayand?INTCMP=SRH.

–. (2006b). *Unspeakable love: Gay and lesbian life in the Middle East*. London: Saqi.

Wilcox, M.M. (2006). "Outlaws or in-laws? Queer theory, LGBTQ studies, and religious studies." *Journal of Homosexuality* 52 (1–2): 73–100. http://dx.doi.org/10.1300/J082v52n01_04.

Willinsky, J. (1998). *Learning to divide the world: Education at empire's end*. Minneapolis: University of Minnesota Press.

Wong, Y.R., and J. Vinsky. (2009). "Speaking from the margins: A critical reflection on the 'spiritual-but-not-religious' discourse in social work." *British Journal of Social Work* 39 (7): 1343–59. http://dx.doi.org/10.1093/bjsw/bcn032.

Yip, A.K.T. (2005a). "Religion and the politics of spirituality/sexuality: Reflections on researching British lesbian, gay, and bisexual Christians and Muslims." *Fieldwork in Religion* 1 (3): 271–89.

–. (2005b). "Taoistic concepts of mental health: Implications for social work practice with Chinese communities." *Families in Society* 86 (1): 35–45. http://dx.doi.org/10.1606/1044-3894.1875.

–. (2008). "The quest for intimate/sexual citizenship: Lived experiences of lesbian and bisexual Muslim women." *Contemporary Islam* 2 (2): 99–117. http://dx.doi.org/10.1007/s11562-008-0046-y.

Yip, A.K.T., and A. Khalid. (2010). "Looking for Allah: Spiritual quests of queer Muslims." In *Queer spiritual spaces: Sexuality and sacred places*, ed. K. Browne, S.R. Munt, and A.K.T. Yip, 81–110. London: Ashgate.

8

Challenging Transmisogyny: From the Classroom to Social Work Practice

JADE PICHETTE

> We have to stand up and speak for ourselves. We have to *fight* for ourselves.
>
> – Sylvia Rivera, in the independent film *Sylvia Rivera, Trans Life Story*

Even in anti-oppressive social work education, the topic of transmisogyny is rarely addressed. Transmisogyny is the intersection between transphobia and misogyny that particularly affects trans women. In social work, if we mention trans women at all, it is usually through authors who appropriate our lives. Increasingly, we need to address the gap in education that places trans women as an invisible part of the LGBTQ community. I discuss my own experiences as a trans woman social worker, and I offer suggestions on how to address transmisogyny in the classroom. In social work, transmisogyny takes many forms, such as not mentioning the lives of trans women, listening to cis authors talk about trans women, and expressing micro-aggressions or outright bigotry toward trans women. This chapter attempts to shed some light on the exclusion of trans women in social work and to provide constructive solutions.

Locating Myself

All scholarship, including the present discussion, is grounded in the implicit bias of the author. I am a white queer trans woman who was born and raised on the unceded territory of the Anishnaabe Algonquin peoples (Ottawa), and I have written this piece on the unceded territory of the Mississaugas of the

New Credit First Nation (Toronto). I completed my bachelor of social work in 2010 at Carleton University and finished my master of social work at Ryerson University in 2013. Due to my ancestry, citizenship status, and high level of education, I enjoy much more privilege than the trans women whom I write about and speak with. These women often come from the volunteer and employment settings, mostly in Ottawa and Toronto, in which I have worked during the past ten years in queer community centres and other social services.

I have worked in trans activism and social work for almost a decade, often with unstable employment, except for a period at a queer community centre. During that time, I met and worked with many trans women. The views and stories in this chapter are mine alone but are drawn from experience, research, and witnessing how trans women have been seen and treated in social work, from the classroom to practice.

An unfortunate limitation of this chapter is the lack of research connecting trans women and the social services. Some of the evidence provided here may be considered anecdotal, as it comes from a combination of my own experiences and those of others, whose names I have chosen to conceal for confidentiality reasons and for their continued safety. I hope that this discussion leads to further research about trans women in social work practice and academia.

Transmisogyny

Trans women are often excluded and forgotten in social work practice. At best, they are seen solely as service users or front-line workers, if they are recognized at all. This is despite the fact that they are one of the most marginalized groups in North America (Brown and Rounsley, 1996; Connell, 2012; Forbes, 2012; Mogul, Ritchie, and Whitlock, 2011; Namaste, 2000, 2011; Rotondi et al., 2011; Rudacille, 2006; Serano, 2007, 2013). This marginalization is compounded by issues of racialization, indigeneity, HIV status (Public Health Agency of Canada, 2012), and engaging in sex work (Namaste, 2011).

Trans women, who were assigned as male at birth but who identify as women, are subject to a unique form of discrimination, a fact that is increasingly being recognized (Connell, 2012; Namaste, 2000; Serano, 2007). The discrimination is called transmisogyny (Serano, 2007) – the hatred of trans women. Transmisogyny is the intersection of the sexism that women experience and the transphobia that trans people encounter (Serano, 2013). As women continue to experience inequality, as compared to men, and as trans people continue to experience violence, trans women are trapped between these two forms of discrimination. Thus, this intersection of sexism and transphobia makes transmisogyny a unique form of discrimination that requires direct analysis.

Some would argue that the term "transmisogyny" is redundant and ask why "transphobia" would not apply in this situation. The reality is that trans women are not treated in the same way as trans men or folks of non-binary genders. This can be seen in the jokes that consistently refer to them (Namaste, 2000; Serano, 2007), in the high rates of HIV among trans women (Bauer, Travers, Scanlon, and Coleman, 2012; Namaste, 2011; Public Health Agency of Canada, 2012), and in the extremely high murder rates of racialized trans women and trans feminine people (Mogul et al., 2011). This would indicate that the discrimination experienced by trans women is not equal to that directed at other parts of the trans community, and that it should be examined though the unique lens of transmisogyny.

Marginalization of Trans Women

The function of the social work profession is to provide services for others. Some people become social workers to ameliorate the marginalization that many oppressed groups encounter. First-year social work students typically say that they want to help people. Despite some oppressive aspects, much of social work's focus is on working with marginalized populations (Carniol, 2005; Lundy, 2004).

Trans women, who experience high levels of marginalization, are one of the least-researched populations. Their risk of suicide is higher than for the general population: nearly half have attempted suicide, and approximately 77 percent of trans people in Ontario have considered it (Rotondi et al., 2011; Scanlon, Travers, Coleman, Bauer, and Boyce, 2010). Many studies have shown that trans women suffer higher levels of depression than other groups (Nuttbrock et al., 2012; Rotondi et al., 2011; Scanlon et al., 2010). Instead of assuming that their depression is related to their gender identity, we need to examine the social conditions that create these high rates of depression and suicide. Trans women's mental health is influenced by societal structures, including education, where they experience more discrimination than their gay, lesbian, and bisexual peers (Sausa, 2005; Taylor et al., 2011), especially as youth. The discrimination at school usually comes from peers and educators but is also compounded by abuse from families (Beam, 2007; Brown and Rounsley, 1996). Because of it, many trans girls drop out of school and never attain higher levels of education later in life.

Those trans women who do pursue higher education do not seem to have as many positive experiences as one would hope. The Trans PULSE Project found that, though 71 percent of trans Ontarians had some post-secondary education, over 50 percent survived on less than $15,000 a year (Bauer et al., 2011). As a result, many trans women participate in sex work or in other criminalized professions (Namaste, 2000, 2011) to survive economically. If they are arrested, the repercussions can be serious, as they are sometimes placed in male prisons where they endure high levels of abuse (Mogul et al., 2011). Ontario has recently made some progress on this front: as of 2015, incarcerated individuals will be housed according to their self-identified gender (CBC News, 2015). All of these issues combine to make life very hard for trans women, especially those who are subject to compounded discrimination by virtue of being Indigenous, racialized, or HIV-positive.

As a result, trans women are often in great need of social services. But, as we shall see, they are often excluded from them (Namaste, 2011; Pyne, 2011; Serano, 2013). In addition, social work education regarding trans women is often incorrect, offensive, or non-existent. If social work is to address the marginalization of trans women, it needs to challenge transmisogyny in its andragogical methods, curriculum, hiring, and admittance policies.

From the Classroom to Social Work Practice: Part 1

During my professional experience, which is mostly in Ottawa and Toronto, I have seen transmisogyny play out in social work academia and practice. It has ranged from covertly excluding trans women from social work services, employment, and education to engaging in overt verbal and physical harassment. The experiences that I describe below are my own and those of trans women whom I have known as service users, acquaintances, and professional colleagues.

Trans women continue to be unrepresented or underrepresented in social work. Like many poor Canadians, who find that higher education is increasingly difficult to access (Mikkonen and Raphael, 2010), few manage to reach undergraduate levels of social work education and even fewer reach graduate levels (Bauer et al., 2012). Furthermore, they are the frequent targets of violence at lower levels of education, including high school (Taylor et al., 2011). As they tend to have low incomes (Bauer et al., 2011), they are often unable to afford university. Thus, despite their knowledge and experience, they may have only high school, college, or no education at all. Social work emphasizes educational credentials, a fact that creates barriers for trans women at many levels of social work practice.

As the discipline has become increasingly professionalized, those who wish to enter social work research and academia require high levels of education. As few trans women enroll in graduate-level academic programs (Bauer et al., 2012), most social work research regarding them is conducted by cis people (those who do not change their gender and/or sex) or trans-masculine people (those who were assigned female at birth but do not identify as women). The resulting research is skewed because it does not represent the experiences of trans women. Namaste (2000, 2011) challenged the trend of using trans women as research subjects, focusing in particular on the work of Judith Butler and Marjorie Garber, both of whom are known for gender theory, in which they conceptualize ideas about gender in society (Butler, 2007; Garber, 1997). Yet, these authors use trans women and trans-feminine people as research subjects, often without their input or consent, concentrating on their bodies and identities instead of their lives, perspectives, and struggles, or the discrimination they face (Namaste, 2011). Butler is often quoted in social work academia, without recognition that her research is grounded in unethical treatment of trans women.

In essence, trans women become tools: researchers use them to prove their own theories regarding gender rather than describing in detail trans women's experiences or needs. As Forbes (2012) puts it, trans women are primary sources in a secondary-source world. In other words, their experiences become valid only when they are interpreted at second-hand by a researcher, who is rarely a trans woman. When they speak from personal experience, their voices are dismissed as non-academic or unverifiable. As a result, they have no ownership or agency regarding the research that deals with them.

When trans women are mentioned in social work education, it is often by cis authors who are describing the concept of gender, or increasingly by trans men discussing transphobia as a whole. In social work education, the only example that I have seen of using research by a trans woman occurred during a graduate class that focused on marginalization. As two students presented the work of Raewyn Connell (2007), which addresses imperialism, each mentioned her birth name, effectively outing her as transsexual, even though this had no relevance to either her work or their topics. Despite occurring in an anti-oppressive social work program and a class that dealt with marginalization, this ethical issue was not addressed by the professor or other students. I later met with the professor and explained that using the birth name of trans people and misgendering them was oppressive. I added that, as the only openly trans student in the program,

I did not feel safe to speak out at the time. Later, during a class presentation on trans youth, I decided to tell the class why the incident was oppressive, which did at least lead to a learning moment for some of my peers.

Trans women who do manage to gain entry into social work programs, as I did, do not see their views represented. Their scholarship has not found a place in social work, and that of trans women academics in the related disciplines of sociology, political science, and women's studies, including Namaste (2000, 2011), Serano (2007, 2013) and others, is rarely discussed. Trans women in social work programs have informed me that they have been misgendered, told that they are not women, verbally and sexually harassed by peers, and harassed by professors and presenters if they challenge their claims regarding trans women. All of these and other factors function to push trans women out of social work programs.

From the Classroom to Social Work Practice: Part 2

What is perhaps Canada's most famous instance of transmisogyny in social work practice comes from Vancouver Rape Relief, a women's shelter and sexual assault counselling service. During the early 2000s, Rape Relief was embattled in a court case due to its treatment of Kimberly Nixon, who had been one of its rape crisis counsellors but was fired when her identity as a trans woman was discovered (Findlay, 2003). Rape Relief argued that, as a trans woman, Nixon could not possibly relate properly to ciswomen service users who were the survivors of rape (Findlay, 2003). This concept both obscures the fact that trans women suffer sexual violence (Namaste, 2000) and inaccurately suggests that all ciswomen have the same experiences of sexual violence (Findlay, 2003; Namaste, 2011). Anti-racist (Carniol, 2005; hooks, 2000), Indigenous (Arvin, Tuck, and Morrill, 2013), and disability (Carniol, 2005; Clare, 2009) theorists have all critiqued this idea of a universal woman's experience, as this essentialization of women's identities privileges a white, Western, and abled perspective. In the end, Rape Relief won its case, as sex is a protected ground against discrimination in the British Columbia Human Rights Code (1996) and the Canadian Human Rights Act (1985). At the time, gender identity and gender expression were not protected legal grounds. This gave Rape Relief the legal ability to exclude trans women from its services and hiring.

Unlike Kimberly Nixon, most trans women do not take their cases to court, deciding to avoid legal action because the criminal (in)justice system rarely treats them kindly (Mogul et al., 2011). Instead, they rely on informal networks for support, such as social groups with other trans women (Beam,

2007), if they have any support at all. Given the high rates of poverty and depression among trans women (Nuttbrock et al., 2012; Rotondi et al., 2011), it is unlikely that these informal networks effectively serve the needs of those who wish to access services.

The only article I was able to find that looks directly at trans women's exclusion in social work is Pyne (2011), which deconstructs cisnormativity in shelter services. A societal structure, cisnormativity presupposes and enforces that not wishing to change gender and sex is not just common, but normal, and that anyone who desires to do so is abnormal. Pyne (2011) recognizes that trans people rarely feel safe or accepted in Canadian shelter services and that they are often abused there. In fact, they are either denied services or avoid the shelter system altogether because they do not feel safe in shelters (Mottet and Ohle, 2003). For their part, trans women are denied access to women's shelters and are unsafe in men's shelters. Thus, they consistently find themselves shut out from equal access to services and must survive via informal networks or without any support at all.

The few trans women who do manage to become social workers often find themselves dealing with certain types of service users, such as sex workers, prison-involved and queer communities, and HIV-positive individuals. The assumption is that they will relate best to these groups because they contain so many trans women (Bauer et al., 2012; Namaste, 2011; Public Health Agency of Canada, 2012). These tend to be front-line positions and some of the most stressful and least paid jobs in social work. They also tend to be part-time and do not provide benefits, thus further marginalizing trans women social workers. In the film *Red Lips* (Williams, 2010), one participant, a trans woman, mentions that though she is employed doing sex worker outreach, she often has the sense that her colleagues do not welcome her presence. Many trans women report feeling unwelcome in social work settings, and every trans woman whom I have met working in social services has said the same thing. This feeling becomes pronounced for racialized trans women, who also face racism from colleagues (Williams, 2010). Overall, the impact is that, as service users and social workers, trans women experience abuse and exclusion, which leads to the continued marginalization of all trans women in society.

Recommendations for Change

To a certain extent, the history of social work and anti-oppressive practice is one in which many marginalized groups have fought constantly for recognition of their experiences and lives (Carniol, 2005; Lundy, 2004). Indeed, only after anti-racist theorists (Carniol, 2005; hooks, 2000) critiqued the racism inherent in social work did anti-racism start to be included in research and curriculum. Only through pressure from Indigenous theorists (Arvin et al., 2013) have anti-colonial struggles been included in social work, and only due to pressure from queer activists, such as the other contributors to this book, have queer discourses entered the discipline. Similarly, only through constant pressure, activism, and advocacy from trans women will transfeminist discourses be included in social work academe and practice. Transmisogyny may be pervasive in social work, but as other social movements and marginalized groups have demonstrated, adversity can be overcome. There is more than one way to challenge transmisogyny. As I am a firm believer in providing solutions, I offer the following suggestions on how to do so.

My first point is addressed to any trans women or trans-feminine people who are reading this essay. Perhaps the greatest challenge to transmisogyny in social work is your continued existence. Being persistent as service users and social workers in challenging and educating service providers or colleagues is imperative. Ultimately, you are your own best advocate in supporting the continued and full participation of trans women of many different marginalized perspectives in the agencies with which you work. This means that your existence as an individual is important and valuable. Joining with trans women who are sex workers, racialized, or HIV-positive, groups that tend to be the most marginalized, is the most important part of making structural change. Trans women service providers – myself included – who come from the more privileged parts of the trans women's community, including being white and educated, need to recognize their privileged position and highlight the voices of marginalized trans women. This does not mean that any of their individual experiences of marginalization are invalid but that theirs are not the only valid narratives in our communities.

Another recommendation is to recognize that many of us have experienced trauma, both inside and outside social work. I am not suggesting that the trauma must be completely healed before we can pursue change in social work, but we must be aware of our own emotional boundaries. As educators, advocates, and members of a marginalized population, we can easily become targets of transmisogyny. I have seen many trans women engage with social services, only to be retraumatized in the process. Self-care is important for everyone who is involved in social work (Lundy, 2004), but this may be especially true for trans women.

To trans men and trans-masculine people who are associated with social work, we need you to work in solidarity with trans women. Please recognize that though you may have had good experiences with an organization and have not been subject to transphobia there, this does not automatically prove that the organization has treated trans women in the same way. Male privilege continues to exist in social work. Women consistently make less money than men, are promoted less often, and have greater need for social services (Carniol, 2005; Lundy, 2004). Although trans men certainly do experience transphobia, they nonetheless benefit from male privilege, a fact that enables them to access social work education and positions that are barred to trans women.

Social service agencies need to be inclusive of all trans people. Having trans men on staff is not enough if there are no trans women or if trans women are confined to low-level positions. Trans men can work in solidarity with trans women, by advocating in their own agencies and others, to include and listen to the voices of trans women. In addition, please recognize that due to transmisogyny, the experiences of trans women are significantly different from those of trans men.

Finally, to cis people who are reading this chapter, there are multiple ways that you can recognize and be inclusive of trans women while redressing transmisogyny. The first is by continuously educating yourself and others, and including trans women speakers and writers in social work events, periodicals, syllabi, and education. Some good sources of education are the works cited in this chapter, including Connell (2012), Namaste (2000, 2011), and Serano (2007, 2013). Research trans women in your community who write or do public speaking, including those who do not have social work academic credentials. Trans women are best placed to describe their own experiences, and it is their writing and voices that need to be emphasized.

The inclusion of trans women also requires hiring them in more social work positions and doing more than just keeping them at the level of direct service provision. We also need to explicitly include trans women's experiences and bodies when describing women's experiences and lives. This entails consistently taking stands against organizations that harass or discriminate against trans women. There is also a need for comprehensive anti-oppression education that addresses cis and male privilege, challenges transmisogyny, and makes spaces safer for trans women, as well as for policy reform that explicitly protects and includes them in social work services. Trans women need a place at the table on a variety of issues, such as academic research, policy creation, and analysis. They also need greater representation in social work management positions.

Overall, the best way to challenge transmisogyny in social work is through the inclusion of a diversity of trans women in research, scholarship, andragogy, and practice. This encompasses trans women of all sexual orientations, those who are racialized, who work in the sex trade, are HIV-positive, and who come from varying educational backgrounds. Having someone visit your agency or classroom to lead a brief training session in "Trans 101" is insufficient to challenge transmisogyny. Instead, the continued physical presence of trans women in all settings and the valuing and embracing of their voices are what is needed to create the conditions necessary for change.

Conclusion

Transmisogyny will continue to be a significant force in social work practice and education. As trans women remain one of the most marginalized populations in Canada, social workers need to step up. We need to recognize our privileges and create change in our classrooms, boardrooms, and practice settings. We need to assume that trans women are already accessing social work services and that if they are not, it is because of a failing on the part of the profession. Social work needs to stand up against transmisogyny. An important initial means of doing so is to listen to more diverse voices.

As more trans women look for inroads into the social work profession, progress will be made. Everyone needs to be concerned about transmisogyny in social work as it reinforces both cisnormativity on trans people and traditional forms of sexism. It also does a disservice to social work as a whole. Progress will be slow, but as in all social movements, the struggle must be embraced by both trans women and their allies.

References

Arvin, M., E. Tuck, and A. Morrill. (2013). "Decolonizing feminism: Challenging connections between settler colonialism and heteropatriarchy." *Feminist Formations* 25 (1): 8–34. http://dx.doi.org/10.1353/ff.2013.0006.

Bauer, G., N. Nussbaum, R. Travers, L. Munro, J. Pyne, **and** N. Redman. (2011). "We've got work to do: Workplace discrimination and employment challenges for trans people in Ontario." *Trans PULSE E-Bulletin* 2 (1). Retrieved from http://transpulseproject.ca/.

Bauer, G., R. Travers, K. Scanlon, and T. Coleman. (2012). "High heterogeneity of HIV-related sexual risk among transgender people in Ontario, Canada: A province-wide respondent-driven sampling survey." *BMC Public Health* 12 (1): 292–304. http://dx.doi.org/10.1186/1471-2458-12-292.

Beam, C. (2007). *Transparent: Love, family, and living the T with transgender teenagers*. New York: Harcourt Books.

British Columbia Human Rights Code. (1996). R.S.B.C., c. 210. Retrieved from http://www.bclaws.ca/Recon/document/ID/freeside/00_96210_01.

Brown, M., and C. Rounsley. (1996). *True selves: Understanding transsexualism for families, friends, coworkers and helping professionals*. San Francisco: Jossey-Bass.

Butler, J. (2007). *Gender trouble: Feminism and the subversion of identity*. New York: Routledge.

Canadian Human Rights Act. (1985). R.S.C., c. H-6. Retrieved from http://laws-lois.justice.gc.ca/eng/acts/h-6/.

Carniol, B. (2005). *Case critical: Social services and social justice in Canada.* Toronto: Between the Lines.

CBC News. (2015, January 26). "Gender identity to guide housing of Ontario's transgender inmates." Toronto. Retrieved from http://www.cbc.ca/news/canada/toronto/gender-identity-to-guide-housing-of-ontario-s-transgender-inmates-1.2932304.

Clare, E. (2009). *Exile and pride: Disability, queerness and liberation.* Cambridge, MA: South End Press.

Connell, R. (2007). *Southern theory.* Malden: Polity Press.

—. (2012). "Transsexual women and feminist thought: Toward new understanding and new politics." *Signs* (Chicago) 37 (4): 857–81. http://dx.doi.org/10.1086/664478.

Findlay, B. (2003). "Real women: Kimberly Nixon v. Vancouver Rape Relief." *University of British Columbia Law Review* 36 (1): 57–76.

Forbes, K. (2012). "'Do these earrings make me look dumb?' Diversity, privilege, and heteronormative perceptions of competence within the academy." In *Transfeminist Perspectives in and beyond Transgender and Gender Studies,* ed. A. Enke, 34–44. Philadelphia: Temple University Press.

Garber, M. (1997). *Vested interests: Cross-dressing and cultural anxiety.* New York: Routledge.

hooks, b. (2000). *Feminism is for everybody: Passionate politics.* Cambridge, MA: South End Press.

Lundy, C. (2004). *Social work and social justice: A structural approach to practice.* Peterborough: Broadview Press.

Mikkonen, J., and D. Raphael. (2010). *Social determinants of health: The Canadian facts.* Toronto: York University School of Health Policy and Management.

Mogul, J., A. Ritchie, and K. Whitlock. (2011). *Queer (in)justice: The criminalization of LGBT people in the United States.* Boston: Beacon Press.

Mottet, L., and J. Ohle. (2003). *Transitioning our shelters: A guide to making homeless shelters safe for transgender people.* Washington, DC: National Gay and Lesbian Task Force.

Namaste, V. (2000). *Invisible lives: The erasure of transsexual and transgendered people.* Chicago: University of Chicago Press.

—. (2011). *Sex change, social change: Reflections on identity, institutions and imperialism.* Toronto: Women's Press.

Nuttbrock, L., W. Bockting, A. Rosenblum, M. Mason, M. Macri, and J. Becker. (2012). "Gender identity conflict/affirmation and major depression across the life course of transgender women." *International Journal of Transgenderism* 13 (3): 91–103. http://dx.doi.org/10.1080/15532739.2011.657979.

Public Health Agency of Canada. (2012). *Population-specific HIV/AIDS status report: Women.* Retrieved from http://www.phac-aspc.gc.ca/aids-sida/publication/ps-pd/women-femmes/es-sommaire-eng.php.

Pyne, J. (2011). "Unsuitable bodies: Trans people and cisnormativity in shelter services." *Canadian Social Work Review* 28 (1): 129–37.

Rotondi, N.K., G.R. Bauer, R. Travers, A. Travers, K. Scanlon, and M. Kaay. (2011). "Depression in male-to-female transgender Ontarians: Results from the Trans PULSE Project." *Canadian Journal of Community Mental Health* 30 (2): 113–33. http://dx.doi.org/10.7870/cjcmh-2011-0020.

Rudacille, D. (2006). *The riddle of gender: Science, activism, and transgender rights.* New York: Anchor Books.

Sausa, L.A. (2005). "Translating research into practice: Trans youth recommendations for improving school systems." *Journal of Gay and Lesbian Issues in Education* 3 (1): 15–28. http://dx.doi.org/10.1300/J367v03n01_04.

Scanlon, K., R. Travers, T. Coleman, G. Bauer, and M. Boyce. (2010). "Ontario's trans communities and suicide: Transphobia is bad for our health." *Trans PULSE E-Bulletin* 1 (2). Retrieved from http://transpulseproject.ca/.

Serano, J. (2007). *Whipping girl: A transsexual woman on sexism and the scapegoating of femininity*. Berkeley: Seal Press.

–. (2013). *Excluded: Making feminist and queer movements more inclusive*. Berkeley: Seal Press.

Taylor, C., and T. Peter, with T.L. McMinn, T. Elliott, S. Beldom, A. Ferry, Z. Gross, S., Paquin, and K. Schachter (2011). *Every class in every school: The first national climate survey on homophobia, biphobia, and transphobia in Canadian schools: Final report*. Toronto: Egale Canada Human Rights Trust.

Williams, K. (Producer and director). (2010). *Red lips: Cages for black girls* [Motion picture]. Canada: Charles Street Video.

PART 3

The Queering Project – Gender and Sexual Diversity in Social Work Education

9

Oh Canada: LGBTQ Students and Campus Climates in Canadian Social Work Programs

SHELLEY L. CRAIG, LAUREN B. MCINROY, AND CHRISTOPHER DOIRON

Many factors influence lesbian, gay, bisexual, transgender, and/or queer (LGBTQ) students' experiences of campus climates. These include the availability of supports and resources for LGBTQ students, LGBTQ curriculum content, institutional policies concerning LGBTQ populations, the risks regarding disclosure of LGBTQ status, and LGBTQ role models and organizations on campus (Dugan and Yurman, 2011; Gortmaker and Brown, 2006). However, little scholarly literature has specifically addressed either LGBTQ social work students' experiences in their programs or the overall climate of the programs regarding LGBTQ populations and concerns, particularly in Canada (Chinell, 2011). For LGBTQ students, the environment of post-secondary campuses and classrooms varies widely, from supportive, to covertly antagonistic, to openly hostile (Longerbeam, Inkelas, Johnson, and Lee, 2007). Thus, it is difficult to depict accurately.

This chapter addresses the gap in the literature by describing the Canadian component ($n = 106$) of a 2012 North American study ($n = 1,310$) that explored the educational climates of English-language social work programs and the experiences and perceptions of LGBTQ bachelor of social work and master of social work students who were enrolled in them. Participants generally stated that their institutions were "somewhat friendly" to LGBTQ issues. However, a third (33 percent) also reported encountering homophobia in their programs, and many participants lacked knowledge regarding whether institutional and program non-discrimination policies existed. They also reported critical shortages of LGBTQ curriculum content. Understanding the experiences of LGBTQ social work students on their campuses, and in their programs, is crucial to supporting their educational participation and achievement, as well as their engagement in the social work profession (Hylton, 2005).

Campus Climates

Waldo (1998) defines campus climate as "measurable perceptions of various aspects of campus life" (p. 748). Like their non-LGBTQ counterparts, LGBTQ students are active participants in campus activities and are "academically and socially influenced by their ... [institutional] environments" (Longerbeam et al., 2007, p. 215). Although numerous institutions have prioritized campus improvements to benefit LGBTQ students (Woodford, Silverschanz, Swank, Scherrer, and Raiz, 2012), negative climates remain problematic for many of them. Students learn most effectively in supportive environments (Hylton, 2005). Yet, LGBTQ students frequently report poor experiences on post-secondary campuses, regularly encountering homophobia, heterosexism, hostility, discrimination, and harassment, as well as other forms of violence and victimization (Dugan and Yurman, 2011; Gortmaker and Brown, 2006; Kwon and Hugelshofer, 2012; Rankin, 2003; Waldo, 1998). In addition, sexual minority students (e.g., lesbian, gay, bisexual, and queer) are also frequently and surreptitiously encouraged by other students, and by faculty, to adapt to the heteronormative collegiate environment (Jurgens, Schwitzer, and Middleton, 2004). This experience is potentially shared by gender minority students (e.g., transgender or transsexual individuals). These reports of negative experiences by LGBTQ students have been corroborated by similar disclosures of discriminatory behaviour on the part of non-LGBTQ students (Kwon and Hugelshofer, 2012). However, the research comes predominantly from the United States, and the Canadian context remains poorly understood and in need of further exploration. Also, much of the research is a decade old (or older), resulting in an incomplete picture of the current situation.

In a large-scale US study of college campuses (Rankin, 2003), a significant proportion of LGBTQ students indicated that their institution failed to address issues or concerns related to their identities (41 percent) and that the curriculum was not representative of their issues (43 percent). Further, 43 percent stated that the climate of their institution was homophobic, 36 percent had experienced harassment during the previous year, and 61 percent felt that sexual minority students were likely to encounter it (Rankin, 2003). Though the students disagreed regarding whether their institutions had "visible leadership" on LGBTQ issues, they generally concurred (72 percent) that institutions provided "visible resources on ... [LGBTQ] issues and concerns" (Rankin, 2003, p. 5). Although LGBTQ students may receive support from their own LGBTQ communities on campuses, either formally or informally, this does not automatically negate the adverse effects of the larger heteronormative campus atmosphere (Waldo, 1998). Further, peer support or the presence of some resources do not decrease the need for post-secondary institutions to develop a discernible leadership strategy in response to the campus environment. Visible LGBTQ role models are important to students' willingness to disclose their LGBTQ status at school (Gortmaker and Brown, 2006).

Unsurprisingly, the negative experiences of LGBTQ students frequently result in detrimental outcomes (Kwon and Hugelshofer, 2012). LGBTQ students often perceive campuses as hostile, and those who attend such institutions typically feel the need to conceal their LGBTQ identity from peers and faculty (Gortmaker and Brown, 2006; Longerbeam et al., 2007), which may result in decreased access to social support and resources for their LGBTQ status. Many students use an adaptive or evasive approach (such as not disclosing their identities, changing their routines, altering their behaviour, or not discussing their personal lives) to avoid potentially hostile environments or encounters (Kwon and Hugelshofer, 2012; Woodford et al., 2012). Taking this approach could inhibit their access to campus resources (e.g., not participating in the campus LGBTQ group, not using the health centre for LGBTQ-related concerns, or not using LGBTQ-trained campus counselling services). More generally, LGBTQ people are subject to hostility, stigma, and violence and commonly experience fear, distrust, isolation, and stress that may adversely affect their mental and emotional well-being and contribute to increased "depression, anxiety, and substance use" (Kwon and Hugelshofer, 2012, p. 63). In the case of LGBTQ students, learning opportunities and academic outcomes may also be negatively affected (Woodford et al., 2012; Woodford, Han, Craig, Lim, and Matney, 2014). Conversely, positive institutional climates provide targeted campus programs to facilitate LGBTQ students' "outness" and educational success (Gortmaker and Brown, 2006; Hylton, 2005).

Canadian Social Work Programs and LGBTQ Students

The education and training of future social work professionals in Canada is the responsibility of numerous post-secondary institutions across the country. The Canadian Association for Social Work Education (CASWE) is tasked with accreditation of bachelor of social work (BSW) and master of social work (MSW) programs; presently, there are forty accredited social work "faculties, departments, [and/or] schools" in Canada, thirty of which offer English-language programs (CASWE, n.d.). Specifically, twenty-eight accredited BSW English-language programs and twenty-two accredited MSW English-language programs are currently offered nationally (CASWE, n.d.). CASWE mandates the integration of diversity and social justice across the curriculum of the programs, including content specifically addressing LGBTQ identities (CASWE, 2014). However, the extent and consistency of the implementation of such mandates remains unclear (Hylton, 2005). In addition, recent research demonstrates that LGBTQ populations are often inadequately represented in the curriculum content of North American social work programs, including those in Canada (Brownlee et al., 2005; Fredriksen-Goldsen, Woodford, Luke, and Gutiérrez, 2011).

Although content specific to sexual minority populations, predominantly gays and lesbians, has recently increased in the curriculum of North American social work programs, the attitudes of social work students regarding LGBTQ populations remain problematic (e.g., negative, homophobic, or heterosexist, such as viewing LGBTQ people or relationships as unnatural) (Black, Oles, Cramer, and Bennett, 1999; Brownlee et al., 2005; Cluse-Tolar, Lambert, Ventura, and Pasupuleti, 2005). Some evidence indicates that social work students have more positive attitudes regarding sexual minority people than do their counterparts in other academic disciplines and the general population (Brownlee et al., 2005; Cluse-Tolar et al., 2005). Yet, negative attitudes do exist among them and may influence their behaviour when they become practising professionals (for example, they may respond judgmentally to LGBTQ people, react poorly to homophobic situations, avoid LGBTQ professional materials, or be unwilling to work with LGBTQ service users) (Black et al., 1999). Due to a lack of attention in research, their attitudes toward gender minority populations are not well known.

With regard to North American faculty, Fredriksen-Goldsen et al. (2011) indicate that the majority of faculty, particularly in Canada, hold "supportive attitudes" regarding LGBTQ populations and are "generally supportive" of including LGBTQ content in their social work programs. However, their support varied depending on which LGBTQ subpopulation was under consideration (e.g., LGB versus T), as well as on the demographic characteristics of faculty (age, race, and ethnic background). The problematic attitudes of faculty and students should thus be a concern to the social work profession and social work education, as a lack of acceptance contributes to discrimination and the potential for inadequate service provision as unaccepting social workers may deliver inappropriate or insufficient services (Brownlee et al., 2005).

Such attitudes may sometimes be unconscious, as social workers, despite training in diversity, often internalize the biases of the larger socio-cultural landscape (Berkman and Zinberg, 1997).

Further, negative attitudes in the social work program and the classroom may be harmful to LGBTQ students, though the impact of this remains unclear and warrants further consideration. One in-depth study of three sexual minority social work students who had recently graduated at a Canadian institution found that they experienced discrimination (e.g., inappropriate or offensive language and assumptions about family structure), both in and out of the classroom. They also encountered stereotyping, a lack of attention to LGBTQ topics in their classes (e.g., a lack of or outdated literature on LGBTQ topics), and a dismissive attitude toward LGBTQ issues from both peers and faculty (e.g., when the participants brought up LGBTQ issues, they were ignored by students and faculty) (Chinell, 2011). The participants also reported that faculty were uninformed regarding policies or community programs related to the LGBTQ community and were unsupportive of them. Unsurprisingly, the participants frequently became somewhat disengaged from their program and were disappointed in it (Chinell, 2011).

When considering campus climates for LGBTQ students, the literature has predominantly focused on US institutions and specific topics such as discrimination, sexual identity development, or the attitudes of non-LGBTQ students toward their LGBTQ (particularly gay, lesbian, and bisexual) classmates (Longerbeam et al., 2007; Waldo, 1998). However, the recent study discussed throughout the rest of this chapter (Craig, Dentato, Messinger, and McInroy, 2016) took a broader approach to explicating educational climates for LGBTQ students in North American social work programs. It achieved this through detailed reporting of a variety of institutional and program characteristics (such as geography and population area), as well as a thorough description of students' perceptions and experiences of support and homophobia or transphobia at their institutions and in their programs.

Methods

As a component of a large-scale North American mixed-methods study ($n = 1,310$), online surveys were systematically distributed to all CASWE-accredited social work schools in Canada that offered a BSW and/or an MSW program in English. The full data collection procedures for the larger North American study are described elsewhere (Craig, McInroy, Dentato, Austin, and Messinger, 2015). For this national study, a survey link was distributed to each

Canadian social work school at least twice, with a request to distribute the survey opportunity to enrolled students. The survey was available online for approximately ten weeks (April–June 2012) and generally took thirty minutes to complete. Participants were asked to read and confirm their acceptance of a declaration of consent prior to answering the questions. The study had a University of Toronto Ethics Board Protocol. Participants had the option of entering a draw for gift cards from an online retailer, and those who wished to provide feedback on the study were encouraged to contact the primary investigator via email. Inclusion criteria encompassed current enrollment in a BSW or MSW program at a Canadian post-secondary institution, self-identification as an LGBTQ individual, and fluency in English sufficient to complete the survey. In total, 112 surveys were completed for the Canadian component of the study. Six did not meet the inclusion criteria because the participants identified as non-LGBTQ, resulting in a Canadian total of 106.

For this study, questions regarding experiences of LGBTQ students in Canadian social work programs and questions concerning Canadian post-secondary campuses to be analyzed – such as the quantity of LGBTQ curriculum content and the presence of LGBTQ non-discrimination policies and program components related to practice with LGBTQ communities – were extracted from the larger survey, which generally defined terms and concepts (e.g., curriculum content, policies, program components) for participants. Dichotomous and likert-scale questions (sometimes including an open-ended option) were used. Descriptive statistics, including frequencies, were generated using SPSS 20 (Field, 2009).

The Students

As illustrated in Appendix A, participants' reported sexual identifications were queer (27 percent), lesbian (24 percent), gay (21 percent), bisexual (20 percent), or other (9 percent). To facilitate analyses, sexual identity responses selected by few participants (e.g., pansexual or asexual) were collapsed into other categories. A number of additional categories were offered for race and ethnicity, but participants identified only as white non-Hispanic (80 percent), multi-racial (13 percent), white Hispanic (3 percent), black (2 percent), South Asian/Middle Eastern (2 percent), or Asian (1 percent). Participants' gender identifications were as cisgender woman (68 percent), cisgender man (26 percent), no gender categories (4 percent), and/or transgender (4 percent). "Cisgender" refers to individuals who are not transgender. For ease of analysis, the transgender category was amalgamated from several smaller categories, including transgender-woman (0.9 percent) and transgender-man (1.9 percent). Participants gave their ages as twenty-nine and under (63 percent), thirty to thirty-nine (18 percent), forty to forty-nine (14 percent), fifty to fifty-nine (2 percent), or sixty and over (3 percent).

Findings

Institutional and Program Characteristics

Participants attended at least eighteen post-secondary institutions across Canada. Eighty-two percent reported the province in which their institution was located: Alberta (13 percent), British Columbia (12 percent), Newfoundland and Labrador (3 percent), Nova Scotia (14 percent), Ontario (48 percent), Quebec (9 percent), and Saskatchewan (1 percent). As indicated in Appendix B, most institutions were located in urban areas (> 50,000 people) (92 percent), were public institutions (90 percent), and had no religious affiliation (84 percent).

Institutional and Program Climates

Asked about the overall LGBTQ friendliness of their institution, with responses on a five-point likert scale ranging from "not at all friendly" to "very friendly," participants reported their institutions as being friendlier to sexual minority identities (M[ean] = 2.97, S[tandard] D[eviation] = 0.90) than to gender minority identities (M = 2.08, SD = 1.06), though neither set of responses was particularly positive (Appendix C). Regarding explicit policies protecting LGBTQ students, many participants noted that their institution had a non-discrimination policy related to sexual minority identities (71 percent). A smaller percentage indicated that their social work program had a non-discrimination policy related to sexual identity (59 percent). However, a notably lower proportion indicated that their institution (34 percent) or program (37 percent) had an equivalent policy related to gender minority identities. Somewhat unsurprisingly, many participants did not know whether their institution had a non-discrimination policy related to either sexual identity (27 percent) or gender identity (57 percent). Similarly, significant numbers did not know whether their program had a non-discrimination policy related to either sexual minority identities (34 percent) or gender minority identities (50 percent).

When asked about applications that incorporated inclusive questions for LGBTQ applicants (e.g., gender options and recognition of LGBTQ identity as a minority category), only a quarter indicated that their institution had such an application (24 percent). A large proportion believed that their institution did not (38 percent), and an equally large percentage did not know (39 percent). Over half did not believe that their institution (53 percent) and their program (54 percent) had a targeted recruitment process to encourage the enrollment of LGBTQ students. Positively, a majority of participants indicated that their institution had LGBTQ organizations or student groups (89 percent), and a moderate proportion also reported that it had LGBTQ student centres or lounges (54 percent). However, relatively few said that their program had LGBTQ organizations or student groups (10 percent), and none stated that their program had LGBTQ student centres or lounges. Yet, it should be noted that some programs have no centres or lounges of any kind. The low number of program-based student lounges could also potentially stem from practical space and resource challenges, particularly for smaller programs, rather than the purposeful exclusion of LGBTQ students. At the institutional level, only a few participants indicated that their institution had mentoring options that were specifically related to LGBTQ identity (16 percent), and many did not know whether mentoring options existed (56 percent). Responses for the social work programs were similar, as only a few had mentoring options that related to LGBTQ identities (4 percent), and again, a notable number of participants did not know whether mentoring options existed (19 percent). The majority of institutions (60 percent) did not have a gender-neutral bathroom (Appendix B).

Program Enrollment
As illustrated in Appendix B, the sample was relatively equally divided between program types, with slightly more students in an MSW program (51 percent) than a BSW program (50 percent). Participants varied significantly in the number of semesters they had completed in their program, ranging from not having finished their first semester to having completed eight semesters or more.

Program Curriculum
As demonstrated in Appendix C, when asked (on a four-point likert scale) about the inclusion of LGBTQ curriculum content, particularly classroom examples and course readings, participants replied that their program offered sexual minority identity content ($M = 1.60$, $SD = 0.69$) notably more frequently than gender minority content ($M = 0.85$, $SD = 0.64$), though both appeared infrequently in the curriculum.

Program Experiences

As Appendix C reveals, when asked (on a five-point likert scale) about their overall feeling regarding how well their program supported their LGBTQ identities, participants reported relatively low levels of support (M = 2.72, SD = 1.14). Similarly, their overall disclosure in their program of their LGBTQ identity (four-point likert scale) was moderate (M = 2.28, SD = 0.89). They indicated that other people in their program were moderately comfortable with their LGBTQ identities (M = 2.31, SD = 0.65, on another four-point likert scale). They had come out to relatively few faculty (M = 1.99, SD = 1.30, measured on yet another four-point likert scale), though a greater proportion were out to other students (M = 2.42, SD = 1.17, measured on the same scale).

As shown in Appendix D, a third (33 percent) of participants had experienced homophobia in their program. Problematically, 16 percent stated that faculty did not intervene when peers displayed homophobia, and 19 percent said that faculty members demonstrated homophobia or bias. Only 11 percent had encountered transphobia in their program, though the low number is probably due to the relatively few gender minority participants (8 percent). Again, 16 percent said that faculty did not intervene when peers displayed transphobia, and 22 percent reported that faculty members demonstrated transphobia or bias. When asked about the percentage of faculty who were supportive of sexual minority identity issues, participants ranked only a little over half (58 percent) as 76 to 100 percent supportive. Importantly, they stated that faculty were less supportive of gender minority identity issues, with only 37 percent as 76 to 100 percent supportive. Positively, a large majority of students (91 percent) knew of an openly LGBTQ classmate, 58 percent knew of an openly LGBTQ faculty member, and 21 percent knew of an openly LGBTQ staff member. However, 47 percent also knew at least one classmate whose LGBTQ status was concealed, 24 percent knew at least one faculty member who was not open about LGBTQ status, and 7 percent knew at least one staff member who was not open about LGBTQ status.

Limitations

Despite the informative and novel findings of the study, some limitations must be acknowledged. The study population consisted largely of white, non-Hispanic, non-Aboriginal women, resulting in low numbers of racial and ethnic minority participants and those who identified as men. No participant identified as Aboriginal. However, the gender distribution of participants may also reflect the proportionally greater representation of women in the social work discipline. The study was also limited to programs that offered instruction in English. Therefore, its findings should not be considered demonstrative of francophone programs. Although efforts were made to recruit participants from all English social work programs in Canada, the sample was relatively small ($n = 106$) and may not be fully representative. Participants attended only eighteen social work schools of the thirty accredited English-language social work faculties, departments, or schools in Canada. Further, they were enrolled as BSW and MSW students during the spring of 2012, when the data were collected, and thus the study may not reflect the current situation. Nor should we assume that their experiences were shared by PhD students or continuing education students. As mentioned previously, it is important to note that many social work programs have limited space and resources, which should not suggest intentional exclusion of LGBTQ students. Social work education must also address a broad range of issues, and thus all areas may not receive the same level of attention; nor do all faculty have expertise in all subject areas. Despite these limitations, this study adds significantly to the current knowledge about the experiences of LGBTQ students in Canadian social work programs.

Recommendations

This study provides valuable information to address climate concerns for social work programs in Canada and elucidates the educational experiences of LGBTQ students in these environments. As discussed above, the on-campus atmosphere can significantly affect student experiences and achievement. A third of the participants in this study reported encountering homophobia in their program (33 percent), which is roughly comparable to Rankin's (2003) study of a decade ago, which found that 43 percent of LGBTQ participants perceived their institution as homophobic. These findings suggest a possible improvement on campuses, but it is nonetheless clear that more progress is needed. It should be acknowledged that many post-secondary institutions have taken steps to facilitate recognition and understanding of LGBTQ populations: they have invited guest speakers on LGBTQ-related topics, conducted positive space campaigns, and established LGBTQ student groups and groups building alliances with non-LGBTQ allies. However, it has been suggested that these interventions are frequently not informed by a systemic awareness of the heteronormative campus climate or the experiences of LGBTQ students (Woodford et al., 2012). Strategies to address the continuing problem of discrimination and underrepresentation of LGBTQ students in Canadian social work programs should be considered. Crucial to this effort is the increased inclusion of LGBTQ curriculum content (e.g., inclusion of LGBTQ case studies and readings in courses and discussions of LGBTQ issues that may affect social work practice with the population), improved institutional supports and resources on campus (e.g., LGBTQ student groups, student centres, and LGBTQ materials and programming in the campus student and health centres), and professional preparation opportunities for LGBTQ students.

Systemic Recommendations

Policies and Procedures

Post-secondary institutions and social work programs should have formal clauses or policies to protect students from discrimination based on their LGBTQ identity. Further, as the responses to the 2012 study indicate, LGBTQ social work students have insufficient knowledge of non-discrimination policies of this type at their institutions and in their programs. Therefore, the policies should be widely publicized to all students. This could be achieved in a variety of ways, including presentations during orientation, letters or emails to students, a statement on the institution and/or program website, inclusion in course outlines and other classroom documents, and physical advertisements and other materials at the school.

This study also found that students perceived targeted recruitment and inclusive applications for potential LGBTQ social work students as insufficient. Research indicates that the majority of social work programs may not place sufficient emphasis on the recruitment of LGBTQ students (Hylton, 2005). However, more research should be undertaken to confirm the state of recruitment in Canada and to investigate how students could be made aware of such initiatives. Canadian social work programs should consider targeted recruitment processes to ensure the representation and retention of LGBTQ people in both the programs and the profession itself. Hylton (2005) suggests that the programs can promote the recruitment of LGBTQ individuals though various factors such as the inclusion of LGBTQ identities in recruitment materials, non-discrimination policies that prohibit harassment of LGBTQ populations, the presence of LGBTQ student groups or organizations in the programs, and outreach to general LGBTQ student groups. Also, the programs and their institutions should offer inclusive applications that are respectful of potential students with LGBTQ identities. Such applications would offer gender options beyond male and female, perhaps through the use of open-ended question formats, with the opportunity to write in the appropriate identity, rather than forced-choice question formats. In applications, students could also identify as minority students, based on their LGBTQ status.

Program Recommendations

Positively, most participants (89 percent) indicated that their institution had LGBTQ organizations or student groups (Appendix B). In previous research, LGBTQ social work students expressed the desire to build community with their peers, and they suggested LGBTQ lounges or student groups specifically for social work students as a means of facilitating this (Hylton, 2005). LGBTQ students, particularly undergraduates, often have their first exposure to LGBTQ communities on post-secondary campuses (Waldo, 1998). However, only 54 percent of students reported that their institution had an LGBTQ student centre or lounge, which would be a substantial physical and financial statement by institutions emphasizing their support of LGBTQ students, infrastructure and resources permitting. In addition, only 10 percent of participants' programs had LGBTQ organizations or student groups, and none had an LGBTQ student centre or lounge – resources that can foster professional support and community among LGBTQ students (Hylton, 2005). However, as mentioned earlier, some programs had no student centres or lounges at all, which potentially explains the low percentage. The institutional and program climates elucidated above probably make it challenging for faculty and students to develop supportive initiatives in programs and to access adequate resources for implementation.

Mentoring of LGBTQ students also ensures the adequate representation of LGBTQ people in the social work profession. Yet, participants indicated that only 16 percent of institutions and 4 percent of programs had mentoring options that focused specifically on LGBTQ identities. Mentoring options for LGBTQ students by either senior students or faculty, such as individual or small-group meetings, work study, or post-doctoral fellowship opportunities with faculty, could be a crucial source of support and could offer professional role models for students. Though 91 percent of students knew of an LGBTQ peer, only 58 percent were aware of an LGBTQ faculty member. There must be sufficient openly LGBTQ senior students and faculty for formal mentoring programs, or even informal mentoring opportunities, to be feasible. Social work programs may place insufficient emphasis on recruitment and retention of LGBTQ faculty and students, and they may create climates in which LGBTQ faculty and students do not feel comfortable disclosing their identities and participating in such programs. The increased presence of LGBTQ faculty and peers may amplify student feelings of support and visibility, and provide role models of LGBTQ social work professionals for LGBTQ students (Hylton, 2005). In addition, 47 percent of participants knew at least one peer, and 24 percent knew at least one faculty member, whose LGBTQ status was hidden. The presence of such classmates, and particularly such faculty, may indicate to LGBTQ students that the campus is unwelcoming or unsafe in some way.

More representative curriculum content has also been recommended to improve climate and as a response to social work students' experiences of discrimination and lack of visibility (Chinell, 2011; Hylton, 2005). However, participants reported a critical lack of LGBTQ-representative curriculum, particularly classroom examples (e.g., case studies and guest speakers) and course readings, especially regarding gender minority populations. Research demonstrates that the inclusion of content about LGBTQ populations in required courses has the potential to positively affect the attitudes of social work students by exposing them to, and increasing their contact with, LGBTQ individuals and populations (Bassett and Day, 2003). Increasing non-LGBTQ students' awareness of LGBTQ populations will also ideally contribute to a more positive climate on campuses and less hostile environments in classrooms (Evans and Herriott, 2004).

Physical Recommendations

In Chinell's (2011) small-scale study, participants also recommended that social work programs increase the visible indicators of LGBTQ populations. In addition to creating space for LGBTQ student centres or lounges, "safe space" programs have been suggested as a physical means to facilitate the identification of allies and to indicate a supportive climate. In such programs, faculty and staff who are knowledgeable about LGBTQ issues display a visible indicator of support, usually a certain symbol (Hylton, 2005). However, when such programs are implemented, both their nature and the meaning of the symbol should be explained to incoming students. Another crucial visible indicator of support is the gender-neutral or single-stall bathroom, ideally flagged as such with a prominent sign or gender-neutral logo and publicized, either in the institution or social work program's literature for prospective students or on their website. In the 2012 study, 60 percent of participants indicated that their institutions did not have a gender-neutral bathroom. The lack of such a facility may particularly inhibit the presence of gender minority students.

Conclusion

This study of campus climates for BSW and MSW students enrolled in English-speaking social work programs in Canada found that although some sources of representation and friendliness do exist, institutions need to make greater efforts to facilitate support for LGBTQ students. In particular, the creation, implementation, and promotion of sexual and gender identity non-discrimination policies, intentional and inclusive recruitment efforts, and strategies to reduce homophobic experiences, increase representation, and expedite access to support and resources should be undertaken and communicated to potential and current students. These measures are essential to encourage the participation and academic success of LGBTQ students in social work programs and to ensure the representation of LGBTQ identities in the social work profession.

Appendix A

Participant demographics

Participant demographics ($n = 106$) Characteristic	n	%
Age ($n = 106$)		
29 and under	67	63.2
30–39	19	17.9
40–49	15	14.2
50–59	2	1.9
60 and over	3	2.8
Sexual orientation ($n = 106$)		
Lesbian	25	23.6
Gay	22	20.8
Bisexual	21	19.8
Queer	29	27.4
Other	9	8.5
Gender[a, b] ($n = 106$)		
Woman	72	67.9
Man	28	26.4
No gender categories	4	3.8
Transgender	4	3.8
Race and ethnicity ($n = 104$)		
White non-Hispanic	83	79.8

Participant demographics (*n* = 106)		
Characteristic	***n***	**%**
Multi-racial	13	12.5
White Hispanic	3	2.9
Black	2	1.9
South Asian/Middle Eastern	2	1.9
Asian	1	1.0
Parental education (n = 105)		
Middle school	6	5.7
High school	16	15.2
Community college/vocational school	20	19.0
University/college	43	41.0
Advanced degree	20	19.0

a Individual percentages calculated using all respondents (*n* = 106).
b Participants could select more than one option.

Appendix B

Categorical institutional and program characteristics

Institutional and program characteristics (*n* = 106)		
Categorical institutional characteristics	***n***	**%**
Population area (n = 106)		
Urban area (> 50,000 people)	97	91.5
Urban cluster (2,500–50,000 people)	4	3.8
Rural area (< 2,500 people)	5	4.7
Public/private (n = 106)		
Public	95	89.6
Private	3	2.8
Unsure	8	7.5
Religious affiliation (n = 106)		
No religious affiliation	89	84.0
Religious affiliation	7	6.6
Unsure	10	9.4
Non-discrimination policy: Sexual identity (n = 106)		
Yes	75	70.8
No	2	1.9
Do not know	29	27.4

Institutional and program characteristics ($n = 106$)		
Categorical institutional characteristics	**n**	**%**
Non-discrimination policy: Gender identity ($n = 106$)		
Yes	36	34.0
No	10	9.4
Do not know	60	56.6
Has LGBTQ organizations/student groups ($n = 106$)		
Yes	94	88.7
No	5	4.7
Do not know	7	6.6
Has LGBTQ student centre or lounge ($n = 105$)		
Yes	57	54.3
No	26	24.8
Do not know	22	21.0
Has LGBTQ mentoring options ($n = 106$)		
Yes	17	16.0
No	30	28.3
Do not know	59	55.7
Has inclusive application ($n = 106$)		
Yes	25	23.6
No	40	37.7
Do not know	41	38.7
Has targeted recruitment process: LGBTQ students ($n = 106$)		
Yes	9	8.5
No	56	52.8
Do not know	41	38.7
Gender-neutral bathrooms ($n = 106$)		
Yes	30	28.3
No	64	60.4
Do not know	12	11.3
Categorical program characteristics	**n**	**%**
Program type ($n = 105$)		
Bachelor of social work	52	49.5
Master of social work	53	50.5
Non-discrimination policy: Sexual identity ($n = 106$)		
Yes	62	58.5
No	8	7.5
Do not know	36	34.0

Categorical program characteristics	n	%
Non-discrimination policy: Gender identity ($n = 106$)		
Yes	39	36.8
No	14	13.2
Do not know	53	50.0
Has LGBTQ organizations/student groups ($n = 106$)		
Yes	11	10.4
No	82	77.4
Do not know	13	12.3
Has LGBTQ lounge ($n = 106$)		
Yes	0	0.0
No	96	90.6
Do not know	10	9.4
Has LGBTQ mentoring options ($n = 105$)		
Yes	4	3.8
No	81	77.1
Do not know	20	19.0
Has targeted recruitment process: LGBTQ students ($n = 106$)		
Yes	15	14.2
No	57	53.8
Do not know	34	32.1

Appendix C

Continuous institutional and program experience

Institutional and program factors ($n = 106$) Variables	M	SD	Skewness	Kurtosis
Continuous institutional experience				
Institution's sexual minority identity friendliness[a] ($n = 106$)	2.97	.899	-.825	.514
Institution's gender minority identity friendliness[a] ($n = 106$)	2.08	1.057	-.202	-.075
Continuous program experience				
Overall level of disclosure about LGBTQ identity in program?[c] ($n = 106$)	2.283	.892	-1.414	1.506

Institutional and program factors ($n = 106$)				
Variables	M	SD	Skewness	Kurtosis
Continuous program experience				
Others' overall level of comfort with your LGBTQ identity in program?[c] ($n = 106$)	2.311	.653	-.627	.379
How many faculty know your LGBTQ identity?[d] ($n = 105$)	1.99	1.297	.018	-1.077
How many other students in your program know your LGBTQ identity?[d] ($n = 105$)	2.42	1.167	-.319	-.657
How supported do you feel in terms of your LGBTQ identity in program?[a] ($n = 106$)	2.72	1.136	-.652	-.311
How often are sexual minority readings/examples provided in classes?[b] ($n = 106$)	1.60	.686	-.022	-.179
How often are gender minority readings/examples provided in classes?[b] ($n = 106$)	.85	.644	.149	-.603

a 0–4 (not, somewhat not, neutral/do not know, somewhat, very).
b 0–3 (never, rarely, sometimes, often).
c 0–3 (not, do not know, somewhat, very).
d 0–4 (none, few, some, most, all).

Appendix D

Categorical institutional and program experience

Categorical variables ($n = 106$)		
Variable	n	%
Did you experience homophobia while in your social work program? ($n = 106$)		
Yes	35	33.0
No	69	65.1
Do not know	2	1.9

Categorical variables ($n = 106$)		
Variable	n	%
Did you experience transphobia while in your social work program? ($n = 106$)		
Yes	12	11.3
No	74	69.8
Do not know	20	18.9
What percent of faculty would you consider supportive of sexual minority identity issues? ($n = 106$)		
0–25%	7	6.6
26–50%	8	7.5
51–75%	20	18.9
76–100%	61	57.5
Do not know	10	9.4
What percent of faculty would you consider supportive of gender minority identity issues? ($n = 106$)		
0–25%	12	11.3
26–50%	15	14.2
51–75%	18	17.0
76–100%	39	36.8
Do not know	22	20.8
Do faculty intervene when students display homophobia? ($n = 106$)		
Yes	28	26.4
No	17	16.0
Do not know	61	57.5
Do faculty intervene when students display transphobia? ($n = 106$)		
Yes	20	18.9
No	17	16.0
Do not know	69	65.1
Do faculty behave and speak in ways that reflect their own homophobia and bias? ($n = 106$)		
Yes	20	18.9
No	67	63.2
Do not know	19	17.9

Categorical variables ($n = 106$)		
Variable	n	%
Do faculty behave and speak in ways that reflect their own transphobia and bias? ($n = 106$)		
Yes	23	21.7
No	53	50.0
Do not know	30	28.3
Are you aware of any openly LGBTQ faculty? ($n = 106$)		
Yes	61	57.5
No	42	39.6
Do not know	3	2.8
Are you aware of any openly LGBTQ administrators or staff? ($n = 106$)		
Yes	22	20.8
No	77	72.6
Do not know	7	6.6
Are you aware of any openly LGBTQ students? ($n = 105$)		
Yes	96	91.4
No	7	6.7
Do not know	2	1.9
Are you aware of any closeted LGBTQ faculty? ($n = 105$)		
Yes	25	23.8
No	60	57.1
Do not know	20	19.0
Are you aware of any closeted LGBTQ administrators or staff? ($n = 103$)		
Yes	7	6.8
No	75	72.8
Do not know	21	20.4
Are you aware of any closeted LGBTQ students? ($n = 104$)		
Yes	49	47.1
No	34	32.7
Do not know	21	20.2

References

Bassett, J.D., and K.J. Day. (2003). "A test of the infusion method: Emphatic inclusion of material on gay men in a core course." *Journal of Teaching in Social Work* 23 (3–4): 29–41. http://dx.doi.org/10.1300/J067v23n03_04.

Berkman, C.S., and G. Zinberg. (1997). "Homophobia and heterosexism in social workers." *Social Work* 42 (4): 319–32. http://dx.doi.org/10.1093/sw/42.4.319.

Black, B., T.P. Oles, E.P. Cramer, and C.K. Bennett. (1999). "Attitudes and behaviors of social work students toward lesbian and gay male clients: Can panel presentations make a difference?" *Journal of Gay and Lesbian Social Services* 9 (4): 47–68. http://dx.doi.org/10.1300/J041v09n04_03.

Brownlee, K., A. Sprakes, M. Saini, R. O'Hare, K. Kortes-Miller, and J. Graham. (2005). "Heterosexism among social work students." *Social Work Education* 24 (5): 485–94. http://dx.doi.org/10.1080/02615470500132756.

CASWE (Canadian Association for Social Work Education). (2014). "Standards for accreditation." Retrieved from http://caswe-acfts.ca/wp-content/uploads/2013/03/CASWE-ACFTS-Standards-11-2014.pdf.

—. (n.d.). "List of accredited programs." Retrieved May 2, 2016, from http://caswe-acfts.ca/commission-on-accreditation/list-of-accredited-programs/.

Chinell, J. (2011). "Three voices: Reflections on homophobia and heterosexism in social work education." *Social Work Education* 30 (7): 759–73. http://dx.doi.org/10.1080/02615479.2010.508088.

Cluse-Tolar, T., E.G. Lambert, L.A. Ventura, and S. Pasupuleti. (2005). "The views of social work students toward gay and lesbian persons: Are they different from other undergraduate students?" *Journal of Gay and Lesbian Social Services* 17 (3): 59–85. http://dx.doi.org/10.1300/J041v17n03_04.

Craig, S.L., M. Dentato, L. Messinger, and L.B. McInroy. (2016). "Educational determinants of readiness to practise with LGBTQ clients: Social work students speak out." *British Journal of Social Work* 46 (1): 115–34. http://dx.doi.org/10.1093/bjsw/bcu107.

Craig, S.L., L.B. McInroy, M.P. Dentato, A. Austin, and L. Messinger. (2015). *Social work students speak out! The experiences of lesbian, gay, bisexual, transgender and queer students in social work programs: A study report.* Toronto: Council on Social Work Education/Council on Sexual Orientation and Gender Identity and Expression. http://www.cswe.org/file.aspx?id=82833.

Dugan, J.P., and L. Yurman. (2011). "Commonalities and differences among lesbian, gay, and bisexual college students: Considerations for research and practice." *Journal of College Student Development* 52 (2): 201–16. http://dx.doi.org/10.1353/csd.2011.0027.

Evans, N.J., and T.K. Herriott. (2004). "Freshmen impressions: How investigating the campus climate for LGBT students affected four freshmen students." *Journal of College Student Development* 45 (3): 316–32. http://dx.doi.org/10.1353/csd.2004.0034.

Field, A.P. (2009). *Discovering statistics using SPSS*. London: Sage.

Fredriksen-Goldsen, K.I., M.R. Woodford, K.P. Luke, and L. Gutiérrez. (2011). "Support of sexual orientation and gender identity content in social work education: Results from national surveys of U.S. and anglophone Canadian faculty." *Journal of Social Work Education* 47 (1): 19–35.

Gortmaker, V.J., and R.D. Brown. (2006). "Out of the college closet: Differences in perceptions and experiences." *College Student Journal* 40 (3): 606–19.

Hylton, M. (2005). "Heteronormativity and the experiences of lesbian and bisexual women as social work students." *Journal of Social Work Education* 41 (1): 67–82. http://dx.doi.org/10.5175/JSWE.2005.200300350.

Jurgens, J.C., A.M. Schwitzer, and T. Middleton. (2004). "Examining attitudes toward college students with minority sexual orientations: Findings and suggestions." *Journal of College Student Psychotherapy* 19 (1): 57–75. http://dx.doi.org/10.1300/J035v19n01_07.

Kwon, P., and D.S. Hugelshofer. (2012). "Lesbian, gay, and bisexual speaker panels lead to attitude change among heterosexual college students." *Journal of Gay and Lesbian Social Services* 24 (1): 62–79. http://dx.doi.org/10.1080/10538720.2012.643285.

Longerbeam, S.D., K.K. Inkelas, D.R. Johnson, and Z.S. Lee. (2007). "Lesbian, gay, and bisexual college student experiences: An exploratory study." *Journal of College Student Development* 48 (2): 215–30. http://dx.doi.org/10.1353/csd.2007.0017.

Rankin, S.R. (2003). *Campus climate for gay, lesbian, bisexual, and transgender people: A national perspective*. Policy Institute of the National Gay and Lesbian Task Force. Retrieved from http://www.thetaskforce.org/static_html/downloads/reports/reports/CampusClimate.pdf.

Waldo, C.R. (1998). "Out on campus: Sexual orientation and academic climate in a university context." *American Journal of Community Psychology* 26 (5): 745–74. http://dx.doi.org/10.1023/A:1022110031745.

Woodford, M., Y. Han, S.L. Craig, C. Lim, and M. Matney. (2014) "Discrimination and mental health among sexual minority college students: The type and form of discrimination does matter, a mediation analysis." *Journal of Gay and Lesbian Mental Health* 18 (2): 142–63. http://dx.doi.org/10.1080/19359705.2013.833882.

Woodford, M.R., P. Silverschanz, S. Swank, K.S. Scherrer, and L. Raiz. (2012). "Predictors of heterosexual college students' attitudes toward LGBT people." *Journal of LGBT Youth* 9 (4): 297–320. http://dx.doi.org/10.1080/19361653.2012.716697.

10

Opening Theory: Polyamorous Ethics as a Queering Inquiry in the Social Work Classroom

BECKY IDEMS

The sea change in societal attitudes toward lesbian and gay (and, to a lesser degree, bi and trans) people is mirrored in social work education's increasing emphasis on aligning anti-homophobia advocacy with its core values (Woodford, Atteberry, Derr, and Howell, 2013). Adopting lesbian, gay, bi, trans, and queer (LGBTQ) identities as the "new normal," undergraduate classrooms increasingly embrace cultural competence approaches to LGBTQ individuals, families, and communities in textbooks, case studies, and skills-focused course content (Van Den Bergh and Crisp, 2004). Proponents of these approaches argue for their capacity to transform the profession by encouraging future practitioners to challenge homophobic and heterosexist beliefs and attitudes, and offering them the resources to work confidently and competently with LGBTQ service users (Camilleri and Ryan, 2006; Crisp, 2006; Van Den Bergh and Crisp, 2004; Woodford et al., 2013).

Cultural competence models are rooted in psychotherapy: gay affirmative practice (GAP) was the earliest example of an LGBTQ-competent approach to practice. GAP sought to challenge prejudicial beliefs and assumptions about "gays and lesbians" in therapeutic contexts (Crisp, 2006; Tozer and McClanahan, 1999). Defined as practice that "affirms a lesbian, gay, or bisexual identity as an equally positive human experience and expression to heterosexual identity" (Davies, 1996, p. 25, as cited in Crisp, 2006, p. 116), GAP models offer six principles, which can be applied across diverse settings. These include not assuming service user heterosexuality; recognizing society's homophobia (rather than sexual orientation) as the core problem; accepting non-heterosexual identification as the desired outcome of intervention; addressing service users' internalized homophobia; understanding the coming out process; and addressing the practitioner's own homophobia and heterosexism (Crisp, 2006, p. 117). These principles hold promise in a variety of social work frameworks, as they align with the tenets of both environmental and strengths-based models and of structural and anti-oppressive approaches (Appleby and Anastas, 1998, as cited in Crisp, 2006).

Based in a large body of scholarship that documents rates of homophobia and heterosexism among social work students and faculty (Camilleri and Ryan, 2006; Trotter, Brogatzki, Duggan, Foster, and Levie, 2006; Woodford et al., 2013), cultural competence approaches emphasize the connection between ignorance and prejudice, suggesting that the invisibility of LGBTQ people in society, and in the curriculum, is connected to the prevalence of these dangerous attitudes (O'Neill, 2006). Thus, these approaches stress the acquisition of particular kinds of knowledge – "the knowledge, attitudes, and skills [to] practice with gay men and lesbians" (Crisp, 2006, p. 123).

Some proponents advocate broadening this knowledge base beyond understanding and acceptance to include advocacy and activism. Focusing on connections between intersectional oppressions, homophobia, and hate crimes against non-heterosexual individuals, Bush and Sainz (2001) call for social workers to develop "the knowledge, skills, and attitudes needed to counter harassment and hate crimes" (p. 206). Accordingly, critical accounts advocate for andragogical approaches that help students, faculty, and social workers move beyond discomfort and defensiveness, and make space for nuanced conversations about the complexities of sexuality and identity (Bush and Sainz, 2001; Crisp, 2006; Trotter et al., 2006).

Although all cultural competence approaches problematize the notion of tolerance and strive to remove the stigma of "other" from non-heterosexual service users, some theorists argue that using the concept of culture is inherently problematic (Bogo, 2006; Hicks and Watson, 2003; Jeyasingham, 2008; Poon, 2011). Bogo (2006, p. 36) reminds us that a focus on "difference" and "culture," in working with any population, often masks the reality of a practitioner's own, often dominant, cultural affiliation. That is, in social work education, a non-culture of heterosexuality is assumed, alongside other dominant and invisible memberships related to class, gender, race, and other value-laden cultural affiliations. In contrast with this, a simplistic, universalized gay and lesbian culture is strategically adopted by the so-called neutral, presumably cisgender, heterosexual social worker. This offloads the responsibility to initiate cultural competence onto the service user, who is (assumed to be) cisgender and straight until proven otherwise, and it ignores key differences and needs for service users whose identities, activities, and life experiences fall outside of recognized categories.

It is in these grey areas, where cultural affiliations and identity labels collide and collapse, that queer theory accounts unsettle the essential or biological roots of binary categories of gender and sexuality, asserting instead their socially constructed, fluid, and mutable natures (Burdge, 2007; McPhail, 2004). Perhaps more importantly, these accounts remind us of the ideological functions of these constructed knowledges (Hicks and Watson, 2003; Jeyasingham, 2008; O'Brien, 1999; Poon, 2011; Willis, 2007). The positioning of non-heterosexual behaviours in a hierarchical binary is central to the social construction of heterosexuality, which requires a negative, socially stigmatized construction of homosexuality to define itself against (Hicks and Watson, 2003). Willis (2007) argues that, though affirmative approaches challenge overtly discriminatory discourses such as sinner, diseased, and unnatural, they simultaneously enact discourses that characterize queer and trans service users as "troubled" or "challenged" (p. 189). It is within this power-laden and regulatory context that Burdge (2007) posits "ending gender" as a central tenet of transformational social work.

Queer theory approaches unsettle the roots of traditional social work, which rely upon a hierarchy of knowledge in which the service user, or "problem population," is merely an object, whereas the (presumed cisgender and straight) practitioner is a participant. The adoption of a hierarchy of culturally recognizable and acceptable behaviours, goals, and outcomes for non-heterosexual service users is not a politically neutral act. This knowledge hierarchy supports hetero- and gender-normativity by constructing the *known* and *knowable* "good gay" while silencing, radicalizing, and marginalizing "bad queer" ways of being (Bush and Sainz, 2001; Hicks and Watson, 2003; Jeyasingham, 2008). Critiquing GAP and cultural competence models of practice uncovers the underlying normative functions of false binaries of gender and sexuality. Herein lies the dangerous paradox of all knowledge-based cultural competence frameworks – the impossibility of alleviating the stigma of the other while relying on knowledge frameworks that impose meaning on non-dominant identities from a position of presumed membership in the dominant group.

Moreover, Hicks and Watson (2003) criticize social work approaches to gender and sexual diversity as an "adding in," which fails to challenge social work's historical role in perpetuating oppression: "Anti-discriminatory practice can be seen as an attempt to assimilate these ideas into existing social welfare theories, whilst concomitantly defending and legitimating the profession as a whole ... Anti-discriminatory versions of challenges to social welfare are very watered down, and ... leave dominant discourses, such as 'heteronormativity,' intact" (para. 2.4). Adopting discourses of anti-discrimination and cultural competence while simultaneously failing to challenge underlying hierarchies of knowledge does more than merely buttress hetero- and gender-normative discourses in practice. These elisions legitimize professional hierarchies and violences across recognized and unrecognized categories of difference, emphasizing the notion of "sexual orientation" as something that is visible and recognizable while failing to challenge transphobic and homophobic violences embedded in practice (Jeyasingham, 2008). Oppressive attitudes are not discrete or exclusive, but co-exist and support each other (Bogo, 2006; Burdge, 2007; Ehrlick, 1992; Jeyasingham, 2008; Willis, 2007). Thus, a transformative queering project requires students, educators, and practitioners to first challenge their dualistic notions of sexual and gender normalcy – to dismantle "appropriate hierarch[ies] of beliefs, attitudes, and behaviour" (Ehrlick, 1992, p. 106) – before laying claim to the capacity to challenge and transform oppressive social structures and relations.

Changes to social work andragogy, then, prioritize attempts at "eliminating" or "expanding" categories of gender and sexuality (Burdge, 2007). Queering approaches offer practical advice for accomplishing these ideological shifts in classrooms. Suggestions include the teaching continuum models of human gender expression and sexual behaviour rather than "discrete" categories of fixed identity. Moreover, students can be encouraged to think critically about the discursive construction of reality by introducing and emphasizing postmodernist and queer theory approaches to critical thinking, which encourage a tentative approach and an acknowledgment of "partial truths" (McPhail, 2004, p. 17). Concretely, Hafford-Letchfield (2010) advocates using debate and role-play, allowing students to recognize and explore multiple perspectives and realities outside of fixed models of human identity.

Similarly, Willis (2007) points to the need for practitioners to assist service users in co-authoring new discourses that emphasize their creativity and agency, instead of reinscribing normative identities and presumed practice needs and outcomes. To assist students in recognizing both the normalizing and transformative potentials of discourses of gender and sexuality, Jeyasingham (2008) affirms the responsibility of social work educators to recognize and call into question the ways that gay and lesbian contributions to service knowledge are ignored and overlooked in the day-to-day teaching of social work practice models. Flipping the script in classroom moments – that is, recognizing queerness and gender non-conformity as something more than a problem to be solved or intervened upon – "enable[s] us to explore how constructs of gender relations, love, family, the body, sickness and caring maintain heteronormativity in social care services more widely" (p. 149). Through a deliberate and consistent emphasis on "queering assumptions" and "reading against the grain" (Hicks and Watson, 2003), the social work classroom emerges as a potential locus of social transformation that begins, first and foremost, in an analysis of the regulatory nature of social work practice.

Therefore, in this chapter I develop an argument that critiques the encroachment of competencies in the social work profession, as well as the contribution of competency approaches to neo-liberal contexts of practice. I then discuss field-based knowledge and practice skills, exploring how both can contribute to theory building in the social work discipline. Drawing in embodied experiences of polyamory, and the attendant values and principles of these relational practices, the final section offers other ways of knowing that resist dominant practice and theoretical discourse. By making these connections, I provide a counter-argument to competency approaches and urge broader queer inquiries in social work classrooms.

Contextualizing "Competence" in Neo-liberal Contexts of Practice

The impact of global neo-liberalism – in particular, the decline of the welfare state in the United Kingdom and North America – is widely recognized as fundamentally changing the character of social work practice and education. In professions and institutions, shifts toward economic accountability and individual responsibility – a trend that scholars have dubbed "managerialism" (Halford and Leonard, 1998) – increasingly shape day-to-day practice realities and contribute to the mounting stress of social workers, managers, and educators (Baines, 2004; McDonald, 2006). In these tense spaces, social workers are charged with divvying up declining resources among increasing numbers of people and keeping up with demands to document, evaluate, and standardize their work. At the same time, they are responsible for honouring professional commitments to praxis, to social justice, and to the ideals that brought them into the field.

In Canada, the debate rages around the recent movement by professional regulators to identify, define, and mandate the skills and actions that comprise professional social work practice (Aronson and Hemingway, 2011; Rossiter and Heron, 2011). Informed by shifts in the health sciences, professional social work education and administration increasingly stress the importance of using evidence-based knowledge as a foundation for practice decisions (Bates, 2007; Witkin and Harrison, 2001). In response to these shifts, post-informed theorists and educators echo queer approaches that challenge simplistic views of the profession as a beacon for progressive values (Fook, 2000; Healy and Leonard, 2000; Rossiter and Heron, 2011). These accounts situate cultural competence approaches in a critique of the impacts of managerialism on social work values, ethics, and practices, and they seek to uncover the normative and regulatory potentials of evidence-based frameworks, tick-box ethics, and competencies profiles, which strip the complexities of practice to a series of decontextualized actions and reactions (Fook, 2000; Healy and Leonard, 2000; Rossiter and Heron, 2011). Thus, the transformative potential of queer and post-informed inquiry emerges in its ability to expose the normalizing and conservatizing roles of professional competencies – cultural and otherwise – and to trace their alignment with the neo-liberal project.

Critical accounts trouble the wholesale adoption of evidence-based frameworks, questioning the degree to which evidence is, or can be, consistently accessed and applied in practice settings. More importantly, these accounts raise questions about the role of knowledge claims in the relationship between service users and practitioners. Bates (2007, p. 154) articulates these questions in her reflexive exploration of evidence in her own practice: "Having the knowledge of experts behind me increased my feelings of confidence and competence as a practitioner. I began to say to students, parents, and staff, 'the research says.' There was an instant authority attached to saying this. Moreover, because what I was saying represented 'the research,' its validity was assumed as well." Witkin and Harrison (2001) point to the dangerous elision that occurs when expertise is thus claimed. The creation of a knowledge hierarchy, wherein empirical evidence trumps all other forms of evidence, carries with it the twin spectres of false legitimacy and the erasure and invisibility of myriad other forms of knowledge, including practice wisdom and the situated knowledges of service users.

Fook (2002) utilizes deconstructionist tactics to uncover the legitimizing and status-making nature of knowledge claims: "When we apply postmodern thinking on a more specific professional level, professions, and the way they are organized, can be seen as features of a modernist state. They represent organized ways of practicing and thinking based on the assumption that universal and scientific knowledge will lead to better, more progressive, ends" (p. 81). Fook and other post-informed social work theorists trouble enlightenment narratives of "evolution" and "progression" in the profession, and they draw our presumed social justice underpinnings into question

(McDonald, 2006). These accounts take up a Foucauldian lens to characterize social work knowledge, within the context of all social science knowledge, as "constitut[ing] what are called *regimes of truth*, which can (at worst) silence or (at best) discount other knowledges and ways of knowing" (McDonald, 2006, p. 84, emphasis in original).

Clarke (2004) cautions us regarding the slippery nature of neo-liberalism – its chameleon ability to uptake, absorb, adapt, and co-opt discourses from both the right and the left, and to sanitize all discourses in the so-called apolitical language of the market. Echoing this caution, queered approaches to competence models attend to the ways that both systemic injustices and individual privileges are embedded and concealed in discourses that presume a one-to-one relationship between individual rights and social progress – as when marriage equality gains are trumpeted as a democratic victory (Jeyasingham, 2008). Recognizing the porosity of discourses of "accessibility" and "human rights" – their susceptibility to co-optation by the neo-liberal project – allows educators, students, and practitioners to uncover the ways that so-called sea changes in public discourse conceal the increasing exclusion and exploitation of individuals and communities, both locally and globally.

In the context of anti-homophobia efforts in the classroom, attention to the slippery nature of discourses allows both students and educators to examine how simplistic adoption of GAP and cultural competence models fails to challenge – indeed, masks – dangerous hierarchical cultural, gender, or class judgments and affiliations in practice. In the market-grounded values of competency approaches, service users emerge as consumers whose problems, experiences, rights, and responsibilities are understood through notions of individual choice and the free market. It is in this context that Rossiter and Heron (2011) characterize competency profiles as an attempt to fundamentally alter the values base of social work – to "[force] its alignment with neo-liberalism" (p. 307). Broadening our discursive lens helps us recognize how championing gains such as marriage equality reifies neo-liberal ideals by proffering basic protections and benefits to individuals and families that fit into a particular mould – that of consumer citizen – rather than addressing broader inequities for all marginalized groups. A transformative andragogy must address the convergence of neo-liberal discourses in LGBTQ practice and advocacy, and promote unceasing questioning of whose lived experiences are recognizable and normalized under market ideologies, and whose are subject to control and punishment.

Indeed, interrogating the economic discourses that underpin competency frameworks begs the question: In embracing rationality of the market, what have we left by the wayside? Or, as Fook (2011) would ask, "who (and what) gets excluded from the debate when it is framed in competency terms?" (p. 296). Opponents of rigid competency approaches contend that standardized practice skills and frameworks, when untethered from other forms of practice knowledge and critical thought, run the risk of ignoring social justice or reducing practice to discrete, decontextualized actions taken by individual social workers (Aronson and Hemingway, 2011).

In light of the conservatizing potential of movements toward professionalization, critical theorists argue for a re-examination of social work ethics that centres social justice (Fook, 2000; Rossiter and Heron, 2011; Weinberg, 2010). In contrast with approaches that conflate evidence-based practice and competencies frameworks with a narrowed-down, rigid conceptualization of ethics centred on the provision of defined services within the terrain of the free market, these accounts make space to politicize ethics and the ethical social worker: "The foundations of social work – thinking, reflecting, and making complex judgments – cannot be represented in the form of competencies. Competencies by definition eliminate the intellectual and ethical foundations of the profession in favor of rudderless behaviours" (Rossiter and Heron, 2011, p. 306). Invoking critical responsibilities such as reflexivity, an awareness and analysis of power, and a commitment to addressing macro contexts that affect service users, critical post-informed social work theorists join the chorus of queer voices calling out for a radical re-visioning of social work ethics and the ethical social worker (Fook, 2000; Weinberg, 2010).

Queering the Gap: Theory Building in the Undergraduate Classroom

Examining the practices of social workers who were identified as "experts" by others in their field, Fook and her colleagues(2000) found that these workers' practice held little resemblance to the practice frameworks they had been taught (Fook, 2000; Fook, Ryan, and Hawkins, 2000). Instead, these experienced, skilled practitioners synthesized social work theory with their own complex experiences and shifting values, particular working contexts, and service users' needs. Moreover, despite their lack of adherence to formal theory, Fook identified a high level of skill and confidence in their practice, which less experienced, by-the-book students did not display. It is into this "widening gap" (2000, p. 107) between theory and practice that Fook argues for "mixing and matching" (2002, p. 91) approaches to research and education. Her call for social work researchers and educators to develop theory continuously as they experience and reflect on practice asks them to explicitly seek situated practice knowledges from outside rigid theoretical frameworks and to draw these knowledges into classrooms as legitimate theories in their own right. As Fook (2002) notes,

> Through a series of reflective (deconstructive) questions, which are designed to uncover hidden assumptions, practitioners are able to reconstruct a desired theory of practice. The process thus involves a theorizing directly from practice itself, rather than through espoused notions of it. The beauty of this reflexive approach of course is that we are able to get closer to the practice as practiced, rather than the formal theory as practiced, so to speak. (p. 90)

Moving social work reflexivity out of the minutiae of the practice moment and into the realm of theory building illuminates the possibility of renegotiating the very purpose of the critical classroom.

In her foundational text *Getting Smart: Feminist Research and Pedagogy with/in the Postmodern*, Lather (1991) describes the purpose of transformative education as one of process over content: "The task is to construct classroom relations that engender fresh confrontation with values and meaning" (p. 144). Challenging the notion of classrooms as spaces where the authoritative educator fills the passive and receptive student with truth, Lather's call for "open, flexible theory-building" (p. 54) joins Fook's exhortation of "inductive theory" in social work classrooms. Acknowledging the classroom as a space to teach theory making, rather than just theories, requires critical educators to equip students with the skills and processes necessary for evaluating information and synthesizing knowledge.

Thus, a broader commitment to theoretical multi-vocality and open, fluid theory-building classroom practices emerges as crucial in supporting the queering potentials of activities such as "ending gender" (Burdge, 2007), "queering assumptions," and "reading against the grain" (Hicks and Watson, 2003). Multi-vocal andragogies promote adopting queered frameworks for thinking about service users, ourselves, and the nature of our work by decentring rigid, static knowledges and by centring "ideological renegades" (Ehrlick, 1992) in knowledge production processes. Conceptualized in this way, queerness emerges as a deliberate and politicized mode of inquiry rather than a practice outcome or a knowable certainty.

The following pages explore polyamorous ethics as a queering mode of inquiry that might broaden student notions of inclusion and exclusion in respect to sexual and gender diversity while simultaneously grounding, challenging, and expanding andragogical strategies to help students unpack tensions between social control and social justice in the neo-liberal context of their practice. In exploring the possibilities of this one "renegade" (Ehrlick, 1992) or "outlaw" theory, this chapter begins to trace a path for the adoption of all manner of queering theories and approaches in the undergraduate classroom.

Open Classrooms: Centring Polyamory in Social Work Education

As outlaw theories go, its practice-based development and process-oriented focus make a polyamorous lens uniquely suited to the queering project in the social work classroom. Although consensual non-monogamy can be traced back as far as written history, the term "polyamory" was coined during the early 1990s to describe non-monogamous "alternative lifestyles" (Robins, 2004; Taormino, 2008). Its literal meaning – "loving many" (Robins, 2004) – conveys little of its ethics or its practice. More fully defined, polyamory is "the practice of openly and honestly participating in a variety of simultaneous love relationships" (Anderlini-D'Onofrio, 2004, p. 3).

Polyamorous practices and communities are rooted in feminist and gay liberation movements. Representing a concrete response to Rich's (1980) assertion of the underlying patriarchal nature of North American "compulsory heterosexuality," poly ethics pose a deliberate challenge to heteronormative patriarchy, prioritizing and politicizing a heightened awareness of the mundane, everyday ways that normative structural power plays out between individuals (Pallotta-Chiarolli, 2004; Robinson, 1997). Indeed, concepts of polyamory and polyfidelity developed within a politics of resistance to sexist, heterosexist dominant cultural practices of non-monogamy such as "free love" and "swinging," and the silent double standard of expected male cheating, which were often based in, or failed to challenge, an assumption of men's ownership of women's bodies (Ritchie and Barker, 2006; Robinson, 1997). At the same time, polyamory challenged the internalized homophobia and sexism manifesting as biphobia in queer communities (Anderlini-D'Onofrio, 2004; Robins, 2004). This politicized and fundamentally intersectional trajectory of polyamorous thought and practice poses a challenge to the dangerous "adding in" (Hicks and Watson, 2003) of lesbian and gay identity as a singular oppressed identity category in cultural competence approaches.

Poly theorists echo Foucault on the discursively constructed nature of sexual identity, seeking to expose the normative and power-laden nature of "monogamy" by recognizing the deceitful nature of these claims, as in Pallotta-Chiarolli's (2004) feminist exploration of three classic texts about polyamory:

"Immersing oneself into each of these books is to have the strange become familiar, and the taken for granted suddenly up for scrutiny. It is to have words like polyamory and polyfidelity introduced, explored, and become the everyday, while words like monogamy are suddenly exposed for all the silences, erasures, denials that it has disguised" (p. 231). Robinson (1997) deepens and politicizes the insights of poly theorists, extending the critical potential of "a critique of monogamy" well beyond the realm of the sexual or the domestic:

> The often unquestioned acceptance of monogamy on the part of both the Left and feminists allows the public discussion of these issues to be carried out in the vocabulary and emotional language of the Right ... A critical consideration of monogamy allows us to respond imaginatively to changing social trends ... The so-called breakdown of family life can give us the opportunity to rethink social arrangements once the central assumption of monogamy has been held up to scrutiny. (p. 144)

Robinson (1997) argues that discourses of monogamy prop up both patriarchy and capitalism simultaneously by ignoring and marginalizing the myriad configurations in which people live and care for each other. Therefore, a politicized critique of monogamy holds the potential to deepen structural accounts of sexism, cissexism, and heterosexism in the social work classroom by offering students the opportunity to unfix and re-vision concepts of attraction, love, commitment, and family, and to develop an awareness of the intersecting ways that structural oppression and privilege play out in the minutiae of everyday life and relationships. This can be accomplished by enriching and expanding the types of families and relationships that are offered in classroom activities such as role-play scenarios (Hafford-Letchfield, 2010), and by engaging students in classroom dialogue and reflective exercises that trace their own assumptions about relationship and family structures within broader social discourses (McPhail, 2004).

Moreover, though there is a small body of poly-theorizing academic literature across gender and sexuality studies, much poly dialogue occurs outside of academia, in grassroots activist communities. In particular, poly activism centres on a large, accessible online community that provides support and resources, and engages in lively dialogue about the liberatory potentials of poly living as it intersects with the most intimate details of individuals' lives and relationships (Easton and Hardy, 2009; Taormino, 2008). It is this grassroots, action-based orientation that has the capacity to inform a queering andragogy

– to help fledgling social workers conceptualize practice in ways that challenge the individualizing forces of neo-liberalism by offering a bridging point between theory and on-the-ground experience. Educators routinely summon grassroots social movements to contextualize historical shifts in practice and to encourage students to engage in advocacy for systemic change. Broadening notions of activism and advocacy to include poly history and communities in classroom discussion and community-based assignments allows space for students to explore, define, and expand their awareness of lived realities and transformative possibilities outside of mainstream LGBTQ activism.

In current contexts of marriage equality activism and gains, locally and globally – of the ushering of gay, lesbian, bisexual, and trans identities into the realm of the "normal" – polyamorous relationships and practices emerge as distinctly queer. Pushing aside normalized and normalizing notions of biologically innate identities and family structures, polyamorous individuals and communities attempt to carve out space for loving, equitable relations outside of hegemonic cissexist and heterosexist social structures (Pallotta-Chiarolli, 2004; Ritchie and Barker, 2006; Robins, 2004; Robinson, 1997). In their popular and often-cited guide to polyamorous relationships, *The Ethical Slut*, Easton and Liszt characterize poly social structures as revolutionary and transformative:

> We want to create a world where everyone has plenty of what they need: of community, of connection, of touch and sex and love. We want our children to be raised in an expanded family ... We want a world where the sick and aging are cared for by people who love them, where resources are shared by people who care for each other. (Easton and Liszt, 1997, pp. 268–69, quoted in Pallotta-Chiarolli, 2004, pp. 233–34)

Poly activism and communities offer an alternative vision of social welfare that is aligned with the core values of the social work profession – in particular, the ethical responsibilities of social workers to "respect ... the inherent dignity and worth of persons," and to commit themselves to the "pursuit of social justice" (CASW, 2005a, pp. 3–4).

Finally, in centring community as the pivot point for social responsibility and transformation, polyamory connects the dots between systemic oppression and individual suffering while breaking down competency's easy slide into individualizing actions and solutions. A poly lens directed toward social welfare promotes deliberate, ongoing work to recognize and explore service users' family and community networks and supports that will not be immediately recognized by hetero- and gender-normative standards such as shared genetics, socially and legally sanctioned kinship ties, geographical neighbourhoods, or socio-cultural distinctions.

Recognizing realities outside knowledge hierarchies opens space for reconceptualizing intervention possibilities, both on an individual basis and in students' internalized practice frameworks. Teaching about families and communities through a poly lens that emphasizes interconnectivity, accountability, and reciprocity does more than merely challenge simplistic representations of individual identities as "troubled," "challenged," or fraught with risk (Willis, 2007). Rather, it requires the rethinking and rewriting of tried-and-true practice models, such as systems theory and ecological models of practice, to more accurately reflect the family, community, and systemic contexts that service users navigate. In doing so, it offers up a map for a politicized social change mission for the profession.

Deliberately centring utopian possibilities for a more just and equitable future in an ongoing analysis of daily actions holds the potential to contribute to a critical social work andragogy that is rooted in both deconstruction and construction – criticism and hope. The rest of this chapter explores poly ethics as one mode of inquiry to encourage educators and students to recognize the fundamental fluidity, relationality, and co-constructed nature of knowledge, and to interrogate their own practices as they align with neo-liberal agendas and with visions of social justice.

Opening Theory: A Poly Lens on Critical Reflexivity

Aligning classroom inquiry with polyamorous ethics requires reconceptualizing the personal, political, and theoretical within a relational field informed by poly values and commitments, including fluidity, careful communication, negotiation, boundary setting, and honesty. This section discusses these values and commitments, focusing on two crucial tenets of poly relationships – consent and boundaries (Taormino, 2008). Using these concepts as an entry point, it explores concrete examples of andragogical strategies that could potentially "construct classroom relations that engender fresh confrontation with values and meaning" (Lather, 1991, p. 144). In this, poly ethics emerge as a mode of inquiry that is "designed to uncover hidden assumptions" (Fook, 2002, p. 90), providing the opportunity to queer social work andragogy in the "here and now" – in the detailed, intentional, moment-by-moment examination of our daily classroom interactions.

Consent

Consent is the foundation of ethical polyamory (Easton and Hardy, 2009; Taormino, 2008). Defined as "an active collaboration for the benefit, well-being, and pleasure of all persons concerned" (Easton and Hardy, 2009, p. 20), poly notions of consent thicken our definition beyond a simple "yes" or "no" answer to encompass a living, breathing process that is constantly renegotiated between two or more individuals: "You are never trying to sneak up on anybody and you are not required to be subtle. It is always okay to ask as long as it is okay for the other person to say no" (Easton and Hardy, 2009, p. 33). Poly consent requires that all parties be vigilant for the moment when a relationship or action steps into the realm of coercion, discomfort, manipulation, or exclusion (Easton and Hardy, 2009; Taormino, 2008).

Moving this fluid conceptualization of consent into social work practice and education critically extends our ethical responsibilities beyond informed consent, requiring an ongoing reflexive stance that obliges practitioners to constantly renegotiate expectations of disclosure in practice relationships. Teaching consent through a poly lens necessitates incorporating sensitivity and humility as core skills in interviewing practice, field placement objectives, student assessments, and assignments. It means reconfiguring what we teach as critical reflexivity – moving beyond identifying personal biases and social locations to recognize and begin to unpack the regulatory and invasive potentials of the most seemingly inert question or plan of action. Initiating classroom discussions and assignments that require students to explicitly juxtapose poly definitions of consent against the operational definitions provided in organizational contexts and mainstream practice models allows space to explore the processual nature of knowledge exchange as it flows between service user and practitioner, and to develop skills to recognize and challenge the knowledge hierarchies that arise in their practice relationships.

Moreover, this approach requires educators to be aware of the ongoing processes by which students are engaged in – or disengage from – course content and classroom discussion. Recognizing consent in the classroom requires critical educators to be sensitive and non-judgmental about the capacity of students to uptake complex political stances and expectations. Indeed, it necessitates tentativeness and openness that extends to concrete acts such as dialogue facilitation and marking. This recognition summons the unsettling question, "To whom does the classroom belong?" (hooks, 1994). Lather (1991) contends that critical theories "position the 'oppressed' as the unfortunately deluded, and critical pedagogues as 'transformative intellectuals' (Aronowitz and Giroux,

1985) with privileged knowledge free of false logic and beliefs" (p. 137). Post-inspired social work theorists disrupt the "temptations of power and certainty" (Amundson et al., 1993, quoted in Healy and Leonard, 2000, p. 35), pointing to the colonial roots of critical knowledge, which

> can lead us to contemplate students or service users as colonial subjects who are expected to benefit from the superior knowledge we, the colonists bring to them ... Critical education reproduces the hierarchical forms of power and authority when resistance to the perspectives of the educator is seen as something to be put down either by an ideological process of working through the resistance until it is undermined internally or, in the last resort, by the exercise of repressive power and exclusion. (pp. 35–36)

By seeing students as consenting partners in the co-construction of knowledge rather than as "'bad' colonial subjects ... who resist our knowledge [and] cling to their own interpretations of what is happening to them and their world" (p. 35), we can begin to imagine consensual curricula and classrooms. Poly consent troubles critical educator subjectivities by drawing into focus the coercive underpinnings of the so-called liberatory classroom and sensitizing poly-informed educators to the dogmatic and polarizing possibilities of critical education.

In difficult moments – when a student makes a "problematic" or "oppressive" remark in class, or after grading one too many papers by students who "just don't get it" – it is easy to slide into an authoritative stance that elides course enrollment (which is often mandatory) with blanket consent to being passively filled with critical theory. Perhaps it is in these moments that taking up a poly-informed reflexive framework centred on consent might be useful in holding educators and students responsible for more deliberately negotiating the various shades of meaning and understanding in classroom spaces.

The poly-informed dialogues and assignments suggested previously are key to introducing a non-normative discourse with the capacity to invoke and provoke reflexive moments that break down binaries of sexuality and gender, and of good gay and bad queer. Considering classroom spaces through a poly lens of consent unsettles knowledge hierarchies that reify divides between educators and students, between students who get it and those who do not, and between elite theory, activism, and multiple forms of practice. This might be accomplished through a deliberate and ongoing utilization of poly notions of consent to challenge normative discourses in classroom discussion. More importantly, it calls for educators to consider their own reflexive praxis – to constantly scrutinize their roles in framing and facilitating classroom discussions and to interrogate their own seemingly routine activities, such as marking and giving feedback.

Boundaries

Easton and Hardy (2009) define boundaries as "quite simply, how you can tell where you end and the next [person] begins." Asserting that "good boundaries are strong, clear, and flexible; bad boundaries are weak, foggy, and brittle" (p. 210), the authors argue that, as for consent, developing good boundaries involves a never-ending process of negotiation:

> Boundaries are invariably in the plural because none of them hold still for long and all of them are individual. They are how we understand where I end and you begin, where we meet and how we are separate as individuals. You need to figure out where your limits are, [and] what constitutes comfortable distance or closeness between yourself and others in various situations. (p. 72)

In poly practice, boundaries are constantly and deliberately negotiated and co-constructed, and require of all parties an ongoing commitment to owning their desires, needs, and fears.

This fluid conceptualization of boundaries is juxtaposed against the cut-and-dried definition of mainstream social work, which invokes neo-liberal discourses of professionalism to narrow the concept so that it includes only the personal actions and interactions that are allowed in practice relationships. For example, the Canadian Association of Social Workers' "Guidelines for Ethical Practice" (CASW, 2005b) relegates the entire discussion of boundaries to the relationship between service user and practitioner, and it frames boundaries prescriptively, as rigidly defined, preventative actions (p. 11). Ethical practitioners "maintain appropriate professional boundaries throughout the course of the professional relationship and after the professional relationship" (2005b, p. 11). Mainstream perspectives create boundaries by shunning physical contact as much as possible and by carefully avoiding any form of dual relationship, whether sexual, social, or professional in nature.

The notion of "professional boundaries" has long been contested by feminist activists and practitioners, who argue that personal empowerment and healing from experiences of gender-based violence and oppression must occur vis-à-vis non-hierarchical, reciprocal relationships of care that embrace alternative visions of social relations and advocate for structural change (Dominelli and

Campling, 2002). Nonetheless, a poly-informed inquiry centred on boundaries extends critical thinking and practice beyond gender- and community-based contexts of practice by offering educators and students an important starting point to explore social justice possibilities outside of individualist conceptions of identity and of practice across social work settings. As previously discussed, weaving narratives of poly activism, experiences, and communities into our representations of history and practice is crucial to creating a foundation for these deeper dialogues. Recognized as a theory in its own right, with the capacity to challenge and extend mainstream practice potentials, a poly conceptualization of boundaries can then be introduced alongside traditional accounts, and students can be asked to reflect on these insights as part of classroom discussions and assignments.

Queer theorist Ahmed (2004) argues that emotions are both relationally generated and generative of collective identities:

> I suggest that emotions create the very effect of the surfaces and boundaries that allow us to distinguish an inside and an outside in the first place. So emotions are not simply something "I" or "we" have. Rather, it is through emotions, or how we respond to objects and others, that surfaces or boundaries are made: The "I" and the "we" are shaped by, and even take the shape of, contact with others. (p. 10)

Drawing on the idea that boundaries are contested, collaborative, and ever-shifting, Ahmed traces how our reactions to each other orient us in the world, forming both our own skins and those of our communities. Thus, poly boundaries echo queer theory by emphasizing interconnectivity over separation. Deliberately engaging in classroom dialogues centred on emotionally reflexive practices of mutual, ongoing boundary construction encourages both students and educators to move beyond fixed notions of identity. It also prompts them to cultivate capacities for mutuality and fluidity in their own practice and in their conceptualization of social transformation. These conversations can be bookended with readings from feminist, poly, and queer theory, which challenge traditional accounts of professional boundaries, and with journalling activities and assignment questions, which encourage students to map the proximities and distances of groups and communities, and to trace the insides and outsides of identity categories, social classes, nations, professional affiliations, and activist communities. In unsettling binarized, individualistic notions of self and practice relationships, poly boundaries hold the potential to radically expand how we define successful social work outcomes, moving us beyond individual changes in static practice settings to recognize possibilities for community-level action and engagement.

Conclusion

This chapter draws preliminary links between diverse knowledge sources that have the potential to critically expand the philosophical foundation of social work practice. Through a brief discussion of the critical and practical possibilities of reconceptualizing consent and boundaries, poly-informed inquiry emerges in the social work classroom as one entry point to "theorize the gap" (Fook, 2002) between theory and practice. In emphasizing connection over content, and process over destination, polyamory as a queered mode of inquiry offers educators and students far more than a distinct collection of facts or identities: bringing poly thought and ethics into the classroom invokes an ever-evolving collectivist vision of socially just practice. It is hoped that these queered explorations will spark research and dialogue about new directions for critical social work education that challenge the normalizing and regulating functions of the profession of social work, within the context of neo-liberalism.

References

Ahmed, S. (2004). *The Cultural Politics of Emotion*. New York: Routledge.

Anderlini-D'Onofrio, S. (2004). "Plural loves: Bi and poly utopias for the new millennium." In *Plural Loves: Designs for Bi and Poly Living*, ed. S. Anderlini-D'Onofrio, 1–6. New York: Harrington Park Press.

Aronson, J., and D. Hemingway. (2011). "'Competence' in neoliberal times." *Canadian Social Work Review* 28 (2): 281–85.

Baines, D. (2004). "Pro-market, non-market: The dual nature of organizational change in social services delivery." *Critical Social Policy* 24 (1): 5–29. http://dx.doi.org/10.1177/0261018304039679.

Bates, M. (2007). "Evidence-based practice and anti-oppressive practice." In *Doing Anti-oppressive Practice: Building Transformative, Politicized Social Work*, ed. D. Baines, 145–59. Halifax: Fernwood.

Bogo, M. (2006). *Social work practice: Concepts, processes, and interviewing*. New York: Columbia University Press.

Burdge, B. (2007). "Bending gender, ending gender: Theoretical foundations for social work practice with the transgender community." *Social Work* 52 (3): 243–50. http://dx.doi.org/10.1093/sw/52.3.243.

Bush, I.R., and A. Sainz. (2001). "Competencies at the intersection of difference, tolerance, and prevention of hate crimes." *Journal of Gay and Lesbian Social Services* 13 (1–2): 205–24. http://dx.doi.org/10.1300/J041v13n01_14.

Camilleri, P., and M. Ryan. (2006). "Social work students' attitudes toward homosexuality and their knowledge and attitudes toward homosexual parenting as an alternative family unit:

An Australian study." *Social Work Education* 25 (3): 288–304. http://dx.doi.org/10.1080/02615470600565244.

CASW (Canadian Association of Social Workers). (2005a). "Code of ethics." Retrieved from http://www.casw-acts.ca/sites/default/files/attachements/CASW_Code%20of%20Ethics.pdf.

–. (2005b). "Guidelines for ethical practice." Retrieved from http://www.casw-acts.ca/sites/default/files/attachements/CASW_Guidelines%20for%20Ethical%20Practice.pdf.

Clarke, J. (2004). "Dissolving the public realm? The logics and limits of neo-liberalism." *Journal of Social Politics* 33 (1): 27–48.

Crisp, C. (2006). "The gay affirmative practice scale (GAP): A new measure for assessing cultural competence with gay and lesbian clients." *Social Work* 51 (2): 115–26. http://dx.doi.org/10.1093/sw/51.2.115.

Dominelli, L., and J. Campling. (2002). *Feminist social work theory and practice.* Basingstoke, UK: Palgrave.

Easton, D., and J.W. Hardy. (2009). *The ethical slut: A practical guide to polyamory, open relationships and other adventures.* 2nd ed. New York: Crown.

Ehrlich, H.J. (1992). "The ecology of anti-gay violence." In *Hate Crimes: Confronting Violence against Lesbians and Gay Men,* ed. G.M. Herek and K.T. Berrill, 105–12. Newbury Park, CA: Sage.

Fook, J. (2000). "Deconstructing and reconstructing professional expertise." In *Practice and Research in Social Work: Postmodern Feminist Perspectives,* ed. B. Fawcett, B. Featherstone, J. Fook, and A. Rossiter, 104–19. New York: Routledge.

–. (2002). "Theorizing from practice: Towards an inclusive approach for social work research." *Qualitative Social Work: Research and Practice* 1 (1): 79–95. http://dx.doi.org/10.1177/147332500200100106.

–. (2011). "The politics of competency debates." *Canadian Social Work Review* 28 (2): 295–98.

Fook, J., M. Ryan, and L. Hawkins. (2000). *Professional expertise: Practice, theory and education for working in uncertainty.* London: Whiting and Birch.

Hafford-Letchfield, T. (2010). "A glimpse of the truth: Evaluating 'debate' and 'role play' as pedagogical tools for learning about sexuality issues on a law and ethics module." *Social Work Education* 29 (3): 244–58. http://dx.doi.org/10.1080/02615470902984655.

Halford, S., and P. Leonard. (1998). "New identities? Professionalism, managerialism, and the construction of self." In *Professionals and the New Managerialism in the Public Sector,* ed. M. Exworthy and S. Salford, 102–21. Buckingham, UK: Open University Press.

Healy, K., and P. Leonard. (2000). "Responding to uncertainty: Critical social work education in the postmodern habitat." *Journal of Progressive Human Services* 11 (1): 23–48. http://dx.doi.org/10.1300/J059v11n01_03.

Hicks, S., and K. Watson. (2003). "Desire lines: 'Queering' health and social welfare." *Sociological Research Online* 8 (1). http://dx.doi.org/10.5153/sro.782.

hooks, b. (1994). *Teaching to transgress.* New York: Routledge.

Jeyasingham, D. (2008). "Knowledge/ignorance and the construction of sexuality in social work education." *Social Work Education* 27 (2): 138–51. http://dx.doi.org/10.1080/02615470701709469.

Lather, P. (1991). *Getting smart: Feminist research and pedagogy with/in the postmodern.* New York: Routledge.

McDonald, C. (2006). *Challenging social work: The institutional context of practice.* New York: Palgrave Macmillan.

McPhail, B.A. (2004). "Questioning gender and sexuality binaries: What queer theorists, transgendered individuals, and sex researchers can teach social work." *Journal of Gay and Lesbian Social Services* 17 (1): 3–21. http://dx.doi.org/10.1300/J041v17n01_02.

O'Brien, C.A. (1999). "Contested territory: Sexualities and social work." In *Reading Foucault for Social Work*, ed. A. Chambon, A. Irving, and L. Epstein, 131–56. New York: Columbia University Press.

O'Neill, B. (2006). "Towards inclusion of gay and lesbian people: Social policy changes in relation to sexual orientation." In *Canadian Social Policy: Issues and Perspectives*, ed. A. Westhues, 331–48. Waterloo, ON: Wilfrid Laurier University Press.

Pallotta-Chiarolli, M. (2004). "'Take four pioneering poly women': A review of three classical texts on polyamory." In *Plural Loves: Designs for Bi and Poly Living*, ed. S. Anderlini-D'Onofrio, 229–44. New York: Harrington Park Press.

Poon, M.K. (2011). "Writing the racialized queer bodies: Race and Sexuality in Social Work." *Canadian Social Work Review* 28 (1): 145–50.

Rich, A. (1980). "Compulsory heterosexuality and lesbian existence." *Signs* (Chicago) 5 (4): 631–60. http://dx.doi.org/10.1086/493756.

Ritchie, A., and M. Barker. (2006). "'There aren't words for what we do or how we feel so we have to make them up': Constructing polyamorous languages in a culture of compulsory monogamy." *Sexualities* 9 (5): 584–601. http://dx.doi.org/10.1177/1363460706069987.

Robins, S. (2004). "Remembering the kiss ..." In *Plural Loves: Designs for Bi and Poly Living*, ed. S. Anderlini-D'Onofrio, 99–108. New York: Harrington Park Press.

Robinson, V. (1997). "My baby just cares for me: Feminism, heterosexuality and non-monogamy." *Journal of Gender Studies* 6 (2): 143–57. http://dx.doi.org/10.1080/09589236.1997.9960678.

Rossiter, A., and B. Heron. (2011). "Neoliberalism, competencies, and the devaluing of social work practice." *Canadian Social Work Review* 28 (2): 305–9.

Taormino, T. (2008). *Opening up: A guide to creating and sustaining open relationships*. San Francisco: Cleis Press.

Tozer, E.E., and M.K. McClanahan. (1999). "Treating the purple menace: Ethical considerations of conversion therapy and affirmative alternatives." *Counseling Psychologist* 27 (5): 722–42. http://dx.doi.org/10.1177/0011000099275006.

Trotter, J., L. Brogatzki, L. Duggan, E. Foster, and J. Levie. (2006). "Revealing disagreement and discomfort through auto-ethnography and personal narrative: Sexuality in social work education and practice." *Qualitative Social Work: Research and Practice* 5 (3): 369–88. http://dx.doi.org/10.1177/1473325006067366.

Van Den Bergh, N., and C. Crisp. (2004). "Defining culturally competent practice with sexual minorities: Implications for social work education and practice." *Journal of Social Work* 40: 221–38.

Weinberg, M. (2010). "The social construction of social work ethics: Politicizing and broadening the lens." *Journal of Progressive Human Services* 21 (1): 32–44. http://dx.doi.org/10.1080/10428231003781774.

Willis, P. (2007). "'Queer eye' for social work: Rethinking pedagogy and practice with same-sex attracted young people." *Australian Social Work* 60 (2): 181–96. http://dx.doi.org/10.1080/03124070701323816.

Witkin, S.L., and W.D. Harrison. (2001). "Whose evidence and for what purpose?" *Social Work* 46 (4): 293–96. http://dx.doi.org/10.1093/sw/46.4.293.

Woodford, M.R., B. Atteberry, M. Derr, and M. Howell. (2013). "Endorsement for civil rights for lesbian, gay, bisexual, and transgender people among heterosexual college students: Informing socially just policy advocacy." *Journal of Community Practice* 21 (3): 203–27. http://dx.doi.org/10.1080/10705422.2013.811623.

11

Social Work Education: Exploring Pitfalls and Promises in Teaching about Black Queer Older Adults

DELORES V. MULLINGS

I approach writing this chapter with caution and from a stance of not knowing in relation to age and sexual orientation. I locate myself as a middle-aged and middle-class, Jamaican-born, Canadian citizen. I self-identify as a black heterosexual woman and mother of two living children. I am a product of a strong Christian family but have long since embraced other forms of spirituality. To ensure that I wrote with integrity, I consulted a self-identified black lesbian and several other black queer individuals. Through this process, I achieved a better understanding of what Bérubé (2001) means in noting that discourse related to lesbian, gay, bisexual, transgender, and queer (LGBTQ) people is centralized so that the white experience is normalized. If that is the case, how do social work educators begin to reshape the andragogical discourse to fully include African Canadian LGBTQ experiences in social work education? Care providers, including social workers, are ill-prepared to work with older LGBTQs in general (Brennan-Ing, Seidel, Larson, and Karpiak, 2014); therefore, administrators and educators need to implement dramatic changes to integrate the experiences of queer people, including older African Canadian queer people, into social work education. This chapter identifies gaps in the education, discusses the challenges that older black queers experience, and proposes a teaching strategy to improve social work education to support student learning in preparation for ethically, culturally, and racially appropriate practice with this population. Given the limited data about African Canadian LGBTQs, I cite work from the United States to generalize the Canadian experience. In addition,

I use a black-focused perspective as a first layer of analysis and then integrate black queer older adults into my arguments.

The US literature uses the terms "African American" and "black." Although blacks in the United States and Canada do share certain factors such as over-policing (Amar, 2010), generalizations are not appropriate in many situations because the two populations have different historical and geographical experiences. Generally, "African Canadian" refers to people of African descent who call Canada home. In this chapter, I use "African Canadian" and "black" interchangeably in referring to individuals who were born in Canada or elsewhere. However, Amadahy and Lawrence (2009) note that white settler society excludes blacks: "the reality then is that Black peoples have not been quintessential 'settlers' in the White supremacist usage of the word" (p. 107). The word "home" refers broadly to a sense of belonging to the land and its people, but African Canadians are "settlers" on territories stolen from Canada's First Peoples (Alcantara, 2007; Fraser, 2005) and therefore cannot enact ownership of stolen properties. In much the same way as "queer" and "LGBTQ" are often used, I employ "black" and "African Canadian" interchangeably, to mean people of the black diaspora in Canada who share a common history and experiences of racism as a result of colonization, identity, slavery, displacement, and "constructing a home away from home" (Clifford, 1994, p. 302). These individuals see a relationship between themselves and others whose self-identification resembles theirs.

Gaps in Social Work Education

What do we know about African Canadians, African Canadian queer people, and African Canadian queer older adults? Do we teach students about the barriers they face, their hopes, and resiliency? Do we honour their ancestors' memories and their contributions to building the Canadian nation-state? How do we include their experiences of historical and contemporary state tyranny? How can social work education improve student understanding of older queer African Canadians? This section addresses some of these questions by identifying gaps in social work education, beginning with the prominence of Eurocentric theoretical underpinnings in schools of social work.

Canadian social work schools continue to improve students' preparedness to work with marginalized populations. This is evident in the contributions of social work scholars who have injected critical andragogy into the classroom: Indigenous theory and practice (Neckoway, Brownlee, and Castellan, 2007;

Sinclair, 2004); anti-colonialism (Adjei, 2007, 2013); anti-racism (Shaikh, 2012); critical race (Adjei, 2013; Mullings, 2012); identity politics (Massaquoi, 2004); queer theory (Swan, 2002); madness studies (LeFrançois, Menzies, and Reaume, 2013); participatory visual media (Sitter, 2012); whiteness (Mullings, 2014); and black mothering (Bernard, 2000; Mullings and Mullings-Lewis, 2013). These theoretical perspectives have helped to decentre traditional andragogy, which is mostly white-focused. Despite these improvements, social work education is still grounded in Eurocentric philosophical foundations: theories taught in social work education are derived from and based on white people's understanding of behaviour, growth and development, aging, child rearing, adaptation, and grief (see Piaget and Play, 1962; Skinner, 1953). Schiele (1996) notes that the social work profession approaches racialized people's experience via add-on techniques such as multiculturalism, cultural sensitivity/competency, and diversity. Although they encourage social work students to become aware of their privilege and understand how their experiences could potentially influence their practice, they fail to account for black experiences in general, and black queer older adult experiences in particular, in any substantive manner. Furthermore, they are not generalizable to all groups of black people, and they certainly do not attend to within-group differences or multiple identities such as sexuality and gender identities. Most strikingly, they can stereotype participants, forcing them into self-debasing caricatures that originated in the white imagination.

To their credit, some schools have introduced Indigenous programs in their curriculum, though not usually in the entire social work program. Regardless of these attempts at integration, the andragogical foundation and theoretical perspectives of Canadian social work schools are still based on white middle-class, mostly male, viewpoints (see Adler, 1927; Merton, 1938; Mullaly, 2010; Parsons, 1991; von Bertalanffy, 1968) and to a lesser extent, those of white middle-class women (Baines, 2011; Dominelli, 2002; McGoldrick, 1988). The relatively recent influx of alternative theories and concepts, including anti-oppressive theory and intersectionality, has also failed to address the experiences of blacks in any comprehensive way. Similarly, queer theory excludes the concerns of black LGBTQs (Robinson, 2007), and my own research has shown that the limited scholarship on older LGBTQs completely excludes black individuals. Racialized scholars have introduced an anti-racist discourse, but this focuses primarily on race and excludes gender and sexual identity. Black queer theory, the most recent theoretical perspective, deals with issues of race, gender, and sexual orientation; this chapter uses it to support its arguments regarding queerness. Despite the premise of black queer theory, its proponents concentrate almost entirely on queerness from a gay male perspective (see, for example, Larcher, 2012; Robinson, 2007; Walcott, 2009). Some scholars have recently discussed lesbian-related issues (see Moore, 2008, 2011), but trans concerns are almost completely silenced. Since anti-racism and black queer theory do not examine black queer older adults in Canada or globally, the knowledge regarding this population is limited, a situation that this chapter seeks to address.

Anti-black Racism

A major gap in social work education is the lack of depth in discussing anti-black racism. There is an extensive anti-black racism scholarship (see, for example, African Canadian Legal Clinic, 2002; Bashi, 2004; Calliste, 2000; Clairmont and Dennis, 1999; Henry, 1994; James et al., 2010; Johnson, 2012; Ladson-Billings, 2009), but predictably, little of the literature discusses anti-black racism in Canadian schools of social work. Therefore, where possible, multi-disciplinary scholarship will support the arguments in this section. As my own experience and discussions with other black students and faculty reveal, social work educators may include sporadic course content about anti-black racism, but they themselves may not be sufficiently knowledgeable about the insidiousness of racism and its complexities, and/or they may not be fully comfortable with discussing the issues. Titone (1998) explains why she as a white educator was misguided in her approach to teaching about racism: "I came to adulthood never realizing that 'White' had been socially constructed just as 'Black' had been and that I too had been racialized. All of my experiences and my knowledge – and, equally important, the experiences and knowledge I did not have – were with my personality identity" (p. 162).

This is not to suggest that all white professors are unaware that race is socially constructed; however, having an awareness is different from teaching effectively to help students understand these complex matters. More importantly, Titone suggests that her education, regardless of the level or institutional affiliation, focused on "issues of diversity" and failed to provide her with adequate education and supports to develop her skills as an anti-racist ally. As mentioned above, social work schools are based on a white-dominated education system, and the major theoretical underpinnings of the discipline are derived from the same source. Therefore, it is reasonable to conclude that many social work educators have little experience in teaching about anti-black racism because, like Titone, they themselves were not instructed in this topic. Howard (2006) argues that educators' inability or lack of skill in facilitating discussions of anti-black racism stems from the overrepresentation of white instructors and a lack of training, mentoring, and support. The relatively recent increase in racialized and black student populations has motivated some educators to integrate content on anti-black racism, though without adequate training and support, these inclusions are probably ineffective.

Like many Canadians, students may be misinformed regarding Canada's historical human rights policies and may want to believe that their country has always been a safe refuge for survivors of persecution (Fleras and Elliot, 2007; Mendes, 1995). Razack (1999) argues that "discussions of racism create feelings of pain, rage, guilt and innocence amongst all students" (p. 237) and states that these emotions can be challenging to navigate. Furthermore, "the skill level and knowledge of the teacher are critical for promoting dialogue and shifts towards change" (p. 237). Educators' commitment to discussing ageism, anti-black racism, heterosexism, and homophobia, as well as support from administrators and colleagues, will help prepare students to work with black queer older adults.

The small number of black educators in Canadian universities, only 1.6 percent of the total professoriate, is troubling (Canadian Association of University Teachers, 2010). This low percentage may be a result of racism (Henry and Tator, 2009). Wane (2012) contends that gendered and racial hierarchies are interrelated inequities in academia. This is evidenced by "first, an underrepresentation of visible minorities and particularly Black scholars in the academy; second, a racial hierarchy in which Black women professors are underrepresented and experience higher rates of underemployment" (p. 2). I was unable to locate any literature on black queer professors in Canadian social work schools, so I employ the parallel literature about queer African American educators to support my arguments. Black queer educators face unique challenges. Holland (2005) notes that her colleagues tend to ignore what she is *actually* saying; instead, they see "black, woman, lesbian – and have very high expectations for the kind of narrative that I might employ" (p. x). Thus, Holland is entrapped in an imaginary space where she is expected to serve the needs of her colleagues based on their stereotypical notions of who she is and how she should behave to best represent a black lesbian. Appropriately, Alexander (2005) states that "our bodies are always already racially historicized, sexualized, physicalized, and demonized" (p. 250). Specifically, Alexander is arguing that blacks are stereotyped as certain types of beings and are historically seen as dangerous and violent (e.g., gang members), meant to be feared (e.g., the boogeyman), and sexually voracious. Alexander adds, "I am first and always black – it is my history and my heritage marked and written in this dark flesh. It is the first thing noticed and remembered" (p. 251). Black educators, therefore, bring a unique perspective to education: their bodies act to disrupt the discourse in the traditional spaces reserved for whites, and as embodied subjects, they combine life experience with critical andragogy, important elements to help advance education about black queer older adults. On the other hand, many black educators, regardless of age, gender, or sexual orientation, may not be adequately equipped to teach students on these issues and populations.

Exploring Black Queerness

A strong and resilient people, African Canadians have overcome and survived various forms of atrocities while developing solid support systems in their families and spiritual/religious communities (Este, 2004; Spencer, 2006). They have also contributed to building Canada as politicians, business owners, artists, and athletes. If students are to learn how to work with older queer African Canadians, they must first get to know them as a people. African Canadians are often portrayed negatively and stereotypically in popular culture; the video and print media (movies and daily headlines) commonly depict them as drug traffickers, prison inmates, gangsters, welfare recipients, and irresponsible parents (Entman, 2006; Mahtani, 2001; Peffley, Hurwitz, and Sniderman, 1997). Unfortunately, black sports and music superstars sometimes reproduce these stereotypes. However, it cannot be denied that the careers of many black musicians are shaped mostly by white male executives in the music industry. Yet, these artists, athletes, and musicians are lauded as spokespersons and role models for all blacks, an unrealistic expectation that is reflective of Fanon's (1967) suggestion that blacks are made to feel responsible for their entire race. Subtleness is yet another way that the insidiousness of racism is hidden by the unrealistic social expectations of individuals who themselves are survivors of racism.

According to Gill (2012), "Black and queerness are articulated differently depending upon the sites and meaning systems within which they appear and each contributes its turbulent dynamism to the conjunction of Black queerness" (p. 33). Evidence of this difference is demonstrated in queer communities, black communities, and black families. Multiple levels of exclusion exist in queer communities, not the least of which is racism. Giwa and Greensmith (2012), Larcher (2012), and Van der Meide (2001) identify problems of racism in Canadian LGBTQ communities, which range from propagating a unified homogeneous "community," sexual stereotyping, exclusion, and exploitation, to the lack of culturally and racially diverse programs and services. Canadian scholars Crichlow (2004), Giwa and Greensmith (2012), and Walcott (2009) note that black gay and bisexual men also experience racism in a unique way.

It can be argued that the cultures of larger white gay communities are based on, shaped, and controlled by white gay men, so that when black men enter these spaces, they need to play by the established rules that sexually stereotype racialized men. They are expected to be sexually promiscuous, aggressive, and endowed with large penises (Robinson, 2007). This is a clear example of how age, race, gender, and sexual orientation intersect and contribute to the marginalization of black gay and bisexual men. Black lesbians, especially those who are mothers and/or unpartnered, are also disadvantaged by a lack of childcare and parent resources; black queers in general are challenged by a lack of acceptance in white queer spaces; and black LGBTQs experience significant disapproval from their families and heterosexual blacks (Cahill, 2009; David and Knight, 2008; Moore, 2008; Robinson, 2007).

Navigating Identity in Community Spaces

Black people pressure black LGBTQ individuals into choosing their blackness over all other identities (Cahill, 2009; Crichlow, 2004). Even black activists who challenge racist systems often fail to see the intersection of social identities such as gender and sexual orientation. Glass and Few-Demo (2013) note that black LGBTQ people fear revealing their identities to families and the wider community because they anticipate rejection. Research also suggests that blacks express stronger disapproval and more negative attitudes toward queer identities than many whites, even when both groups have similar religious and educational backgrounds (Lewis, 2003). Consequently, some black LGBTQ people "cover" themselves by acquiescing to the expected norm of behaving like heterosexuals to avoid being harassed or stereotyped (Robinson, 2007). "Covering" also helps black queer people remain in the inner circles of families without having to explain themselves. They omit personal and intimate details about their lives, accept alternative names or the downgrading of their partners' status (families may refer to partners as "friends"), refrain from demonstrating affection at family gatherings, and alter their behaviour to suit family expectations (Glass and Few-Demo, 2013; Miller, 2011; Moore, 2011). An important fact for social work educators to be cognizant of, and to help students understand, is that black queer people constantly negotiate their identities – many do not leave their families, communities, or churches, attempting instead to negotiate safer spaces within these relationships and venues (Crichlow, 2004; Ward, 2005).

A recent Canadian study of black gay and bisexual men found that 30 percent of participants were connected to their black communities through recreational, religious, social, or cultural groups, and between 60 and 79 percent spent their time with other blacks (Larcher, 2012). These findings demonstrate that African Canadian queer people have strong attachments to their black communities, a reality that educators need to be aware of. African Canadian queers also remain attached by not giving their families ultimatums to totally accept their lifestyles. Although extended families deny or fail to accept their queer lifestyles, black lesbians in one study "voiced a strong emotional attachment and loyalty to their extended families and Black communities" (Glass and Few-Demo, 2013, p. 720). Miller (2011) suggests that black lesbians manage their minoritized identities by choosing when to share their sexual orientation. Black gay men manage their identities by having sex with men, also referred to as MSM (men who have sex with men), and being "on the down low," but do not self-identify as or with the LGBTQ umbrella term. Crichlow (2004) notes that MSM, for example, create private relationships with male sexual partners while maintaining committed heterosexual relationships with women (e.g., marriage). Families and communities function to shield black queer people from racism in the larger society and offer them a sense of belonging (Cahill, 2009); therefore, having support in black spaces is important in the lives of black queer people. It is understandable that many would remain connected to families, churches, and communities despite their homophobic experiences.

Many blacks grow up in families with strong religious and spiritual connections; thus, being a part of organized religious communities is important to many. Church communities provide informal support, religiosity, and connection to black families and black communities (Este, 2004; Gillard, 1998; Mensah, 2002; Spencer, 2006). In fact, the church community is a first line of defence in times of crisis and has historically provided various forms of welfare services (Este, 2004; Spencer, 2006). Although church may be important to black queer people, they may not be comfortable being out and discussing their relationships in church communities (Glass and Few-Demo, 2013). From my experience, it is not unusual to attend African Canadian church services and hear pastors preaching hate against queer people, with the most virulent attacks often directed at "battymen" – a Jamaican term used to describe gay men (Crichlow, 2004). Sometimes these attacks come in the wake of congregational gossip about individuals' sexual orientations. After being subject to this vilification and derogatory comments, LGBTQs are forced to relinquish leadership roles and are either relegated to the back pews and shamed into repenting for their "evil" ways or are expelled from their churches altogether (personal communication, November 12, 2013). Even for those who hide their sexual orientation and stay, unrelenting homophobia often compels them to withdraw from their congregations, at least in the early stages of sexual identity exploration (Glass and Few-Demo, 2013). Many religious and spiritual leaders deny black queer people's connection to black communities, suggesting that LGBTQ rights pertain to upper-middle-class white people who enact their sexuality in ways that have no link to black people and black life (Moore, 2010). The disconnection between racial, sexual, and gender identities implies that blacks are not members of the LGBTQ population and provides legitimacy for the assumption that they experience racism but not homophobia. This assumption invariably renders black LGBTQ people invisible, in both their families and their churches.

Despite the exclusion and homophobia that queer older blacks have historically experienced in their families and churches, some improvements have been made. Some black leaders and churches have engaged in relationship building with black LGBTQ communities, resulting in successful ally development. One of the more prominent church movements to support black LGBTQ people in the United States is Many Voices. In one of its activities, on December 14, 2014, thousands of congregants of historically black churches across the United States wore black clothes "to protest the criminalization, disproportionate incarceration, and killing of black and brown people by law enforcement" (Many Voices, 2014b, para. 1). More importantly, the church leaders linked this violence to sexual identity: "As a Black church movement for gay and transgendered justice, we envision a community that embraces the diversity of the human family and ensures that all are treated with love, compassion, and justice" (Many Voices, 2014a, para. 1). Reverend Reggie Longcrier (2014) of the Exodus Missionary Outreach Church in Hickory, North Carolina, clarifies that he no longer worries about what others think of him as an LGBT ally. Reverend Palmer (2013) challenges the claim that black churches are homophobic, dismissing it as a myth:

> Because of this myth black Christian allies like myself are seen as an oddity even though our numbers are growing by leaps and bounds. There are many of us and yet the actions and words of the vile get the spotlight and the focus. Not only do they get the focus, they leave us with the bill. We are the ones who pay for their religious based homophobia. It is us who are met with the hostility and rage from those who have been hurt by those who are filled with hate. (para. 4)

Reverend Dr. Nabors, a prominent Detroit minister, recently publicized himself as an ally; as Stevenson (2014) suggests, "the highly respected African

American pastor and scholar was so appalled by a group of black pastors' recent demonstration against same-sex marriage in Detroit that he could not stay silent any more" (para. 1). As is the case in all groups, there are tensions in the black churches, traditionally cisgendered organizations, with respect to agreement regarding the existence of homophobia and how it is enacted and challenged by black church leaders. Social work educators need to help students understand these nuances without inserting biases about religion and blacks. This is especially important, given that many social work educators appear to oppose the inclusion of religious material in social work education. To support this claim, I recall my own experience in school: Throughout my social work education, I never saw religious material in any course that I took. In my teaching experience, I frequently receive questions and comments, mostly from African Canadian students, about the lack of religious material in their programs. My experience parallels Furman, Benson, Grimwood, and Canda's (2004) research, which surveyed 789 social work practitioners across the United Kingdom. More than 75 percent of respondents reported that their social work education had no religious or spirituality content. In addition, Wong and Vinsky (2009) challenge the discourse of "spiritual-but-not-religious," arguing that the exclusion of religiosity in social work education may continue to extend the colonial embodiment, which has historically marginalized racialized groups.

The Challenges of Being Old, Black, and Queer

Like heterosexuals, older black queers typically turn to partners, friends, and families for informal support when they cannot independently care for themselves (Glass and Few-Demo, 2013; Lewis and Marshall, 2012; Moore, 2008, 2011). When they deteriorate physically or emotionally, so that informal care providers can no longer manage, they seek formal help from health-care systems. And yet, according to Almack, Seymour, and Bellamy (2010), Averett and Jenkins (2012), Brennan-Ing, Seidel, Larson, and Karpiak (2014), and Knochel, Croghan, Moone, and Quam (2012), we know little about the care needs of these populations. A scan of Canadian institutional living facilities for queer older adults confirms that "little is known about the prevalence, health concerns, and aging experiences of LGBT older residents of long-term care homes, retirement residences, and assisted living facilities" and that these populations remain relatively invisible (Sussman et al., 2012, p. 2). There is increasing scholarly interest in all aspects of LGBTQ life, but this development has not remedied the dearth of knowledge on issues affecting older LGBTQ adults (Fredriksen-Goldsen et al., 2011; Knochel et al., 2012). My own research shows that even less is known about older queer adults who are black; arguably, the recent interest and study of queer people have primarily focused on white middle-class concerns (see the work of Averett, Yoon, and Jenkins, 2012; Biblarz and Savci, 2010; Brotman, Ryan, and Meyer, 2006; LaSala, 2002; McIntyre and McDonald, 2012; Sinding, Barnoff, and Grassau, 2004; Sussman et al., 2012). This, however, is not surprising. It is another example of how black queer people are excluded from the larger white LGBTQ communities, and consequently there is even less information about black queer older adults and their unique challenges.

The care needs of older queer adults differ from those of heterosexuals (e.g., fear of being outed); similarly, the needs of older black LGBTQ people differ from those of their white counterparts (e.g., racially specific services). Within-group marginalization also occurs, as is the case with trans people. This exclusion offers unique challenges to systemically cisgendered institutions because older trans adults have "complex social or bodily needs relating to their gender reassignment treatments" (Age UK, 2010) and because as a society, we have limited knowledge about the aging trans body (Age UK, 2010). For example, a trans woman who lives in an institution may require additional space and privacy because she may still have a penis or an "old style" vagina. If she has a vagina (usually made from parts of the colon), it will not naturally remain open, so she will need to do certain things to maintain the opening. A trans man may still have breasts or need to catheterize to take special care of his penis (Age UK, 2010). Where institutional knowledge deficits affect white queer people, African Canadian LGBTQs are even more deeply disadvantaged. For example, black trans people have additional concerns for privacy around genitalia, and this is especially important given the racist exoticism and stereotypes about enlarged genitals for both men and women. These current challenges cannot overshadow the historical misunderstanding, neglect, and mistreatment in health-care settings, mainly through the practice of institutionalized heterosexism (Cahill, 2002). Racist and heterosexist social "policy reinforces strong feelings of isolation and powerlessness, and a sense of being a 'second class' citizen for older LGBTQs" (Concannon, 2009, p. 405). Black queer older adults experience homophobia, racism, and sexism at the personal, community, and institutional levels. Despite these experiences, social work educators can make a difference by preparing future practitioners to work with these individuals. Effective learning and teaching strategies are vital to students' preparedness to engage in fieldwork with vulnerable populations such as African Canadian queer older adults.

Teaching Methods

How can educators encourage students to deconstruct what they may know about older African Canadian queers and also engage them in critical, insightful, and exciting education? I believe that community service learning (CSL) is an appropriate andragogical tool to help students learn about older black queers in a critical and transformative manner. Why do I choose CSL? Quite simply, I have seen its effectiveness in helping students to connect theory with practice, and it makes a tremendous difference to how much material they retain, the quality of their reflection, and the depth of their analysis. In their reflections and debriefing, students have commented positively on their CSL experience and recommend that other students have the opportunity to engage in this liberatory type of learning. In undergraduate courses that I facilitate, I have used CSL with much success during the last five years. I am committed to CSL because it combines class-based theoretical instructions with meaningful community participation to enhance students' academic experience (Baggerly, 2006; Giles and Eyler, 1994). Social work educators encourage students to collaborate with others and to critically reflect on their experiences; CSL is firmly aligned with these principles. For example, collaboration between community partners and the academic institution, facilitation of reflective exercises (e.g., written reflection), and reciprocal (mutual learning) processes are three key components of CSL (Espino and Lee, 2011; Green, 2003; Mink and Twill, 2012). The CSL projects that I design with the help of student co-ordinators are learner-centred and self-directed; they promote student interdependence, effective group and teamwork, and community partnership. A CSL project can also help "students understand racism and privilege and, in particular, how these are manifested in everyday life. It also provides students the chance to confront their social identities and positions" (Mullings, 2013, p. 18), to work collaboratively with others, to develop collegial and community partnerships, and to enhance their leadership skills. When students engage with the community in unstructured ways (e.g., by making a documentary), they can develop critical thinking skills, a sense of civic responsibility, and a commitment to social justice (Boyle-Baise, and Kilbane, 2000; Eyler, Giles, and Braxton, 1997; Giles and Eyler, 1994; Lowe and Clarke, 2009; Myers-Lipton, 1996). To demonstrate how CSL can be an effective model for teaching students about black queer older adults, I provide suggestions to facilitate transformative learning using this andragogical method.

Community Service Learning Model

In this section, I explain how I integrate CSL into teaching, discussing student reactions, my approach and response to student anxiety, and examples of CSL projects. I then provide an example of how CSL may be used to collaborate with black queer older adults. The CSL projects that I help students to initiate are not the usual ones, such as planting trees, cleaning up neighbourhoods, and tutoring. Our projects take the form of community events. With the help of a student services' co-ordinator, students are introduced to the principles of event planning (such as intended audience, date and time of event, and promotion schedule). They organize and manage their projects with guidance from me. In the past, they have held a half-day conference on sexual violence, produced a documentary about street-involved people in St. John's, Newfoundland, and helped low-income parents register their children in the Canada Learning Bond program. These projects were done in collaboration with community partners, which also include individuals who have lived experience with the subject. In helping students organize their projects, I follow a sequence of steps, which I detail below to demonstrate how social work educators could integrate CSL to help students learn about African Canadian queer older adults.

I favour CSL projects in which the entire class is involved because they enable students to build relationships and develop organizational and conflict resolution skills. The project is initiated in the first class of the course. I introduce CSL as a student-centred approach to learning, explain its values, and stress the excitement of this type of learning. I also assign a small paper that is due the following week, explain why it is due so early, and commit to returning the papers one week after the submission date. This process helps to lay the foundation for the project and to encourage student participation.

To complete their assignments, students review the required readings on CSL, write a paragraph in which they define it, search the Internet for information about black queer older adults, and create a detailed outline for a CSL project to work with this population. The outline must show that the project is large enough to encompass the entire class, that it can realistically be finished within the term, and that it will benefit black queer older adults and the students themselves.

During the second class, students submit their assignments. As I collect their papers, I remind them that I will return them the following week. CSL involves action and learning (Green, 2003), so I immediately establish this environment by having students engage in small and large group discussions about their chosen topic – in this case, black queer older adults. Topics for these discussions are chosen in one of two ways: I offer three to five options from which students can choose a topic or they chose the topic themselves by individually suggesting subject areas and then choosing a topic together as a class. The class separates into small groups so that students can share the findings from their Internet search and their understanding of CSL. I also give them some points to address: for example, they can share two new pieces of information that they found; detail what they learned about African Canadian queer older adults; discuss a piece of information that conflicts with popular culture; or explain what CSL means to them or what they feel about it. Every small group tackles two topics, spending approximately ten minutes on each one, after which a fifteen-minute full class discussion ensues. Next, I provide positive feedback to reduce misunderstanding, build confidence, and correct misinformation. For example, I highlight students' depth of analysis, amount of information gathered, group dynamics, and courage to discuss difficult subjects. I also share examples of CSL projects from past classes.

During week three's class, I list the potential projects that I selected from the students' submitted papers. These are chosen based on how well they adhere to assignment specifications. Students then pick their top five preferences from the list and subsequently discuss them with the community groups or organizations with whom they choose to collaborate. One of the five proposals is finally selected as the class CSL project.

Alternatively, rather than completing an assignment in which they themselves propose CSL projects, the students can ask the community groups and organizations for suggestions regarding their needs and will then choose a project from among these recommendations.

After students have established a partnership with a community group or organization, the planning process can begin. In my experience, CSL assignments are time consuming and non-linear; when projects appear unstructured, students can become anxious and/or can exhibit low group confidence. If this occurs, I remind them of their strengths, skills, and knowledge (which they shared at the beginning of the course), and I affirm my belief in their ability to complete the project.

Once students have a clear idea of the project and how they want to participate individually, I create an online list of tasks (such as handling media, co-ordinating, fundraising, storyboarding, writing, editing, and updating). Using our university's online electronic learning and teaching tool, about three to six students sign up for each task and remain responsible for it throughout the project or until they complete it. When the work is finished, they join other groups. Some students may belong simultaneously to more than one group, depending on their interests and the tasks and responsibilities of certain groups. Each group is a subgroup of the class, has its own responsibilities, and can make decisions on behalf of the class. Group members are responsible for posting updates so that everyone knows what is happening in all the groups and with the overall project. These online groups help students facilitate discussions, provide updates, seek suggestions, and ask for help. Everyone is expected to review these postings for pertinent information about the project (such as a change in plans, to confirm an invited guest, to report donations received, or to seek help to distribute posters). This process also helps to create transparency, reduces power imbalances, and increases accountability among students. I frequently review the posts to determine how they are proceeding and to identify potential strengths and areas to be improved as the project unfolds.

Students provide project updates during class time. With large projects, they are divided into subgroups. Because all students may not be aware of specific information, large class updates are important to ensure that everyone knows about the various activities of the project. They also enable students to reflect on the project, identify areas of concern, think about how they feel, and assess the group's progress. In addition, they allow me to offer guidance. I co-facilitate time-limited updates with students at the end of certain classes, and we create clear boundaries to focus on updates rather than process.

While the project is under way and after it is completed, I schedule reflective exercises. I ask students to individually submit written reflections, and I co-facilitate entire class reflections with guided questions. In my experience, these exercises are challenging for students, and they initially offer only surface reflection that is safe and non-threatening. For example, they may describe an experience as "interesting." To strengthen critical reflection, I encourage them to "dig deeper" and to "think with your bellies" (Mullings, 2013, p. 18), not their heads. I also rephrase questions, maintain silence when the class appears uncomfortable, and deconstruct shame and guilt (Mullings, 2013). I have noted that students' priorities change during their participation in CSL projects. As they remarked during one class reflection, "We don't even care about the marks anymore; we just want to make a great documentary."

The suggestions offered above are merely the initial steps to begin a CSL project in which students can learn about black queer older adults. They may need support to help resolve group conflicts, to secure resources (such as grants), and to determine how to share final products. They will also need generous amounts of encouragement. Each group of students is different and its experiences will be unique. Therefore, especially in the early stages of a CSL project, instructors can expect to spend extra time outside of class supporting students. Students will encounter challenges, but their feelings of accomplishment and pride when the project is completed will outweigh negative experiences. Their feedback has suggested that CSL provides a valuable learning experience. For example, at the end of a semester, one student sent me the following message: "I'm just emailing you because I don't think I stressed my gratitude today. This has been a difficult and oftentimes frustrating course, but I am incredibly grateful for every second. I cannot narrow down the specific reasons but I've changed so much and grown. To think of entering the social work world without this growth is a scary thought" (personal communication, November 30, 2013).

Conclusion

This chapter is a contribution to an initial national dialogue about queerness in social work education. Although a great deal of the literature is devoted to black gay and bisexual men and male youth and increasingly to lesbians, black queer older adults are almost completely ignored in the Canadian, American, and global literature. Research and education are urgently needed to fill this gap, a task that this chapter begins to address.

Over the last two decades, schools of social work have improved their attempts to be racially and culturally inclusive. They have introduced dynamic educational models designed to help transform learning, teaching, and andragogy – strategies that have created exciting opportunities for students and educators alike. Despite the gains, social work education remains predominantly white, cisgendered, heterosexist, and ageist, with minimal practical theories, strategies, or movements to change this reality. This chapter outlined several key areas in social work education that have persistent gaps and that require immediate rectification to include black queer older adults. Like those of other groups, the lives of African Canadians consist of layers of complexities; social identities are not static, and it is important to address these complexities comprehensively in social work education. Although black people have lived in Canada for more than five generations, their experiences are largely absent from social work education. Given this – predictably – nothing is taught about black queer older adults, an exclusion that is just one aspect of the challenges faced by this population. A range of literature provided a brief insight into what social work students need to know about this population, including racism in white LGBTQ communities and homophobia in black families, black churches, and black queer communities. The chapter also introduced community service learning as a method that social work educators could use to help students understand some of the concerns of black queer older adults.

Dedication

This chapter is livicated to the memories of sister Sharona Hull, Toronto's original self-identified black lesbian mother and community activist.

Acknowledgment

Special thanks to my sister-friend Leslie Ramsay Taylor, four individuals who wish to remain unnamed, and Tessa South.

References

Adjei, P.B. (2007). "Decolonizing knowledge production: The pedagogic relevance of Gandhian Satyagraha to schooling and education in Ghana." *Canadian Journal of Education* 30 (4): 1046–67. http://dx.doi.org/10.2307/20466678.

–. (2013). "The non-violent philosophy of Mahatma Gandhi and Martin Luther King Jr. in the 21st century: Implications for the pursuit of social justice in a global context." *Journal of Global Citizenship and Equity Education* 3 (1): 80–101.

Adler, A. (1927). "Individual psychology." *Journal of Abnormal and Social Psychology* 22 (2): 116–22. http://dx.doi.org/10.1037/h0072190.

African Canadian Legal Clinic. (2002). *A report on the Canadian government's compliance with the International Convention on the Elimination of All Forms of Racial Discrimination*. Toronto: African Canadian Legal Clinic.

Age UK. (2010). *Transgender issues in later life*. Fact sheet 16. London: Age UK. Retrieved from http://www.ageuk.org.uk/Documents/EN-GB/Factsheets/FS16_Transgender_issues_in_later_life_fcs.pdf?dtrk=true.

Alcantara, C. (2007). "Explaining Aboriginal treaty negotiation outcomes in Canada: The cases of the Inuit and the Innu in Labrador." *Canadian Journal of Political Science* 40 (1): 185–207. http://dx.doi.org/10.1017/S0008423907070060.

Alexander, B.K. (2005). "Embracing the teachable moment: The black gay body in the classroom as embodied text." In *Black Queer Studies: A Critical Anthology*, ed. E.P. Johnson and M.G. Henderson, 249–65. Durham, NC: Duke University Press. http://dx.doi.org/10.1215/9780822387220-015.

Almack, K., J. Seymour, and G. Bellamy. (2010). "Exploring the impact of sexual orientation on experiences and concerns about end of life care and on bereavement for lesbian, gay and bisexual older people." *Sociology* 44 (5): 908–24. http://dx.doi.org/10.1177/0038038510375739.

Amadahy, Z., and B. Lawrence. (2009). "Indigenous peoples and black people in Canada: Settlers or allies?" In *Breaching the Colonial Contract*, ed. A. Kempf, 105–36. Dordrecht, Netherlands: Springer Netherlands. http://dx.doi.org/10.1007/978-1-4020-9944-1_7.

Amar, P. (2010). "Introduction: New racial missions of policing: Comparative studies of state authority, urban governance, and security technology in the twenty-first century." *Ethnic and Racial Studies* 33 (4): 575–92. http://dx.doi.org/10.1080/01419870903380862.

Averett, P., and C. Jenkins. (2012). "Review of the literature on older lesbians: Implications for education, practice, and research." *Journal of Applied Gerontology* 31 (4): 537–61. http://dx.doi.org/10.1177/0733464810392555.

Averett, P., I. Yoon, and C.L. Jenkins. (2012). "Older lesbian sexuality: Identity, sexual behavior, and the impact of aging." *Journal of Sex Research* 49 (5): 495–507. http://dx.doi.org/10.1080/00224499.2011.582543.

Baggerly, J. (2006). "Service learning with children affected by poverty: Facilitating multicultural competence in counseling education students." *Journal of Multicultural Counseling and Development* 34 (4): 244–55. http://dx.doi.org/10.1002/j.2161-1912.2006.tb00043.x.

Baines, D., ed. (2011). *Doing anti-oppressive practice: Social justice social work.* Black Point, NS: Fernwood.

Bashi, V. (2004). "Globalized anti-blackness: Transnationalizing Western immigration law, policy and practice." *Ethnic and Racial Studies* 27 (4): 584–606. http://dx.doi.org/10.1080/01491987042000216726.

Bernard, W.T. (2000). "Bringing our boyz to men: Black men's reflections on their mother's childrearing influences." *Journal of the Motherhood Initiative for Research and Community Involvement* 2 (1): 54–65. Retrieved from http://qe2a-proxy.mun.ca/login?url=http://pi.library.yorku.ca/ojs/index.php/jarm/article/viewFile/2178/1386.

Bérubé, A. (2001). "How gay stays white and what kind of white it stays." In *The Making and Unmaking of Whiteness*, ed. B.B. Rasmussen, I.J. Nexica, and M. Wray, 234–65. Durham, NC: Duke University Press. http://dx.doi.org/10.1215/9780822381044-011.

Biblarz, T.J., and E. Savci. (2010). "Lesbian, gay, bisexual, and transgender families." *Journal of Marriage and the Family* 72 (3): 480–97. http://dx.doi.org/10.1111/j.1741-3737.2010.00714.x.

Boyle-Baise, M., and J. Kilbane. (2000). "What really happens? A look inside service-learning for multicultural teacher education." *Michigan Journal of Community Service Learning* 7 (1): 54–64. Retrieved from http://quod.lib.umich.edu/cgi/p/pod/dod-idx/what-really-happens-a-look-inside-service-learning-for.pdf?c=mjcsl;idno=3239521.0007.107.

Brennan-Ing, M., L. Seidel, B. Larson, and S.E. Karpiak. (2014). "Social care networks and older LGBT adults: Challenges for the future." *Journal of Homosexuality* 61 (1): 21–52. http://dx.doi.org/10.1080/00918369.2013.835235.

Brotman, S., B. Ryan, and L. Meyer. (2006). *The health and social service needs of gay and lesbian seniors and their families in Canada.* Montreal: McGill School of Social Work. Retrieved from https://www.academia.edu/2751086/The_health_and_social_service_needs_of_gay_and_lesbian_seniors_and_their_families_in_Canada.

Cahill, S. (2002). "Long term care issues affecting gay, lesbian, bisexual and transgender elders." *Geriatric Care Management Journal* 12 (3): 4–8.

–. (2009). "The disproportionate impact of antigay family policies on black and Latino same-sex couple households." *Journal of African American Studies* 13 (3): 219–50. http://dx.doi.org/10.1007/s12111-008-9060-7.

Calliste, A. (2000). "Nurses and porters: Racism, sexism and resistance in segmented labour markets." In *Anti-racist Feminism: Critical Race and Gender Studies*, ed. A. Calliste, G.J.S. Dei, and M. Aguiar, 143–63. Halifax: Fernwood.

Canadian Association of University Teachers. The Changing Academy? (2010). *CAUT Education Review* 12 (1). Retrieved from https://www.caut.ca/docs/education-review/the-changing-academy-a-portrait-of-canada-rsquo-s-university-teachers-(jan-2010).pdf?sfvrsn=14.

Clairmont, D.H.J., and W.M. Dennis. (1999). *Africville: The life and death of a Canadian black community.* 3rd ed. Toronto: Canadian Scholars' Press.

Clifford, J. (1994). "Diasporas." *Cultural Anthropology* 9 (3): 302–38. http://dx.doi.org/10.1525/can.1994.9.3.02a00040.

Concannon, L. (2009). "Developing inclusive health and social care policies for older LGBT citizens." *British Journal of Social Work* 39 (3): 403–17. http://dx.doi.org/10.1093/bjsw/bcm131.

Crichlow, W.E.A. (2004). *Buller men and batty bwoys: Hidden men in Toronto and Halifax black communities.* Toronto: University of Toronto Press.

David, S., and B.G. Knight. (2008). "Stress and coping among gay men: Age and ethnic differences." *Psychology and Aging* 23 (1): 62–69. http://dx.doi.org/10.1037/0882-7974.23.1.62.

Dominelli, L. (2002). *Anti-oppressive social work theory and practice.* London: Palgrave Macmillan.

Entman, R.M. (2006). "Blacks in the news: Television, modern racism, and cultural change." In *Communication and Law: Multidisciplinary Approaches to Research,* ed. A. Reynolds and B. Barnett, 205–27. Mahwah, NJ: Lawrence Erlbaum.

Espino, M., and J.J. Lee. (2011). "Understanding resistance: Reflections on race and privilege through service-learning." *Equity and Excellence in Education* 44 (2): 136–52. http://dx.doi.org/10.1080/10665684.2011.558424.

Este, D.C. (2004). "The black church as a social welfare institution: Union United Church and the development of Montreal's black community, 1907–1940." *Journal of Black Studies* 35 (1): 3–22. http://dx.doi.org/10.1177/0021934703261938.

Eyler, J., D.E. Giles, Jr., and J. Braxton. (1997). "The impact of service-learning on college students." *Michigan Journal of Community Service Learning* 4 (1): 5–15. Retrieved from http://quod.lib.umich.edu/m/mjcsl/3239521.0004.101/1.

Fanon, F. (1967). *A dying colonialism.* New York: Grove Press.

Fleras, E., and J.L. Elliot. (2007). *Unequal relations: An introduction to race, ethnic, and Aboriginal dynamics in Canada.* Toronto: Pearson Education Canada.

Fraser, S. (2005). "Indian and Northern Affairs Canada: Meeting treaty land entitlement obligations." Chapter 7 in *Report of the auditor general of Canada to the House of Commons, November 2005.* Ottawa: Office of the Auditor General of Canada.

Fredriksen-Goldsen, K.I., H.J. Kim, C.A. Emlet, A. Muraco, E.A. Erosheva, C.P. Hoy-Ellis, J. Goldsen, and H. Petry. (2011). *The aging and health report: Disparities and resilience among lesbian, gay, bisexual, and transgender older adults.* Seattle: Caring and Aging with Pride. Retrieved from http://caringandaging.org/wordpress/wp-content/uploads/2011/05/Full-Report-FINAL-11-16-11.pdf.

Furman, L.D., P.W. Benson, C. Grimwood, and E. Canda. (2004). "Religion and spirituality in social work education and direct practice at the millennium: A survey of UK social workers." *British Journal of Social Work* 34 (6): 767–92. http://dx.doi.org/10.1093/bjsw/bch101.

Giles, D.E., and J. Eyler. (1994). "The theoretical roots of service-learning in John Dewey: Toward a theory of service-learning." *Michigan Journal of Community Service Learning* 1 (1): 77–85.

Gill, L.K. (2012). "Situating black, situating queer: Black queer diaspora studies and the art of embodied listening." *Transforming Anthropology* 20 (1): 32–44. http://dx.doi.org/10.1111/j.1548-7466.2011.01143.x.

Gillard, D. (1998). "The black church in Canada." *McMaster Journal of Theology* 1. Retrieved from http://www.mcmaster.ca/mjtm/1-5.htm.

Giwa, S., and C. Greensmith. (2012). "Race relations and racism in the LGBTQ community of Toronto: Perceptions of gay and queer social service providers of color." *Journal of Homosexuality* 59 (2): 149–85. http://dx.doi.org/10.1080/00918369.2012.648877.

Glass, V.Q., and A.L. Few-Demo. (2013). "Complexities of informal social support arrangements for black lesbian couples." *Family Relations* 62 (5): 714–26. http://dx.doi.org/10.1111/fare.12036.

Green, A.E. (2003). "Difficult stories: Service-learning, race, class, and whiteness." *College Composition and Communication* 55 (2): 276–301. http://dx.doi.org/10.2307/3594218.

Henry, F. (1994). *The Caribbean diaspora in Canada: Learning to live with racism.* Toronto: University of Toronto Press.

Henry, F., and C. Tator, eds. (2009). *Racism in the Canadian university: Demanding social justice, inclusion, and equity.* Toronto: University of Toronto Press.

Holland, S.P. (2005). "Foreword: 'Home' is a four letter word." In *Black Queer Studies: A Critical Anthology,* ed. E.P. Johnson and M.G. Henderson, ix–xiii. Durham, NC: Duke University Press.

Howard, G.R. (2006). *We can't teach what we don't know: White teachers, multiracial schools.* New York: Teachers College Press.

James, C.E., D. Este, W. Thomas-Bernard, A. Benjamin, L. Bethan, and T. Turner. (2010). *Race and well-being.* Halifax: Fernwood.

Johnson, M.A. (2012). "'To ensure that only suitable persons are sent': Screening Jamaican women for the West Indian Domestic Scheme." In *The Jamaican in the Canadian Experience,* ed. C. James and A. Davis, 36–53. Halifax: Fernwood.

Knochel, K.A., C.F. Croghan, R.P. Moone, and J.K. Quam. (2012). "Training, geography, and provision of aging services to lesbian, gay, bisexual, and transgender older adults." *Journal of Gerontological Social Work* 55 (5): 426–43. http://dx.doi.org/10.1080/01634372.2012.665158.

Ladson-Billings, G. (2009). "'Who you callin' nappy-headed?' A critical race theory look at the construction of black women." *Race, Ethnicity and Education* 12 (1): 87–99. http://dx.doi.org/10.1080/13613320802651012.

Larcher, A.A. (2012). "Black gay and bisexual men in Toronto: A snapshot of results from the MaBwana Black Men's Study." Retrieved from http://www.accho.ca/Portals/3/documents/resources/MaBwana_Factsheet_Snapshot_Oct2012.pdf.

LaSala, M.C. (2002). "Walls and bridges: How coupled gay men and lesbians manage their intergenerational relationships." *Journal of Marital and Family Therapy* 28 (3): 327–39. http://dx.doi.org/10.1111/j.1752-0606.2002.tb01190.x.

LeFrançois, B.A., R. Menzies, and G. Reaume, eds. (2013). *Mad matters: A critical reader in Canadian mad studies.* Toronto: Canadian Scholars' Press.

Lewis, G.B. (2003). "Black-white differences in attitudes toward homosexuality and gay rights." *Public Opinion Quarterly* 67 (1): 59–78. http://dx.doi.org/10.1086/346009.

Lewis, M.K., and I. Marshall. (2012). "Cultural complexities and conflict." In M.K. Lewis and I. Marshall, *LGBT Psychology: Research Perspectives and People of African Descent,* 119–37. New York: Springer Science and Business Media. http://dx.doi.org/10.1007/978-1-4614-0565-8_7.

Longcrier, R. (2014). "Leading by example." Retrieved from http://www.manyvoices.org/blog/2014/12/leading-by-example/.

Lowe, L., and J. Clarke. (2009). "Learning about social work research through service-learning." *Journal of Community Engagement and Scholarship* 2 (1): 50–59. Retrieved from http://jces.ua.edu/learning-about-social-work-research-through-service-learning/.

Mahtani, M. (2001). "Representing minorities: Canadian media and minority identities." *Canadian Ethnic Studies* 33 (3): 99–133.

Many Voices. (2014a). "About." Retrieved from http://www.manyvoices.org/about/.

–. (2014b). "Black LGBT religious leaders: Black bodies matter." Retrieved from http://www.manyvoices.org/black-lgbt-religious-leaders/.

Massaquoi, N. (2004). "An African child becomes a black Canadian feminist: Oscillating identities in the black diaspora." *Canadian Women's Studies* 23 (2): 140–44.

McGoldrick, M. (1988). "Ethnicity and the family life cycle." In *The Changing Family Life Cycle: A Framework for Family Therapy,* 2nd ed., ed. B. Carter and M. McGoldrick, 69–90. New York: Gardner Press.

McIntyre, M., and C. McDonald. (2012). "The limitations of partial citizenship: Health care institutions underpinned with heteronormative ideals." *Advances in Nursing Science* 35 (2): 127–34. http://dx.doi.org/10.1097/ANS.0b013e31824fe6ca.

Mendes, E., ed. (1995). *Race discrimination: Law and practice*. Toronto: Carswell.

Mensah, J. (2002). *Black Canadians: History, experiences, social conditions*. Halifax: Fernwood.

Merton, R.K. (1938). "Social structure and anomie." *American Sociological Review* 3 (5): 672–82. http://dx.doi.org/10.2307/2084686.

Miller, S.J. (2011). "African-American lesbian identity management and identity development in the context of family and community." *Journal of Homosexuality* 58 (4): 547–63. http://dx.doi.org/10.1080/00918369.2011.556937.

Mink, T., and S. Twill. (2012). "Using service-learning to teach a social work policy course." *Journal of Community Engagement and Scholarship* 5 (1): 5–13. Retrieved from http://jces.ua.edu/using-service-learning-to-teach-a-social-work-policy-course/.

Moore, M. (2008). "Gendered power relations among women: A study of household decision making in black, lesbian stepfamilies." *American Sociological Review* 73 (2): 335–56. http://dx.doi.org/10.1177/000312240807300208.

–. (2010). "Articulating a politics of (multiple) identities." *Du Bois Review* 7 (2): 315–34. http://dx.doi.org/10.1017/S1742058X10000275.

–. (2011). *Invisible families: Gay identities, relationships, and motherhood among black women*. Los Angeles: University of California Press.

Mullaly, B. (2010). *Challenging oppression and confronting privilege*. 2nd ed. Don Mills, ON: Oxford University Press.

Mullings, D.V. (2012). "Racism in Canadian social policy." In *Canadian Social Policy*, 5th ed., ed. A. Westhues, 95–113. Kitchener, ON: Wilfrid Laurier University Press.

–. (2013). "Community service learning: A teaching tool to help students acknowledge their own racism." *Race Equality and Teaching* 32 (1): 15–21.

–. (2014). "The racial institutionalization of whiteness in contemporary Canadian public policy." In *Unveiling Whiteness in the 21st Century: Global Manifestations*, ed. V. Watson, D. Howard-Wagner, and L. Spanierman, 115–40. New York: Lexington Books.

Mullings, D.V., and R. Mullings-Lewis. (2013). "How black mothers 'successfully' raise children in the 'hostile' Canadian climate." *Journal of the Motherhood Initiative for Research and Community Involvement* 4 (2): 105–19. Retrieved from http://jarm.journals.yorku.ca/index.php/jarm/article/view/37832.

Myers-Lipton, S.J. (1996). "Effect of a comprehensive service-learning program on college students' level of modern racism." *Michigan Journal of Community Service Learning* 3 (1): 44–54. Retrieved from http://quod.lib.umich.edu/m/mjcsl/3239521.0003.105/1.

Neckoway, R., K. Brownlee, and B. Castellan. (2007). "Is attachment theory consistent with Aboriginal parenting realities?" *First Peoples Child and Family Review* 3 (2): 65–74. Retrieved from http://journals.sfu.ca/fpcfr/index.php/FPCFR/article/view/43.

Palmer, G. (2013). "Five lessons I've learned as a black Christian LGBT ally." Retrieved from http://www.truthwinsout.org/opinion/2013/03/34022/.

Parsons, T. (1991). *The social system*. London: Routledge.

Peffley, M., J. Hurwitz, and P.M. Sniderman. (1997). "Racial stereotypes and whites' political views of blacks in the context of welfare and crime." *American Journal of Political Science* 41 (1): 30–60. http://dx.doi.org/10.2307/2111708.

Piaget, J., and D. Play. (1962). *Imitation in childhood*. New York: Norton.

Razack, N. (1999). "Anti-discriminatory practice: Pedagogical struggles and challenges." *British Journal of Social Work* 29 (2): 231–50. http://dx.doi.org/10.1093/oxfordjournals.bjsw.a011444.

Robinson, R.K. (2007). "Uncovering covering." *Northwestern University Law Review* 101 (4): 1809–49.

Schiele, J.H. (1996). "Afrocentricity: An emerging paradigm in social work practice." *Social Work* 41 (3): 284–94.

Shaikh, S.S. (2012). "Antiracist feminist activism in women's social service organizations: A review of the literature." *Intersectionalities: A Global Journal of Social Work Analysis, Research, Polity, and Practice* 1: 70–92. Retrieved from http://journals.library.mun.ca/ojs/index.php/IJ/article/view/351.

Sinclair, R. (2004). "Aboriginal social work education in Canada: Decolonizing pedagogy for the seventh generation." *First Peoples Child and Family Review* 1 (1): 49–62. Retrieved from http://journals.sfu.ca/fpcfr/index.php/FPCFR/article/view/10.

Sinding, C., L. Barnoff, and P. Grassau. (2004). "Homophobia and heterosexism in cancer care: The experiences of lesbians." *Canadian Journal of Nursing Research* 36 (4): 170–88. Retrieved from http://ingentaconnect.com/content/mcgill/cjnr/2004/00000036/00000004.

Sitter, K.C. (2012). "Participatory video: Toward a method, advocacy and voice (MAV) framework." *Intercultural Education* 23 (6): 541–54. http://dx.doi.org/10.1080/14675986.2012.746842.

Skinner, B.F. (1953). *Science and human behavior*. New York: Simon and Schuster.

Spencer, E.B. (2006). "Spiritual politics: Politicizing the black church tradition in anti-colonial praxis." In *Anti-colonialism and Education: The Politics of Resistance*, ed. G.J.S. Dei and A. Kempf, 107–27. Rotterdam: Sense.

Stevenson, J. (2014). "Prominent Detroit minister 'comes out' as ally: Nabors rejects black pastors' bigotry." Retrieved from http://www.pridesource.com/article.html?article=65449.

Sussman, T., M. Churchill, S. Brotman, L. Chamberland, A. Daley, J. Dumas, et al. (2012). "Identifying barriers, developing solutions: Addressing the health and social needs of gay, lesbian, bisexual and transgender older adults who reside in long-term care homes." Montreal, Canadian Institutes of Health Research. Retrieved from http://www.yorku.ca/lgbthome/documents/olderlgbtinltchomes.pdf.

Swan, T.A. (2002). "Coming out and self-disclosure: Exploring the pedagogical significance in teaching social work students about homophobia and heterosexism." *Canadian Social Work Review* 19 (1): 5–23. Retrieved from http://www.jstor.org/stable/41669744.

Titone, C. (1998). "Educating the white teacher as ally." In *White Reign: Deploying Whiteness in America*, ed. J.L. Kincheloe, S.R. Steinberg, N.M. Rodriguez, and R.E. Chennault, 159–75. New York: St. Martin's Press.

Van der Meide, W. (2001). "The intersection of sexual orientation and race: Considering the experiences of lesbian, gay, bisexual, transgendered ('GLBT') people of color and two-spirited people." Ottawa, Egale Canada. Retrieved from http://arc-international.net/wp-content/uploads/2011/08/egale-wcar-report-e.pdf.

Von Bertalanffy, L. (1968). *General systems theory*. New York: George Braziller.

Walcott, R. (2009). "Reconstructing manhood; Or, the drag of black masculinity." *Small Axe: A Caribbean Journal of Criticism* 13 (1): 75–89. http://dx.doi.org/10.1215/07990537-2008-007.

Wane, N.J. (2012). "Status of black women in the academy on International Women's Day." Retrieved from http://www.ideas-idees.ca/blog/status-black-women-academy-international-womens-day.

Ward, E.G. (2005). "Homophobia, hypermasculinity and the US black church." *Culture, Health and Sexuality* 7 (5): 493–504. http://dx.doi.org/10.1080/13691050500151248.

Wong, Y.L.R., and J. Vinsky. (2009). "Speaking from the margins: A critical reflection on the 'spiritual-but-not-religious' discourse in social work." *British Journal of Social Work* 39 (7): 1343–59. http://dx.doi.org/10.1093/bjsw/bcn032.

12

Queering Space in Social Work: How Simcoe County Has Moved from Queerful to Queerious

JAN YORKE, LIGAYA BYRCH, MARLENE HAM, MATTHEW CRAGGS, AND TANYA SHUTE

Rural and northern experiences for lesbian, gay, bisexual, transgender, or queer (LGBTQ) individuals are frequently isolating and fraught with abuse, sexual prejudice, sexual stigma, and homonegativity that can parallel the stress experienced by other non-dominant groups (Dermer, Smith, and Barto, 2010; Kosciw and Diaz, 2006). Prevailing social forces, including government and educational and other institutions in rural and northern Canada, may not champion the needs of LGBTQ individuals. Small towns may not have the resources to support advocacy for LGBTQ funding and policy priorities. In addition, rural isolation, lack of safety, limited transportation, or fear of the consequences of being "visible" could play a role in individual needs not being met. Finding ways to bring the concerns and needs of rural and northern LGBTQ communities to the forefront can be challenging and may take efforts on a number of fronts. Queering social work has an important role to play in this regard.

This chapter represents the views of a collective of faculty, social work students, and community members. It is guided by a discussion of queer theory and a critique of the relationship between queerness and the social work profession. LGBTQ-friendly curriculum, field placements, and spaces will be explored. The discussion employs research, examples, and critical analysis to scrutinize the barriers, opportunities, and contexts that can face LGBTQ communities. The examples draw on rural and northern Canada, specifically Simcoe County, which lies a hundred kilometres north of Toronto, in central Ontario. In this case, rural Ontario is defined as including both agricultural zones and small towns, and as being situated a hundred to a thousand kilometres from a large urban centre such as Toronto, London, or Ottawa.

Through an examination of LGBTQ history in Simcoe County and the use of a community engagement model (Ham and Byrch, 2012), the discussion will show how local social work students and academics have used community-level knowledge for LGBTQ policy development and implementation, transforming "queerful" (fearful of queers) to "queerious" (curious about queers). If queerness is to be legitimized, dialogue needs to occur across community, academia, and social service environments. Opportunities for queering social work education in rural and northern Ontario accompany action-oriented recommendations for prioritizing LGBTQ issues. Discussions of the theoretical concepts that underpin these recommendations are an important place to start.

Theoretical Framework and Instruments of Oppression

Queer theory emerged in institutional academic settings that challenged dominant and pervasive notions regarding sexuality and gender. Queer theorists challenge three assumptions: first, that LGBTQ individuals wish to assimilate into the unchanged status quo; second, that all LGBTQ people share an essential character/identity among themselves; and third, that sexuality is a private issue with no place in the public realm (Slagle, 2006). Queer theory effectively reclaims a subjugated term, with the intent to make fluid sexual/gendered practices (Gibson, 2010). Furthermore, it moves away from early lesbian feminist notions of sexual identity, which had mostly been couched in terms of correcting a misogynist ideology that ignored lesbians. Queer theory escapes the limitations of the binary discursive of early gay liberation and of lesbian feminist liberation (Jagose, 1996), evolving from a single hegemony to one of sexual pluralism (Altman, 1993; Hawkes, 1996). As Foucault (1990) suggests, sexual categorization of individuals follows from and reinforces power relations, situated within a particular historical and cultural context (Gibson, 2010).

The fluidity of "queer" challenges the binary notion of gender and suggests a broader sexual identity (Gorman-Murray, Pini, and Bryant, 2013). Gender and sexuality are constructed through a combination of thought, physical and sensual activities, language, and symbolic systems or images, all of which are part of a social process (Kinsman, 1996).

Heteronormativity, homophobia, transphobia, and cisgenderism are instruments of oppression used against LGBTQ people in Canada. Hillock (2012) describes oppression as a complex constellation of power, privilege, and domination that occurs across and between contexts and that contributes to various kinds of inequality. Understanding these forces is vital for the discussion in this chapter. Heteronormativity (heterosexuality as the norm) is one example of a common form of oppression experienced by LBGTQ individuals (Lundy, 2008). It is socially pervasive and it enables homophobia, which threatens personal safety for the LGBTQ community. Homophobia is "the irrational fear, hatred, and intolerance of gay men and lesbian women based on myths and stereotypes" (Lundy, 2008, p. 82).

Homophobia is similar to transphobia, which is the feeling of unease, or even revulsion, toward those who present with transgendered (trans) expressions of gender identity (Lombardi, 2009). Traditional attitudes regarding biological sex and social gender are the basis of transphobic beliefs and behaviours. Transphobic individuals voice concerns about the appearance of trans people and see them as being disruptive and threatening, which is used as grounds for discrimination (Lombardi, 2009).

Finally, cisgenderism, as an instrument of oppression, has historically described individuals who are non-transgendered. Current use of the term moves beyond that notion to describe the disenfranchisement of individuals to claim their own gender designations (Blumer, Ansara, and Watson, 2013). Together, all of these instruments effectively oppress LGBTQ people, and thus social work must reflect upon them in class discussions, curriculum development, and the creation of safe queer space.

Queerness in Canadian Rural and Northern Communities

Social work strategies for rural and northern communities require evidence-based practices. Rainbow Health notes that there is a limited amount of Canadian academic research on LGBTQ issues (Rainbow Health Ontario, 2013), and few peer-reviewed journal articles or research projects examine LGBTQ needs and concerns in rural and northern Canadian communities (Byrch, 2000; Kennedy, 2010; Marple, 2005; Murray, 1999). Social work scholars in Australia (Fish, 2012; Napier and George, 2001; Willis, 2007; Willis, Ward, and Fish, 2011), the United Kingdom (Fairtlough, Bernard, Fletcher, and Ahmet, 2013), and the United States (Fredriksen-Goldsen, Woodford, Luke, and Gutiérrez, 2011; Sperling, 2010) have started to write about LGBTQ issues and their impact on the social work profession. However, little has been heard from Canadian scholars (Hillock, 2012; Mulé, 2005, 2006). Nonetheless, it is important to examine the literature on urban versus rural LGBTQ experiences and the implications for social work to facilitate change.

The current discourse regarding LGBTQ people in Canada is largely urban focused. Wienke and Hill (2013) note that gay and lesbian research studies have historically concentrated on urban settings. Johnson (2007) explains that there is a "widely cherished belief" (p. 5) that LGBTQ people belong in urban areas and do not belong in rural areas. Cities typically have greater diversity, and LGBTQ people tend to gravitate to them, which naturalizes the urban space as a gay haven of open expression that is free of negative consequences (Gorman-Murray et al., 2013; Johnson, 2007). Alternatively, the rural context is presented as a place where LGBTQ people are silenced and hidden (Gorman-Murray et al., 2013).

Some American research suggests that rural communities are less socially tolerant than their urban counterparts of queer folk. They are less likely to uphold the rights of LGBTQ individuals and families with regard to housing, employment discrimination, and human rights violations such as inequitable parenting laws (Eldridge, Mack, and Swank, 2006; Leedy and Connolly, 2007; Watkins and Jacoby, 2007). The lack of acceptance and support in urban or rural settings can often result in LGBTQ people being harmed, mistreated, and oppressed, particularly those who are immigrant refugees (Onishenko, 2013). Social norms and values in small rural towns may historically represent dominant, white, conservative, Judeo-Christian or other dogmatic religious assumptions that describe gender in binary terms (male or female) (Wilcox, 2006). LGBTQ individuals may leave small-town Ontario for these reasons, gravitating toward urban areas that are not dominated by these ideologies and can also provide privacy, acceptance, and "community" (Kennedy, 2010).

Conversely, literature also suggests that rural and northern communities are populated by LGBTQ individuals who may be as healthy and happy, if not more so, than some of their urban counterparts (Wienke and Hill, 2013). Gray (2009) suggests that rural queer life is not deficient or less than urban queer life: rather, it is different. Rural LGBTQ people develop coping strategies related to being public (i.e., they avoid cities and find acceptance through community involvement), they create space and community in their own rural areas, or they remain private for safety purposes (Gorman-Murray et al., 2013). For example, if they have difficulty finding adequate resources and community spaces for meeting and organizing, they locate alternative means for collaborating. This is where it becomes important to understand the cultural differences in rural spaces. Specific ethnic or cultural groups in the rural and northern context might actually be more historically open than other groups and contexts to sexual diversity. For example, First Nations' communities often celebrate the importance of two-spirited people to traditional and cultural ways of life (Brotman, Ryan, Jalbert, and Rowe, 2002). Various religious denominations, cultural groups, and ethnic communities have also welcomed LGBTQ individuals into their services and gatherings, performing same-sex marriages and providing space and resources to gay-straight alliances (GSAs), community-funded non-profit services, and youth groups.

In Ontario, LGBTQ individuals may move to small northern or rural communities for employment or education because of the regional health care, federal, and provincial public-sector departments or educational institutions (colleges and universities) placed there. Government-funded and public-sector services are obliged to be inclusive, directed by policy and employment standards (Ministry of Labour, n.d.). These may provide fertile ground for the increased LGBTQ awareness to which Marple (2005) refers.

Marple contends that the generalist approach required in small rural and northern agencies and institutions can contribute to a better understanding among non-queer professionals of how to meet the needs of LGBTQ individuals. This strategy could apply in many ways to social work agencies and institutions in small, rural, or northern communities, including social work educational institutions. A critique of the social work profession will be used to help guide this discussion of queering social work education in the rural context.

Social Work and Queerness

As Burdge (2007) acknowledges, queer theory is consistent with social work values and ethics. To support her point, she quotes the National Association of Social Workers (NASW): "Social workers must be able to appreciate ambiguous terminology – along with ambiguous genders" (p. 243). The "Code of Ethics" of the Canadian Association of Social Workers (CASW, 2005) uses the Canadian Human Rights Act (1985) and the Ontario Human Rights Code (1990) to define discrimination, respect the inherent dignity of the individual, and uphold "each person's right to self-determination, consistent with that person's capacity and with the rights of others" (CASW, 2005, p. 4). However, social work is not immune to the larger societal or essentialist constructs that define individual behaviour, physical ways of being, policy, practice, research, and education (McPhail, 2004). The profession's role in the disenfranchisement of Canada's First Nations people through involvement in the well-known sixties scoop attests to this (Blackstock, 2009).

Despite mandates such as those of the Ontario College of Social Workers, the Social Service Workers "Code of Ethics and Standards of Practice

Handbook" (2011), and the Canadian Association of Social Workers "Code of Ethics" (CASW, 2005), social workers produce and re-produce binary definitions of sexuality and gender, reinforce myths and stereotypes, ignore queer issues in practice, curricula, and field placements, and use language that is non-inclusive (Chinell, 2011; MacKinnon, 2011). These issues are also problematic and difficult to address in the rural and northern context. The literature suggests that social work tends to make sense of oppression through a heterosexist model and has thus packaged the notions of lesbian, gay, and bisexual as fixed types, with needs often defined around perceived sexuality (Gibson, 2010; MacKinnon, 2011). Burdge (2007) recommends that social work practice should abandon the dichotomous character of gender in favour of gender pluralism and should empower people to take control of the language representing them, to make sense of their lived experience, and to define themselves, particularly when no definition exists. Queering social work relies on its capacity to respond to the notion of gender and sexual pluralism. As MacKinnon (2011) argues, even social work's use of anti-oppressive theory and practice is limiting in that this method of theorizing the social excludes the nuances of LGBTQ, human sexuality, and in particular, the experience of trans individuals.

The evidence shows that homophobia and transphobia are kept in place by structures of heterosexism and cisgenderism, including social work's conformist practices, which have had dire consequences for the LGBTQ community (Gibson, 2010; MacKinnon, 2011; Schilt and Westbrook, 2009). Trauma, mental health, illness, substance use, violence, harassment, and exclusion continue to frame the lived experience of being an LGBTQ person. Issues such as acceptance, aging communities, family planning, and the pathologization of trans communities are often ignored and are taking their toll (Altman, 1993; Burdge, 2007; Lee and Quam, 2013; Lev, 2004). On the periphery are public organizations and institutions that have a responsibility to engage and support LGBTQ communities, yet individuals continue to struggle to find services that meet their needs (Ham and Byrch, 2012). These struggles are complicated by issues of race, class, gender, ability, and language.

The social work profession too often remains in a queerful place. "Queerful" refers to the fearfulness that helps to perpetuate privacy, invisibility, and confinement to closed systems within the broader dominant heterosexual community and in LGBTQ communities themselves (Ham and Byrch, 2012). The challenge for social work is to develop strategies toward the "queerious," or curiosity regarding queers, which refers to the notions of public discourse, visibility, and open, integrated, and overlapping systems within and between heterosexual and LGBTQ systems and communities (Ham and Byrch, 2012). LGBTQ individuals and their needs become visible or remain invisible, depending on how safe and supported they may feel (Daley, 2010; Schneider and Dimito, 2008). These ideas draw on the notion of open and closed systems, which refers to the capacity that local hard and soft infrastructures (i.e., social networks and institutions) have or create to serve the needs of everyone who lives in a given community. In queerful places, LGBTQ needs may be disregarded or not "privileged" in terms of priority, or they may be purposely ignored in the dominant heterosexual discourse. Kinsman (1996) describes heterosexual privilege as "a social practice through which heterosexuals empower themselves through daily participation in the relations of heterosexual hegemony" (p. 9). In rural and northern queer and heterosexual communities, the movement from queerful to queerious (from private to public and closed to open systems) challenges the social work profession to develop action-focused strategies. Laurentian University is one example of an academic institution that has endeavoured to queer social work education through collaborating with the queer community and advocating for queer scholarship opportunities.

Social Work Education in Our Rural Context

Laurentian University has a small satellite campus in Barrie, a Simcoe County town, which has operated out of a community college for over twelve years. At this campus, the university's social work school has offered a bachelor of social work (BSW) for three years. It currently serves over two hundred full and part-time students with a forty-five-student annual enrollment rate. Offered by a tricultural university (French, First Nations, and English), the BSW "is concerned with structural and individual change, and is committed to the eradication of social inequalities based on race, ethnicity, language, religion, marital status, gender, sexual orientation, age, abilities, economic status, political affiliation, national ancestry, and all other forms of oppression" (Laurentian University, 2013a). The school employs a structural social work perspective, grounded in critical theory, situated in a social context rather than the notion of individual deficits (Carniol, 2010; Mullaly, 2010). In our opinion, this mandate makes the Laurentian School of Social Work a prime location for queer scholarship. Despite this, the student authors of this chapter determined that its curricula and field placement sites and acknowledgment of LGBTQ issues were limited. We believe that theoretical constructs alone cannot move the social work profession into the queerious.

Indeed, understanding the shift in social work education regarding LGBTQ awareness on a small rural campus requires an exploration of the community in which it is ensconced. Simcoe County, which is situated approximately one hour north of Toronto, consists of both urban and rural communities. Its population of 446,063 spans a vast geographical region encompassing 4,819.16 square kilometres (County of Simcoe, 2013). The largest town, Barrie, is centrally located and is surrounded by the small communities of Orillia, Midland, Penetanguishene, Collingwood, Wasaga Beach, and Innisfil, as well as broad rural townships.

In Simcoe County, the historical contribution of queer community organizing and practice has been a major factor in facilitating action and advocacy for queer scholarship at Laurentian University.

Case Study: Moving from Queerful to Queerious in Simcoe County

The Simcoe County LGBTQ Network, comprised of community members, health services, and community organizations across various sectors, was formed in 2009 to provide an opportunity for collaboration, relationship building, and open dialogue about the need for more formal services for LGBTQ residents. To work toward increasing the capacity of organizations and educational institutions to respond, *The Simcoe County LGBT Youth Needs Assessment Report* was written (Ham and Byrch, 2012). The two authors of this report, social work students and out lesbians living and working in Simcoe County, had been LGBTQ advocates for well over two decades. As social workers, they emphasized the importance of service user history (i.e., using techniques such as eco-maps and family histories) for accurate assessment, appropriate intervention, and reaching a full understanding of the depth of service users' experiences. To that end, the report drew on survey and focus group feedback from LGBTQ youth to identify their priorities with respect to needed services. As a result, the assessment was the largest of its kind in Simcoe County, with over 157 participants. As mentioned previously, the environment that gave rise to the development and acceptance of this report was created by decades of community activism.

Although the report indicated that 82 percent of organizations provided safe space, only 4 percent of youth who participated in the study had accessed a community organization to support them with LGBTQ-related issues. These results suggest a disconnect between an organizational perception of service provision specifically for queer individuals and the queer individuals' perception of service provision. The message that became clear was that social workers need to be more involved by taking the initiative when dealing with invisible LGBTQ communities.

As a result of the report, the Child Youth and Family Services Coalition-Simcoe County, affectionately known as the Coalition, passed a motion to support becoming more inclusive of those who identify as LGBTQ. A similar motion was presented at the Child and Adolescent Project Steering Committee of the local health planning body and was tabled at the North Simcoe Muskoka Local Health Integration Network (NSM LHIN) in May of 2013. Thus, relationships between social services and other publicly funded sectors (such as health, education, and government planning bodies) were gradually built over time, access was gained to key stakeholders, and advocacy for local LGBTQ issues was advanced.

Privilege and Legitimizing of LGBTQ Work in Simcoe County

Over the past four decades, the political landscape in rural Ontario has seen neoliberal shifts in policy and planning, which many people have resisted (Coulter, 2009; Smith, 2005). Moreover, three provincial acts have been passed into law, namely, the Excellent Care for All Act (ECFA, 2010); Bill 33, Toby's Act (Right to be Free from Discrimination and Harassment Because of Gender Identity or Gender Expression) (2012); and Bill 13, Accepting Schools Act (2012), an amendment to the Ontario Education Act. The ECFA was intended to ensure excellent health care for all, at the right time and in the right place. As a result, the Ministry of Health and Long-Term Care developed the Health Equity Impact Assessment (HEIA) tool in 2009–10 to advance the quality of and equity within health-care service design and delivery. In this tool, LGBTQ people are clearly identified as a marginalized population.

For LGBTQ residents of Simcoe County, the situation has improved over time. Current funding requirements, changes in the legislation previously discussed, and the evolving social climate seem to have helped them become more accepted. Both the Simcoe Muskoka District Health Unit and the NSM LHIN have engaged in training stakeholders, requiring all their planning groups to discuss how the social determinants of health affect marginalized and vulnerable populations and how to implement the HEIA tool. Bill 13 requires the Simcoe County District School Board (SCDSB) to address anti-bullying, including LGBTQ-specific bullying, and it has done so by inviting presentations of the LGBTQ needs assessment results and recommendations to superintendents and staff (Ham and Byrch, 2012). In addition, the SCDSB has supported the need for training on LGBTQ issues among special education workers and social workers. Late in 2014, it released a guidebook to help education professionals better support and work with trans-identified students (SCDSB, 2014). There has also been significant face-to-face training of professionals, and work continues to better serve LGBTQ students. The SCDSB guidebook made use of the needs assessment recommendations (Ham and Byrch, 2012), which also inform the work of the Simcoe County LGBTQ Network. The queering of social work therefore relies not just on theoretical reconstruction and analyses that identify the nuances of power, privilege, inclusion, and oppression, but also on community partnerships, collaboration, and finding viable ways to pursue change through scholarship and training of front-line social workers and researchers (Walls et al., 2009; Willis, 2007; Willis et al., 2011).

Queering Social Work Education

Social work curriculum is often a barometer of social conditions. Thus, comprehensive curriculum development involves presenting a full range of perspectives on material, including oppositional views and dialectical tensions. Critical curriculum development seeks to uncover privileged perspectives and tensions related to those who are marginalized by dominant interests (Giroux and McLaren, 1994; Levy, 2009). The outright omission of material that is directly relevant to queer experiences should be considered structural suffocation and dismissal, one of a range of strategies for "keeping gayness out of education" (Gilbert, 2006, p. 25). In contrast, queering social work curricula and learning environments would be designed to emphasize a queerious andragogy that privileges queer voices. This andragogy would also address and include the knowledge of all students/educators about matters important to and affecting diverse queer communities, families, groups, couples, and individuals, thereby transgressing the heteronormativity that is dominant in much mainstream social work discourse and curricula. This parallels social work education's explicit anti-oppressive orientation and the expectation that social work professionals will foster critical awareness of structural injustice and inequity (Lundy, 2008).

Students' Perspective

In 2012, the faculty at the Laurentian University School of Social Work in Barrie responded to students' advocacy for and requests to work in LGBTQ-centred community-based research, policy development, and knowledge sharing in their local communities. Ham and Byrch's (2012) report was one example of this advocacy. Indeed, the gradual shift toward privilege and legitimacy (queerful to queerious) on the Barrie campus was in some ways brokered through the student, community, and advocacy involvement of Ham and Byrch. Their activism and academic involvement provided access to support and acceptance for the recommendations of the needs assessment. Developing a partnership with the Laurentian University School of Social Work has also provided the local LGBTQ community with access to faculty allies, research, field practicums, and funding in an educational institution for LGBTQ-related issues. Through faculty-supervised practicums, students built on existing community development work, moved into community-engaged research with the local AIDS Committee, and even successfully published with faculty support. Faculty members further supported the students' work in knowledge transfer back into the curriculum by encouraging students to present their work and findings in applied research classrooms. Presentations of the LGBTQ youth needs assessment results were also incorporated into the contract objectives for one student's field placement practicum (Ham and Byrch, 2012).

Despite this, the student authors of this chapter encountered (and still encounter) queerful or even some heteronormative responses from faculty at Laurentian University and other universities. In some instances, faculty expected LGBTQ students to speak as experts on all aspects of queer material. Even when professors were queer themselves, they were not always comfortable with engaging students in LGBTQ theorizing. This may have arisen because they were not fully out in the workplace, were afraid for their own jobs, tenure, and promotion, or were not supported by members of the academic institution or the social work department. Perhaps it reflected a general reluctance among faculty and students to unpack their own homophobia/transphobia. One openly LGBTQ student author, taking distance courses from an out-of-province university, had an unfulfilling experience. This student developed a qualitative research project that asked her/his peers to share their experiences with discussion of LGBTQ topics in the classroom and curriculum. The students responded that the curriculum was void of queer content and said that if it were raised at all, it was through the comments shared by LGBTQ students who were out. Students also stated that they would benefit greatly from a course dedicated to LGBTQ learning and would welcome the opportunity to have greater LGBTQ-related content in all courses.

Faculty Perspective

As Laurentian University structural social work educators, concerned with the eradication of social inequality, the faculty agreed that all course texts must include content that is written from an emancipatory orientation. For many social work topics, Canadian-centred texts are limited and are rarely inclusive of rural and northern contexts (Chappell, 2014; Hicks, 2014; Turner and Turner, 2009). Most texts present queer communities as just one in a growing web of community interests for social policy consideration or merely as a dimension of pluralism (Lundy, 2008; Mullaly, 2010). One only hopes to find a text that does not reflect or reinforce white, heterosexual, male, middle-class dominance as well as an urban and geographically southern orientation. Texts can subordinate or use a reductionist approach to matters of identity, specifically related to the interaction of oppressions that First Nations, racialized, and sexual and gender groups already experience. This can result in significant social exclusion or invisibility, especially in northern and rural contexts (hooks, 1994).

Social work departments are complex and subject to a number of competing forces that can interfere with making LGBTQ content part of the dominant discourse in curriculum. To begin with, increased numbers of part-time faculty positions, including for queer theory scholars and advocates, should provide enough diversity of experience and knowledge in varied areas of interest to social work schools. Laurentian University has human resource policies that ensure gender, age, ability, and ethnic inclusivity in hiring qualified applicants (Laurentian University, 2013b). The reality, however, is that faculty and curricula in small, rural, or northern communities may not reflect this diversity, because of geography (limited access to scholars/tenure track positions dedicated to specific subject expertise), faculty association collective agreements regarding part-time seniority, and/or the degree of departmental collegial governance regarding hiring. As well, the subject expertise of any given faculty member may or may not be specifically applicable to all courses that he or she teaches. Regardless of their subject expertise, faculty (especially part-time) are expected to be "janes/jacks-of-all-trades," their flexibility allowing them to maintain sufficient tenuous employment (Boesenberg, 2014; Canaan and Shumar, 2008; Rajagopal and Farr, 1992).

Having fewer tenured faculty members in social work departments means fewer academic resources dedicated to advocacy and scholarly research with and for marginalized groups, LGBTQ being one example. Queer part-time faculty may not have input to the internal department curricula design, and neither they nor any part-time faculty are paid to participate on committees. Unless full-time faculty, accreditation standards, and professional associations advocate for queer theory, in course design or in the development of electives, it can remain on the periphery.

Heteronormative power structures and priorities (publishers, university administrations, and corporate funders) may prevail in decisions about the distribution of resources across the educational institution, using a rationale of austerity and a neo-liberal paradigm to make efficiencies (Boesenberg, 2014; Bauder, 2006; Canaan and Shumar, 2008; Coulter, 2009; Giroux, 2002; Smith, 2005). The number and focus of elective courses may be limited (to assure fuller classes), so unless the majority of students prioritize or choose LGBTQ issues as important, they may not emerge in a stand-alone course. Satellite campuses appear to be designed to operate more efficiently than the parent institution, with even fewer resources or access to them. This can limit a social work school's ability to respond to LGBTQ community concerns as well.

The social work faculty at Laurentian's Barrie and Sudbury campuses are no strangers to some of these dynamics. They have, however, attempted to address LGBTQ issues in a number of ways across the undergraduate curriculum, such as developing independent material as addendum for course texts (that do not include this information); customizing student practicums; using critical analysis to review case studies; inviting guest speakers; reviewing peer-reviewed material in policy discussions; and encouraging students to write essays about LGBTQ issues that can be submitted for publishing. Currently, neither the Sudbury nor the Barrie campus offers a mandatory or elective credit course, specifically in social work, that is dedicated to LGBTQ concerns.

Finally, it is important to note that faculty, as members of the northern and rural communities in which they work, can also participate in local coalitions and planning networks. In an expansive, rural context, faculty need resources and infrastructure to participate in these networks. Government austerity is pervasive, driving community networks into survivor mode. This is affecting faculty's ability to participate as well as preventing the proliferation of LGBTQ services other than "disease-based AIDS organizations" (Mulé, 2005, p. 86).

Recommendations and Conclusions

Drawing on our experience in Simcoe County, we offer a number of recommendations. Social work will finally be queered when efforts are mounted on a number of fronts to make it safe and welcoming to LGBTQ students, when it builds alliances with LGBTQ agencies and community members, and when it encourages supportive environments in which LGBTQ scholars, researchers, and faculty can work. Indeed, collaborative community partnerships, advocacy, and visible support for the LGBTQ community, as described in this chapter and as we have found at Laurentian University, have made for a more queerious environment.

To begin with, rural and northern libraries in the community, educational institutions, and social work faculties need to populate their public and institutional collections with LGBTQ literature, including LGBTQ-authored peer-reviewed journals, articles/books, and research. LGBTQ material should be prominent in the curricula. In addition, social work schools should adopt affirmative action policies for LGBTQ student recruitment and for the hiring of LGBTQ faculty. Social work schools should seek out (or create) more placements, especially in social justice and community development settings that serve the LGBTQ community. Field instructors need to receive training and knowledge related to the service needs of the LGBTQ community. Field placement co-ordinators should ensure that all LGBTQ students have safe placements. Organizations that provide training and education, such as David Kelley Services (at Family Service Toronto), offer LGBTQ counselling internships for those faculty or students who wish to establish support for LGBTQ communities elsewhere. This is especially important for social work student placement opportunities in a rural or northern context. Such areas are typically under-serviced and under-served, and placements may not be available for students who wish to work with queer communities.

Schools of social work need to invest in relationships with local organizations through participation in social service planning bodies, for knowledge exchange and to encourage the full integration of anti-oppressive and queer practice and theories. Students could invite supportive faculty into these mutually beneficial academic-community partnerships. Faculty and field placement co-ordinators must work with organizations to ensure that the practicum environment will complement social justice and queer concepts and theories that students have learned in class. Otherwise, students could end up "checking their university knowledge at the door." Similarly, they must learn to put theory in the context of the lived experience of service recipients. Field supervisors should understand from field consultants (university faculty) that anti-oppressive practices regarding sexual or gender identity/orientation are important in social work field education, particularly in small, northern, and rural communities, where matters of anonymity and the pressure and obstacles to disclose may be challenging (Newman, Bogo, and Daley, 2008). This should occur especially in placements where students are not always supervised by masters of social work graduates.

Faculty should encourage discussions with students, and curricula should include sexuality, gender, queer theory, and related LGBTQ issues. Also, faculty have the academic freedom to address (or not address) topics as they see fit. Regardless of whether a faculty member is queer or not, recommendations that support LGBTQ theory and practice should be prioritized as part of course curriculum. Deans and school directors should advocate for resources for workshops and lifelong learning on LGBTQ issues and for the use of social workers who have knowledge and expertise in this area. Faculty can gain expertise as professors by acting as field supervisors for research placements. Social work researchers should put emphasis on community-based research skill development in their own research programs, using less jargon, less discussion of heteronormative theory, and more theory development grounded in LGBTQ community experiences (Filax, 2006). First-year social work students should be oriented by social work faculty and students in the upper years of the program about gender, sexuality, and oppression.

Especially in introductory social welfare and social work texts, publishers should be encouraged to include chapters that discuss LGBTQ issues as they relate to social policy, practice, scholarship, and research. Faculty should consider employing an addendum of custom courseware that includes LGTBQ scholars and scholarly works, and they should invite speakers from the local LGBTQ community to address their classes. It is recommended that future social work research should include a universal, national scan of LGBTQ content in texts and in social work courses. Publishers, scholars, and teaching faculty should use social policy statutes related to LGBTQ populations as examples for discussion and should invite queer scholars to contribute to textbook development to support queering social work curriculum.

Academia in general must advocate for the inclusion of LGBTQ issues in policy and other decision-making processes. It also needs to create safe out spaces (as at the University of Windsor, which designated its human rights office as a safe space) and to have an accountability structure that deals with complaints about spaces that are declared unsafe. Faculty must assist in the transformative process in their institutions, becoming allies in supporting the community to resist assimilation (Stein, 2013). Finally, the Canadian Association for Social Work Education can play a role in developing a national strategy for professional development regarding LGBTQ issues, which should be addressed in accreditation processes.

References

Altman, D. (1993). *Homosexual oppression and liberation.* New York: New York University Press.

Bauder, H. (2006). "The segmentation of academic labour: A Canadian example." *ACME: An International E-Journal for Critical Geographies* 4 (2): 228–39.

Bill 13, Accepting Schools Act. (2012). S.O. 2012, c. 5. Retrieved from http://ontla.on.ca/web/bills/bills_detail.do?locale=en&BillID=2549.

Bill 33, Toby's Act (Right to be Free from Discrimination and Harassment Because of Gender Identity or Gender Expression). (2012). S.O., c. 7. Retrieved from https://www.ontario.ca/laws/statute/S12007.

Blackstock, C. (2009). "The occasional evil of angels: Learning from the experiences of Aboriginal peoples with social work." *First Peoples Child and Family Review* 4 (1): 28–37.

Blumer, M.L.C., Y.G. Ansara, and C.M. Watson. (2013). "Cisgenderism in family therapy: How everyday clinical practices can delegitimize people's gender self-designations." *Journal of Family Psychotherapy* 24 (4): 267–85. http://dx.doi.org/10.1080/08975353.2013.849551.

Boesenberg, E. (2014). "Productive investments: Masculinities and economies in Fisher's *The Walls of Jericho*." In *Black intersectionalities: A critique for the 21st century,* ed. M. Michlin and J. Rocchi, 51–67. London: Oxford University Press.

Brotman, S., B. Ryan, Y. Jalbert, and B. Rowe. (2002). "Reclaiming space-regaining health: The healthcare experience of two-spirited people in Canada." *Journal of Gay and Lesbian Social Services* 14 (1): 67–87. http://dx.doi.org/10.1300/J041v14n01_04.

Burdge, B. (2007). "Bending gender, ending gender: Theoretical foundations for social work practice with the transgender community." *Social Work* 52 (3): 243–50. http://dx.doi.org/10.1093/sw/52.3.243.

Byrch, L. (2000). It's not just about HIV: An investigation of the relationship of HIV positive women to a northern Ontario AIDS service organization. Unpublished master's thesis, Laurentian University, Sudbury.

Canaan, J.E., and W. Shumar, eds. (2008). *Structure and agency in the neoliberal university.* New York: Routledge.

Canadian Human Rights Act. (1985). R.S.C., c. H-6.

Carniol, B. (2010). *Case critical: Social services and social justice in Canada.* Toronto: Between the Lines.

CASW (Canadian Association of Social Workers). (2005). "Code of ethics." Retrieved from http://www.casw-acts.ca/en/what-social-work/casw-code-ethics.

Chappell, R. (2014). *Social welfare in Canadian society.* Toronto: Nelson Education.

Chinell, J. (2011). "Three voices: Reflections on homophobia and heterosexism in social work education." *Social Work Education* 30 (7): 759–73. http://dx.doi.org/10.1080/02615479.2010.508088.

Coulter, K. (2009). "Women, poverty policy, and the production of neoliberal politics in Ontario, Canada." *Journal of Women, Politics and Policy* 30 (1): 23–45. http://dx.doi.org/10.1080/15544770802367788.

County of Simcoe. (2013). "Economic development: County demographics." Retrieved from http://edo.simcoe.ca/stats.

Daley, A. (2010). "Being recognized, accepted and affirmed: Self-disclosure of lesbian/queer sexuality within psychiatric and mental health service settings." *Social Work in Mental Health* 8 (4): 336–55. http://dx.doi.org/10.1080/15332980903158202.

Dermer, S.B., S.D. Smith, and K.K. Barto. (2010). "Identifying and correctly labelling sexual prejudice, discrimination and oppression." *Journal of Counseling and Development* 88 (3): 325–31. http://dx.doi.org/10.1002/j.1556-6678.2010.tb00029.x.

ECFA (Excellent Care for All Act). (2010). S.O., c. 14. Retrieved from https://www.ontario.ca/laws/statute/10e14.

Eldridge, V.L., L. Mack, and E. Swank. (2006). "Explaining comfort with homosexuality in rural America." *Journal of Homosexuality* 51 (2): 39–56. http://dx.doi.org/10.1300/J082v51n02_03.

Fairtlough, A., C. Bernard, J. Fletcher, and A. Ahmet. (2013). "Experiences of lesbian, gay and bisexual students on social work programmes: Developing a framework for educational practice." *British Journal of Social Work* 43 (3): 467–85. http://dx.doi.org/10.1093/bjsw/bcs001.

Filax, G. (2006). "Politicising action research through queer theory." *Educational Action Research* 14 (1): 139–45. http://dx.doi.org/10.1080/09650790600585632.

Fish, J. (2012). *Social work and lesbian, gay, bisexual and trans people: Making a difference.* Bristol, UK: Policy Press.

Foucault, M. (1990). *The history of sexuality.* Vol. 1, *An introduction.* Trans. R. Hurley. New York: Vintage. (Original work published 1978.)

Fredriksen-Goldsen, K.I., M.R. Woodford, K.P. Luke, and L. Gutiérrez. (2011). "Support of sexual orientation and gender identity content in social work education: Results from national surveys of U.S. and anglophone Canadian faculty." *Journal of Social Work Education* 47 (1): 19–35. http://dx.doi.org/10.5175/JSWE.2011.200900018.

Gibson, M. (2010). "Building research, building justice: Epistemology, social work and lesbian parents." *Canadian Social Work Review* 27 (2): 239–58.

Gilbert, J. (2006). "'Let us say yes to who or what turns up': Education as hospitality." *Journal of the Canadian Association for Curriculum Studies* 4 (1): 25–34.

Giroux, H. (2002). "The corporate war against higher education." *Workplace: A Journal for Academic Labor* 9: 103–17.

Giroux, H.A., and P. McLaren, eds. (1994). *Between borders: Pedagogy and the politics of cultural studies.* New York: Routledge.

Gorman-Murray, A., B. Pini, and L. Bryant. (2013). *Sexuality, rurality, and geography.* Lanham, MD: Rowman and Littlefield.

Gray, M. (2009). *Out in the country: Youth, media and queer visibility in rural America.* New York: New York University Press.

Ham, M., and L. Byrch. (2012). *The Simcoe County LGBT youth needs assessment report: Making it better today.* Barrie, ON: Byrch Consulting & Associates. Retrieved from http://www.rainbowhealthontario.ca/wp-content/uploads/woocommerce_uploads/2014/08/Making%20It%20Better%20Today%20Report.pdf.

Hawkes, G. (1996). *A sociology of sex and sexuality.* Philadelphia: Open University Press.

Hicks, S. (2014). *Social welfare in Canada: Understanding income security.* Toronto: Thompson Educational.

Hillock, S. (2012). "Conceptualizations and expressions of oppression: Gender differences." *Affilia* 20: 27–38.

hooks, b. (1994). *Teaching to transgress: Education as the practice of freedom.* New York: Routledge.

Jagose, A. (1996). *Queer theory: An introduction.* New York: New York University Press.

Johnson, C.R. (2007). "Homosexuals in unexpected places? An introduction." *American Studies* 48 (2): 5–8.

Kennedy, M. (2010). "Rural men, sexual identity and community." *Journal of Homosexuality* 57 (8): 1051–91. http://dx.doi.org/10.1080/00918369.2010.507421.

Kinsman, G. (1996). *The Regulation of Desire.* 2nd ed. Montreal: Black Rose Books.

Kosciw, J.G., and E.M. Diaz. (2006). *The 2005 National School Climate Survey: The experiences of lesbian, gay, bisexual, and transgender youth in our nation's schools.* New York: Gay, Lesbian, and Straight Education Network.

Laurentian University. (2013a). "Human resources and professional development policies." Retrieved from https://laurentian.ca/policies-accountability, February 2, 2013.

–. (2013b). "Social work." Retrieved from https://laurentian.ca/program/social-work.

Lee, M., and J.K. Quam. (2013). "Comparing supports for LGBT aging in rural versus urban areas." *Journal of Gerontological Social Work* 56 (2): 112–26. http://dx.doi.org/10.1080/01634372.2012.747580.

Leedy, G., and C. Connolly. (2007). "Out in the cowboy state: A look at lesbian and gay lives in Wyoming." *Journal of Gay and Lesbian Social Services* 19: 19–34.

Lev, A.I. (2004). *Transgender emergence: Guidelines for working with gender-variant people and their families.* Binghampton, NY: Hawthorne Clinical Press.

Levy, D.L. (2009). "Gay and lesbian identity development: An overview for social workers." *Journal of Human Behavior in the Social Environment* 19 (8): 978–93. http://dx.doi.org/10.1080/10911350903126866.

Lombardi, E. (2009). "Varieties of transgender/transsexual lives and their relationship with transphobia." *Journal of Homosexuality* 56 (8): 977–92. http://dx.doi.org/10.1080/00918360903275393.

Lundy, C. (2008). *Social work, social justice and human rights: Structural approach to practice.* Toronto: University of Toronto Press.

MacKinnon, K.V.R. (2011). "Thinking about queer theory in social work education: A pedagogical (in) query." *Canadian Social Work Review* 28 (1): 139–44.

Marple, L. (2005). "Rural queers? The loss of the rural in queer." *Canadian Women's Studies* 24 (2–3): 71–74.

McPhail, B.A. (2004). "Questioning gender and sexuality binaries: What queer theorists, transgendered individuals, and sex researchers can teach social work." *Journal of Gay and Lesbian Social Services* 17 (1): 3–21. http://dx.doi.org/10.1300/J041v17n01_02.

Ministry of Labour. (n.d.). "Employment standards." Retrieved from http://www.labour.gov.on.ca/english/es/, January 10, 2015.

Mulé, N.J. (2005). "Beyond words in health and well-being policy: 'Sexual orientation' – from inclusion to infusion." *Canadian Review of Social Policy* 55: 79–98.

–. (2006). "Equity vs. invisibility: Sexual orientation issues in social work ethics and curricula standards." *Social Work Education* 25 (6): 608–22. http://dx.doi.org/10.1080/02615470600833527.

Mullaly, R. (2010). *Challenging oppression and confronting privilege.* Toronto: Oxford University Press.

Murray, G. (1999). "Northern Ontario access to HIV care project." A report submitted to the Ontario HIV treatment network. Sudbury, ON.

Napier, L., and J. George. (2001). "Changing social work education in Australia." *Social Work Education* 20 (1): 75–87. http://dx.doi.org/10.1080/02615470020028382.

Newman, P.A., M. Bogo, and A. Daley. (2008). "Self-disclosure of sexual orientation in social work field education: Field instructor and lesbian and gay student perspectives." *Clinical Supervisor* 27 (2): 215–37. http://dx.doi.org/10.1080/07325220802487881.

Onishenko, D. (2013). "Equal rights discourse: A shifting terrain for sexual minority refugee claimants." Paper presented at Congress 2013, Canadian Association of Social Work Educators' Conference, June 3–6, Victoria, BC. http://congress2015.ca/sites/default/files/sites/default/uploads/programs/50-cssr-scer-2015-05-29.pdf.

Ontario College of Social Workers and Social Service Workers. (2011). "Code of ethics and standards of practice handbook." Retrieved from http://www.ocswssw.org/professional-practice/code-of-ethics/.

Rainbow Health Ontario. (2013). "About LGBT health research." Retrieved from http://www.rainbowhealthontario.ca/research/about.cfm, February 7, 2013.

Rajagopal, I., and W.D. Farr. (1992). "Hidden academics: The part-time faculty in Canada." *Higher Education* 24 (3): 317–31. http://dx.doi.org/10.1007/BF00128449.

SCDSB (Simcoe County District School Board). (2014). "Creating positive spaces for trans* students." Retrieved from http://scdsb.on.ca/About%20Us/About%20Us%20Documents/Equity_Inclusive_TransStudents.pdf.

Schilt, K., and L. Westbrook. (2009). "Doing gender, doing heteronormativity: 'Gender normals,' transgender people, and the social maintenance of heterosexuality." *Gender and Society* 23 (4): 440–64. http://dx.doi.org/10.1177/0891243209340034.

Schneider, M.S., and A. Dimito. (2008). "Educators' beliefs about raising lesbian, gay, bisexual, and transgender issues in the schools: The experience in Ontario, Canada." *Journal of LGBT Youth* 5 (4): 49–71. http://dx.doi.org/10.1080/19361650802223003.

Slagle, R.A. (2006). "Ferment in LGBT studies and queer theory: Personal ruminations on contested terrain." *Journal of Homosexuality* 52 (1–2): 309–28. http://dx.doi.org/10.1300/J082v52n01_13.

Smith, M. (2005). "Resisting and reinforcing neoliberalism: Lesbian and gay organizing at the federal and local levels in Canada." *Policy and Politics* 33 (1): 75–93. http://dx.doi.org/10.1332/0305573052708483.

Sperling, R.L. (2010). "Conspicuously absent: Lesbians in professional social work." *Affilia* 25 (3): 250–63. http://dx.doi.org/10.1177/0886109910375375.

Stein, M.R. (2015). "Size matters: Power and politics in the 1968 Philadelphia study of prison sexual violence." Sex talk @ York II. http://people.laps.yorku.ca/people.nsf/researcherprofile?readform&shortname=mrstein.

Turner, J.C., and F.J. Turner, eds. (2009). *Canadian social welfare*. Toronto: Pearson Education Canada.

Walls, N.E., R. Griffin, H. Arnold-Renicker, M. Burson, L. Johnston, N. Moorman, J. Nelsen, and E.C. Schutte. (2009). "Graduate social work students' learning journey about heterosexual privilege." *Journal of Social Work Education* 45 (2): 289–307. http://dx.doi.org/10.5175/JSWE.2009.200800004.

Watkins, F., and A. Jacoby. (2007). "Is the rural idyll bad for your health? Stigma and exclusion in the English countryside." *Health and Place* 13 (4): 851–64. http://dx.doi.org/10.1016/j.healthplace.2007.02.002.

Wienke, C., and G.J. Hill. (2013). "Does place of residence matter? Rural-urban differences and the wellbeing of gay men and lesbians." *Journal of Homosexuality* 60 (9): 1256–79. http://dx.doi.org/10.1080/00918369.2013.806166.

Wilcox, M.M. (2006). "Outlaws or in-laws? Queer theory, LGBT studies, and religious studies." *Journal of Homosexuality* 52 (1–2): 73–100. http://dx.doi.org/10.1300/J082v52n01_04.

Willis, P. (2007). "'Queer eye' for social work: Rethinking pedagogy and practice with same-sex attracted young people." *Australian Social Work* 60 (2): 181–96. http://dx.doi.org/10.1080/03124070701323816.

Willis, P., N. Ward, and J. Fish. (2011). "Searching for LGBT carers: Mapping a research agenda in social work and social care." *British Journal of Social Work* 41 (7): 1304–20. http://dx.doi.org/10.1093/bjsw/bcr114.

Conclusion

NICK J. MULÉ

The discipline of social work carries with it a high level of responsibility in that it is committed not only to working with people who are vulnerable and oppressed but also to improving their lives. Throughout its history, social work has advocated for and worked with a variety of marginalized service user populations, including LGBTQ people. In doing so, it has taken on an important social role and mandate to conduct research and to educate itself, students, and society in general regarding the critical work of improving the social lives of the marginalized. Formalized and focused education of this type tends to occur in academia. Although the literature does address LGBTQs in social work and in numerous disciplines, this book questions how we engage from epistemological, theoretical, policy, and programming with implications for practice perspectives. This is a reflexive process that addresses this important responsibility, which is specific to social work education.

In North America and globally, prevailing definitions of gender and sexuality have long marginalized LGBTQ communities and benefitted dominant groups. Regrettably, mainstream society's rigid notions of gender and sexuality have often been upheld by social work. However, LGBTQs and their allies in the discipline have challenged social work to shift from contributing to hegemonic oppression to critically contesting it so that the subjugation of a marginalized population can be interrogated and addressed via alternative perspectives and material changes. The contributors to this book have taken up this queering project.

Part 1: From Absence to Presence – Queers Positioning Themselves in Social Work

Part 1 of this anthology focuses on contextual perspectives that enable readers to deepen their understanding of the complexities that make up LGBTQ populations. These contexts include historical, theoretical, and andragogical/pedagogical issues that address LGBTQs in social work education. In addition, each chapter contributes unique perspectives from LGBTQ lenses and explores their implications for the study of social work and social work's obligations, in relation to these communities.

Chapter 1, Susan Hillock's wide-spanning history, highlights the challenges faced by LGBTQ-identified individuals, communities, and movements, many of which persist today, and all of which social work needs to be cognizant. In Chapter 2, Nick J. Mulé exposes the dominance of queer theory in sexuality studies and LGBT mainstreamed assimilationism in the broad LGBTQ movement. He offers a critical, progressive queer liberationist perspective that aligns with social work principles as a theoretical and practical alternative to queer theory. In Chapter 3, Jake Pyne critiques the dominance of queer theory and its implications for trans individuals. Like Chapter 2, this chapter calls for social work to provide a comprehensive theoretical curriculum that includes queer theory as well as other theories and perspectives. In Chapter 4, Susan Hillock moves beyond theory to reveal the extent to which formal recognition of LGBTQs is absent from numerous aspects of social work academe.

Given the diversity of LGBTQ communities and the history of their formations and development, social work education needs to consider such history when researching, teaching, and developing practice models. Furthermore, social work must learn how best to engage in theoretical discussions and debates that dialectically influence gender and sexuality studies and community activist discourses, both in terms of theory and practice approaches. That is, can a commitment to the queering project assist to address queer issues in these numerous aspects of the social work discipline? This book invites the profession to critically think about and take action regarding these issues.

Part 2: Coming Out and the Academic Closet – Rainbow Narratives

Through the act of coming out, the contributors in Part 2 of this volume personify a particularly powerful stimulus that has propelled the LGBTQ movement forward, as they both stake out their queer presence in social work and, importantly, confront and challenge social work academe to be more reflective and responsive. The issues they raise include the intersectionalities between feminism and queer perspectives; the implications of heterosexist curriculum for social work students; the intersections of race, religion, and gender; and the forms of misogyny that particularly target trans women. Their chapters deal specifically with intersectional subjective experiences and are nuanced in their analyses regarding the highly sensitive approach that social work education needs to take to address such concerns. Queer voices on being queer in social work academic settings, whether as students, faculty, or administrators, provide powerful narratives and messages that can influence the future queering of social work education.

In Chapter 5, Norma Jean Profitt and Brenda Richard provide a historic overview of social work education's evolution, in which they share their experiences as feminists. They reflect on a time when feminist thought was first emerging in academia and discuss subsequent queer studies and the challenges they had, and have continued, to face. In Chapter 6, Karolyn Martin and Robyn Lippett share their insightful experiences, as undergraduate social work students, of being taught a curriculum that they deconstruct as heterosexist. They offer suggestions on how to queer the curriculum for the benefit of all students and the field in general. In Chapter 7, Maryam Khan challenges heterosexist, religious, sexist, and to some extent, racist stereotypes in the academy. She outlines the problematics of stigma-based normative thinking about religion, sexuality, and spirituality in social work academic settings. Such stigmatization is also taken up by Jade Pichette in Chapter 8, with regard to the misogyny that is directed at trans women, in both social work academe and the field.

First-person narratives play an invaluable role in informing the discipline of subjective experiences. How can social work education be cognizant of the importance of queer perspectives and resist silencing such views? What role can it play in providing spaces for queer voices? How can we learn from these experiences and use these authors' lessons to inform social work theory, andragogy, and practice?

Part 3: The Queering Project – Gender and Sexual Diversity in Social Work Education

Part 3 focuses on the project of queering social work academe. The project begins with questioning the current state of Canadian social work academia and then urges it to rise to a higher level of effective responsiveness related to LGBTQ issues. In the true sense of critically pursuing the queering project, the contributors in Part 3 offer recommendations on ways to queer social work education that hold instructors accountable to the principles and standards of practice of the discipline. Furthermore, these chapters call for a sensitivity that both reflects the diversity of LGBTQ communities and strengthens the profession's role in working with them.

In Chapter 9, Shelley L. Craig, Lauren B. McInroy, and Christopher Doiron map the climate of BSW and MSW English-language social work programs in Canada, detailing a 2012 study that revealed the persistence of homophobia and transphobia among social work faculty. Faculty were unfamiliar with non-discrimination policies, LGBTQ topics were underrepresented in the curriculum, and both students and faculty were uncomfortable with LGBTQ identities. In Chapter 10, Becky Idems discusses and challenges both theory and ethics, arguing for a more progressive and diversified approach to the issue of relationships. She challenges the neo-liberal implications of competencies by highlighting a few ethical principles of polyamorous relationships and how they can contribute to the queering of social work education. Issues relating to age, race, and sexuality are explored in Chapter 11 by Delores V. Mullings, who looks at the challenges and opportunities for older black queer adults. She presents a community services learning approach as a method to queer social work education. In Chapter 12, Jan Yorke, Ligaya Byrch, Marlene Ham, Matthew Craggs, and Tanya Shute provide a community development trajectory on embracing LGBTQs in a rural setting involving social work academia and the community. In all these chapters, the authors provide practical recommendations on how to queer social work education.

The queering project is a challenging one, involving as it does the dismantling of heterosexism, cisgenderism, and homo-, bi-, and transphobia in the social work discipline. Thus, the themes of a challenge and the act of challenging run through this book, reflecting the extent to which social work education needs to go to address both LGBTQ issues and their diversity and complexity. As students, faculty, and administrators, the contributors to this volume represent such diversity within social work academe, and they provide entry points for readers of all kinds to consider how social work education could be queered. How can social work academe rectify past inactivity and oppression related to LGBTQ issues, service users, faculty, and students? In what ways can social work education engage in the exploration of the complex realities of LGBTQ people? In addition, to meet a queer project mandate, can social work education commit itself to staying current regarding LGBTQ issues?

Given the histories of social work as a profession and of LGBTQ movements and communities, a book of this nature – one that looks specifically at social work education and how it addresses queer issues – is long overdue. The first of its kind in North America, this anthology examines an issue that, to date, has been minimally considered. The diverse issues, needs, and concerns put forth in nuanced and insightful ways by the contributors to this volume paint a picture of the current challenges that face the social work discipline. In recognizing that the queering project is an ongoing endeavour that requires us to stay vigilant and to engage in ensuring that social work academe provides a more inclusive and comprehensive education, these chapters provide us with ways of moving forward. In so doing, they envision a social work education that strengthens its principles and standards of practice so that social work with LGBTQs is conducted in accessible, equitable, ethical, and sensitive ways. Effective education on these important issues will produce more informed and responsive social workers and ultimately a more sensitized and relevant profession. We picture teaching/learning endeavours where homo-, bi-, intersex-, and transphobia, cisgenderism, and heterosexism are critically, systematically, and systemically interrogated, dismantled, and transformed. Correspondingly, we hope that this book begins to motivate the profession to take on the queering project in social work education by contributing relevant and valuable knowledge, insight, and experience on social work with LGBTQ people and communities.

Contributors

LIGAYA BYRCH (BA, MA, CHE, MSW), an Ontario LGBTQ organizer, was named "Woman of the Year" by Windsor's Lesbian/Gay Community Council, has hosted a community radio program called LesBiQ Airwaves, completed a thesis on HIV-positive women in northeastern Ontario, and most recently co-wrote *The Simcoe County LGBT Youth Needs Assessment Report: Making It Better Today*. She works for the North Simcoe Muskoka Local Health Integration Network as the senior manager for health system integration.

MATTHEW CRAGGS (BSW, MSW, RSW) completed his fourth-year BSW practicum working with a community-based research team, organized by the AIDS Committee of Simcoe County, exploring rural and urban gay and MSM health in Simcoe County and Muskoka. His MSW major research focused on the experiences of rural queer youth in Ontario. He currently practises social work in Toronto.

SHELLEY L. CRAIG (PhD, RSW, LCSW) is an associate professor at the Factor-Inwentash Faculty of Social Work at the University of Toronto. Recognized with the 2015 "Inspirational Social Work Leader" award by the Ontario Association of Social Workers, she publishes extensively on community-based interventions for sexual and gender minority youth, on the effects of online and offline media on this population, and on affirmative social work education.

CHRISTOPHER DOIRON (BSc, MSW, RSW) completed a research practicum during his MSW program at the Factor-Inwentash Faculty of Social Work at the University of Toronto. Currently, he is a family therapist at Catholic Family Services Bureau in Charlottetown, Prince Edward Island. His research interests include sexual and gender minority youth populations, male body image, and knowledge translation relating to social work.

MARLENE HAM (BSW) has worked as a community organizer and advocate. In 2001, she joined the Toronto Women's Bathhouse Committee and was co-chair of the LGBTQ Youth Line from 2003 to 2007. In Simcoe County, where she lives, she has been instrumental in queer capacity building. In 2012, she co-authored *The Simcoe County LGBT Youth Needs Assessment Report: Making It Better Today*, and she has enhanced local knowledge on queer issues. She has contributed her time to a local research team to explore rural and urban gay and MSM (men who have sex with men) health, and she coordinated the Simcoe County LGBTQ Network from 2012 to 2015. In 2015, Marlene accepted the position of provincial coordinator for the Ontario Association of Interval & Transition Houses, where she currently works.

SUSAN HILLOCK (BA, BSW, MEd, PhD) is an associate professor of social work at Trent University, in Peterborough, Ontario. She has twenty-five years of clinical social work practice and over seventeen years of undergraduate and graduate teaching experience. She teaches anti-oppressive and critical theory and practice (queer theory, social justice/change, intimate partner violence, feminism, structural social work, human rights, anti-racism, community development/organization, family practice, and diversability) at the undergraduate and graduate levels.

BECKY IDEMS (BA, Diploma in Counselling, MSW, PhD candidate) has practised in a variety of settings since 2001, including rape crisis centres, homeless shelters, supportive housing providers, and queer community organizations. She is currently a doctoral candidate at McMaster University. Her research focuses on challenging the regulatory violences of post-secondary education and social work practice in neo-liberal contexts, and on centring marginal voices in practice and the classroom.

MARYAM KHAN (BSW, MSW, PhD candidate) has over ten years of clinical experience in mental health and addictions, working with queer youth, women, and homeless and street-involved youth. Her research interests include social policy and analyses, race and racialization, sex work, Islam and sexual diversity, intersectional identities and identity politics, social policy and access to health care for racialized trans and queer persons, cultural imperialism and privilege, gender and sexuality, anti-colonial thought, and decolonization. Maryam has also taught part-time in the social work departments at Centennial College, Seneca College, and York University.

ROBYN LIPPETT (BA, BSW) holds an Honours English BA from Acadia University and a BSW from St. Thomas University. She is a project co-ordinator at Partners for Youth Inc., where she co-ordinates the New Brunswick Youth in Care Network. She has worked with LGBTQ youth around issues of bullying and relationship violence. Her current interests include food justice and permanency for LGBTQ youth in care.

KAROLYN MARTIN (BA, BSW, MA) holds a BA and a BSW, both from St. Thomas University, and an MA from Trent University. Currently, she is the field education co-ordinator at the St. Thomas University School of Social Work. She is passionate about social justice in Atlantic Canada.

LAUREN B. MCINROY (BA, BEd, MSW, RSW, PhD candidate) is a student at the Factor-Inwentash Faculty of Social Work at the University of Toronto. Her research interests include vulnerable children and adolescents, sexual- and gender-variant populations, and the implications of new media participation for youth and young adults.

NICK J. MULÉ (SSW Dipl., BA, MSW, PhD) is an associate professor at the School of Social Work, York University, where he teaches policy, theory, and practice. His research interests include social inclusion/exclusion of LGBTQ populations in social policy and service provision. He also engages in critical analysis of the LGBTQ movement and the development of queer liberation theory. The founder and former chairperson of Queer Ontario, Nick is a psychotherapist in private practice who serves LGBTQ populations in Toronto.

DELORES V. MULLINGS (BA, BSW, MSW, PhD) is an assistant professor at Memorial University of Newfoundland in the School of Social Work. Her scholarly interests include mothering, service learning, teaching andragogy, interdisciplinary collaboration, international distance collaborative teaching, health and social needs of older black and racialized adults, black queer older adults, critical race theory and policy, newcomers in rural and small urban centres, and working with racially/culturally diverse families.

JADE PICHETTE (BSW, MSW) is an anti-oppressive educator who works as the volunteer + community outreach coordinator at the Canadian Lesbian and Gay Archives. She previously worked at Kind in Ottawa as the education programs coordinator. Jade has worked with over fifty organizations across Ontario to develop queer/trans inclusive practices. Her MSW research focused on the use of religion as resistance against transmisogyny.

NORMA JEAN PROFITT (MSW, PhD) has a long history of activism in feminist movements in Nova Scotia and Costa Rica, with a focus on violence against women. From 1999 to 2011, she was an associate professor in the School of Social Work, St. Thomas University, where she taught the women and social work course and developed the first course on lesbian, gay, bisexual, and two-spirit people and social work. Her present research interests include women, substance abuse and gender violence, and the intersection of institutional and relational trauma.

JAKE PYNE (BSW, MSW, PhD candidate) is a doctoral candidate in the School of Social Work and the Gender Studies and Feminist Research Program at McMaster University. Over the past fifteen years, Jake has worked in a wide range of community development and advocacy roles in Toronto's trans community. His doctoral research is focused on the current generation of trans youth who are transitioning young, and it poses questions about how these futures have become thinkable in this time and place. Jake's research is supported by Trudeau and Vanier Scholarships.

BRENDA RICHARD (BA, MSW) is an associate professor at the Dalhousie University School of Social Work. A long-time faculty member, she has taught a variety of courses, including "Queer Centered Social Work Practice," and has served in a number of capacities, such as interim director. She has been active in feminist and queer rights movements and community initiatives.

TANYA SHUTE (BSW, MSW, PhD candidate) worked for fifteen years in women's shelters and community mental health centres, community research, policy analysis, advocacy, and administration. She was the executive director of two drop-in centres. She is a sessional instructor in the Laurentian University

School of Social Work and a faculty member at Seneca College in the Social Services Worker Program. Her PhD focuses on critical andragogy and policy.

JAN YORKE (BA, MSW, PhD) is an assistant professor in the School of Social Work at Laurentian University. Since 1973, she has been a front-line crisis worker, an agency director, and a tenured instructor. In 2000, she facilitated the consultation process for HIV/AIDS strategies for the Province of Nova Scotia, emphasizing rural, First Nations, and Afro–Nova Scotian community recommendations. The environment and its impact on healing and change figure prominently in her work. Along with community stakeholders, she recently completed a study on the health needs of rural men who have sex with men.

Index

Accepting Schools Act, Bill 13, 2012 (ON), 235
Addams, Jane, 1, 22–23, 83
adolescents. *See* LGBTQ youth
aging populations
    black queers, 11, 205–21
Alexander, Bryant Keith, 209
andragogy. *See* social work education
anti-essentialism
    queer theory and, 38, 39, 42, 43, 45, 57, 59, 61–69, 120, 228
anti-oppressive practice, 9, 37, 83, 135, 232, 236, 240
anti-war movement, 27, 28
archival collections, 75
Asian queers, 31

BC Teachers' Federation, 78
Belanger, Ken, 98
Belle Époque, 18, 22
Benkart, K.M., 18, 20
Berdaches, 24
bisexual individuals, 6, 22, 31
black LGBTQ individuals, 31
    danger of rejection by family and home communities, 211–12
    danger of rejection by religious communities, 212–14
    experiences of racism, 210–11, 215

    older adults, 11, 205–21
    See also black queer theory
Black Power movement, 27, 28
black queer theory, 207–8
black queers. *See* black LGBTQ individuals
Bornstein, Kate, 66
Boston marriages, 22
boundaries
    polyamorous ethics related to social work education, 200–2
Bryony House, 99
bullying of LGBTQ youth, 75–76, 77, 78, 150, 235
Butler, Eleanor, 22
Butler, Judith, 59, 60–61, 68, 152
Byrch, Ligaya, 234, 237, 251

Canada. Human Rights Commission, 78
Canadian Association for Social Work Education, 80–81, 241
Canadian Association of Social Workers, 80, 124, 231, 232
Canadian Centre for Gender and Sexual Diversity, 78
Canadian Charter of Rights and Freedoms, 31
Canadian Lesbian and Gay Archives, 75
Canadian Teachers' Federation, 78
children. *See* LGBTQ youth; parenthood

cisgendered
  definition, 36
  cisgendered privilege, 12, 17, 37, 42
  See also cisgenderism; heteronormativity; heterosexism
cisgenderism, 17, 79, 228, 229, 232
City College of San Francisco, 74
City University of New York, 74
civil rights movements
  role in queer activism, 27–28, 43, 45
Coalition nationale pour les droits des homosexuels, 30
codes of ethics, 80–81, 124, 192, 231
Combahee River Collective, 100
coming out
  as politicized act, 38, 43, 247
  as queer Muslim, 130–31, 137, 138, 139
  self-reflexive role play, 121
communism, 25
community service learning projects, 216–20
  See also field placements
Concordia University, 74
consent
  polyamorous ethics related to social work education, 198–200
criminalization of homosexuality, 19–20, 23, 25–26, 27, 29
critical social work, 33, 37, 38, 197
CSL. *See* community service learning projects
cultural competence models, 10, 84, 185–88, 189–92
Cunts (lesbian group), 28

Daughters of Bilitis (lesbian organization), 27
Day of Pink, 78
Diagnostic and Statistical Manual of Mental Disorders, 21, 28, 29, 37
Dias, Jeremy, 78
discrimination. *See* oppression
diversity. *See* gender diversity; sexual diversity
DSM3. *See Diagnostic and Statistical Manual of Mental Disorders*

England
  historical attitudes, 18, 19–20, 25
essentialism, 63, 115, 119–20
  anti-essentialism and queer theory, 38, 39, 42, 43, 45, 57, 59, 61–69, 120, 228

  trans experience and, 45, 61–63
ethics, 80–81, 124, 192, 231
ethnic identities, 31
  See also racialized queers
Excellent Care for All Act, 2010 (ON), 235
experience (concept), 94

faculty
  affirmative hiring, 240
  lack of diversity, 209, 238–39
  marginalization of queer faculty, 96, 108
  Profitt, Norma Jean, 93, 99, 100–1, 103
  Richard, Brenda, 93, 95, 97
  rural and northern campuses, 238–39
  understanding of queer issues, 10, 107
  See also teachers
fascism, 25
feminist movement, 93, 95, 99–100, 101
  polyamory and, 194
  queer theory and, 45, 55, 57, 93
feminist theory, 95, 99–100
  framing of transsexual women, 58
field placements, 48–49, 123–24, 237, 239, 240
  See also community service learning projects
Fook, Jan, 192–93
France
  historical attitudes, 18
Freud, Sigmund, 21
Front de libération homosexuel, 29

GAP. *See* gay affirmative practice
Gay Action and Community Homophile Association of Toronto, 29
gay affirmative practice, 185–86, 187, 191, 194
Gay American Indians, 28
gay and lesbian liberation movements, 25–31, 43, 46, 57
  compared to queer liberation, 40–41, 46–47
  documentation and research of, 26–27
  polyamory and, 194
  See also queer activism
gay and lesbian studies, 74–75
  tensions with queer theory, 38–40, 41–42, 57
Gay Asians of Toronto, 31
gay culture
  history of, 18–19

Gay Liberation Front, 29
Gay Manifesto, 29
gay-straight alliances, 32, 78
  hostility to, 37
gender
  essentialism, 45, 61–63
  relationship to sexuality and sex, 104–5
gender diversity, 36, 38, 104–6
  complexities of, 40–41, 232
  Indigenous peoples, 23–24
gender queer
  definition, 40
Germany, 25
Gesch, Lyn, 132–33

Halberstam, Judith/Jack, 66, 68
Ham, Marlene, 234, 237, 252
harassment. *See* bullying
hate crimes, 76, 186
health and well-being issues, 32, 37, 46
  Diagnostic and Statistical Manual of Mental Disorders, 21, 28, 29, 37
  HIV/AIDS, 30–31, 46, 79, 150–54
  trans individuals, 32, 37, 58, 150, 154, 215
heteronormativity, 94, 229, 232–33
  effects on distribution of university resources, 239
  heterosexuality as master status discourse, 114, 125
  within social work, 98
  in social work education, 101–4, 113, 136, 186–87
  universities and, 96, 112
heterosexism, 232, 233
  definition, 30, 36
  in education, 11–12, 101–4, 114, 116–17
  minoritization, 111–12, 116–18, 120, 124, 125
  within social work education, 81, 84, 111–12, 118, 135–37
  tokenization, 112, 118–20, 124, 125, 237
  unlearning via self-reflexivity, 120–23
  See also heteronormativity
heterosexuality
  as master status discourse, 114, 125
  See also heteronormativity
historical overview, 6–7, 17–33, 37, 83
  gay and lesbian studies, 74–75
HIV/AIDS, 30–31, 46, 79, 150–54
Holland, Sharon P., 209

homophobia, 30, 75–77, 229, 232
  in educational institutions, 76–78, 96–97, 107
  experiences of black LGBTQ individuals, 211–14, 216
  in government services, 97, 118
  related to nexus of religion and sexuality, 135–37
  in social work education, 11–12, 81, 82, 96–97, 111
  social workers and, 8, 10, 12, 79–80, 81, 96–97, 112
homosexual rights movements, 25, 27
  See also gay and lesbian liberation movements
homosexuality, 18, 30
  criminalization of, 19–20, 23, 25–26, 27, 29
  decriminalization, 18, 25–26, 27, 29
  in historical records, 17–21
  viewed as mental illness/deviance, 18, 19–21, 23, 28, 29, 80, 96
Hudler, Richard, 75
Hull House, 22–23, 83
human rights, 32–33, 43
  discourse, 31, 39, 46
  legislation, 46, 47, 78, 97

identity politics, 31, 46
  coming out, 38, 43, 247
  queer theory and, 38, 39, 42, 43, 45, 57, 59, 61–69, 120, 228
  trans self-representation and, 54, 56, –59, 60–61, 65–68
Indigenous peoples
  diversity, 23–24
Indigenous queers, 23–24
  activism, 28
International Association of Schools of Social Work, 81
International Federation of Social Workers, 81
intersectionality, viii, 8, 23, 27, 32, 112, 248
  nexus of spirituality, religion and sexuality, 130–43
  See also transmisogyny
intersex individuals, 32
  infants and children, 37
Islam
  Muslim queers, 9, 130–43
  sexual diversity and, 138–39

Islamophobia
  Muslim queers and, 137–38

Kertbeny, Karl Maria, 18
Khan, Maryam, 9, 248, 252–53
  marginalization of Muslim identity, 130–43
Kinsey Report (1948), 27
knowledges. *See* ways of knowing
Krafft-Ebin, Richard von, 20

Lambda Legal, 74
Laurentian University
  social work education, 233–34, 236–39
Lesbian Gay Rights Nova Scotia, 97
lesbian liberation movements. *See* gay and lesbian liberation movements
lesbians
  criminalization, 23
  early activism, 27, 28
  early gay rights movement and, 28
  historical record, 17, 21–23
LGBT populations
  definitions, 40–41
  See also LGBTQ populations
LGBTQ populations
  definitions, 40–41
  See also lesbians; LGBTQ service users; LGBTQ youth; racialized queers
LGBTQ service users, 44
  marginalization of, 97, 117
  marginalization of trans women, 149, 150–51, 152, 153–54
  struggles to find services, 232
LGBTQ studies, 74–75
LGBTQ youth
  bullying of, 75–76, 77, 78, 150, 235
  school drop-out rates, 150
  Simcoe County (ON), 234–36, 237
  social work literature concerning, 79
  suicide, 75, 77, 98
  trans girls, 150
  trans students, 236
Lippett, Robyn, 8–9, 112, 248, 253
Livingston, Jennie, 60
Long Time Coming (journal), 28

Many Voices, 213
marriage rights, 32, 41
Martin, Karolyn, 8–9, 112, 248, 253

Mattachine Action Committee, 29
Mattachine Society, 27
McCarthyism, 25
men
  gender essentialism, 59, 61
mental illness, 76, 96–97, 150
  Diagnostic and Statistical Manual of Mental Disorders, 21, 28, 29, 37
  See also health and well-being issues
minoritization, 111–12, 116–18, 120, 124, 125
misogyny. *See* transmisogyny
monogamy, 194–95
Muslim queers, 9, 130–43

Namaste, Viviane, 60
National Association of Social Workers, 231
National Gay Rights Coalition, 30
neo-liberalism, 191
  competencies and, 10, 189–92, 249
  impact on social work, 189–91, 200
  impact on social work education, 239
  queer theory and, 43, 49
  spirituality and, 133
Nichiwakan Native Gay and Lesbian Society, 24
Nixon, Kimberly, 153
northern contexts. *See* rural and northern life
Nova Scotia. Human Rights Act, 97

older adults
  black queers, 11, 205–21
Ontario
  health care provision, 235
oppression, 26, 27–28, 43, 76, 98–99, 107, 228–29
  bullying of LGBTQ youth, 75–76, 77, 78, 150, 235
  cisgenderism, 17, 79, 228, 229, 232
  criminalization of homosexuality, 19–20, 23, 25–26, 27, 29
  hate crimes, 76, 186
  Islamophobia, 137–38
  minoritization, 111–12, 116–18, 120, 124, 125
  police harassment, 27–29, 31
  tokenization, 112, 118–20, 124, 125, 237
  See also heteronormativity; heterosexism; homophobia; racism; transphobia

Index

259

oral sex, 20
Ottawa Council on Religion and the Homosexual, 29

parenthood, 41, 118
Paris Is Burning (film), 60
persecution of queers. *See* police harassment
Pichette, Jade, 148–49, 248, 254
police harassment, 27–29, 31
polyamorous ethics, 11, 194–202
polyamory
    definition, 194
Ponsonby, Sarah, 22
postmodernist thought, 38
    See also queer theory
Pride movement, 12, 30
prisons
    conditions for trans women, 151
Profitt, Norma Jean, 8, 93, 99, 100–1, 103, 248, 254
Prosser, Jay, 60–61
psychiatry, 20–21
    Diagnostic and Statistical Manual of Mental Disorders, 21, 28, 29, 37

queer
    definitions, 5, 40, 41, 42, 47, 55, 94, 113, 115–16, 131–32
    reclamation of word, 5, 31–32, 40, 42, 115
queer activism, 32–33, 37
    community groups, 42
    marginalization of trans individuals, 115
    origins of, 27–29, 46
    questioning of heterosexual norms, 46, 47
    reclaiming of "queer," 31–32, 40, 42, 47, 115
    social change focus, 38–39, 40–41, 42–43, 46–47
    tensions with queer theory, 38–39, 42–43, 45–46
queer liberation perspective, 47–48
    See also queer activism; social justice
Queer Nation, 31, 77
queer sexuality, 30
    in historical records, 17–24
queer theory, 4, 7, 38, 247
    definition, 30, 55
    black queer theory, 207–8
    critique of, 60

    disapproval of trans choices, 58, 59–61, 62–68
    exclusion of black LGBTQs, 207
    focus on fluidity and anti-essentialism, 38, 39, 42, 43, 45, 57, 59, 61–69, 120, 228
    origins, 56–57, 228
    practical application and, 43, 45–46
    "queer" and, 41–42
    in queer approach to social work education, 39, 112, 114–16, 188
    tensions with queer activism, 38–39, 42–43, 45–46
    trans subjectivity and, 7–8, 54–56, 57, 59–60, 61, 62–69
queers
    faith-based spirituality and, 132
    older black queers, 11, 205–21
    othering of black queers, 210–11, 215
    othering of religious queers, 137–38, 139
    See also LGBTQ populations; queer; racialized queers

racialized queers, 31, 130–32
    absence from the historical record, 23, 24–25
    Indigenous peoples, 23–24, 28
    trans individuals, 60–61, 154
    See also black queers; racism
racism, 23, 97–98, 136, 137, 154, 155
    black LGBTQ experiences, 208–11, 212, 213, 215, 216
    See also racialized queers
Raymond, Janice, 58
religion
    black churches, 213–14
    nexus of spirituality, religion, and sexuality, 130–43
    related to spirituality, 132–33
    stereotyping of religious beliefs, 135–37
religious queers
    marginalization of, 130–43, 214
    othering by queers, 137–38, 139
    othering by religious peers, 138–39
research and scholarship, 3–4
    improvements in, 85, 241
    lack of, 4, 78–79, 85, 96, 149
    narrow focus of, 96
    trans women as research subjects, 9, 152
Rich, Adrienne, 100

Richard, Brenda, 8, 93, 95, 97, 248, 254
Richmond, Mary, 83
Riddell, Caroll, 58
Roof, Wade Clark, 132–33
rural and northern life
    LGBTQ individuals, 11, 227–28, 230–31, 234

same-sex relationships, 26, 32
    historical references to, 17–24
    marriage rights, 32, 41, 191
    See also homosexuality; lesbians
Sappho, 17, 22
schools of social work. See social work education
self-determination, 39–40, 44, 45, 231
service users. See LGBTQ service users
Settlement House movement, 22–23, 83
sex-change. See transitioning
sexology, 19
sexual diversity, 36, 38, 119
    complexities of, 40–41, 232
    Indigenous peoples, 23–24
    Islam and, 138–39
    lack of reflection on, 117–18, 120–23
sexualities
    social construction of, 112–15
sexuality studies, 38, 74–75, 77
    tensions with queer theory, 38–40, 41–42, 57
shelter services
    for trans individuals, 45, 154
Simcoe County (ON), 11, 227–41, 234
Smith, Mary Rozet, 83
social constructionism, 112, 113–14
social justice
    queer liberation perspective and, 46–47
    social work focus on, 7, 9–10, 39, 43–44, 80–81, 83, 111, 116, 166, 189, 192, 196
    spirituality and, 133–34
social work
    critical social work, 33, 37, 38, 197
    ethics, 80–81, 124, 192, 231
    exclusion of sexuality and gender issues, 37, 80
    "invisibility" of LGBTQ individuals, 11, 232–33
    male privilege and, 155–56
    neo-liberalism and, 189–91, 200
    principle of respect for subjectivities, 39, 44, 45, 248
    principle of self-determination, 39–40, 44, 45, 231
    principle of social justice, 7, 9–10, 39, 43–44, 80–81, 83, 111, 116, 166, 189, 192, 196
    professional boundaries, 200–1
    queer roots, 1, 22–23, 83
    role in perpetuating oppression, 8, 10–12, 37, 79–80, 81, 96–97, 112, 185–88, 246
    theory related to practice, 36–37, 43–46, 49, 96, 247
    See also LGBTQ service users; social work education; social workers
social work education, 74
    accreditation standards, 80–81, 116
    attitudes to diversity, 37–38
    classroom power dynamics, 141–42
    cultural competence models and, 10, 84, 185–87, 189–92
    Eurocentric foundations, 134, 206–7
    exclusion of trans women, 151–53, 156–57
    failure to address anti-black racism, 208–10
    fear of controversy, 135–36
    heteronormativity, 101–4, 113, 136, 186–87
    "invisibility" of LGBTQ individuals, 82–83, 96, 116, 137–38, 186
    issues in anti-homophobic advocacy, 185–88
    lack of LGBTQ content, 4, 75, 80, 236, 237
    lack of LGBTQ teaching resources, 75, 78–79, 83–84, 238, 239
    lack of reflection on sexualities, 37–38, 117–18
    Laurentian University, 233–34, 236–39
    LGBTQ courses, 101, 103
    nexus of spirituality, religion, and sexuality, 9, 130–43, 214
    othering of religious/spiritual believers, 134–37, 139, 214
    See also faculty; social work education recommendations; social work students; teaching resources; universities

social work education recommendations, 249–50
  affirmative action faculty and student recruitment, 240
  alliances with LGBTQ communities, 239–40
  analyses of intersectionality, 107, 146
  challenging of heteronormativity, 101–4, 106–7, 112, 113
  community service learning projects, 216–20
  critical discussion of race and racism, 136
  critical discussion of sexualities, 118, 136–37, 241
  critical reflection assignments/discussions, 120–23, 135, 188
  disruption of binary assumptions, 104–7
  faculty opportunities to learn about LBGTQ issues, 10, 107
  field placements, 48–49, 123–24, 237, 239, 240
  guest speakers, 124, 156, 239
  inclusion of LGBTQ contributions, 188–89
  inclusion of spiritual praxis, 139–42
  inclusion of trans women, 156–57
  interdisciplinary andragogy, 48
  LGBTQ content throughout curriculum, 48, 49, 188–89
  polyamory-informed inquiry in bridging theory and practice, 11, 195–202
  practice informed theory-building, 192–93, 240, 241
  queer approach to, 10–11, 112, 114–16, 120–25
  recognition of LGBTQ oppression, 107
  respect of trans subjectivities, 68–69
  role play and debate, 121, 188
  safe spaces in classrooms, institutions, and practica, 10, 107, 121–23, 240, 241
social work research. *See* research and scholarship
social work students
  experiences of queer-identified students, 111–20
  lack of LGBTQ role models, 82–83
  maginalization of religious/spiritual identities, 131
  minoritization of queer-identified students, 111–12, 116–18, 120, 124, 125
  reluctance to come out, 82–83
  tokenization of queer-identified students, 112, 118–20, 124, 125, 237
social workers
  Addams, Jane, 1, 22–23, 83
  homophobic attitudes, 8, 10, 12, 79–80, 81, 96–97, 112
  non-disclosure as self-protection, 82–83, 97–98
  trans women, 151–52, 154, 156–57
  transphobic attitudes, 8, 10, 12, 79–80, 81, 112
spirituality
  definition, 133–34
  nexus of spirituality, religion, and sexuality, 130–43
Starr, Ellen Gates, 83
Stone, Sandy, 58–59, 63, 65
Stonewall riots, 28–29
strengths-based approaches, 37–38
structural social work theory, 105–6
suicide
  LGBTQ youth, 75, 77
  trans women, 150

teachers
  gay-straight alliances and, 78
  homophobic treatment of, 77, 107
  knowledge systems, 134–37
  lack of diversity training, 77
  lack of knowledge concerning LGBTQ communities, 84
  underrepresentation of black educators, 209
  See also faculty
teaching resources
  archival collections, 75
  improved inclusion of LGBTQ resources, 48, 239, 240, 241
  lack of LGBTQ content, 75, 96, 97, 238
  lack of LGBTQ social work resources, 78–79, 81, 83–84, 96
  perpetuation of discrimination, 81, 84
textbooks. *See* teaching resources
theory, 192–93, 240, 241
  black queer theory, 207–8
  feminist theory, 58, 95, 99–100

related to practice, 36–37, 43–44, 192–93, 240, 241
social constructionism, 112, 113–14
structural social work theory, 105–6
See also queer theory
Titone, Connie, 208
Toby's Act, 2012 (ON), 235
tokenization, 112, 118–20, 124, 125, 237
Toronto
mass arrests, 31
trans
definition, 55–56
transgender, 55, 57–58, 59
transsexual, 55, 57–59, 60
See also trans individuals; trans women; transitioning
trans individuals, 55–56
acknowledgment of, 32
availability of shelters for, 45
exclusion from gay rights movement, 28
health and well-being issues, 32, 37, 58, 150, 154, 215
identity and, 58, 60–67
importance of gendered space, 68
intersectional analysis and, 32
male privilege, 155–56
queer representation of, 7–8, 54–56, 57–68, 115
racialized, 60, 61, 154
self-representation, 7–8, 54, 56, 58–59, 60–61, 65–68
See also trans women
trans women, 155
lack of research into social services for, 149
lack of support systems, 153–54
marginalization of, 9, 149, 150–52, 157
mental health, 150
Pichette, Jade, 148–49, 248, 254
as research subjects, 9, 152
shelter services, 154
as social work practitioners, 9, 153, 154, 156–57
suicide, 150
Venus Xtravaganza, 60
See also transmisogyny
transgender, 57–58, 59
definition, 55
See also trans individuals; transitioning

transitioning
heteronormative order and, 41, 54–55, 59–61
medical control and, 58, 60, 64, 65
See also trans individuals
transmisogyny, 9
definition, 149–50
activism against, 154–57
firing of Kimberly Nixon, 153
violence, 150
transphobia, 66–67, 156, 229, 232
related to nexus of religion and sexuality, 135–37
in social work education, 111
social workers and, 8, 10, 12, 79–80, 81, 112
See also transmisogyny
transsexual, 57–59, 60
definition, 55
See also trans individuals; transitioning
two-spirited individuals, 24, 32
Two-Spirited People of the First Nations, 24

unemployment, 76
United States
early activism, 27
female same-sex relationships, 22
universities, 29, 74, 75
heteronormativity, 96, 112
homophobia, 76–78, 96–97
Laurentian University School of Social Work, 233–34, 236–39
See also faculty; sexuality studies; social work education
University of Alberta, 77
University of California–Berkeley, 74
University of Saskatchewan, 75, 77
University of Toronto, 75, 77

Vancouver Association for Social Knowledge, 29
Vancouver Rape Relief, 153

ways of knowing, 134
See also spirituality
Western University, 75
Wilde, Oscar, 20
Wittman, Carl, 29

women
- exclusion from early gay rights movement, 28
- gender essentialism, 59, 61
- viewed as non-sexual, 21–23
- *See also* feminist movement; feminist theory; lesbians; trans women

women's movement
- civil rights influence of, 28

Xtravaganza, Venus, 60–61

York University, 77
youth. *See* LGBTQ youth